JEWISH EXPRESSIONS ON JESUS

JEWISH EXPRESSIONS ON JESUS

An Anthology

Edited with an Introduction

By

TRUDE WEISS-ROSMARIN

KTAV PUBLISHING HOUSE, INC.
NEW YORK
1977

Library of Congress Cataloging in Publication Data

Main entry under title:
Jewish expressions on Jesus.

  Reprint from various sources, 1943-1973.
  Includes bibliographical references.
  1. Jesus Christ—Jewish interpretations—Addresses,
essays, lectures. I. Trude Weiss—Rosmarin 1908-
BM620.J48   296.3'87'2   76-45387
ISBN 0-87068-470-1

Jesus Christ, Jewish interpretation

MANUFACTURED IN THE UNITED STATES OF AMERICA

Contents

Contents

ACKNOWLEDGMENTS

Grateful acknowledgment is made for permission to reprint to the following:

Ben Zion Bokser, "Jesus: Jew or Christian?" Reprinted from *Judaism and the Christian Predicament*. New York: Alfred A. Knopf, 1967. Copyright Ben Zion Bokser.

Haim Cohn, "The Crucifixion." Reprinted from *The Trial and Death of Jesus*. New York: Harper & Row, 1971. Copyright Haim Cohn.

Jules Isaac, "Deicide." Reprinted from *Jesus and Israel*. New York: Holt, Rinehart & Winston, Inc., 1971. Copyright Claire Huchet Bishop.

Walter Kaufmann, "Jesus vis-à-vis Paul, Luther and Schweitzer." Reprinted from *Faith Of A Heretic*. New York: Doubleday & Company, Inc., 1961. Copyright Walter Kaufmann.

Joseph Klausner, "The Jewishness of Jesus." Reprinted from *Jesus of Nazareth*. New York: The Macmillan Company, 1943. Copyright The Macmillan Company.

Jacob Z. Lauterbach, "Jesus in the Talmud." Reprinted from *Rabbinic Essays*. New York: Ktav Publishing House, 1973. Copyright The Hebrew Union College Alumni.

Franz Rosenzweig, "Franz To Eugen." Reprinted from *Judaism Despite Christianity. The Letters on Christianity and Judaism between Eugen Rosenstock-Huessy and Franz Rosenzweig*. University, Ala.: University of Alabama Press, 1969. Copyright University of Alabama Press.

Samuel Sandmel, "The Historical Jesus." Reprinted from *A Jewish Understanding of the New Testament*. Cincinnati: Hebrew Union College Press, 1957. Copyright The Alumni of the Hebrew Union College-Jewish Institute of Religion.

Hans Joachim Schoeps, "The Messiahship of Jesus." Reprinted from *The Jewish Christian Argument*. Translated by David E. Green. New York: Holt, Rinehart and Winston, 1963. Copyright Holt, Rinehart and Winston, Inc.

INTRODUCTION

By Trude Weiss-Rosmarin

I

The readings presented in this volume address themselves to the two principal Jewish interests in the founder of Christianity; Jesus' Jewishness, and his trial and death on a Roman cross.

Generally, Jewish historians tend to accept the Gospel data on Jesus as basically factual, although colored by the partisan rivalry and enmity of the early Church. Jewish scholars know, of course, that the Gospels are not history as historians understand and define it. Nevertheless—and this is inconsistent—they delineate Jesus' Jewish identity and his identification with the Jewish people and its faith and hopes in consonance with the Gospel reports. Also, they take issue with the Gospel accounts of his trial and death as if they were history.

In this respect, Jewish students of nascent and early Christianity tend to be more "Gospel true" than modern and contemporary Christian New Testament scholars, who are in agreement that the "Historical Jesus" is beyond recovery, and that this need not be deplored, since "the Gospels are not historical records but documents of faith." [1] Gonzelmann expresses the virtual consensus of contemporary New Testament scholars that "for a great portion of the tradition there is no possibility of establishing the exact place in the life of Jesus. We no longer know the sequence of events, and, above all, we cannot reconstruct an outer and inner development. . . . The Gospels in their entirety are witnesses of faith. . . . For that reason they have no interest in the 'portrait' of Jesus." [2]

As a consequence of the emphasis on the "Jesus of Faith" and the relegation of the "Historical Jesus" to relative unimportance, Jesus' "Jewishness" and his trial and crucifixion are of no interest to most contemporary New Testament scholars. This does not imply, however, a denial that Jesus *lived*, taught, and suffered the kerygmatic death on the cross. Jesus' life as kerygma is taken for granted. It is axiomatic truth, although the facts of his life are not verifiable by the methods of historical research. Far from being a source of frustration, this inaccessibility is considered an

---

1. Hans Gonzelmann, *Jesus* (Philadelphia: Fortress Press, 1973), p. 7.
2. Ibid., p. 15.

advantage by many New Testament scholars. As they see it, it liberates the Jesus of the kerygma from the limitations of time and place.

"We need no longer consider it disastrous," asserts James M. Robinson, "that the chronology and causality of the public ministry [of Jesus] are gone." [3] But if this is the case, what is the purpose of the "new quest of the historical Jesus" Robinson attempts? It aims at "an existential encounter with a historical person, Jesus, who can also be encountered through the mediation of modern historiography." [4] For Robinson, this "modern historiography" is existential historiography—a historiography not concerned with dates and facts. Therefore, it "cannot verify the truth of the kerygma, that this person actually lived. . . . But it can test whether this *kerygmatic* understanding of Jesus' existence corresponds to the understanding of existence implicit in Jesus' history, as encountered through modern historiography." [5] Robinson emphasizes that "the totality of the person [Jesus] is not to be sought in terms of chronological and developmental continuity." [6] All that matters is the kerygma, that is, the encounter of the believer with the Christ—the Christ whom the Gospels do not present as "the historical—Jesus in distinction from the *kerygma.*" [7]

The exclusive emphasis on the existential-experiential Jesus of the kerygma is also the stance of liberal Catholic theologians. Thus, Malachi Martin professes that "Jesus has no past, will not come again, and in loving action is dissolving the molds of our spent society." For Martin, "the Jesus Self . . . is love, not merely a loving person; spirit, not simply a spirit. . . . He did not come in order to depart, and need not come again because he never went away." [8]

Martin describes *Jesus Now* as "a journey through the quagmire of distortions, defamations and illusions piled around our view of Jesus by historians and theologians who are insensitive to the experiential-existential awareness of Jesus." Among the distortions that gave rise to "The Non-Christian Jesus Figures" [9] Martin also analyzes the dual Jesus image pro-

---

3. James M. Robinson, *A New Quest of the Historical Jesus,* 7th imp. (London: SCM Press, 1971), p. 69.
4. Ibid., p. 94.
5. Ibid.
6. Ibid., p. 95.
7. Ibid., p. 80. For the history of the evolution of modern New Testament scholarship, see Werner George Kuemmel *The New Testament: The History of the Investigation of its Problems* (Nashville: Abingdon Press, 1972).
8. Malachi Martin, *Jesus Now* (New York: E. P. Dutton, 1973), pp. xvi f.
9. Ibid., pp. 21–109.

jected by Jews—the Jesus of the crucifixion, in whose name Jews were persecuted, and the "Jesus-One-of-Us-After-All" of Jewish scholars, who emphasize the Jewishness of Jesus. Martin avers that neither image does justice to the Jesus whom Christians should encounter as "savior, healer, compassionate God," [10] not in a dogmatic sense but in an existential encounter.

One may well ask whether these trends and orientations of New Testament scholars and theologians do not render irrelevant the works of Jewish scholars who take issue with the Gospel accounts of Jesus' trial and death. These works are, indeed, irrelevant for the Gonzelmanns and Martins, who know that while the Gospels tell about a historical person, that is, a person who lived, the story they tell is not history. However, the vast majority of Christians—laity and clergy—do believe in the Gospels as history by the historian's definition. They lack the sophistication of the New Testament scholars who, so as to encounter the kerygmatic Jesus, cleanse his image from what they consider pseudohistorical accretions of the Gospels. Still, the Jesus of the Gospels is preached and taught in the pulpit and the church classroom by Christian clergymen who are at home in New Testament form criticism.

Notwithstanding the critical scholars' unconcern with the "Historical Jesus," it is the "Historical Jesus"—the Jesus presented by the Gospels—who is worshipped as the Christ. In the context of *normative* Christianity, the Gospels are truth, even as in *normative* Judaism the Hebrew Bible is truth. By way of an analogy, it should be said that the "Historical Moses" is also an enigma. He is as enigmatic as the "Historical Jesus." But faith is not concerned with historical certainty. It claims the superior certainty of revelation. There is no to-scholarship-acceptable proof and evidence of the "Historical Moses." Yet he is alive in the historical consciousness of the Jewish people. "If it were not for the Bible we should know nothing of Moses," writes David Daiches. He points out that "the biblical account of Moses is not history as we understand it: it represents the coming together of a variety of traditions. . . . It includes elements of myth and ritual, symbolic situations . . . yet the history underlying it is real; Moses was a real person, the exodus from Egypt and the entry into the Promised Land were real events." [11]

The "realness" of Moses, like the "realness" of Jesus, is certain, al-

---

10. Ibid., p. 27.
11. David Daiches, *Moses* (New York: Praeger Publishers, 1975), p. 9.

though it cannot be proved by history as history is generally defined and understood.

II

Considering that what matters in Christian belief is, as the Catholic theologian Gerard S. Sloyan states his credo, that "after having taught the future certainty of God's reign, Jesus died and rose from the dead," [12] one may wonder whether Jewish scholars need adduce evidence (as if such evidence were still needed) that the Gospel accounts of the Jewish "guilt" in Jesus' death are, as Sloyan writes, "faith literature, like the Hebrew Bible." And as a result, like the Hebrew Bible, "they bristle with antipathies and identify the enemies of the authors with the enemies of God. An important difference is that the evangelists are believers who have taken on new enemies, 'the scribes and pharisees' or 'the Jews,' much in the manner of 'the priests and prophets' of Jeremiah's day or 'the church' for contemporary Christians who mean the church's leadership." [13] If the insights of New Testament scholars were the Christian *norms*, there would be no need for the Jewish expressions on Jesus included in this volume. And, of course, there would have been no need for Vatican Council II *actually* to study and reexamine Jewish culpability in the death of Jesus.

The fact that the eminent theologians who constituted Vatican Council II spent many months studying the problem of Jewish guilt in Jesus' death and finally issued a Declaration that is far from being an unequivocal exoneration of the Jewish sin of deicide, proves that there is still a need for "apologetics."

The Council Declaration on Judaism states:

> The Jewish authorities and those who followed their lead pressed for the death of Christ; still, what happened in his passion cannot be charged against all the Jews, without distinction, then alive, nor against the Jews of today. Although the Church is the new People of God, the Jews should not be represented as rejected by God or accursed, as if this followed from the Holy Scriptures. All should see to it, then, that in catechetical work and in the preaching of the word of God they teach nothing save what conforms to the truth of the Gospel and the Spirit of Christ.

---

12. Gerard S. Sloyan, *Jesus on Trial* (Philadelphia: Fortress Press, 1973), p. 18.
13. Ibid., p. 133.

This is the text. But there is also to be considered its exposition on what conforms to "the truth of the Gospel and the Spirit of Christ."

An authoritative commentary on the Council Declaration on Judaism was provided by Augustine Cardinal Bea, president of the council's Secretariat for Christian Unity and principal spokesman on the relation of the Church to non-Christian religions at Vatican Council II.[14] It was he who worded—with the advice and counsel of other Fathers of the Council—the Declaration on Judaism. One may therefore conclude that Bea's commentary is not mere personal opinion but expresses Catholic doctrine, and therefore it deserves careful study.

Let us commence with his commentary on: "Still what happened in the passion cannot be charged against all the Jews, without distinction, then alive, nor against the Jews of today." According to Bea this means that: "The guilt is in the *personal* order and falls upon anyone who in some way *associates* himself with the 'perverse generation' which is primarily guilty, or who directly cooperated in the condemnation of Jesus, as did the Sanhedrin and the crowd which cried out before Pilate's judgment-seat." [15]

Association with the "perverse generation which is primarily guilty" (it should be noted that Bea draws a distinction between primary guilt and guilt by association) means to be guilty by not believing in Jesus as the Christ. In the section entitled "The Cultivated Olive Tree and the Wild Olive Branches," [16] Bea noted that the Jews were "the cultivated olive tree," cultivated by God. However, they refused to accept the Gospel and therefore "remained excluded from the new people of God because of their refusal to believe. The gentiles, on the other hand, the 'wild olive shoot,' who till then had been excluded . . . are now grafted onto the good olive, the new people of God," that is, the Church.

But what about the Jews of today? Do they share in "the guilt" which is "in the personal order?" Bea's opinion is as follows: "Generally speaking, refusal to believe in the Gospel and in Jesus is a factor in this judgment, and so, in one way or another, is a free decision to ally oneself with the 'perverse generation, with the powers opposed to God." [17]

Yet the Jews were not *collectively* condemned and punished. "Christ directly offers the possibility of escaping the judgment visited on Jerusalem

---

14. *The Church and the Jewish People* (New York: Harper & Row, 1966).
15. Ibid., p. 78.
16. Ibid., pp. 61–65.
17. Ibid., p. 85.

to those who have segregated themselves from the 'perverse generation' and submitted to the Gospel." [18]

The guilt, as the Declaration points out, is not imputed to "all Jews." Again and again Cardinal Bea stresses: "In these passages of the Gospels responsibility for the crucifixion of Jesus is never founded on the membership of the people of Israel but on concurrence with the attitude of the mind of the leaders of the people in Jerusalem." [19]

The Council Declaration that "the Jews should not be represented as rejected by God" means, therefore, that salvation is still available to the Jews. "Even after the condemnation of Jesus, God did not in any way reject the people he had chosen. On the contrary, he continued to offer them the Gospel of salvation." [20]

However, they do not avail themselves of the offer, and thus the inevitable conclusion is: "It is not God who rejects and, suddenly without more ado, sends down the lightning of his punishments. He continues to hold out the good news of salvation . . . but through an unhappy chain of circumstances, strains and stresses and social influences, the members of the Jewish people again and again reject the Gospel until at last, respecting man's freedom of choice, God sends his messengers elsewhere." [21]

God has not rejected, and does not reject, the Jews, because the freedom of accepting the Gospel is still theirs.

III

It is Christian belief that Jesus died on the cross, by the will of God, so as to atone for the "original sin" in Paradise and for the "salvation" of all those who believe that he is the Christ and Son of God who rose from the dead.

It would seem, therefore, that in the context of God's plan-and-intent with Jesus, it is *heresy* to accuse the Jews of "deicide"—heresy because the deicide accusation is a denial of God's will-and-action with Jesus.

But granted that some Jews (or even all Jews) of Jesus' time were guilty as charged in the Gospels, is it fair and justified to associate the descendants of "the perverse generation" with their ancestors' sin, after the lapse of almost two thousand years?

---

18. Ibid., p. 85.
19. Ibid., p. 87.
20. Ibid., p. 91.
21. Ibid., p. 93.

Twenty years after the Holocaust, Israel established diplomatic relations with Germany, while German youth angrily protested against being held responsible for their fathers' crimes in the Final Solution. Definitely, sin is "in the personal order," as Cardinal Bea stated; that is to say, it is not "inherited." This is why Jeremiah (31:29) and Ezekiel (18:2) denounced those who invoked the ancient proverb, "the fathers have eaten sour grapes, and the children's teeth are set on edge." Not so, they proclaimed. Only "the sinner shall die; the son shall not bear the iniquity of the father, neither shall the father bear the iniquity of the son; the righteousness of the righteous shall be upon him, and the wickedness of the wicked shall be upon him" (Ezek. 18:20).

It was in this tradition that many Americans, upon learning of the plight and poverty of the widow and children of President Kennedy's murderer, sent gift checks to the Oswald family. They did not hold the wife and children of the slayer of the President responsible for the crime.

More recently, in the first week of October 1975, when Emperor Hirohito visited this country, American and Japanese leaders, notably President Ford and Emperor Hirohito, emphasized that the memory of the unhappy and bloodstained past must not becloud the present and future relations of the United States and Japan. And yet it is only thirty years since U.S. atomic bombs killed and maimed hundreds of thousands of Japanese in retaliation for Pearl Harbor and its aftermath. James Reston paid this tribute in "The Glory of America: She Has No Memory":[22]

> Thirty years after the last World War, there must still be many American families that feel amputated by the loss of their men and women, but there is no general hatred or bitterness in this country toward either Japan or Germany, not even much surprise at seeing the same Emperor of Japan laying a wreath on the Tomb of the Unknowns in the Arlington cemetery. "Remember Pearl Harbor," Roosevelt warned us, but America forgot to remember.

And the Pearl Harbor Survivors Association declared, on the eve of Emperor Hirohito's arrival in the United States, "The governmental regime which made war in the nineteen-thirties and nineteen-forties and pressed the attack on Pearl Harbor has long since disappeared and with it has gone any reason for us to bear a grudge against the Japanese people." [23]

---

22. *New York Times*, October 5, 1975, Op. Ed page.
23. Ibid., September 30, 1975.

Considering the many American families whose dear ones were killed by Japanese and Germans—to say nothing of the survivors of the six million Jews who were murdered by the Nazis (and most of the survivors grant that they cannot bear a grudge against thhe Germans who were too young to participate in the Final Solution or who were born after 1945), it is surely not unreasonable to wonder why the Churches—Catholic and Protestant—continue to discuss, and seriously, Jewish culpability in the death of Jesus. And all this *after* the scholars' consensus that the Gospels are not history as history is generally defined, and that the Cross is *the* Christian glory. The reason, I suggest, is the Christian belief in *original sin*—the sin of Adam and Eve—that taints, and will taint, all humans till the end of time. Original sin is at the core of Christian faith, together with the belief that Jesus, the "Second Adam," by his death on the cross, atoned for the sin of the "First Adam."

In the context of Christianity, it is not illogical to believe that original sin is inherited by all men, and that all Jews who do not accept Jesus as their savior are guilty of deicide.

IV

Walter Kaufmann argues that Christian belief derogates reason. Thus "Tertullian believes what he considers impossible; Kierkegaard tries to believe what he considers absurd. Paul speaks triumphantly of the *skandalon* and jubilates that he is able to believe what to reason must seem foolishness; Luther exults: Whoever wants to be a Christian should tear out the eyes of his reason." [24] Orthodox Jewish beliefs, too, strain reason, to wit, the belief in the Sinaitic revelation and the Torah as the word of God, *literally*. However, there is the insistence that the revelation was not a visible manifestation of God, for, as Moses was told when he pleaded to see God's Presence, "you cannot see My face, for man cannot see Me and live" (Exod. 32:23).

Obviously, as a self-confessed "heretic" and rationalist, Kaufmann is judgmental in his characterization of basic Christian beliefs. But then, at the other end of the spectrum, there are Jewish thinkers of note who, in the style of Martin Buber, castigate rationalizing Jewish monotheism as "cruel." Buber deplored that "the late-Jewish priesthood" has virtually demythologized the Hebrew Bible. [25] For Buber, as for Freud, a myth is

---

24. Walter Kaufmann, *Critique of Religion and Philosophy* (New York: Harper & Bros., 1958), p. 200.
25. Martin Buber, *On Judaism* (New York, 1967), pp. 97, 102, 105 ff.

an eternal function of the human soul. In the context of myth, Jewish deicide makes as much sense as the Oedipus complex, that is, the innate-inherited desire for patricide of every *male* child, suppressed (because of the impact of socialization) and, on account of this suppression, the source of "universal guilt."

Myths become dangerous when they are accepted as fact-and-truth, in the manner of the "Aryan race" myth, which provided the rationale for Hitler's instigation of the murder of six million Jews. Obviously, Jews as deicides is a myth, because even if it were a fact that Jesus was crucified as a result of Jewish action, it is only in the context of myth that today, almost two thousand years after Golgotha, Christians and Jews think it necessary to "disprove" the deicide charge. And even so they do not succeed fully, as is demonstrated by the Vatican Council II Declaration and, especially, by Cardinal Bea's commentary on the Declaration.

Indeed, Christian New Testament scholars and theologians[26] do not fall into the trap of mythology. And they do not consider Jesus the "fulfilment" of the Old Testament promises and expectation in the *literal* sense. Yet it would be difficult (if not impossible) to find a Christian New Testament scholar and theologian who does not avow that Jesus is Judaism's fulfilment in the *spiritual* sense, that is, that Jesus is the Lord. For example, J. Lindblom, the Scandinavian Bible scholar, writes that it was "a peculiar idea of the early Christians concerning the significance of the Old Testament that historical facts and events of the Old Testament prefigured and foretold facts and events in New Testament times." [27] And the noted German Bible scholar, Walter Eichrodt, expressed the consensus of the scholars that,

> There can be no question today of reviving the old orthodox view that a complete picture of Christ is foreshadowed in the messianic prophecies. To work out *a prophetic proof* of the truth of the NT Gospel by piecing together from the OT the various traits of the messianic King and the salvation mediated through him, and making them into a coherent picture, would involve insoluble contradictions with the history of OT prediction and its significance with OT prophecy.[28]

26. See above, nn. 1–13.

27. J. Lindblom, *The Bible: A Modern Understanding* (Philadelphia: Fortress Press, 1973), p. 146.

28. Walther Eichrodt, *Theology of the Old Testament* (Philadelphia: Westminster Press, 1961), 1:502.

Eichrodt emphasized: "There is no further point in talking about a 'fulfilment' of OT prediction, for all the internal links between OT hope and NT reality of salvation have been severed." [29]

The Hebrew prophets and psalmists, and all those whose writings have been canonized in the Hebrew Bible, did not "predict" or allude to Jesus. Gurdon C. Oxtoby, dean and professor of Old Testament at San Francisco Theology Seminary, asserts that "the historical study of the Bible has emphasized the fact that those who wrote it did so in response to actual situations." [30] He dismisses the New Testament claim that the events of Jesus' life and death were "prophesied" by the Hebrew Bible as "a kind of religious soothsaying; that incredible visionary powers were possessed by prophets and psalmists so that they could describe in detail events that had not yet come to pass, and indeed would not occur until many generations later." [31]

Oxtoby insists that the prophets and psalmists wrote for their own age. "As an instance in point," he analyzes Psalm 118:22–23:

> The stone which the builders rejected
> has become the chief cornerstone.
> This is the Lord's doing;
> it is marvelous in our eyes.

"This passage" writes Oxtoby, "is quoted five times in the New Testament" as a prediction of the rejection and victory of Jesus and the Gospel. However, the meaning of the passage is that "the stone which the builders rejected—is Israel, despised among the nations, deemed of no value among her neighbors, rejected in the eyes of the world, but whom God has chosen and made his own, raising her to a position of significance in his dealings with men. The rejected stone is Israel." [32]

Oxtoby sees what he calls "religious soothsaying" also in Matthew's interpretation of Isaiah 7:14, "Behold, a young woman shall conceive and bear a son and his name shall be called Immanuel." Matthew wrongly translates *alma* with "virgin" and declares that Jesus was the son of a virgin, in keeping with Isaiah's prophecy. Oxtoby, however, asserts:

---

29. Ibid., p. 504.
30. Gurdon C. Oxtoby, *Prediction and Fulfilment in the Bible* (Philadelphia: Westminster Press, 1966), p. 62.
31. Ibid., p. 62.
32. Ibid., pp. 63 f.

> There is a general agreement among Old Testament scholars that the reference is to an anticipated birth to occur within the experience of Ahaz. It was a sign that the coalition with the Northern Kingdom of [Israel] would not succeed. . . . The young woman who is with child is for Isaiah a present personality. . . . What the child signified to Ahaz was therefore the coming of God to deliver Judah from the present threat by Syria and Israel. . . . This is the background of the text quoted by Matthew. The fact that the Greek translation known to him, used the word "virgin" to translate "young woman" may have seemed of special significance to the evangelist.[33]

Lindblom noted, as did numerous other scholars, that "the idea of Jesus' supernatural birth" should be seen in the context of the fact that "the idea of persons fathered by some god was common in the history and mythology of the contemporary non-Christian world."[34]

With respect to Jesus' resurrection, Lindblom points out that "there are undeniably several legendary features which indicate how the first Christians sought to explain and illustrate what happened on the first Easter morning." As for proof of the resurrection, Lindblom avers: "But there were no witnesses to the event. It is and remains inaccessible."[35]

Of course, this does not invalidate belief, because belief is not in need of evidence and proof. Lindblom rightfully asserts that, as Christians should regard it, "the great gift of the New Testament to us is the central content of the divine revelation, the message about God and his work." It is this which matters in the New Testament, and not "a more or less capricious selection of proof texts as a basis for the true faith."[36]

Jewish Expressions on Jesus should be seen as the work of scholars who accept the Gospels *as if* they were history as historians understand and define it. And, when all due allowance is made for the existentialist interpretation of the Gospels, the fact remains that the preponderant majority of Christians—clergy and laity—believe that the Gospels *are* history. Were it otherwise, there would have been no basis for the Vatican Council II reexamination of Jewish culpability in Jesus' death, a reexamination which did not result in an unqualified decision of "innocent of deicide."[37]

---

33. Ibid., pp. 23–25.
34. Lindblom, op. cit., pp. 174 f.
35. Ibid., p. 175.
36. Ibid., p. 186.
37. This anthology is limited to material available in English. For the history of the literature by Jews on Christianity in the corpus of the *Wissenschafts des Judentums,* see Walter Jacobs, *Christianity Through Jewish Eyes* (New York: Hebrew Union College Press, 1974).

Jesus in the Talmud

By Jacob Z. Lauterbach

A STUDY of the relation between Judaism and Christianity, their reactions towards one another and their mutual appreciation or deprecation is of interest not only to the Jewish and Christian theologian, but also to the student of religion in general. In such a study a comparison of the Talmud with the N. T., or an examination of their respective teachings, their agreements or disagreements on fundamental theological questions, occupies a very prominent place. For in the literature of these early centuries, comprising the formative period of Rabbinic Judaism and the beginnings and unfoldment of Christianity, we can best study the fundamental difference between these two religions and their attitudes towards one another. In later years these two religions became more estranged, with the result that frequently only differences are recognized and emphasized while agreements are but rarely acknowledged and appreciated. Both mother and daughter frequently lost their tempers in later years. And whatever parental love and filial respect there may have existed in the earlier days was almost completely forgotten. The representatives of both religions became embittered and irritated, and they spoke harsh words of and to one another and rather sought to deprecate and minimize the truths contained in the religion of their opponents.

We must first seek to ascertain whether the Talmud and the authentic Midrashim have some information to give us about Jesus and his disciples and the birth of Christianity. We must leave out of our discussion later rabbinic works on this subject as well as works of Jewish legendary literature about the life of Jesus in their various forms and versions, such as *Tam u-Mu'ad*, *Toledot Yeshu*, *Ma'aseh d'oto v'et B'no*.[1] We may indeed consider

---

[1] See S. Krauss, *Das Leben Jesu nach Jüdischen Quellen*, (Berlin, 1902), for the various versions; also L. Ginzberg, מעשה.ישו, in *Ginze Schechter*, (New York, 1928), 324 ff.

them occasionally insofar as they may sometimes throw light on older works and help us to a better understanding of the authentic reports or allusions in the Talmud. For while it is possible that all these later works depend upon older sources and in some of their statements go back to older works of Talmudic times, they are not authentic Midrashic works. They do not cite their sources nor mention them by name, so that we cannot judge the character of these supposed sources nor decide upon their reliability. Furthermore, it is most likely to assume that whatever information these later works may have drawn from older authentic works is not reproduced in its original form. It is given in a later legendary form, embedded in layers of popular fancies. We are not so much interested in this study at least, in popular Jewish sentiment toward Jesus. We want to know what the authorities of Judaism, as represented in the literature of the Talmud and the authentic Midrashim, have to say about the beginning and very earliest history of Christianity. We want to find out whether the authentic literature of the Talmud and Midrashim have some information to give us about Jesus and his disciples — and what this information is. And in examining the information on these subjects which we may find in the Talmud, we must be careful to distinguish between such as comes from early sources, or sources contemporary with Jesus, and such as comes from later times. For the Talmud embodies documents and teachings originating in the four pre-Christian as well as in five or six Christian centuries. And some of the contents of the Midrashim represent material of even later centuries. Accordingly, the statements found in the Talmud are not all of equal value, and the reports found in the Talmud and in the Midrashim are not all of equal historical reliability. A report about any event given by an eye-witness is of course of greater historic value and more reliable than a report by a later historian or teacher, who may have drawn his information from older records but may also have obtained it from mere hearsay. In other words, we shall have to consider who the authors of the information found in the Talmud were, and when and where they lived. And yet we cannot set out to ascertain what these early teachers of Judaism actually knew about Jesus and Christianity. We can only seek those reports which were embodied in the literature that has come down to us.

For it is quite possible that these earlier teachers knew more about the origins of Christianity than they cared to report or had occasion to express even to their contemporaries and disciples. If for one reason or another they did not care to speak about these things publicly and explicitly, it would be futile for us to attempt to find out what they knew about them. We cannot make them talk now. We can only guess sometimes and draw conclusions from a veiled allusion or from a side remark about other questions that may have been prompted by what they knew or thought of early Christianity. But all our interpretations of such allusions or indirect remarks cannot claim absolute accuracy and certainty. They are only guesses. Again, it is quite conceivable that not all the information given by these early teachers and embodied in the original works of the Talmudic literature have been preserved to us. Perhaps in their original form the Talmud and Midrashim contained some information about the New Testament characters or some express references to Christianity which in the course of time were eliminated either by Christian censors, by Jews themselves for fear of censors,[2] or even because such information was not considered worth preserving by the later Jewish editors. Some of this early material may have been omitted or lost by sheer negligence or accident without any intentional effort by friend or foe, just as so much other literary material even of an halakic nature, which was certainly regarded as important, as well as haggadic information from ancient times, became lost in the course of the centuries before the age of printing. We must content ourselves with an investigation of the material which is available to us.

---

[2] Even in some Spanish MSS some passages were omitted. See H. L. Strack, *Einleitung* . . ., 68 and R. N. Rabbinovicz, מאמר על הדפסת התלמוד, 24. Jewish printers like Soncino exercised censorship. See Strack, *ibid.*, 84 and 88. Cf. also the letter of the Jewish authorities in Poland in 1631 demanding elimination of references to Jesus in printed editions, see Strack, *ibid.*, 87. Censor-free editions are Bomberg I, 1520–1523; II, 1531; Justinian, 1548. (First censored, Basel, 1578–80, Amsterdam 1644–48 partly restored the omitted passages.)

That is to say, we must deal with the literature as we have it now and consider the talmudic-midrashic works in the form in which they have come down and been preserved to us in those early editions or manuscripts which were, comparatively speaking, free from censorship.

In the later editions the censors expunged passages from the Talmud which though not expressly mentioning Jesus or Christians, were considered by the censors as unfavorable to Jesus or Christianity. Some of these omitted or stricken passages are found in the older editions or have been saved and preserved in separate works.[3] But, as already stated, there may have been many more passages stricken out from the Talmud before the first printed editions appeared or even before the time of the oldest existing MSS.

I said that this study is of interest to both Jew and Christian. But I should add that this interest is — or should be — purely scientific and not apologetic or polemic. It should not aim to prove or disprove the New Testament reports about the central figure of Christianity or its earliest advocates and teachers. For, it must be acknowledged, that from a strictly scientific point of view, the question of the historicity of Jesus cannot be answered either way on the basis of the little information about him found in the Talmud or the lack of such information in the contemporary Jewish literature, that is, in those parts of the Talmud which date from the first century of the common era.

The lack of available information about Jesus in contemporary talmudic literature, i. e., in sayings by Tannaim of the first generation, even if it could be assumed with certainty that the talmudic literature never contained any such passages would not necessarily argue against his historicity. Such an *argumentum e silentio* in this case cannot be regarded as valid or cogent. Such silence may have been purely accidental, in that the earliest redactors of the Talmud may not have had an occasion to embody a report about Jesus by a contemporary in their collections; or such a silence may have been due to ignorance about him on the

---

3 Like ספר חסרונות הש״ס or ספר חסרונות והוא קבוצת ההשמטות (Krakau, 1893); another edition קונטרס למלאות חסרונות הש״ס (Königsberg, 1860); and קונטרס אומר השכחה, 1861; also ספר השבת אבדה (Lemberg [?] 1858).

part of his contemporaries who may not even have noticed his existence or his activity, the reports in the New Testament as to the great excitement caused by Jesus in his days notwithstanding.[4] After all the Talmud does not furnish a complete history of *all* the important events or great personalities of the first century of the common era. Many such events and personalities may have gone unnoticed by the earlier teachers and actually are not mentioned in the Talmud. Jesus and his activity may have been one of these. But aside from these considerations, accepting the historicity of Jesus, the silence could be explained on other grounds. Thus it might be assumed that the Jewish authorities of his days did not consider Jesus of sufficient importance or worth to discuss him or report about him.

But above all, there is the other possibility, that the Jewish teachers of his time *did* discuss Jesus and did refer to him, favorably or unfavorably, but their references to him and their statements about him were later suppressed and ultimately became lost to us.

On the other hand, the scanty references to him that are still to be found in the Talmud and in the Midrashim do not at all prove his historicity, any more than the records of the New Testament.

The references and allusions to Jesus found in the Talmud and in the Midrashim are of such a nature that they cannot be considered convincing proof that he actually existed. For, as will be shown, not even one *single statement* preserved to us in the talmudic-midrashic literature can be regarded as authentic in the sense that it originated in the time of Jesus or even in the first half century of the Christian era. The Talmud does not record even one *talmudic teacher* who lived at the time of Jesus or in the first half century of the Christian era as mentioning Jesus by name, telling something about him, or expressly referring to him in any way. In other words, the Talmud does not furnish any contemporary evidence for the historicity of Jesus.

The references to Jesus recorded in the Talmud are mostly

[4] This is actually assumed by Klausner as one of the causes of the *silence* of the contemporary Jewish authorities about Jesus. See his ישו הנוצרי, 4th ed., (Jerusalem, 1933), 9. Cf. however M. Guttmann in *MGWJ*, (1931), 252.

5

from teachers who lived a long time after Jesus. A very few of them come from teachers who lived in the beginning of the second century of the common era, or at the earliest, in the later part of the first century, but not earlier than the first or the original authors of the synoptic gospels.[5] Whatever these teachers have to say about Jesus simply refers to the person *legendary* or historical — who was believed by the people of their time, especially by the Christian sect, to have been the originator of the Christian sect. The rabbis may have contented themselves with, or relied upon, current stories about him. They certainly knew, and came into contact with, the Christians of their days. And in the second century most of the synoptic gospels, giving the life story of Jesus as the originator of the new faith or the founder of the sect and of the new religion were already redacted. The Christians of the second century among whom these were circulated, certainly believed in a Jesus, as the originator of their new faith or the founder of their new religion. The Jewish teachers of that time, in polemics or in casual references, merely referred to that person, the real or alleged founder, who was the central figure of Christianity. They never argued the question whether such a figure had actually existed or not, since Christianity was an actual reality. They probably were not even interested in this question. For their purpose or from their point of view, which concerned itself merely with the truth or falsehood, the correctness or the incorrectness of the Christian teachings, it really was of no great consequence, or at least it made no difference to them, whether the person in whose name these teachings were given had actually lived or not. To deny that he had lived would not have disproved the teachings ascribed to him. They could accept or believe the legends current about him, and believe that such a person had lived, and nevertheless dispute his greatness or reject and argue against his teachings. But they had no interest in inquiring whether and when he

---

[5] The composition of the present Mark dates from about 70 C. E., that of Matthew and Luke between 70 and 110 C. E. All of them used older sources or gospels, which go back to about the year 50 C. E. though not earlier. See James Moffatt, *Introduction to the Literature of the New Testament*, (New York, 1923), 212 ff.

6

lived. They usually did this only in case of people in whom they were especially interested or in whose teachings they believed, e. g., when they seek to determine who Elijah was,[6] or from what tribe he came,[7] or fix the time and generation of Job.[8] But they probably did not care to inquire whether a person whose teachings they rejected and whose mission or importance they did not believe, actually lived or was merely a myth. Hence, we need not expect to be able to decide the question of Jesus' historicity on the basis of the references made to him by those rabbis of the Talmud who lived after his time. Of course there is a possibility that these references to Jesus by Rabbis of the second century, came from earlier times. Sayings or teachings quoted in the Talmud in the name of a teacher may sometimes be not his own original teaching, but such as he received from older teachers. It is therefore possible — though not plausible — that these later rabbis of the Talmud, when mentioning Jesus or making any statement about him or his disciples, do not give their own original views, but merely quote or repeat what they have heard from their teachers or received by tradition from teachers of former generations — among whom there may have been contemporaries of Jesus. In the latter case, then, we would have the evidence as to Jesus' historical existence coming from his contemporary Jewish teachers, preserved to us and quoted by Rabbis who lived a long time after him. But since in the case of any statement made by a teacher without giving the source, we cannot decide whether that teacher gives his own saying or the view of another teacher, and if this latter is so, when that other teacher lived, it still remains doubtful, to say the least, whether the information contained in that saying, is of an older or of recent date. So the statement that we cannot find in the Talmud *contemporary* evidence of the historical existence of Jesus remains unchallenged.

Yet these references to Jesus made by later rabbis of the Talmud are of great importance and of interest to us. For even if they cannot help us to decide the question of the historicity

---

[6] B. M. 14b. פנחס זה אליהו.

[7] Gen. r. 71.12 אליהו משבט גד (או) משבט בנימין; אליהו כהן היה.

[8] B. B. 15a,b מעולי גולה or איוב בימי משה היה etc.

7

of Jesus, we can still learn from what the rabbis of the Talmud, beginning with the second century, thought about Jesus. It is of no small interest to know what the reaction of Judaism to Christianity, in its formative period, was, and what the rabbis thought about Christianity, its teachings and its alleged or real founder. In other words to know, what information the authoritative Jewish literature, the Talmud and the Midrashim, has about the attitude of the Jewish people, as voiced by their representative teachers, toward Christianity in the first three or four centuries of its history.

In seeking to answer this question we shall proceed in the following manner. We shall first seek to find out what information the Talmud and Midrashim have to give us about Jesus himself — whether they have something to say about the person of Jesus; whether they mention him by his name, Jesus, or designate him by any other name, or refer to him under any special designation like בן פנטירא or בן סטרא or under the disguise of a biblical name like בלעם or allude to him by certain terms unmistakably pointing to him like אותו האיש, פלוני or describing his personality when speaking of him as "man" or "son of man."

Then we shall see whether any mention is made in the talmudic-midrashic literature of his family, relatives, mother and brothers, disciples and followers. In the case of the latter we shall seek to discover also whether some of them are mentioned by their real names, by a substitute name, or merely referred to under the general designation of his disciples, followers or Christians, נוצרים. In connection with a discussion of the latter group, we shall also consider whether, and in which cases, the designation מינים refers to Christians or merely designates heretics in general. Then again we shall consider the various heretical writings or books mentioned in the Talmud ספרי מינים, or ספרי קוסמים, to determine whether they refer to or include also writings of the early Christians or collections of their teachings; also what other general reference to the New Testament, as עון גליון or גליונות or אורייתא אחריתא are found in the Talmud, and whether quotations from it, agreeing or disagreeing with the existent versions of the New Testament, can be discovered in the talmudic-midrashic literature.

8

Beginning with the question whether Jesus is mentioned by his name in the Talmud, we shall first consider the following passage which connects him with an older teacher, a teacher living long before the time in which the Jesus of the Gospels is supposed to have lived.

In the Tractate Sanhedrin[9] of the Babylonian Talmud in a Baraita which reads: ת"ר לעולם תהא שמאל דוחה וימין מקרבת ולא כאלישע שדחפו לגחזי בשתי ידים, there are — although omitted in the present censored editions but found in the Munich manuscript (written 1343) as well as in the older uncensored editions (i. e., those printed before the edition of Basel 1578–81) — following the words בשתי ידים, this additional remark: ולא כיהושע בן פרחיה שדחפו לישו הנוצרי בשתי ידים.[10] This Baraita then declares that Jesus had been a disciple or follower of Joshua b. Peraḥyah by whom he was then repulsed. On the same page in the Talmud about ten lines below, after the words א"ר יוחנן ניחזי ושלשת בניו there is found in the MSS and in the earlier editions a story which seeks to explain the unrelenting attitude of Jeshua b. Peraḥyah towards Jesus referred to in the above Baraita, and to explain how, when and why the latter left Judaism after having been excommunicated and repulsed by his teacher. It reads as follows: ר' יהושע בן פרחיה מאי הוא כדקטלינהו ינאי מלכא לרבנן אזל רבי יהושע בן פרחיה וישו (כת"י מ הנוצרי) לאלכסנדריא של מצרים כי הוה שלמא שלח ליה שמעון בן שטח מיני ירושלים עיר הקודש ליכי אלכסנדריא של מצרים אחותי בעלי שרוי בתוכך ואנכי יושבת שוממה קם אתא ואתרמי ליה ההוא אושפיזא עבדו ליה יקרא טובא אמר כמה יפה אכסניא זו אמר ליה רבי עיניה טרוטות אמר ליה רשע בכך אתה עוסק אפיק ארבע מאה שיפורי ושמתיה אתא לקמיה כמה זימנין אמר ליה קבלן לא הוה קא משגח ביה יומא חד הוה קא קאי קריאת שמע אתא לקמיה סבר מידחא לקבולי אחוי ליה בידיה הוא סבר מידחא דחי ליה אזל זקף לבינתא והשתחוה לה אמר ליה הדר בך אמר ליה (כת"י מ ישו) כך מקובלני ממך כל החוטא ומחטיא את הרבים אין מספיקין בידו לעשות תשובה ואמר מר ישו (כת"י מ הנוצרי) כישף והסית והדיח.[11] Let us consider first a few minor details and the meaning of some words in this story before

[9] Sanh. 107b.

[10] The designation הנוצרי after לישו is omitted in some of the older prints; see R. N. Rabbinovicz, *Diḳduḳe Soferim*, ad loc.

[11] Read the text in the Venice edition; also Soṭah 47a, Amsterdam edition, or in חסרונות הש"ס (Krakau, 1893).

we examine its contents as a whole to determine its reliability and accuracy. The name ישו by which Jesus is here mentioned is probably merely a shortened form of the name ישוע (the abbreviation sign on top is a later addition.)[12] But since such an abbreviated form of the name is not used in any other case of a person named ישוע or יהושע, but persistently and consistently used when the name refers to Jesus, it may be assumed that this shortening of the name was probably an intentional mutilation by cutting off part of it. The rabbis mention other instances of the names of persons being shortened because of their misconduct,[13] but here in the case of the name Jeshua there may have been an additional special reason for shortening it into Jeshu. Elias Levita[14] thinks that the reason was that the Jews, unwilling to even suggest that Jesus might have been a savior, or redeemer, which the name ישוע with an *ayin* at the end signifies, dropped the letter *ayin* from his name.[15]

At any rate, here in the talmudic text, this shorter form of the name was *not* meant to represent the curse ימח שמו וזכרו, "May his name and memory be blotted out," although in the later Jewish works about the life of Jesus this form of the name was understood to be an abbreviation of the three words constituting this curse.[16]

The meaning of the designation הנוצרי which, as we have seen, the MS text adds to the name ישו in our passage, we shall discuss further on in connection with the name נוצרים used as a designation for the Christians.[17] Here I will only point out that

[12] Cf. the shorter form עדו in Zech. 1.1 and in Ezra 5.1 and see S. Krauss, *op. cit.*, 250; also אשתמוע, Josh. 21.14, shortened to אשתמה and Keri אשתמו, *ibid.*, 15.50. See Ch. D. Ginsburg ed. of the Hebrew Bible.

[13] See Mekilta, *Amalek* III, (Friedmann 576, Lauterbach II, 165), the case of עפרן for עפרון and יונדב for יהונדב.

[14] Tishbi as quoted by Krauss, *op. cit.*, 250.

[15] שהיהודים אינם מודים שהוא היה המושיע לפיכך אינם רוצים לקראו ישוע והפילו העין וקורין לו ישו. See also H. L. Strack, *Jesus Die Häretiker und die Christen, nach den Ältesten Jüdischen Angaben*, (Leipzig, 1910), 8.

[16] Thus the author of the מעשה דאותו ואת בנו in Krauss, *op. cit.*, 68 says ואז החרימו חרם בישראל שלא יקרא שמו יהושע אלא ישו כלומר ימח שמו וזכרו וכן קראו משם ואילך בזה השם.

[17] b. Ta'an. 27b. See older editions and *Dikduke Soferim*.

the derivation of this name from Nazareth, presents many difficulties.[18] First, it is doubtful whether there was at that time a
town by that name. If, however, there was, we would have to
read the name Nozaret נוצרת or Nozerah נוֹצְרָה in order to derive
the gentilic נוצרי after the fashion of תמני from חמנה.[19] In the Greek
text of Matthew 2.23 and John 19.19, he is called Ναζωραῖος,
i. e., Nazoraios. This would be a transliteration from נוצריה, which
cannot mean "a man from Nazareth," but must be derived from
נוֹצֵר or נוֹטֵר, "observe," "watch." נוצרי then would mean "an
observer" equal to נוטר, שומר, in this case an observer of a rule or
of the law. נוצרי or נצורא, the Syriac name for Christians, would
be a *nomen agentis* equal in form to סבורא, אמורא, and in the
plural נְצוֹרַיָא would designate people characterized as being strict
"observers" or "keepers of the law" נוצרי תורה or שומרי תורה. It
may have designated a group from a much older period than the
time of Jesus, whose name the Christians, wishing to be regarded
as of similar character, as the true observers of the law, or the
observers of the new or true law, borrowed.[20]

Another detail in this report concerns the meaning of the
expression זקף לבינתא, "put up a brick." We do not know of any
satisfactory explanation for this phrase as it stands, for it can
hardly be assumed that even in a later report Jesus should have
been accused of having worshipped an idol consisting of a
"brick." R. Jeḥiel of Paris in his disputation which took place
in the year 1240 in Paris, suggests that the brick was in the
form of a cross.[21] According to these emendations or explanations,

---

[18] Some Christians would derive the name from נצר = צמח = משיח.

[19] See Herford, *Christianity in Talmud and Midrash*, 52, note, 164–170,
344 and 379.

[20] See Mark Lidzbarski, *Mandäische Liturgien*, (Berlin, 1920), XVI ff.,
and *Ginza, Der Schatz oder das grosse Buch der Mandäer*, (Göttingen and Leipzig), 1925, IX. See below the discussion of passage in Matthew and Talmud
Taanit.

[21] ויכוח רבינו יחיאל, ed. Grünbaum, (Thorn, 1873), 5; ed. R. Margulies,
Lemberg, (*s. d.*), 17. He says, והכי משמע שהשתחווה ללבינה איכא למימר דההיא
לבינה עשויה כשתי וערב כמעשיהם. In the work חם ומועד (no date or place of publication given) 10, it is suggested that there were two bricks — reading לבינתא —
one placed on top or across the other and held by magic: וילך הרשע וזקף לבינה
על גבי לבינה בכשפים.

this sentence would contain a reference to the worship of the cross. But how could Jesus worship the cross before he was crucified? Had the cross some significance before the crucifixion? The same allusion to the cross is found in this sentence, if we emend the text with A. S. Kamenetzki to read צליבתא instead of לבינתא.[22] But there is no basis for this emendation in the MSS. At any rate, the phrase as it stands in our text makes no sense.

Another detail in the report is the phrase אפיק ד' מאה שיפורי ושמתיה. "He sounded four hundred trumpets and excommunicated him." We find a similar statement in b. M. Ḳ. 16a in the report that Barak declared the ban over Meroz (Judg. 5.23) with four hundred blasts of the trumpet, which may also mean that four hundred trumpets were used in declaring or announcing the ban בד' מאה שיפורי שמתיה ברק למרוז. Meroz there is taken by some to have been a person and by some a star,[23] but in this case the trumpets may have been for purposes of proclamation or making it known to the whole camp. What, however, would be the significance of the four hundred trumpets here? To proclaim it to the whole world? As to the use of the Shofar in connection with proclaiming a ban, we have the statement מאי שיפורא שנפרעין ממנו[24] which seems to pre-suppose the use of a Shofar when proclaiming a ban. The significance of its use appears to derive not from its *sound*, but from the mere name שופר which, as a pun on the word שנפרעין ממנו was to serve as a sort of reminder either to the people that the heavenly powers *will*, or to the heavenly powers themselves that they *should*, exact punishment of the man put in ban. Since other definite explanations of the use of the Shofar, or express prescription that it should be used in connection with the act of proclaiming a ban are, to my knowledge, not found in tannaitic literature, it is doubtful whether Joshua b. Peraḥyah used it. I cannot even find any reference to it in a Palestinian source. In b. Sanh. 7b it is said that R. Huna when going out to hold court would say, "Bring

22 A. S. Kamenetzki in התקופה XVIII, (Warsaw, 1923), 511, וכבר בארתי במקום אחר שבמקום ''לבינתא'' צריך להיות ''צליבתא'' (זקף מורה בארמית ''תלה'' ''צלב'') ובכן יש כאן רמז אנדי על עבודת הצלב לנוצרים.

23 Cf. also b. Shebu. 36a.

24 b. M. K. 17b.

out for me the implements of my office, the whip, the staff, the Shofar and the sandal;" which Rashi explains to mean שופר לשמעתא ונדוי. So here, if Rashi is correct the Shofar was one of the means used not only for proclaiming but actually in imposing or pronouncing a ban. Although even here it may mean only to announce the ban, that is, to make it known to the public by means of the Shofar. Likewise the saying of Samuel, "The blow (the sound of the Shofar) binds; the blow releases"[25] is understood by R. Ḥananel[26] and Rashi[27] to mean that by the sound of the Shofar the ban is pronounced or imposed and by the sound of the Shofar the ban can also be removed or lifted. This would mean then that the Shofar sound in itself was the very means of imposing the ban and making it effective.[28] There seems to have been the practice in later, amoraic times, and certainly in gaonic times of using the Shofar as a means by which a ban was pronounced.[29] At any rate we do not find any reference in tannaitic sources to the use of the Shofar in connection with the imposition of ḥerem, though in Tannaitic times it may have been used to proclaim the ban. The manner in which Joshua b. Peraḥyah is reported to have excommunicated Jesus reminds one rather of the later amoraic or gaonic practice and speaks against the authenticity of this report. The whole tone of the story is legendary. At any rate it is not a contemporary document. It is a later report and as a whole has no real historic value, though it may have some elements of truth in it, as we shall see.

In the first place, the whole report about Joshua b. Peraḥyah's flight to Egypt is questionable. It is rather doubtful whether

---

[25] b. M. K. 16a, טוט אסר טוט שרי.

[26] *Ad loc.*   [27] *Ad loc.*

[28] Cf. however, Tosafot Men. 34b, *s. v.* טט בכתפי where one explains the phrase טוט אסר in the saying of Samuel to mean two scholars or judges can pronounce the ban, and two others have the power or authority to remove it. According to this interpretation Samuel had no reference at all to the Shofar.

[29] A full description of the חרם with the use of the Shofar and other horrifying means is given in a responsum of R. Paltoi Gaon in תשובות הגאונים (Lyck, 1864), No. 10, page 8. [May it also have been used to ward off danger from the persons who pronounce the ban?] Cf. also as to the use of the Shofar for mere announcing or proclaiming a prohibition the saying in 'Ab. Zarah 40a, נפק שיפורי דרבא ואסר שיפורי דרב הונה.....ושרי.

Joshua b. Peraḥyah ever went to Egypt. One report which, as we shall see, seems more authentic, names Judah b. Tabbai, and thus casts doubt on our story, which names Joshua.[30] It is very likely that the story in the Babli is but a modification of the other report found in p. Ḥagigah[31] about Judah b. Tabbai who had to run away to Alexandria and later on was recalled to Jerusalem. A later reporter who had heard the story about Judah b. Tabbai confused him with Joshua b. Peraḥyah and mixed with the story other legendary reports about persons who went from Palestine to Alexandria. Out of this confusion of the story about Judah b. Tabbai with other stories, emerged the story as we have it in the Babli, with the suspiciously legendary features of the "brick" and "four hundred shofars" and the specific name of Jesus.

The story about Judah b. Tabbai in p. Ḥagigah[32] reads as follows: מאן דאמר יהודה בן טבאי נשיא עובדא אלכסנדריא מסייע ליה יהודה
בן טבאי הוון בני ירושלם בעון ממניתיה נשיא בירושלם עדק ואזל ליה
לאלכסנדריאה והיו בני ירושלם כותבין מירושלם הגדולה לאלכסנדריאה
הקטנה עד מתי ארוסי יוסב מרתא דביתא דקבלתן מה הוות חסירה (חסידה?)
א"ל חדמן תלמידוי רבי עיינה חות שברה א"ל הא תרתי גבך חדא דחשדתני
וחדא דיסתכלת בה מה אמרית ואייא ברייא לא אמרית אלא בעובדא וכעס
ואזל עלוי. This story has nothing legendary about it and may actually have happened. The expression ואזל at the end may mean simply, "he went away," that is, left the teacher, without any other implication as to the subsequent career of the disciple. It may, however, also mean, he went away and left Judaism, corresponding to the phrase יצא לתרבות רעה. Possibly also it means that he died אזל מן עלמא. Z. Frankel assumes that the whole account of Joshua b. Peraḥyah's going to and coming back from Alexandria is unhistoric. But if we should assume that there is some truth in this legend, and it is based on a traditional report that Joshua b. Peraḥyah had a disciple by the name of Jesus who was expelled by the teacher and who left Judaism, it would not prove anything in regard to the Jesus of the Gospels, who is reported to have been born about 130 years after Joshua b. Peraḥyah. And indeed, some people assume on the basis of this story that there were two

[30] See Z. Frankel, *Darkhe ha-Mishnah*, 35–36.
[31] II, 2, (77d).   [32] *Loc. cit.*

14

men named Jesus.[33] Some Christian scholars likewise assume that there had been a pre-Christian Jesus. Some of those who deny the historicity of the Jesus of the Gospels claim that the Jesus of the Gospels is unhistorical and that the story of the Gospel is but a myth woven around the name of Jesus b. Pandera, a certain person who had been put to death under the reign of Alexander Jannai (106–79 B. C. E.).[34]

One Christian scholar assumes that Jesus indeed lived in the time of Joshua b. Peraḥyah, but that the Gospel writers confused him with a false prophet who lived in the time of Pontius Pilate.[35] He assumes, then, that our story has some historical value. In fact, many of the later Jewish sources do put Jesus in the time of Joshua b. Peraḥyah and Simon b. Shetaḥ.[36]

Likewise, Abraham ibn Daud (1110–1180) in his *Sefer ha-Kabbalah*[37] says: וכותבי זכרונות בישראל אומרים שיהושע בן פרחיה רבו של ישו הנוצרי.[38] He takes notice of the difference between this and the non-Jewish reports and concludes with what he considers a true tradition: קבלת אמת בידינו כי בשנת ארבע לאלכסנדר המלך נולד ומת בן שלשים ושש בשנת שלש למלכות אריסטובולים בן ינאי. This would put Jesus about 70 years before the Gospel date. At any rate, the Jesus of the Gospels, said to have been born under the reign of Herod the Great, could not have lived in the time of Alexander Jannai and could not have been the disciple of Joshua b. Peraḥyah.

The story about Jesus as given in our passage in b. Sanhedrin

---

[33] See R. Jehiel in his ויכוח, ed. R. Margulies (Lemberg), 16–17, who says that this story refers to another Jesus.

[34] For the literature, see Albert Schweitzer, *Von Reimarus bis Wrede, eine Geschichte des Leben Jesu Forschung*, (Tübingen, 1906).

[35] Cf. Maurice Goguel, *Jesus the Nazarene, Myth or History*, (1926).

[36] See S. Kraus, *op. cit.*, 65, 118, 147. In a MS of a Midrash in the British Museum, (Margoliouth, *Catalogue* II, [1915], 21) there is found the following statement, דע שישוע הנוצרי היה קודם חרבן הבית כמאה וחמש ושלשים שנה. Cf. Margoliouth's reference to Steinschneider as to another MS containing the same statement.

[37] Neubauer, *Medieval Jewish Chronicles* I, 53.

[38] Why does he not say "The Talmud says" if our passage in the Talmud was regarded as authentic? In other words the story in our Talmud passage was not regarded by him as קבלת אמת, true tradition.

cannot be considered an historical account of the Jesus of the
Gospels and certainly cannot be considered as contemporary
evidence or as proof for his historicity. It is merely a legend. In
this case we can at least guess, if not explain, how this legend
originated and on the basis of the following assumptions show the
process by which it may have developed and how it became
associated with the name of Joshua b. Peraḥyah. It may be
considered a historic fact that when in the second half of the
second century B. C. E. one of the teachers of Jerusalem, Judah
b. Tabbai (or Joshua b. Peraḥyah) went to Alexandria, he was
accompanied by some of his disciples. It may also be assumed
as historically true, as we have no reason to consider it improbable, that one of the disciples accompanying the teacher, coming
under the influence of the Alexandrian heretical doctrines, disgraced himself and left Judaism. Such a sad occurence seems to
be supposed in the saying of Abtalyon in Ab. 1 12: אבטליון אומר
חכמים הזהרו בדבריכם שמא תחובו חובת גלות ותגלו למקום מים הרעים וישתו
התלמידים הבאים אחריכם וימותו ונמצא שם שמים מתחלל. Whether it
happened to a pupil of Joshua b. Peraḥyah or to one of Judah
b. Tabbai is of no significance. At any rate it was not Jesus.
It must have happened to a disciple of one of the teachers preceding Shemayah and Abtalyon, for Abtalyon apparently
based his saying on this unfortunate event. It seems more likely
that it happened to a disciple of Judah b. Tabbai as the story
in the Yerushalmi has it. This story does not mention Jesus, in
fact, it does not give any name but merely refers to "one of his
disciples." In the Babylonian Talmud, however, the story was
enlarged and the name Jesus added. One might argue that the
original story named Jesus but the Yerushalmi omitted the reference. This, however, would not be likely. We can well understand
how the original story about "one of the disciples" was misunderstood in Babylon as referring to Jesus. They may have
heard the legend told in the gospels, that Jesus had been to
Egypt.[39] They also heard that Jesus was a wizard, who wrought
witchcraft, and enticed and led men astray. They also had heard,
as we shall see below, that Jesus was originally a disciple but

[39] Matth. 2.13-15.

16

later became corrupted in his doctrine.[40] And so they jumped
to the conclusion that the disciple who became corrupt and who
was in Egypt was Jesus. Hence they told the story about Jesus
instead of about "one of the disciples." (Of course it is possible
that even in the Babli the name Jesus is a later insertion.)

There was also another confusion of persons and names which
may have caused the Babylonians to assume that this "disciple"
was Jesus. The Babylonians had heard of a Jesus Sirach, the
grandson of the older Sirach, who came to Egypt about 132
B. C. E., approximately the time of Joshua b. Peraḥyah, and
translated his grandfather's work into Greek. This book of ben-
Sirach was regarded as one of the external books, ספרים חיצונים.[41]
Thus the Babylonians knew of a Jesus who was the author or
translator of one of the ספרים חיצונים, for they confused Sirach
the grandfather.with Sirach the grandson who went to Egypt,
that is, the author with the translator. There were many legends
about this Jesus Sirach, the author of the book, which resemble
the legends about Jesus of Nazareth. His mother, too, was a
virgin, the daughter of Jeremiah, who conceived indirectly from
her father Jeremiah, (the numerical value of whose name ירמיהו
is the same as סירא = 271)[42] by means of a bath-tub.[43] These
legends the Babylonians may have vaguely known, just as they
vaguely knew or heard of the legends about Jesus who was taken
as a child to Egypt. Having in their mind identified the two men
named Jesus, they, therefore, assumed that it was Jesus of
Nazareth who went to Egypt about the year 132 B. C. E., the
time that Jesus Sirach, the younger, went. Likewise, they made
him go not as a child with his father Joseph but with his teacher.
The name Jeshua may indeed have suggested the teacher's name
Jehoshua b. Peraḥyah instead of Judah b. Tabbai, that is a יהושע

---

[40] תלמיד שהקדיח תבשילו ברבים, Ber. 17b, Sanh. 103.

[41] See p. Sanh. 10.1 (28a), ספרים חיצונים כגון ספרי בן סירא ובן לענה and b.
Sanh. 100a where Rab Joseph forbids the reading of Ben Sirach.

[42] See *Yuḥasin* 103, *s. v.* אבוה, in the name of Judah ha-Nasi. See also
Rashi to Ḥag. 15a, *s. v.* , כאמבטי.

[43] See Steinschneider's edition of אלפא ביתא דבן סירא (Berlin, 1858), 16b,
17, a work containing parts from different ages, one from about the end of the
Gaonic period and another part of later date.

17

with a ה to contrast him with his pupil. The teacher with ה in his name had the true belief in God which saved him.[44] The disciple did not have a ה in his name and was lacking in the true belief in God hence was not saved from the bad influence, the מים הרעים of Alexandria.[45]

To sum up, then, the story in b. Sanhedrin is a later legend about Jesus and not a contemporary report, not even a reliable tradition, as is evident from R. Abraham ibn Daud. It merely reflects the vague knowledge of the legends about Jesus that were current about Jesus in later times, about the fifth or sixth century of the Christian era. All it knows of him is that he left Judaism, and caused others to do so and leave their true Jewish religion. He is an enticer who led Israel astray. It knows him as a sorcerer, or one practicing witchcraft, which was the common opinion among the Jews even in the time of the Gospel writers.[46] But it is significant that they speak of him as a one time disciple. Even the later rabbis of the Talmud among whom this legend circulated considered Jesus as having once been a disciple, as one שהקדיח תבשילו, i. e., held false doctrines and followed the practices of magic.

The next passage in the Talmud in which Jesus is mentioned by name and in which he is also referred to and described as a misleader, מסית, is — or rather was — to be found in b. Sanh. 43a,b. It is omitted in the later editions but is found in the earlier printed editions and in the manuscripts. It reads as follows: לפניו אין מעיקרא לא והתניא בערב הפסח תלאוהו לישו והכרוז יוצא לפניו ארבעים יום קודם שהוא ליסקל על שכישף והסית והדיח את ישראל כל מי שיודע לו זכות יבא וילמד עליו ולא מצאו לו זכות ותלאוהו בערב פסח: אמר עולא ותסברא בר הפוכי זכות הוא מסית הוא ורחמנא אמר (דברים י"נ) לא תחמול עליו ולא תכסה עליו אלא שאני ישו דקרוב למלכות הוה: Before we consider this Baraita let us first attempt to ascertain on what day Jesus was executed so as to be able to decide whether this Baraita could have had reference to Jesus and whether it agrees or disagrees

----

[44] Cf. Soṭah 34b, the case of Joshua the son of Nun — יהושע = יה יושיער מעצת מרגלים.

[45] Cf. in addition R. Herford, *Christianity in Talmud and Midrash*, 54 and Heinrich Laible, *Jesus Christus in Talmud*, (Berlin, 1891), 41 ff.

[46] See Matth. 9.34 and 12.24.

18

with the New Testament reports about his execution. Now,
according to the Synoptic Gospels,[47] Jesus was executed on the
first day of the Festival.[48] But according to John 17.8 ff. it was
on the fourteenth of Nisan, before the priests prepared and ate
the Passover lamb, that Jesus was executed, although Jesus had
already eaten his Seder meal the evening previous.[49] Yet they all
agree that he was executed on Friday, for on the third day thereafter, on Sunday, he is said to have arisen. Was Friday *Yom
Ṭob*,[50] so that Jesus could have held Seder on the preceding
night, Thurday evening, as assumed by the Synoptists, or was
it *Ereb Yom Ṭob*, i. e., the fourteenth of Nisan, as John assumes,
and if so, how could Jesus have conducted his Seder before?
The answer is given by Daniel Chwolson.[51] Friday was *Ereb
Yom Ṭob*, but in certain groups בין הערבים was understood as
twilight, i. e., בין השמשות. Those who held that אין פסח דוחה שבת,
for even after Hillel there were some who did not accept his
decision that פסח דוחה שבת,[52] could not slaughter the lamb on
Friday at twilight because בין השמשות ספק יום, hence ספק שבת.
John must have had a report that Jesus was supposed to have
belonged to one such group, hence he reports him as having
offered the Passover sacrifice and celebrated the Seder the night
before.[53] According to John, then, the day in which Jesus was
executed was the fourteenth of Nisan, Friday, *Ereb Shabbat* and
also *Erev Pesaḥ*. The other contradictions in the Gospels do
not concern us.

   Not let us consider our Baraita and see whether it does have

[47] Matth. 26.17 ff. and parallels, Mark 14.12 and Luke 22.7.
[48] Cf. Matth. 27.15 ff. We need not concern ourselves with the difficulty
of Matth. 26.17 "The first day of unleavened bread" = יום ראשון דחג המצות,
i. e., the 15th of Nisan. See Chwolson, *Das letzte Pessahmahl Christi*, (Leipzig, 1908), for it is possible that the fourteenth day, on the afternoon of which
leaven is already forbidden — though Matzah could not yet be eaten — was
regarded by some as the first day of the unleavened bread.
[49] See John 12.2 ff.
[50] The rule לא בד'ו פסח is of a later date.
[51] *Op. cit.*
[52] b. Pes. 66a.
[53] [Ed. note: See J. Lauterbach, "זמן שחיטת הפסח" *Proceedings American
Academy for Jewish Research*, (New York, 1942), vol. 12, Heb. section 1–5.]

reference to Jesus. It contains a few minor difficulties but they
are sufficient to prove that the Baraita is comparatively young
and not entirely authentic. We must remember that this Baraita
is merely cited in a discussion seeking to understand the Mishnah
which says והכרוז יוצא לפניו. The Gemara challenges the implied
interpretation of לפניו as "immediately before but not previous
to that time," by quoting this Baraitha, the authenticity of which
is at all times open to question as is not infrequent in talmudic
discussion.

In the first place, the statement והכרוז יוצא לפניו ארבעים יום, is
rather strange. Does it assume, taking לפניו literally, that for
forty days they would, on each day, lead out the victim with the
herald walking in front of him proclaiming that he was going to
be executed.

But such a procedure is unknown in Jewish law. Aside from
the fact that the Mishnah[54] speaks only of the herald actually
going in front of the victim on his way to the place where he was
to be executed, there is no precedent for forty days of such an-
nouncements. One might possibly expect such a precedent in the
case of a זקן ממרא, a rebellious teacher[55] whose execution was
announced sometime before it actually took place.[56] But there it
is said that they would announce it through letters — but not
by a herald. And even there, no mention is made of a period of
forty days. All it says is: וכותבין ושולחין בכל המקומות which was
probably an announcement of the execution yet to be performed.
It is possible, however, that someone computed as follows: if a
"rebellious elder" (whose execution had to take place during the
time of a pilgrim festival) was judged and convicted on the first
day after Pesaḥ, they would keep him till the next pilgrim festival, i. e., till Shabuoth. Of course, they would not execute him
on the holiday itself (for the phrase "they execute him at the
festival" means at the time or season of the festival)[57] but on

54 Sanh. 6.1.   55 Mishnah Sanh. 11.4.

56 As to whether Jesus could have been considered a זקן ממרא, see above,
The Pharisees and Their Teachings, page 92, note 7, to which is to be added that
Jesus was merely a תלמיד, not yet a זקן and תלמיד שהורה לעשות פטור (Mishnah
Sanh. 11.2).

57 "Zur Festzeit;" see N. Brüll, *Jahrbücher*, VII, 96.

the day before, which was close to the time of the festival when all the prilgrims were already assembled in Jerusalem. In this case, there would be forty days between the sentence and the execution. This Baraita, then, would regard Jesus as a זקן ממרא, "rebellious elder," who denied the traditions of the teachers, and in such a case an elapse of forty days between the sentence and the execution was possible. The author of this Baraita must then have assumed further that Jesus was sentenced about forty days before Pesach, so that they had to keep him forty days until Pesaḥ. To fill out these forty days with some activity, the reporter put in the unheard of practice of the *herald* proclaiming for forty days, instead of the sending out of the letters. But even if we assume this, it will show that the author of this Baraita was badly confused.[58]

Unless we assume that the author of our Baraita somehow heard or believed that Jesus was sentenced about forty days

[58] It is interesting to note the theory of M. Joel, *Blicke in die Religions-geschichte usw.*, (Breslau, 1882), II, 58, who assumes a similar confusion in a Baraita. In Tosefta Sanh. 11.7, (Zuckermandel, 432), the rule about משמרין אותו עד הרגל which the Mishnah applies only to זקן ממרא is extended to others, *viz.*, to מסית ומדיח ונביא השקר which would fit the case of Jesus. The Tosefta passage reads: ומשמרין אותו עד הרגל וממיתין אותו ברגל שנ' וכל העם ישמעו ויראו ולא יזידון עוד דברי ר' עקיבא אמר לו ר' יהודה וכי נאמר וכל העם יראו ויראו אלא כל העם ישמעו ויראו ולמה מענין את דינו של זה אלא ממיתין אותו מיד וכותבין ושולחין בכל המקומות איש פלוני נגמר דינו בבית דינו של פלוני ופלוני עדיו וכך וכך עשה וכן עשו לו. That the execution of these other offenders should be delayed is said to be the opinion only of R. Akiba. Now Joel maintains that this opinion of R. Akiba was constructed by him on the basis of a guess. Akiba had heard the report that Jesus was executed on the first day of Pesach, as the Synoptic Gospels expressly say. He considered Jesus a מסית ומדיח ונביא השקר, if not a זקן ממרא and he accordingly concluded that since in this case Jesus a מסית etc. was executed on the holy day — (or if we take ברגל to mean "Zur Festzeit;" i. e., on Erev Pesaḥ, so that the "first day" in Matthew would be on the 14th of Nisan as in Pes. 5a י"ד נקרא ראשון — the day on which the paschal lamb was sacrificed) then the law must be that a זקן ממרא or מסית should be kept until the time of the festival. The Baraita here, however, had already heard the latter report found in John (18.25 ff.) that Jesus was executed on Erev Pesaḥ, hence it says expressly ותלאוהו בערב פסח. The Mishnah which Joel assumes is also later than this passage in the Tosefta left out מסית ומדיח and speaks only of זקן ממרא whom they ממיתין אותו ברגל. See Brüll, *op. cit.*, *loc. cit.*, against Joel's theory. Joel does not explain how the Tosefta came to include in the practice בן סורר ומורה and עדים זוממים for whom there was no such alleged precedent.

before Pesaḥ, we cannot account for the statement הכרוז יוצא לפניו ארבעים יום. Heinrich Laible[59] says that there is nothing in the history of, or in the legends about, Jesus to account for this period of forty days reported by our Baraita. He suggests that perhaps the practice now obtaining in the church of fasting forty days before Easter was already observed in the ancient church by some people, and the Jews believed that the reason why the Christians fast forty days around that time is because Jesus suffered those forty days before the crucifixion by being led out every day to the execution place with the herald before him. Hence the mistake of our Baraita. But the custom of Lenten fast, which begins about six weeks before Easter, is not mentioned by any church father before the Council of Nicea, 325 C. E. Before that time they fasted only a few days. Even after the Council of Nicea they fasted only six weeks, excluding Sundays, which are only thirty-six days. At any rate the forty days of fasting originated in the seventh century, probably in imitation of Jesus' fasting forty days[60] and thus could not influence our text.

Strack, in a note to Laible's work[61] suggests that perhaps the report of Jesus' fasting forty days may have caused some Jews to think that he fasted that period because his execution was delayed for that period. He also suggests that the forty days are an echo of the forty days between the day of resurrection and the "Feast of Ascension" held forty days after Easter.[62]

Another difficulty in our Baraita is furnished by the phrase ותלאוהו, "they hanged him," which follows the statement יוצא ליסקל, "he is going out to be stoned." Indeed, according to this Baraita, Jesus was guilty of the crimes of witchcraft, enticement and misleading for which death by stoning is prescribed.[63] Thus,

---

[59] *Op. cit.* 81.   [60] Matth. 4.2.   [61] *Loc. cit.*

[62] See *Britannica*, (11th Ed.) I, 717 *s. v.* This festival was celebrated already in the 4th century, though it may have been from even an earlier time.

[63] Mishnah Sanh. 7.4, המסית והמדיח והמכשף ... אלו הן הנסקלין. The Gospel reports do not mention his having been tried and found guilty of these offenses. But this would only prove that neither the Gospels nor the Talmud knew the exact circumstances of the trial and execution of Jesus.

the phrase ותלאוהו cannot refer to a mode of execution, for he had
been killed by stoning. It must therefore mean, they *hung* him
up after he had been stoned to death, merely to expose the body.
This would represent the opinion of Rabbi Eliezer only who holds
that *all* who have been stoned must be hanged.[64] According to
the majority of the teachers, however, only he who is stoned
for blasphemy is afterwards exposed in this fashion. Now the
question is: Was Jesus a blasphemer? According to Matthew
26.64–65 and Mark 14.63–64, Jesus was accused of blasphemy,
but this is rather doubtful. Joel[65] claims that Jesus was not a
blasphemer, for according to M. Sanh. 7.5, a blasphemer is one
who curses the Name, a crime of which Jesus was not guilty.[66]
N. Bruell,[67] however, proves that according to Sifre[68] Jesus, while
not literally blaspheming, could have been considered a blasphemer because of his claim to have the same power as, or share
in, the power of God, or "because he called himself the son of
God."[69] I personally cannot see how he could have been regarded
as a blasphemer, מגדף.[70] At any rate our Baraita itself says that
he was convicted as having been a wizard, enticer and misleader
but not as a blasphemer.

Still it may be that our Baraita is correct on this point.
Rabbi Eliezer the *traditionalist* has probably preserved the
correct tradition in his statement that all those who were stoned
were hung. So Jesus was first stoned as an enticer and misleader
and then hanged. This tradition has also been preserved in
Acts 5.20, "Jesus whom ye slew and hanged on a tree;" and also
Acts 10.39 "whom they slew and hanged on a tree."[71] Our

[64] Mishnah Sanh. 6.4.   [65] *Op. cit.* II, 48 ff.
[66] The Mishnah there says עד שיפרש השם which may however have been
understood to mean merely "pronounce the Divine Name," an offense of which
Jesus may have been guilty. See *Mekilta*, ed. Lauterbach, III, 48, note 6.
[67] *Loc. cit.*
[68] To Deut. 22.1, מה מגדף מיוחד שפשט ידו בעיקר אף כל שפשט ידו בעיקר.
[69] John 19.7.
[70] See *The Pharisees and Their Teachings*, above p. 92, n. 7.
[71] Cf. also Harold P. Cooke, "Christ Crucified — and by Whom," *Hibbert
Journal* XXX, (Oct. 1930), 61–74, though he relies too much on the later
work תולדות ישׁו which also assumes that Jesus was actually first killed by the
Jews and then hanged on a tree.

Baraita then would also report a stoning and a subsequent
hanging. But it is rather strange that our Baraita does not mention the stoning. It does not say וסקלוהו ותלאוהו. Maybe it merely
wants to emphasize the fact that the Halakah is according to
R. Eliezer and although Jesus was not tried or sentenced as a
blasphemer he was nevertheless hanged. It did not deem it
necessary to explicitly state that he was stoned for this is implied
in the words יוצא ליסקל.

There is no doubt that the Baraitha here has no explicit
reference to the execution as such, but merely to the subsequent
exposing of the body. Certainly the expression ותלאוהו does not
mean: they crucified him. To express this the Baraita would
have said וצלבוהו. When the Mishnah wishes to designate one
executed by crucifixion, it uses the expression צלוב[72] so there is
no reason to assume that the Baraita here uses the term ותלאוהו
to indicate crucifixion as assumed by Laible.[73] It is true that
Onkelos to Deut. 21.22 renders the words ותלית אותו על העץ with
ותצלוב יתיה על צליבא from which it would seem that תלה can mean
also צלב. But the Mishnah or Baraita does not use it in this
sense. Laible's reference to the Targum on Esth. 7.9 does not
prove anything. In Esther, the word תלה means 'henken,' i. e.,
execute, kill. In our Baraita here the word תלאוהו after יוצא
ליסקל, necessarily refers to the exposing of the corpse for a while
after death, according to the law in Deut. 21.22. This hanging
or exposing of the body after the person had been killed is expressly distinguished from hanging as a mode of execution,
whether by strangulation or crucifixion.[74]

There is another difficulty in our Baraita. It assumes that
the Jews executed Jesus by stoning and then exposed him by
hanging, all according to Jewish law, and the Romans had
nothing to do with the whole procedure. The Gospels on the
one hand do not report any stoning and on the other hand

---

[72] See M. Yeb. 16.3.

[73] Op. cit., 81 ff.

[74] See Sifre, loc. cit., where it says: יכול יהו תולים אותו חי כדרך שהמלכות
עושים ת״ל והומת ואח״כ ותלית, "perhaps they are to follow the practice of other
nations and hang him alive? No!, Scripture explicitly says, "he shall die"
and afterwards "Thou shalt hang."

expressly mention that the Roman soldiers crucified him.[75] It is not likely that the Gospel writers would have made any changes in the accepted report about the execution in order to exonerate the Jews. It is more likely that they reported correctly that the Romans executed him by crucifixion. Our Baraita then does not represent an authentic historic account. It seemingly represents a later legend, consisting of confused and contradictory reports. The author had heard the report that Jesus was hung upon a beam, עץ. He did not know that this hanging was crucifixion. He also heard another legend preserved in Toledot Jeshu and reflected in Acts, that Jesus was actually hanged on a tree. He had heard that Jesus was accused of being a wizard, enticer and misleader and he knew that as such he had to be stoned. So our author reconciled the report of Jesus having been hung, i. e., crucified, with the other report that he was a misleader, etc., for which he was to be punished by stoning. He assumed that the hanging was not crucifixion, but was performed in compliance with the law of Deut. 21.22 as interpreted by Rabbi Eliezer. In other words, the account of this Baraita is a legend made up by guesswork and misunderstanding of various legends and popular reports about Jesus. Herford[76] suggests that Jesus was known as a תלוי (i. e., hanged one) in early times, and the Jews may have known of him as a or the תלוי. Perhaps Onkelos' translation of Deut. 21.22 כי קללת אלהים תלוי by ארי על דחב קדם קדם כי קללת אלהים תלוי ד' אצטלב is an allusion to Jesus hinted at as a תלוי or צלוב. Thus Paul in Galatians 3.13: "Christ redeemed us from the curse of the Law, having become a curse for us, for it is written: 'Cursed is everyone that hangeth on a tree.'" applied the phrase קללת אלהים תלוי to Jesus. The Jews then having heard of a Jesus as a תלוי deemed it correct to use in the report in connection with the execution of Jesus on the eve of the Passover the phrase ותלאוהו בערב פסח.

This brings us to the discussion of another statement or expression in this report made by the Gemara — or by Ulla — which also points to a late date of the whole report, showing that it does not represent a knowledge of facts. This statement

[75] Matth. 27.27–35; Mark 15.16–32; Luke 23.36.
[76] Op. cit., 85–86.

is: שאני ישו דקרוב למלכות הוה, "The case of Jesus was different for he — or it (the case) — was near the kingdom or government." The meaning of this phrase is very doubtful to say the least, and many suggestions have been offered to explain it. We have to explain the meaning of each word, and each word can have several different meanings. ישו can refer both to the person, Jesus, as well as to the *case* of his death. קרוב can mean related, near, connected with or of concern to. מלכות can mean the kingdom of God, the kingdom of the house of David, the kingdom or government of Rome, or the kingdom of the Messiah. With these various possibilities of the meaning of each word in the report, the report as a whole naturally likewise can have many different interpretations. Krauss[77] would understand this phrase to mean: קרוב למלכות בית דוד, alluding to a relationship or connection with, or descent from, the house of David claimed for Jesus. This interpretation, however, is not plausible. Of course, from the reports in the Gospels, the Jews could have heard that Jesus claimed to be the "son of David" or a descendant of the Davidic house. And in later Jewish works like מעשה דאותו ואת בנו,[78] Miriam, the mother of Jesus, claimed to have come from the Davidic family: אמרה מרים ממשפחת דוד המלך אני. This is the same legend which is reported in the Book of James, or Protoevangelium[79] where Mary is said to have been of the tribe or the *House of David*. But it is nowhere stated that the Rabbis believed Mary, or that the Jews admitted this claim of Davidic descent for Jesus. And it is likely that even if it had been true the Rabbis would rather have hesitated to admit it. Furthermore, it is not clear how this fact, assuming that it was a fact, that he was related to the house of David would have changed the course of law, so as to delay his execution for forty days. We do not find any reference to a special procedure in the announcement of the execution of one sentenced to death, in the case of princes of the

[77] *Op. cit.*, 215.

[78] Krauss, *op. cit.*, 67.

[79] See *The Apocryphal New Testament*, by M. R. James, (Oxford, 1924), 43, "The child Mary, that she was of the tribe of David;" and "Protevangelium des Jakobus," 10, Hennecke, *Neutestamentliche Apocryphen*, 2te Auflage, (1924), 89.

house of David. Above all, in the time of the Second Temple there was no longer a Davidic kingdom, and hence one could not claim connection with such a kingdom. The people who claimed descent from the Davidic house, like the family of Hillel and others, are usually described as ממשפחת דוד or מבית דוד as even Miriam in *Ma'ase d'oto v'et B'no* said: ממשפחת דוד המלך אני.[80] Nowhere, to my knowledge, can we find that people claiming descent from David are described as קרובים למלכות בית דוד, related to the royal house of David. The expression קרובים למלכות[81] usually means connected or influential with the Roman government. So the מלכות here cannot mean מלכות בית דוד which no longer existed at that time. We may, therefore, take the phrase קרוב למלכות in the sense of קרוב למלכות רומי. This statement then would allude to the reports in the N. T. that Pilate hesitated to execute Jesus.[82] The Rabbis may have heard of those legends and concluded that Jesus stood in the good graces of Roman government. The report then would mean that the Jews were afraid to execute him immediately, but showed the governor, who was friendly to Jesus, that they were giving Jesus a fair chance to find proof for his innocence; they were making an exception in his case and allowing an announcement of forty days to find evidence justifying a new trial.[83]

It is also possible that this statement of the Gemara echoes the report in Luke 23.8–12, that Herod (probably Herod of Chalcis) was friendly to Jesus; hence the later legend describes Jesus as being close to royalty, taking קרוב למלכות as referring to a *ruler* of the House of Herod. Of course, such an interpretation would presuppose that the Babylonian teachers (or Ulla?) knew the reports of the Gospel and even accepted these reports. While the latter may be unlikely and as Herford[84] remarks, it is

[80] *Loc. cit.*

[81] See B. K. 83 where it is used for the descendants of Hillel.

[82] John 18.38–19.16. Cf. also Matth. 27.19–24 where Pilate's wife sends word to him: "Have thou nothing to do with that righteous man," and Pilate washes his hands, saying: "I am innocent of this . . . . man's blood." Also Mark 15.12–15 and Luke 23.13–20.

[83] Cf. Laible, *op. cit.*, 80–81 and Herford, *op. cit.*, 89, both of whom favor this interpretation of the passage.

[84] *Loc. cit.*

27

not at all warranted to assume a knowledge of the Gospel reports by the Rabbis, yet it is not altogether impossible. In a vague and confused manner some of the Gospel reports may have penetrated into the circles of the Rabbis even in Babylon. Herford's suggestion, that because Jesus spoke so often of the "Kingdom," meaning the kingdom of heaven, some people may have misunderstood him to boast of his connections with the earthly government, and this gave rise to a current belief about his being related to or connected with royalty, is far fetched. Perhaps some people may have made a joking or ironical remark, that he was — according to his preaching — so near to the kingdom of heaven, or the coming of the kingdom.

All these interpretations of the phrase קרוב למלכות are not satisfactory. Hence one may offer still another interpretation which, at least, is not less satisfactory than all the others.

I suggest that since this statement שאני ישו דקרוב למלכות הוה was made by Ulla, an Amora of the third generation living in the first half of the fourth century or by the Gemara in answer to Ulla's argument, it may refer to the Roman government. At that time, i. e., after Constantine's conversion, the government was friendly to and even associated and connected with Christianity. The people of the fourth century, judging from conditions of their own times, assumed that the friendly relations between Christianity and the government must have existed also in the time of the founder of Christianity; hence they called Jesus "close to the government," in the sense of having influence with the Roman government.[85]

Another direct reference by name to Jesus is found in b. Sanh. 103a ונגע לא יקרב באהלך שלא יהא לך בן או תלמיד שמקדיח תבשילו ברבים כגון ישו הנוצרי.[86]

---

[85] Like B. K. 83a של בית ר"ג קרובים למלכות. This is also echoed in the later legend of the *Toledot Jeshu* (Krauss, 131) according to which Mary the mother of Jesus is related to Queen Helen. This legend confuses Helena, wife of Monobaz of Adiabene (about 50 C. E.) with Helena, mother of Constantine the Great — called St. Helena (247–327 C. E.).

[86] Thus in the old printed editions and MSS. See *Dikduke Soferim*, *ad loc*. Parallel to this is b. Ber. 17b, שלא יהא לנו בן או תלמיד שמקדיח .... אין פרץ, תבשילו ברבים כגון ישו הנוצרי, in MSS and uncensored texts. Some MSS read כגון ישו הנוצרי in place of כישו הנוצרי.

The phrase שמקדיח תבשילו, 'spoil the soup' or 'burn the food' is figurative. It means spoil the teaching, causing the good food, the doctrines of Judaism to become spoiled, harmful and of bad taste.[87] As to the word ברבים, among the masses, it means that the masses take this *corrupted Judaism* for the genuine Judaism, the real spiritual food. Thus the Aruk *s. v.* קדח has כגון ישו הנוצרי שהיה מעמיד ע"ז בשוקים וברחובות. It seems the author considered the later Christian practice of burning incense before shrines and images as idolatrous, and assumed that Jesus, the founder of the religion, was the author of these practices.[88] The date of these two sayings is about the second half of the third century. The saying in Berakot, if it be by R. Joḥanan (died 275) or his disciple R. Eleazar b. Pedat, is not earlier than the second half of the third century. The saying in Sanhedrin is given by Ḥisda, a Babylonian Amora of the third century (died 309) in the name of R. Jeremiah b. Abba, an Amora of the second generation, a pupil of Rab who for a time lived in Palestine where he probably heard this saying with its reference to Jesus and thus is also not earlier than the third century. Both sayings, then, are of a comparatively late date, at any rate, they are not tannaitic and certainly not contemporary with Jesus. It is, however, interesting to note that Jesus was still considered as a disciple of the wise, though he disgraced them by corrupting the teachings which he received from them. In the later *Toledot Jeshu* he is also described as having once been a disciple; they simply could not imagine anyone who had never studied capable of leadership or even of heresy.

The next passage which in the uncensored editions contains a reference to Jesus by name, is in b. Giṭ. 56b–57a where it is reported that Onkelos the nephew of Titus conjured up the spirit of Jesus, or brought him up from hell, or dragged him up from the grave, and asked him for his advice in regard to the attitude to be assumed toward the Jews. Before we discuss this passage it may be advisable to examine first the passage in 'Ab.

---

[87] Jastrow's "disgraces his education" misses the point.
[88] See Strack, 39; Laible, 50: also Herford, 56–62, who has some interesting remarks.

Zarah 10b–11a and its parallel in Midrash Deut. r. 2.15 in order to identify this Onkelos.

The passage in 'Ab. Zarah speaks of an Onkelos b. Clonimos. Clonimos is probably corrupted from Clemens and the passage has reference to Flavius Clemens, a Roman Consul and nephew of the Emperor Domitian, hence also a nephew of Titus, who was sentenced to death and executed in the year 95 or 96 on the charge of atheism, i. e., of having denied the Roman gods. He was probably a proselyte to Judaism, hence he was confusedly identified with Onkelos or Akylos אונקלוס הגר or עקילס הגר who lived (a little later?) in the time of R. Eliezer and R. Joshua.[89] The similarity of names often led to the confusion and identification of different personalities. In passing, I may remark that probably the Titus who is so condemned in the Talmud as טיטוס הרשע and who is charged with having burned the Temple and committed other crimes, was not Titus the son of Vespasian who later became emperor and who is so highly spoken of by Josephus and other historians. It was a stepson of Vespasian whose name likewise was Titus and who was in command of the soldiers who burned the Temple.[90]

Now to return to our story in Giṭ. 56b–57a. Clemens or Onkelos called Jesus up from Hell, for the term אסקיה, "brought him up," suggests that he was believed to have been somewhere down below, unless we interpret it simply "dragged him up from the grave" which is very unlikely since the expression בנגידא, "by necromancy," points to his spirit coming up.

Jesus is described here — in the substitute reading as פושע ישראל — in the original form as one who scoffed at the Pharisaic teachings or the rabbinical interpretation of the law. This legend then echoes, or presupposes a knowledge of the charges reportedly made by Jesus against the Pharisees.[91] It is to be noticed that he is still regarded as a Jew — even in the substitute reading of "transgressor," with sympathies for his people, advising others

[89] See Graetz, *Geschichte*, IV, 4th ed., 109–110 and note 12, 402 ff.

[90] Cf. Mendel Wohlman החלמוד ויוסיפוס פלאוויוס in the periodical מזרח ומערב edited by Abraham Almaleh, vol. V, (June, 1930).

[91] Matth. 15.3 ff., against tradition; 16.6–12 against the leaven of the Pharisees *et al.*

to do good and no harm to the Jews. He is markedly distinguished here from Balaam in his attitude towards the Jews. He is still one of them.[92]

Likewise the later legend about Simon Peter[93] — שמעון כיפא, who told the Christians to be friendly to the Jews, טובתם תדרוש, and the legend of an Elijah (אל יה?) חכם אחד שנקרא אליה, who simulated Christianity and proclaimed to the Christians in the name of Jesus, ולא תעשו רע ונזק ליהודים לא בגופם ולא בממונם,[94] echo this report here that Jesus wished the Jews well and did not want his people to suffer. Whether the Jews really believed this of him, or whether it was put forward by them as a precaution against possible persecutions on the part of the Christians, we cannot decide. In ancient times the former may have been the case; in later times the latter motive may have prompted the legend.

In the above passage we have seen that Jesus is mentioned by name or as פושע ישראל alongside of, but distinguished from, Balaam. Let us now consider another passage in the Talmud which is understood by some to refer to Jesus though not mentioning him by his real name but alluding to him by the name of Balaam.[95]

The passage is found in Sanh. 106b (the preceding part and saying of Rab Papa on 106a will be considered later) and reads as follows: א"ל הוא מינא (צדוקי) לר' חנינא מי שמיע לך בלעם בר כמה הוה א"ל מיכתב לא כתיב אלא מדכתיב אנשי דמים ומרמה לא יחצו ימיהם בר תלתין ותלת שנין או בר תלתין וארבע א"ל שפיר קאמרת לדידי חזי לי פנקסיה דבלעם והוה כתיב ביה בר תלתין ותלת שנין בלעם חגירה כד קטיל יתיה פנחס ליסטאה א"ל מר בריה דרבינא לבריה בכולהו לא תפיש ביה למדרש לבר מבלעם הרשע דכמה דמשכחת ביה דרוש ביה. We must first seek to ascertain the identity of the persons in this dialogue. R. Ḥanina b. Ḥama, a Palestinian Amora of the first generation, pupil and successor to Judah Ha-Nasi, flourished in the first

---

[92] See M. Friedmann, *Onkelos and Akylos*; and Marmorstein, *HUCA*, X, (1935), 228, note 22.

[93] Krauss, 86–88.   [94] *Ibid.* 84.

[95] The other passages mentioning the name ישו but referring to his disciples and followers as תלמידי ישו will be discussed later. Here we deal only with references to his person.

half of the third century. But who was the heretic or Sadducee
who conversed with him on this question? If we assume that he
was a Christian, then it is difficult to maintain that the person
about whom he sought information was Jesus. A Christian would
not have spoken about Jesus in such a disrespectful manner
referring to him as "lame Balaam." Against this one might argue
that, possibly, we have not in this report the exact words of
the heretic. The latter may have used, in his question as well
as in his reference to the Book = פנקס which he later cites, the
real name ישו, but the reporter — or a later copyist, perhaps
a very later scribe, fearful of the censor — changed the name
and substituted בלעם חגירא for ישו הנוצרי. But there is another
difficulty in identifying this heretic as a Christian, if we assume
that he sought information about Jesus. Why should a Christian
ask Ḥanina whether he knows or had heard how old Jesus was?
It would, therefore, be more likely to assume that this heretic
or Sadducee was a non-Christian heretic, a member of one of
the many sects that existed in Palestine in those days. He
agreed with Ḥanina's attitude toward Jesus and in denying his
claims to Divinity or messiahship and may have sought only
to obtain information or compare notes with him about Jesus.
On this assumption there is at least no objection to assuming
the possibility that Jesus is meant when they talk about "Balaam
the lame." But we have, as yet, no positive reason for the
assumption that Jesus is here designated as Balaam. We must
therefore examine the contents of the dialogue and see whether
there is any positive justification for identifying the Balaam
mentioned here with Jesus. It has been suggested that the
Balaam mentioned here is a designation of Jesus.[96] [97]פנחס ליסטאה
would then be a corrupted form of Pontius Pilate. This description might fit Jesus who was probably 33 years old when he was
executed, for according to Luke 3.23, Jesus was about thirty
years old[98] when he began his teaching and his career did not

---

[96] See J. Levy, Wörterbuch, s. v. בלעם, 236; and Geiger, "Bileam und
Jesus" in Jüdische Zeitschrift, VI, 34 ff.

[97] J. Perles in Monatschrift, (1872), 266–7, suggest here פנחס פליסטאה.

[98] This, by the way, was said in order to make him resemble Moses who,
according to the Midrash, Num. r. 14.29, began his teaching at the age of
thirty-two.

last more than three years. The *Pinkas* which this heretic here cited could then have been one of the Gospels, containing the life story of Jesus. The name Balaam might have been chosen as a designation for Jesus to indicate as the Talmud elsewhere[99] fancifully explains the meaning of his name, that he is עם בלא, "without the people," or as the Aruk *s. v.* בלע reads עם בלא פירוש שאין לו חלק עם ישראל, "*Belo'-'am* means that he had no portion in Israel,"[100] or it might mean עם בלע, *Bala'-'am*, "one who sought to devour, i. e., destroy and harm, the people" by leading them away from God — alluding to the charge that he sought to lead Israel away from their Father in Heaven.

The description חגירה, "the lame one," cannot so easily be made to fit Jesus, since there is no record elsewhere of his having been lame. There is not any record in the Bible about Balaam having been lame either. It was merely a tradition among the Rabbis that Balaam was lame on one foot.[101] It may therefore be argued since the Rabbis were accustomed to refer to Balaam as "the lame Balaam" when they came to use his name as an epithet for Jesus, in order to characterize him as being like Balaam, they applied to him the full name with the adjective "the lame."

Perhaps the saying of Jesus in Mark 9.45: "If thy foot cause thee to stumble, cut it off: it is good for thee to enter into life halt, rather than having two feet to be cast into Hell" suggested to some people that Jesus was lame on one foot. There may have been some legend current among the Jews that Jesus was lame. It is possible that the legend found in the later *Toledot Jeshu*[102] that Jesus was polluted by Judas Iscariot and thrown down to the ground from the air where he was flying, originally also contained the additional statement that Jesus became lame as a result of the fall.[103]

[99] Sanh. 105a.

[100] No portion with all Israel in the world to come?

[101] Sanh. 105a; R. Joḥanan said: Balaam limped on one foot. The proof verse Num. 23.3 is of course questionable. Perhaps the tradition is based on Num. 22.25 "and crushed Balaam's foot against the wall."

[102] Krauss, 43–44.

[103] Thus Simon Magus who was brought down from the air by Peter — in the story which is the prototype of the story of the fight in the air between

It may also be that since according to the legend in *Toledot Jeshu*,[104] Jesus is supposed to have cut open the flesh on his hip or thigh and put into the open wound the pieces or parchment containing the letters of the sacred name and then closed again the wound with the skin of the flesh, some people assumed that he limped as a result of this operation and they called him "the lame." It is also possible that since the Christians considered Jesus "the lamb," i. e., the lamb of the Passover sacrifice, פֶּסַח, the Jews in derision made a pun on this designation and called him פִּסֵּחַ, "the lame one," in Aramaic חגירא.[105] These are all possible, though far fetched, interpretations which might explain how the designation "Balaam the lame" could have been chosen as a descriptive epithet for Jesus.

Likewise Phineas the robber besides being possibly a corrupted form of Pontius Pilate, might be an allusion to the High Priest who in his zeal was instrumental in the apprehending and crucifying of Jesus, thus proving himself a worthy descendant of the great zealot Phineas the son of Eleazar, the son of Aaron — who was zealous for his God.[106] Of course, this Christian source cited by the Sadducee (heretic) characterized Phineas as a murderer instead of a zealot. It will thus have to be assumed that the reporter in quoting the Sadducee (heretic) substituted for the name Yeshu used by him the epithet Balaam the lame, but left the uncomplimentary characterization of Phineas, as "the murderer" unchanged, which would be rather strange. Of course it is also possible that this Sadducee (heretic) belonged to a sect that objected to acts like that of Phineas, hence he called him "Phineas the robber" to indicate that he, his successors, descendants or imitators, were to be thought of as murderers. However, while he regarded Jesus as an innocent victim of these priestly zealots, he rejected him and described him as "Balaam the lame."

Jesus and Judas Iscariot — became lame. See Krauss, 175 and B. Heller in *MGWJ*, (1932), 36.

[104] Krauss, 40.

[105] See Rashi *ad loc.* חגירא תרגום של פסח.

[106] Num. 25.11–13.

Then again "Phineas the robber" may be a variation of the
name פאפא בן רצצתא or another characterization of the person
by that name, who according to *Toledot Jeshu*[107] betrayed Jesus,
thus causing his death.

Admitting that all these possible interpretations are rather
forced, it may nevertheless be said that at least it is not impossible
to assume that Jesus was the subject of the discussion between
R. Ḥanina and the heretic and that he is designated by them,
or at least by one of them, as "the lame Balaam." I say advisedly,
it is not impossible. But is it plausible? We must ask ourselves
the question: what cogent reason is there against taking this
report about the discussion between Ḥanina and the heretic in
its plain and literal meaning, as referring to the Biblical personage, Balaam, the contemporary of Balak and Moses, whom
Phineas the son of Eleazar, the commander of the army in
the campaign against the Midianites is said to have killed as
stated in Num. 31.8: "Balaam also the son of Beor they — i. e.,
the soldiers under the command of Phineas — slew with the
sword."[108] Balaam's Chronicle which the heretic cites may have
been an apocryphal work containing the story of Balaam with
some additions to and embellishments of the biblical story.[109]
Perhaps it was a gnostic work, and the circles among whom
this book was preserved rather favored Balaam and hence
called Phineas who killed him, a robber, since Balaam was
a lame and helpless man who could not defend himself. Perhaps
indeed in that apocryphal book it was reported that Phineas
personally slew Balaam with the sword, not "they slew" as
in Numbers.

There seems to be no reason at all to assume that the name
Balaam was used by the Rabbis as a substitute for the name

[107] Krauss, 78–79.

[108] See Rashi here *s. v.* כד קטיל יתיה where it is said פנחס שר צבא ואפילו קטליה
אחר כל המלחמה נקראת על שמו.

[109] Perhaps the פרשת בלעם mentioned in b. B. B. 14b "Moses wrote his
Book [presumably the Pentateuch] and the פרשת בלעם" refers to such a separate story about Balaam and not to the account in Numbers, which was
part of Moses's Book. See Isaiah Horowitz של"ה (Fürth, 1764), 362a where
it is indeed assumed that the Talmudic saying refers to such a separate book
written by Moses in addition to the Pentateuch and subsequently lost.

Jesus. Such usage could not have been meant to indicate or to suggest that Jesus was in character like Balaam, for, as we shall see below, such was not the case. Since, we find that in many passages he is called by his real name Jeshu, why then should another name have been substituted in this passage? Even if there had been some reason for not using his real name, a better substitute could have been used, either the term פלוני or אותו האיש or even פושע ישראל and not the name of an ancient heathen prophet. The use of the latter name as a substitute would not be advisable as it might mislead people into thinking that it was actually the ancient heathen prophet who was meant and not another person who was supposed to have been like him and therefore called by his name.[110]

This argument becomes even stronger, since, as we have seen in the passage in Giṭṭin,[111] Jesus is distinguished from and contrasted with Balaam, the heathen prophet, in that he is called פושע ישראל, "a Jewish sinner." Against this it might be argued that not all tractates of the Talmud were redacted by the same person or even the same school, hence the terminology need not be alike in all the tractates. While the redactor of Giṭṭin may have distinguished Jesus' character from that of Balaam, the redactor of Sanhedrin may have identified them and hence he called Jesus by the name of Balaam. But the mere fact that some people, like those who redacted the tractate Giṭṭin, made a distinction between Jesus and Balaam, shows that it was not a general practice to designate Jesus as Balaam. Why then should we assume that the redactor of Sanhedrin used as a substitute for Jesus a name which some people might take literally when he could have used any of the other substitutes about which there were no disputes and which were less likely to be misunderstood? Above all, we would have to assume that both the heretic and R. Ḥanina regarded Jesus as having had the same character as Balaam and hence both would call him by that name. But we do not find anywhere else that the Rabbis of the Talmud ascribed to Jesus the sins and vices of Balaam.

---

[110] See also W. Bacher in *JQR* [o. s.], III, (1891), 356–357 against Geiger.
[111] *Supra.*

Why then assume that R. Ḥanina did characterize him as another Balaam? An examination of the passages of the Talmud describing the character of Balaam provides no justification for interpreting them as referring to Jesus. Thus the passage in Ab. 5.19, characterizing the followers or disciples of Balaam, as possessing "an evil eye, a haughty spirit and a proud mind," does not refer to the Christians, the disciples of Jesus.[112] The Christians were not regarded by the Tannaim as having a haughty spirit, proud mind and an evil eye. Hence the application of the verse Ps. 55.24 "Men of blood and deceit shall not live out half their days," applied also by R. Ḥanina to Balaam, could not refer to the disciples of Jesus who preached meekness and a humble spirit.[113] But the description actually fits the biblical Balaam as understood by the Rabbis.[114] This condemnation by the Rabbis of Balaam and his disciples cannot refer to Jesus and his followers, especially since the same condemnation of Balaam and his disciples was current among the Christians and finds strong expression in the N. T. writings, where it certainly cannot be thought of as an allusion to Jesus and his disciples. Why then should we assume that the same condemnation when found in Talmudic literature refers to Jesus and his disciples?

The following are the references to Balaam and his disciples in the N. T. writings: In the second Epistle of Peter 2.1–3 and 10–15 there is a reference to a false sect which indulged in lust and "forsaking the right way, they went astray, having followed the way of Balaam the son of Beor." In verse 18 we read "For uttering great swelling words of vanity, they entice in the lusts of flesh by lasciviousness," which latter description compares with the Rabbinic characterization of Balaam.[115] Further reference is made in Revelation 2.14–15: "But I have

---

[112] Cf. Herford, *Pirke Aboth*, (New York, 1925), 140–141, where he modifies his former opinion about the undercurrent of a reference to Jesus in the Balaam passages, expressed in his *Christianity in Talmud and Midrash*, 69.

[113] Matth. 5.3–12.

[114] See Midrash Num. r. 20.9.

[115] In the Midrash Num. r. 20.8 עמד בלעם והטעה את הבריות בעריות, and in b. Sanh. 106a שנתן לו עתה על הזנות. Cf. Graetz, *Geschichte* IV, 4th ed., 92.

a few things against thee, because thou hast there some that hold the teachings of Balaam, who taught Balak to put a stumbling block before the sons of Israel, that they might eat food sacrificed to idols and practice immorality. So hast thou also some that hold the teachings of the Nicolaitans in like manner." This description agrees with the description of the disciples of Balaam in Abot[116] and fits those gnostic sects or the Nicolaitans but not the Christians. Hence, even if we did not take the name Balaam in our passage literally, as referring to the ancient heathen prophet — which as we have seen is not the case — and we had to assume that Balaam is a epithet for a person who lived in later times, it would be more likely that the person referred to was the founder or teacher of the Nicolaitans, or of another gnostic sect referred to also in N. T. writings.[117]

Dr. H. P. Chajes in *Markus Studien*[118] declares that in those passages of the Talmud where Balaam's lasciviousness and immorality are emphasized or described, the reference is to the Nicolaitans and not to Jesus or the Christians.[119] Even Geiger, who interprets our passage in Sanhedrin as referring to Jesus admits that Balaam is not a substitute for Jesus in all the passages of the Talmud.[120] In other words, he admits that it was not the general practice of the Rabbis to refer to Jesus under the name of Balaam. What reason then have we to interpret any passage in which Balaam is mentioned as referring to Jesus, if we can just as well interpret it to refer to the Biblical personage himself or to some other person of whom we know at least that he had the characteristics or was of the type of Balaam, like the Nicolaitans?[121]

---

[116] *Loc. cit.*

[117] See M. Friedländer, *Der Antichrist* (Göttingen, 1901), 191–193.

[118] Berlin, 1899, p. 25.

[119] Cf. also Klausner, *Jeshu Hanozri*, p. 23, note 3.

[120] *Jüdische Zeitschrift* VI, (1868), 36–37.

[121] In the passage from the Yalḳuṭ to be discussed later on, where Balaam is opposed to Jesus and utters a prophetic warning against him, there may be an illusion to Balaamites or some other false sect who were against Jesus and the Christians. See Friedländer, *Antichrist, loc. cit.* Hyamson's statement

Coming back to our passage in Sanhedrin, we have seen that it could well be interpreted as referring to the biblical Balaam himself, and there is no reason whatever to interpret it as referring to Jesus. It is, however, possible that the redactor of the Talmud or the compiler of this Tractate, in putting this report about the discussion between Ḥanina and the heretic in this particular setting and context, knew that certain people did sometimes consider Jesus, the would-be Jewish prophet, in a class with the heathen prophet Balaam. Hence he put this passage next to the saying of R. Papa (106a) which may contain an allusion to Mary, the mother of Jesus. R. Papa, to illustrate the saying of R. Joḥanan about Balaam, cites a popular proverb about a woman who was the wife or daughter of princes and rulers and yet has so fallen that she would go a whoring after carpenters היינו דאמרי אינשי מסגני ושלטי הואי אייזן לנגרי נגרי. This may also be interpreted that she had to marry a carpenter after she had become a whore. We then would have to supply another word like אינסבא after the word אייזן. Or it may mean she committed adultery after being married to a carpenter like זנתה תחת אישה הנגר. This then would allude to Mary who claimed descent from princes, the royal house of David and yet had to be married to a lowly carpenter and then — or because — she committed adultery. But the saying of R. Joḥanan refers to Balaam himself and not Jesus. In commenting upon the passage in Josh. 13.22 בלעם בן בעור הקוסם, "Balaam also the son of Beor, the soothsayer, did the children of Israel slay with the sword," the question is asked קוסם? נביא הוא!, "Soothsayer? But he was a prophet!" And R. Joḥanan's answer בתחלה נביא ולבסוף קוסם, "First he was a prophet then he became merely a soothsayer," no doubt refers to the biblical Balaam, who, so R. Joḥanan thought, started out as a prophet, for the Torah reports that God spoke to him, but later degenerated and became a magician קוסם or a soothsayer.

If one should interpret this saying of R. Joḥanan as an

that "there are many references to Jesus in Talmudic literature." But the references are veiled under the name of Balaam, (JQR, [n. s.], XXII, Oct. 1931, 216) is rather hazardous and certainly not proven.

allusion to Jesus then it would mean that the Rabbis actually acknowledged that Jesus had originally been a prophet or possessed prophetic powers and then lost them, which is very unlikely. We have seen that the Rabbis considered him as a disciple who spoiled the good doctrine but we never find any reference to his having had, misused and subsequently lost any prophetic powers. Of course, one could argue that the Rabbis were making fun of him when they said בתחלה נביא and meant that originally he started out with prophetic pretensions although he was most certainly not such. But it was too serious a question for the Rabbis to joke about.[122]

The passage in the Mishnah Sanh. 10.2 that mentions Balaam as one of the four commoners who had no share in the world to come, has also been understood by some scholars as referring to Jesus under that name and not to the Biblical personage. The argument, given in favor of this interpretation, is that since those four are mentioned as exceptions to the rule that all Israel, or every Israelite, has a share in the world to come כל ישראל יש להם חלק לעוה"ב they must be a part of Israel. Hence the Balaam mentioned could not refer to the heathen prophet of old.[123] Klausner's counter-argument[124] that Doeg the Edomite, also mentioned as one of the four exceptions, was likewise not a Jew, is not strong enough to disprove this theory. For, in the first place, Doeg was considered by the Rabbis as a Jew, even though he may have been of Edomitic descent. Secondly, as Klausner himself notices, the scholars who consider the name Balaam in this Mishnah passage an epithet for Jesus also consider the other three biblical names, Doeg, Ahitophel and Gehazi as substitutes for the real names of some of the disciples of Jesus, as we shall see below. But there is no cogent reason to assume that Balaam is a substitute for Jesus. Since, according to the Rabbis, the pious men of the gentiles have a share in the world to come,[125] there was reason to state that Balaam though a prophet and as such expected to be counted among the צדיקים

---

[122] See below discussion of passage in Num. r. 20.7.

[123] Geiger, *Jüdische Zeitschrift* VI, 32–33; Laible, *op. cit.*, 52–53; Herford, *Christianity etc.*, 66.

[124] *Jeshu Hanozri*, 4th ed., 23.   [125] Tosefta Sanh. 13.2.

חסידי אומות העולם or באומות who have a share in the world to come, is excluded from this privilege.

The passage in Midrash Num. r. 20.7 describing Balaam as one who began as an interpreter of dreams, then turned (חזר does not necessarily mean, returned), to magic or soothsaying and then turned to — became a recipient of — the holy spirit, or to prophecy ויש אומרים בתחלה פותר חלומות חזר להיות קוסם וחזר רוח הקודש is interpreted by Stier[126] as referring to Jesus and describing his career, as first performing miraculous cures (קוסם?) and then claiming the holy spirit. As a reason for his thus interpreting this midrashic passage, Stier assumes that the Rabbis, wishing to criticize Jesus and fearing to do so openly, mentioned him under the disguise of Balaam.[127] But this is a very poor reason. As we have seen, they mention his name ישו when they criticized him as a מכשף and מסית ומדיח and as a disciple who spoiled the good doctrine, why then should they be afraid to mention him by his name when they rather compliment him by saying חזר לרוח הקודש? Stier's interpretation, that this merely means "claiming prophecy" is not correct.

His argument, that Jesus was like Balaam in that both of them used their prophetic powers to hurt Israel is also weak. For this would mean that the Rabbis admitted that Jesus, like Balaam of old, was actually a prophet and not merely a prophetic claimant. Furthermore, Jesus never, in the opinion of the Rabbis, sought to do harm to Israel. We have seen above, that the Rabbis believed him friendly to his people, so that even after his death he is supposed to have given advice to do good and no harm to the Jews. He certainly cannot be held responsible for all the harm that has come to the Jews as a result of the misunderstanding of his teaching on the part of his followers. Besides, the first stage of Balaam's career as described in this passage, that of being an interpreter of dreams פותר חלומות does not fit Jesus. Further קוסם soothsayer or even magician, does not necessarily mean one who performs miraculous cures by magic, as Jesus was accused of doing. So it seems to me that it is very

[126] In Rahmer's *Das Jüdische Literaturblatt* X, (1881), Nos. 31 and 32.
[127] *Ibid.*, 122.

questionable, to say the least, whether this midrashic passage can mean all that which Stier would read into it. And we still have to find proof for the statement that Balaam was used as an epithet for Jesus.

There are still other names by which, according to some modern scholars and even some Amoraim, Jesus is supposed to have been mentioned in tannaitic literature. One of these is the name Ben Satada or Ben Sateda בן סטרא.[128] There has been so much speculation about this alleged designation of Jesus, both by the Amoraim in the Talmud and by modern scholars, that for the sake of clarity, it is advisable to divide the material. We shall, therefore, first consider the older material, that is, the references found in the tannaitic statements. We shall examine these statements and seek to ascertain their meaning independently of the amoraic comments on them. For it is doubtful, to say the least, whether the latter's interpretations of the tannaitic statements are correct. At any rate, we have a right to investigate for ourselves the meaning of the tannaitic statements, and we must not be prejudiced by the amoraic comments.[129] Then after we have independently come to some conclusions as to the meaning of the tannaitic statements, we shall proceed to consider the amoraic comments separately. For even if we should find that the Amoraim did not correctly interpret or even misunderstand the tannaitic utterances on this point, the amoraic remarks are in themselves of interest to us, as we can at least learn from them that some of the Amoraim referred to Jesus under the name of בן פנטירא or בן סטרא and how they understood these names as fitting Jesus or adequately describing him.

---

[128] The passages in which this name occurs are: Tosefta, Shab. 11.15 Zuckermandel, 126); Sanh. 10.11 (Zuckermandel, 431); b. Shab. 104b and b. Sanh. 67a; p. Shab. 12.4 (13d); p. Yeb. 16.6 (15d end).

[129] A method of procedure which I pursued with good results in interpreting the statements about the three books found in the Temple "The Three Books found in the Temple at Jerusalem" JQR, [n. s.] VIII, (1917–18), 385–423, and about the chronological data concerning the Second Temple "Misunderstood Chronological Statements in the Talmudic Literature," Proceedings of the American Academy for Jewish Research V, (New York, 1934).

In Tosefta Shab. 11.15 the question is discussed of whether tattooing, or scratching and making marks on one's body, המסרט על בשרו, is to be considered a form of writing, so that one who does this on a Sabbath has violated the Sabbath law prohibiting writing. R. Eliezer, against the opinion of the majority of the teachers, considers tattooing a form of writing and cites in support of his opinion, the case of a certain person, whom he designates as בן סטדא, who used this method of writing only. Said R. Eliezer to the other teachers: "But did not Ben Satada learn [what?] (or teach) only by this form of writing?" אמר להם ר' אליעזר לחכמים והלא בן סטדא לא למד אלא בכך. To this, his opponents, the other teachers, answer: "Because of one fool shall we lose or destroy all sane people?" אמרו לו מפני שוטה אחד נאבד את כל הפקחין. Here we are not told what this man learned in this manner, nor is it clear how through or because of (this) one fool we may lose or destroy all sane people. Does it mean that although one man, a fool, used tattooing as a form of writing, we cannot consider it as such, for to do so would in effect destroy all sane people by sentencing them to death, should they happen to do tattooing on a Sabbath? This would certainly be an exaggeration to say the least. For not all sane people tattoo, and even those who do, do not all do so on the Sabbath. Besides, we do not say that we lose or destroy people when we forbid them to do any other, more useful, work on Sabbath, even though the performance of such prohibited work involves a death sentence. Why then should we specifically consider the prohibition of tattooing on the Sabbath a cause of losing or destroying people, even though as in other cases one's disregard of this law might lead to a death sentence? This Baraita as it stands in the Tosefta is certainly cryptic. But we may learn more about the subject under discussion from the versions in which this Baraita is reported or quoted in the palestinian and babylonian Talmuds.

In p. Shab. 12.4 (13d) we read תניא אמר להן ר' אליעזר לחכמים והלא בן סטדא לא הביא כשפים ממצרים אלא בכך? אמרו לו מפני שוטה אחד אנו מאבדין כמה פקחין? And in b. Shab. 104b we read: תניא אמר להן ר' אליעזר לחכמים והלא בן סטדא הוציא כשפים ממצרים בסריטה שעל בשרו? אמרו לו שוטה היה ואין מביאין ראיה מן השוטים. The difference between these two versions is only that the Palestinian version still retains an allusion to the loss or destruction of many (not all!) sane people in connection with or as a result of the insane conduct of Ben Satada, while the Babylonian version ignores or does not know of these sad consequences but simply says: "We cannot cite in proof the action of a fool or insane person." Both the palestinian and the babylonian versions, however, agree that it was magic formulae, incantations or charms, that Ben Satada wrote on his body.[130] They also tell us that he brought these magic charms from Egypt, or he came from Egypt with these magic formulae tattooed on his body, thus bringing them to Palestine. The presumption is that the officials in Egypt, or the custodians, who watched over the palace-library, museum, or archives where these charms were kept, would not allow anyone to make copies of them. Ben Satada, therefore, could not copy them on papyrus or parchment, for he feared such copies, if found on him, would be taken from him. Hence he resorted to the unusual method of tattooing or writing them on his body. The Ben Satada, then, here alluded to was a magician who came to Palestine from Egypt, and apparently directly or indirectly caused the destruction of many innocent and sane people; or many naive people came to harm as a result of his coming to Palestine; or at least were threatened with harm; though it is not clear what kind of harm or destruction was done or threatened and how it was connected with Ben Satada's appearance. The question presents itself, why did R. Eliezer not mention this magician by his own name, but only mentions whose son he was? And if this should be an allusion to Jesus, who was believed to have been a magician and to have visited Egypt, why did not R. Eliezer mention him by the name by which he, himself, elsewhere designates Jesus, namely ישוע בן פנטירא.[131] Considering the fact that the

---

[130] The word למד in the Tosefta version then means למד כשפים.

[131] Tosefta Ḥul. 2.24 (Zuckermandel, 530). Of course one could assume that בן סטדא is indeed a mistake for or corruption of בן פנטירא though it would be forced and as we shall see, unnecessary, even though we ourselves assume that סטדא is a slightly corrupt form of another name. R. Hananel in his commentary to Shab. 104b reads בן פטיא and not בן סטדא so it may just be the name of an unknown man. See *Aruk* II, 180, *s. v.* בר פטר where he says פירוש שם

reading סטדא is not certain, and many suggestions as to the original of which it may have been a corrupted form have been made previously, one feels justified in making a slight emendation which would suit the context in which this name occurs. I propose to read סרטא instead of סטדא. Further the term בן does not here mean son, so that the words Ben Satada, or better Ben Sarata does not intend to give the parentage of the person referred to. The term בן means rather "adept" or "expert" as in בן קמצן.[132] and in בן חמסן or בן קמצן and in בר אוריין or בן תורה Ben Sarata then means an *adept at tattooing* or *an expert tattooer*. R. Eliezer, interested merely in proving his point that סריטא is a form of writing and as such is prohibited on the Sabbath, cites as evidence the case of a certain expert tattooer without giving his proper name or the name of his father or mother. There is no reason whatever to consider either term בן סטדא or the reading בן סרטא a designation for Jesus.[133] True Jesus was also considered a מכשף

אדם. See also *Aruk*, *s. v.* בר פחתי or בר פאתי, though the *Aruk* reads here סטדא; see also Kohut, *ibid.*, *s. v.* סטדא where there is much material but not correctly understood. B. Königsberger in Rahmer's *Literaturblatt* XX, (1891) No. 36, 140–141 suggests that Satada (or as R. Ḥananel reads פטיא) is corrupted from פטרא and refers to Peter. בן would mean not son but disciple. He says: Ohne Zweifel ist nämlich פטיא und סטדא corruptiert aus פטרא, das nichts Anderes bedeutet als "Petrus" .... Das בן ist dabei vielleicht überflüssig (wenn nicht als "Jünger" zu übersetzen)." See *Magyar Zsido Szemle*, (Juli, 1891), 458, to which Königsberger refers. He could have made a better suggestion by referring it to "pater" "son of the father." See below, the discussion of בן פטורי.

[132] Tosefta, Soṭah 13.8. N. Brüll, *Jahrbücher* VII, 95 also suggests that originally it read בן סירטא. But he thinks it refers to Jesus who was so designated to distinguish him from בן סירא. In this he is wrong. The designation never referred to Jesus and there is no reason to seek to distinguish him from Ben Sira.

[133] After having written this, I found a remark (by Reifman?) in *Ha-Lebanon* V, No. 8, (Paris, 1868), 116, as follows: ונראה לי ברור כי תחת בן סטדא צ"ל בן סרטא וכן הוא אמת הגירסא בתוספתא שבת פ' י"ב. ונקרא כן לפי שסרט על בשרו כישופי מצרים וקסמיהם (מיסטעריעוון?) כאמור (תוספתא שם ושאר מקומות וכאשר האמינו גם הרומים ועיין גרטץ ח"ד) והוספת בן לפעל היתה נהוגה הרבה בימי קדם להורות על מי שדרכו בפעולה ההיא כמו (תוספתא סוטה פ' י"ג) מעשה בכהן אחד בציפורי שנטל חלקו ... והיו קורין אותו בן חמסן. ועיין פסחים מ"ט וקרו ליה בר מחם תנורי .... בר מרקיד בי כובי (ולא צורך מה שפירש רש"י שם: קרו ליה לבנו). Königsberger in Rahmer's *Literaturblatt*, *loc. cit.*, also states that the printed edition (Venice?) has בן סירטא and not בן סיטרא

and was also believed to have been in Egypt and returned to Palestine, but he was not the only one supposed to have practiced witchcraft. He was also believed as reported in the later Toledot Jeshu to have copied — not charms — but the letters of the holy name for purposes of witchcraft, but he copied them on parchment and hid the parchment in an open wound of his flesh.[134] So this is no reason for identifying Ben Satada (Sarata) with Jesus.

Perhaps, however, the basis for such an identification is to be found in a matter mentioned in connection with the name Ben Satada which occurs in tannaitic statements which we shall now examine. In Tosefta Sanh. 10.11,[135] in connection with the discussion of the procedure in the case of a trial of a מסית "one who beguiles others to idolatry," it s said חוץ מן המסית וכן עשו לבן סטדא (כת"י וויען: לביה סטרא; דפוסים: לאיש אחר) בלוד נימנו (הכמינו) עליו שני תלמידי חכמים וסקלוהו. But even here we have as yet no reason to assume that the Ben Satada mentioned designates Jesus, as we shall see in the discussion of this passage. In p. Sanh. 7.12 (25d) it reads כך עשו לבן סוטר (דפוס וווילנא: לבן סוטרא) בלוד והכמינו לו והביאהו לבי"ד וסקלוהו. Here, בן סוטרא, according to the reading in the Wilna edition, cannot possibly be an allusion to Jesus, although he claimed to be the son and the redeemer סוטרא. Likewise in p. Yeb. 16.6 (15d end) we read: שכן עשו לבן סטרא בלוד שהכמינו . . . . . . והביאוהו לבי"ד וסקלוהו where there is not the least indication that it refers to Jesus. Only in b. Sanh. 67a where it reads: וכן עשו לבן סאדא בלוד ותלאוהו בערב הפסח is there a suggestion that it refers to Jesus who was sentenced and crucified (ותלאוהו?) on the eve of Passover. But as this additional remark ותלאוהו בערב הפסח is found only in the babylonian Talmud, we have reason to regard it as an amoraic comment — which we shall consider when we discuss how the Amoraim understood the name Ben Satada — and not as part of the

---

as given by Zuckermandel in the variants. Reifman, however, seems still to have believed that בן סרטא was a designation of Jesus because he, Jesus, tatooed the charms on his body. In this R. is wrong as there is no reason why it should refer to Jesus and not to any other tatooer or magician.

[134] See above p. 506, and Krauss, op. cit., 40.

[135] Zuckermandel, 431.

original text of the Baraita. Thus, even though we identify
the Ben Satada in Tos. Sanhedrin and parallels with the one in
Tos. Shabbat and assume that they both refer to one person, we
can still maintain that the מסית in Sanhedrin and the מכשף in
Shabbat have reference, not to Jesus[136] but to another person
whom we shall soon identify.

That Jesus is not referred to in these tannaitic statements can
be stated with all certainty. This has been recognized by Derenbourg[137] and he is followed by most modern Jewish scholars.[138]
I say most modern scholars recognized that B. Satada is not a
designation of Jesus, even though some Jewish teachers, following the amoraic comments in the b. Talmud, understood it as
such. But there are some exceptions even among modern scholars.
Thus Paulus Cassel in his *Aus Literatur und Geschichte*[139] still
maintains that even in the tannaitic sources Ben Satada is a
designation of Jesus, but he assumes בן סטרא is a corrupt form of
בן.סטרא[140] He explains the name to be like בר כוכבא a designation

---

[136] I cannot refrain from quoting here the ingenious but nonetheless incorrect remark of A. S. Kaminetski in *Hatekufah* XVIII, (Warsaw, 1923), 511 ff.,
where, assuming that Ben Satada refers to Jesus who was killed by Pontius
Pilate, he merely seeks to explain how Ben Satada could be a corrupted form
of the designation Christ and hence a name for Jesus. He says: אולם בן סטדא
(ברסטדא =) הוא באמת כנוי לישו ונשתבש או נסתרס בכונה (על דרך 'בית כריה' במקום
'בית נליה' וכדומה) מהשם כרסטוס (או 'כריסטא' בתמונת הקריאה כמו גם 'ישו' = בקריאה)
והמלה 'בלוד' נכתבה בטעות השמיעה במקום 'פלט' ובכן הנוסח העקרי היה 'וכן עשה לכרסטא
(פלט' (מפני שהנציב הרומי פלט קים את פסק הדין נקרא על שמו). Even if it were absolutely
certain that Jesus is referred to in this fanatic statement, such an interpretation בן סטרא or בלוד would not be plausible. One can certainly not base the
identification of Jesus with Ben Satada on such an interpretation involving
a series of mistakes and mispronunciations.

[137] *Essai sur l'histoire etc.*, 468. In the Hebrew translation of this work,
this passage has been omitted. Long before Derenbourg, R. Jeḥiel of Paris in
his disputation in 1240 declared — and it was not merely for apologetic
purposes — that the passage in Sanhedrin about Ben Satada does not refer
to Jesus. See ויכוח רבינו יחיאל, ed. Samuel Grünbaum, (Thorn, 1873), 4–5,
and ed. R. Margulies, (Lemberg) 18. Cf. Rahmer's *Literaturblatt* II, No. 10,
p. 40 and also *MGWJ*, (1869), 195, the remark by Lewin.

[138] See M. Joel, *Blicke* II, (Breslau, 1883), 55 ff. Exception are Kohut in
Aruk completum, s. v., and Jacob Levy in his *Wörterbuch*. See their remarks.

[139] (Berlin-Leipzig, 1885), 338, 340–41.

[140] See the variants mentioned above p. 517 and note 133.

47

for the Messiah. "Im Orient, in Persien mag Christus, weil die Magier daher kamen, zumal diesen Namen wie Bar Kochba getragen haben."[141] "Die Talmudisten welche Ben Satada erwähnen, kennen, wie bei Panther nicht mehr den Grund[142] sonst würden sie solche Erklärungen nicht gebildet haben, wie die dass darin der Name Maria enthalten sei."[143] All this is far-fetched, for there is no warrant for identifying Ben Satada with Jesus.

The tannaitic statements taken by themselves do not justify an identification of Jesus with Ben Satada, and do not contain any indication pointing to Jesus. From these statements we learn only that a certain man, considered a misleader of the people, מסית and a magician מכשף, who came from Egypt, was executed in Lud — not in Jerusalem. Hence, as R. Jeḥiel already pointed out it could not refer to Jesus who was executed in Jerusalem. Suppose we read with the Palestinian Talmud: וכן עשו לבן סטדא בלוד הביאוהו לבי"ד וסקלוהו and interpret it in a forced manner to mean: So did they to B. Satada in Lud, i. e., "they apprehended him in Lud, by hiding witnesses and thus laying a trap for him." Only this much was done in Lud. Subsequently they brought him to court in Jerusalem where they stoned him. I say, even if we could accept such a forced interpretation of the statement in the version of the p. Talmud, we could not identify this Ben Satada with Jesus. For, as far as we know, Jesus is never mentioned as being in Lud, and the sources state that he was apprehended in Jerusalem. So the statement of the Baraita itself speaks against any identification of Jesus with Ben Satada. The additional remark in the Babli ותלאוהו בערב הפסח is due to the misunderstanding of the Amoraim, who, as we shall see, apparently felt they had enough reasons for identifying B. Satada with Jesus.[144]

[141] He is apparently referring either to the Messianic interpretation of the verse דרך כוכב מיעקב (Num. 24.17) or to the son whose coming was heralded by the star which the magi saw.

[142] I. e., that it means בן אסטרא, בר כוכבא, משיח.

[143] *Ibid.*, 341, as to Papus being a shorter form from Josephus, as the modern Italians have Pepi.

[144] Or rejecting a late dating for this phrase, we can make the not impossible assumption that the otherwise unknown Ben Satada actually was executed on the eve of the Passover.

Possibly the reading בן סוטרא, "savior" or "redeemer,"
suggested to the Amoraim that the passage refers to one, who
wanted to be or was called by others, the Son and the savior.
There were many features, as we shall see, in the story of this
anonymous B. Satada, that could have caused this misunderstanding on the part of the Amoraim. But no matter how we
may explain the manner in which the mistake on the part of
the Amoraim came about, the mistake remains a mistake, and
the fact remains that Ben Satada was not Jesus.

Acknowledging this latter fact, some scholars apparently
unable to rid themselves of the suggestion of the Amoraim, still
try to find in Ben Satada a designation, if not for Jesus himself,
then of a person connected with Jesus. Thus one scholar[145]
thought that Ben Satada referred to or designated Jacobus, the
brother of Jesus who,[146] according to Josephus,[147] was sentenced
to death by the High-Priest Ananus. This Jacobus, a brother of
Jesus, could also be called בן סטרא for he and Jesus had one and
the same mother, though not the same father. This theory, of
course, would indirectly preserve the identification of Jesus with
Ben Satada, or Mary with Sata-Da,[148] as understood by the
Amoraim. But the theory is false. The same considerations which
speak against the identification of Jesus with B. Satada, force
us to reject the identification of the brother of Jesus, Jacobus,
with Ben Satada, or with the man tried and executed — or merely
trapped and apprehended — in Lud. For Jacobus likewise was
sentenced and executed — not in Lud, we have no record that he
ever was in Lud, — but in Jerusalem during the absence of the
Roman governor; Festus was dead and his appointed successor
Albinus was on the way to Jerusalem but not yet arrived.

Furthermore, Ananus the High-Priest was a Sadducee and,
as Josephus tells us, the law-abiding citizens, especially the
Pharisees, were outraged by this unlawful act of Ananus and
demanded his removal from office. It is therefore unlikely
that the Rabbis should cite this unlawful act of a Sadducean

---

[145] Löwy in Rahmer's *Literaturblatt* VII, No. 4, (1878), 15.
[146] Matth. 13.55.
[147] *Antiquities* XX, 9.1.   [148] See below p. 529.

High Priest as a precedent, or an illustration, for the legal procedure to be followed in the case of a beguiler מסית and to refer to
this highhanded act of Ananus as the act of a legal court הביאוהו
לבית דין.[149]

Having lost one Jacobus whom he tried to identify with
Ben Satada, the same scholar might claim that possibly another
Jacobus could play the role of Ben Satada. This other Jacobus
(called *major*) or James the brother of John[150] was killed with
the sword by King Herod.[151] It appears from the context in Acts
that this happened shortly before the Passover, or during "the
days of unleavened bread." For we are told that when Agrippa
saw that it pleased the Jews he also seized Peter during the
Passover festival. Agrippa was a pious king and his action may
not have been so condemned as the act of Ananus, hence the
later Rabbis might have regarded an act of his as a precedent.
But we have no express record that the act of killing Jacobus
was done in Jerusalem — though from the context in Acts it
would seem that the seizure of Peter during the Passover festival
was in Jerusalem — hence it could have happened in Lud. Yet,
with all these possibilities, this Jacobus cannot be identified with
the Ben Satada of the Talmud. For this Jacobus was killed
with the sword — when it says killed by Agrippa it may mean
by order of Agrippa through a court process — not stoned or
hanged and the death of a מסית is by stoning not by the sword.
How then could the Rabbis cite this execution of a man by
the sword as a precedent for their law in regard to a מסית who
must be killed by stoning only?

Now, there is still left another, or a third, Jacobus, *viz.*,
Jacobus Alpheus[152] also called Jacobus *minor*,[153] the lesser. Hence,
if we read בן זוטרא בן סוטרא = the younger, or the little one,
instead of בן סטדא, the designation could refer to Jacobus minor.
But we have no record elsewhere of this younger one having
been killed. Löwy[154] made the mistake of imagining that this

---

[149] Cf. Grünbaum, in Rahmer's.*Literaturblatt*, No. 8, 20.
[150] Acts 12.2.
[151] Agrippa, grandson of Herod the Great.
[152] Matth. 10.3; Mark 3.18; Luke 6.15; Acts 1.13.
[153] Mark 15.40.   [154] *Loc. cit.*

Jacobus minor — and not James the brother of Jesus — was
executed by the High Priest Ananus. Grünebaum[155] therefore
suggests that an *unknown person* — not Jesus! — whom they
called Ben Satada, is referred to in b. Sanhedrin. The reason why
they called him so was — so Grünebaum imagines — because
that unknown person was a מסית and a מכשף and the Rabbis
would not believe that such a bad man could have been the
son of a good, decent mother. And on the principle מדחציף
כולי האי ש״מ ממזר הוא, "his impudence proclaims him a bastard,"
they assumed that he must have been the son of a bad woman
סטא דא . . .[156] One can see that Grünebaum, though he has some
good ideas and was on the track of discovering who this Ben
Satada was, could not entirely free himself from the idea
suggested by the later Amoraim that the designation סטדא was
meant to refer to the mother.

He does not, however, follow the Amoraim in assuming
that it refers to the mother of Jesus but explains that from
the bad character of the son the Rabbis concluded that the
mother must have been a bad woman, a סוטה. But not every
bad man is a בן סוטה.

Thus far we had only negative results. We have found that
Ben Satada was not Jesus nor any of the followers of Jesus by
the name of Jacobus, and, we may add, not even that "unknown
man" who was so designated merely on the presumption that
a bad man must have had a bad mother. Considering the fact
that the very reading of this strange designation is doubtful and
it is found in different forms in the various readings of the texts,
such as סוטר, סוטרא, סירטא, סטדא, סטר[157] we must ask: why limit
our efforts to identify the man so designated by accepting just
one form of the name סטדא and concentrate our search upon
the explanation of the meaning of this one form of the name
merely because the Amoraim had this reading and in a fanciful
manner sought to explain its significance? We have found

---

[155] *Loc. cit.*

[156] See below the discussion of the amoraic comment. Grünbaum does not
discuss the question whether Ben Satada in Tosefta Shabbat was identical
with the one mentioned in Sanhedrin.

[157] R. in *HaLebanon, loc. cit.*, etc.

above, that judging from the context of the Baraita in the
Tosefta Shabbath, the reading סרטא gives a better sense and
explains the significance of this designation satisfactorily. On
the basis of this reading and understanding of the name we can
seek with some hope of finding the identity of the person so
designated or characterized, and we may even be able to find
the causes that led the Amoraim to the mistake which they
made in the identification of the person so named. We must
approach this question without prejudice and independent of
the amoraic comments, and seek to find a person believed to
be both a מסית and a מכשף who came from Egypt and could
properly and befittingly have been described or designaged
as בן סרטא as I prefer to read this name, and who might have
been caught and entrapped in Lud and perhaps even executed
there. *We indeed find such a person.* H. P. Chayes[158] suggests
the following. Josephus in *Antiquities* XX, 8.6 reports an incident
which happened in Jerusalem during the time of the Roman
Procurator Felix, i. e., between 52 and 60 C. E. as follows:
"Moreover there came *out of Egypt* about this time to Jerusalem
one who said he was a prophet and advised the multitude of the
people to go along with him to the mount of Olives. He
said further that he would show them from hence how at his
command *the walls of Jerusalem would fall* down . . . But the
Egyptian himself escaped out of the fight [with Felix's soldiers]
and did not appear again." In *Wars* II, 13.5 Josephus again
mentions this false prophet, as follows: "But there was an
Egyptian false prophet that did the Jews more mischief than the
former; for he was a *cheat* and pretended to be a prophet . . . But
Felix prevented his attempt . . . The Egyptian ran away."
Mention of this Egyptian is also made in Acts where we learn
that the Jews to whom he caused so much harm did not give
up hope of catching him, and when they caught one whom they
believed to be that Egyptian they sought to harm him and take
revenge on him. For in Acts 21.27–38 we read: "The Captain
said to Paul: 'Art thou not then the Egyptian who before these
days stirred up to sedition?' " This was also during the time

---

[158] *HaGoren* IV, 33–37; also Herford, *op. cit.*, 345.

of Felix's procuratorship.[159] We see then that the Jews, seeking
to harm Paul, did so because they believed him to be that
Egyptian. They were mistaken this time and suspected the wrong
person. But, we may safely assume, they continued to be on the
lookout and did not relax their search for him. It may have
happened that this Egyptian, who had misled the multitude
and hence was a מסית and who was believed to have been a
מכשף who had brought witchcraft tattooed on his flesh from
Egypt, and hence was called בן סטרא, may have at some later
time turned up again in Lud, Josephus' statement that "he
appeared no more" nothwithstanding. Or, at least, some people
in Lud became suspicious of a person whom they believed to be
that Egyptian, and entrapped him by hiding witnesses and by
getting him to repeat the seductive speeches whereby they
identified him as indeed being that Egyptian; they brought him
to court, where the witnesses who listened to him in hiding
testified against him and thus he was sentenced to death and
executed, and if the reading in the Babylonian Talmud is
accepted, this could have happened around the Passover time
or even on the eve of the Passover. The saying of the teachers
in answer to R. Eliezer[160] מפני שוטה אחד אנו מאבדין פקחין הרבה
then has reference to this Egyptian whom Josephus describes
as a "madman" from Egypt who was the cause of the death of
many sane people who followed him and were killed by the
soldiers of Felix. It is not an argument against R. Eliezer as
would appear from the Babli version: שוטה היה ואין מביאין ראיה
מן השוטה, but, is a sad comment at the mere mention by R. Eliezer
of this בן סטרא, the "madman," on the great harm caused by
him: "Yes, because of one madman we lost many sane people."

Now let us consider the mistake of the Amoraim and attempt
to find out what led them to identify this Ben Satada with
Jesus. In the story about Jesus as known among the Jews in
Babylon in later amoraic times, both according to reports from
the Gospels which reached them in some form and according to
other legends that were current among them, there are many

[159] See Acts 23.24.
[160] Tosefta, *loc. cit.*

features which resemble the story about the Egyptian false
prophet, or "madman," as told by Josephus.

1) Like the Egyptian, Jesus was considered a beguiler of
people and a magician. This is mentioned in the Gospels: "The
Pharisees said, 'By the prince of the demons [i. e:, by Beelzebub]
casteth he out demons' "[161] i. e., he is a magician. This report
of the Gospels about the opinion of the Pharisees reached the
Amoraim in Babylon. Further, in the legend about Jesus having
gone with Joshua b. Peraḥyah to Egypt[162] — and come back
from Egypt, he/is referred to as שכשף והסית והדיח, "one who
does magic, entices and misleads."

2) Like the Egyptian, a man who "came out of Egypt,"
as Josephus describes him, Jesus also came out from Egypt
as a child, according to the Gospels,[163] to fulfill the word, "Out
of Egypt did I call my son," and according to the Jewish legend
in Sanhedrin discussed previously, as a grown up man, a disciple
of Joshua b. Peraḥyah.

3) Jesus was believed to have learned the arts of magic or
witchcraft in Egypt. Thus in מעשה דאותו ואת בנו Chapter XI[164] it is
said: והלך למצרים וישב שם הרבה ימים ולמד שם הרבה כשפים ואח״כ
חזר לירושלים. And while this is found only in a later source, it
no doubt echoes an older legend which must have already been
current in amoraic times.

4) Later Jewish legends, which may echo an older legend,
make Jesus also a sort of a שורט, or מסרט, or סרטא. He is supposed
to have cut in the letters of the holy name, by means of which
he performed his miracles, on his thigh. Thus we read in מעשה
דאותו ואת בנו, Chapter V[165] הזכיר האותיות על יריכו וקרע אותה בלי כאב.
The text is not quite clear, and while it describes the act as
consisting of hiding the parchment with the letters in his open
wound, it originally may have read simply וקרע האותיות על יריכו,
"he tattooed the letters on his thigh." The verb וקרע like ושרט
can mean cutting the letters into his flesh, for in p. Shab. 12.4

[161] Matth. 12.24; also Matth. 9.34.
[162] See above pp. 481 et seq.
[163] Matth. 2.15–23.
[164] Krauss, 78.
[165] Krauss, 68.

(13d) the phrase הקורע על העור is used in the sense of השורט
על בשרו. Although this legend reports that Jesus learned the
letters of the holy name שם המפורש and not magic formulae, the
idea is the same. Some Jewish people would not admit that
with magic formulae one could perform miracles, so they reported
his having used for this purpose the letters of the שם המפורש
which were guarded in the Temple and could not be brought
out . . . . . just as the magic formulae were guarded in the
temples or museum of Egypt. We must remember that these
whispering rumors or legends are not reported clearly nor
accurately; they are given in hints and confused indications.
It is significant, however, the the Tosefta Shabbat[166] does not
specify כשפים or מצרים but merely says cryptically לא למד אלא
בכך which may mean "he learned the means by which he could
perform miracles only in this manner" which might thus echo
or have given rise to the later legend that Jesus learned in this
manner the letters of the holy name by which he performed his
tricks or miracles. Other people were less hesitant to admit that
with כשפים, which in the words of Sanh. 67b שמכחישין פמליא של
מעלה, "lessened the powers of the Divine agencies," one could
perform miracles. Knowing that Egypt was the land of witchcraft
and magic, they reported accurately הוציא כשפים ממצרים. Even
after the identification of Ben Satada with Jesus, they still
preferred to say that Jesus, who as they knew from other legends
and reports went to Egypt, learned in Egypt the magic arts by
which he performed his miracles rather than to say that he did
them by means of the שם המפורש.

In the latter case God is made to be rather helpless in the
hands of him who knows the trick of using the holy name.
Against His will He must help Jesus, who got control of His
name, to do whatever Jesus wanted Him to do.

5) The Egyptian is reported to have led the people to the
Mount of Olives and there to have boasted that by his command
he could cause the walls of Jerusalem to fall. We are not told
what the significance of this boast was. It could not have meant
that he could thus be able to enter Jerusalem, for we have not

---

[166] *Loc. cit.*

heard, and it does not seem likely that he was prevented from entering the city. It probably meant that he could by his command also raise other, stronger, or fiery walls. Now Jesus, likewise, is reported to have sat *on the Mount of Olives* when he said: "Verily I say unto you there shall not be left here one stone upon another,"[167] which probably meant that he could bring it about by his command. For he was accused of having said: "I am able to destroy the Temple of God and to build it in three days,"[168] or: "I will destroy this Temple made with hands and in three days I will build another made without hands."[169] While Jesus is reported to have made this boast in regard to the Temple and the Egyptian made his about the walls of Jerusalem, both reports may have been understood by some people at a later time, especially in Babylon, as referring to the same thing. At any rate in both cases the boast is of the same nature and could well have been confused with one another or mistaken one for another.

Thus we see that there are or were sufficient resemblances between the story about this Egyptian false prophet and the legend current among the Jews about Jesus. And the Amoraim in Babylon, in time and place far removed from these supposed or real events, and not sufficiently interested to examine critically the exact facts underlying these reports, could well have confused these two reports with one another and mistaken the report about the otherwise unknown Egyptian false prophet as referring to Jesus who in their opinion was also a false prophet and not better than the other. But once they identified Jesus with the Egyptian madman, they soon realized that there are some difficulties inherent in this identification. For, again by hearsay and inaccurately, they got other information or rumors about Jesus and his family which seemed to be in conflict with his identification with the man designated as Ben Satada. So they set about in their fashion to smooth out these difficulties and to harmonize various conflicting reports about Jesus and Ben

[167] Matth. 24.2-3; Mark 13.1-4; Luke 21.5-7.
[168] Matth. 26.61.
[169] Mark 14.58.

Satada, and to explain the meaning of the different designations used for him in these different reports. These harmonizing efforts at explaining away the difficulties in the conflicting designations or descriptions are expressed in the amoraic comment to the Baraita in Sanh. 67b and Shab. 104b which reads as follows: בן סטדא (בתמיה) (והלא) בן פנדירא הוא? אמר רב חסדא בעל סטדא בועל בן פנדירא בעל פפוס בן יהודה הוא אמו סטדא אמו מרים מגדלא שער נשיא היא כדאמרין בפומבדיתא סטת דא מבעלה.

The Gemara finds the identification difficult. How could Jesus be called Ben Satada when in another Baraita[170] he is called בן פנדירא which indicates that his father's name was Pandera and not Satada? Rab Hisda (an Amora of the third generation, died about 309) then tries to solve this difficulty by assuming that Satada was the name of the legal husband, the man to whom the mother had been betrothed or married, and Jesus was sometimes called after the name of his mother's husband,[171] since not all people knew that her husband was not the father of her child. The real father, however, was the paramour of the mother, a man by the name of Pandera, and people who knew this called Jesus by the name of his real father, Ben Pandera. But against this assumption of Rab Hisda an objection is raised. The Amoraim had heard a report that the name of Mary's legal husband was Pappos (which is probably a short form of Josephus),[172] whom they confused with Pappos ben Jehudah (who lived in the time of Akiba, first half of the second Christian century.) Hence, they argued, his name could not have been Satada. So they tried to argue, perhaps the name of the mother was Satada, but this too they found incorrect, for they heard that his mother's name was Miriam, whom they designated מרים מגדלא שער נשיא.[173] They finally came to the conclusion that Satada indeed designates the mother although it was not her proper name. It was merely a characterization of her conduct, indicating that she had committed adultery סטת דא מבעלה.[174] That

---

[170] Tosefta, Ḥul. 2.20–24; to be discussed below.

[171] See Rashi, ad loc., ונקרא על שם בעל אמו אעפ"י שהוא ממזר.

[172] See Cassel, op. cit., 341.

[173] See below.

[174] They were correct in their suggestion that סטדא is not a proper name but

the Gemara here was mistaken and confused in the identification of all these names — Josephus, Pappos and Miriam, was recognized by medieval rabbinic authorities. Thus, Tosafot to Shab. 104b *s. v.* בן סטדא objects to the identification of Ben Satada with Jesus and מרים מגדלא שער נשיא with Mary the mother of Jesus. They quote Rabbenu Tam (1100–1171) as follows: אומר רבינו תם דאין זה ישו הנוצרי דהא בן סטדא אמרינן הכא דהוה בימי פפוס בן יהודה דהוה בימי רבי עקיבא ... וישו היה בימי יהושע בן פרחיה. Then again *s. v.* אמו מרים Tosafot remarks: והוא קאמר בפ"ק דחגינה רב ביבי הוה שכיח גביה מלאך המות כו' אמר ליה לשלוחיה זיל אייתי לי מרים מגדלה נשיא משמע שהיתה בימי רב ביבי מרים מגדלא נשיא אחרת היתה אי נמי מלאך המות היה מספר לרב ביב מעשה שאירע כבר מזמן גדול.[175] Tossafot's objection to those identifications are mainly on the basis of the chronological discrepancies. But Tosafot assumes that as is stated in the question of the Gemara in Shab. 104, Miriam Magdala or Megadla was the mother of Jesus. For in b. Ḥag. 4b *s. v.* הוה שכיח גביה Tosafot remarks: מספר מה שאירע לו כבר דהאי עובדא דמרים מגדלא נשייא בבית שני היה דהיתה אמו של פלוני.

Let us now consider here the question whether this identification is correct, i. e., whether מרים מגדלא שער נשיא was the mother of Jesus.[176] From the amoraic discussion here it is evident that there was current a legend among the Jews that Mary the mother of Jesus was מגדלת שער נשיא, a dresser of women's hair.[177] This legend is also found in the later *Toledot Jeshu*. This legend that Mary the mother of Jesus was a hair dresser or *Haarflechterin* was also current in Christian circles.[178] But the understanding of מגדלא שער נשיא to mean "dresser of woman's hair"[179] or " Frauen-

---

a characterization; however, they did not know to whom it referred and what it originally meant.

[175] See these quotations in קבוצת ההשמטות (Krakau, 1893), 3, and cf. R. Jeḥiel in his ויכוח ed. R. Margulies (Lemberg), 16–17, referred to above.

[176] Strictly speaking this should come later in the section discussing the relatives and followers of Jesus.

[177] See Krauss, 186 and note 9 on p. 274. והיא היתה מרים קודם שנשאת מגדלת שער נשיא.

[178] See Lagarde, *Mittheilung* III, 257–260; but cf. Dalman, *Grammatik des Jüd.-pal. Aramäisch*, 141, note 7 and Krauss, *ibid.*, 275.

[179] Herford, 33.

haarflechterin"[180] is in itself not correct. For why should there be specified "a dresser of woman's hair," why not simply a hair-dresser? It seems to me that there was in the mind of the Rabbis, who had heard of only one Mary in connection with Jesus,[181] a confusion not alone with Mary Magdalene, as assumed by Laible and by Winer[182] but also with Mary the sister of Martha and Lazarus who anointed the Lord with ointment and wiped his feet with her hair.[183] She must have had long hair, since she could conveniently reach the feet of Jesus with it. They iden-tified this Mary with Mary Magdalene, understanding it to mean not the Mary of Magdala, but the Mary who had especially long hair, and they further identified her with the mother. This would explain the reference in the *Toledot* קודם שנשאת, "before she was married" she had long hair, for after she had been married she could not be expected to show her hair and no one could see whether it was long or short. Had the reference been to hair-dresser, the remark קודם שנשאת would not make good sense, for a woman could follow this profession even after she was married.[184]

Having once confused this Mary with the mother of Jesus, they may have thought that the legend of the woman by that name who escaped death merely by the stupidity of the agent of the angel of death (as reported in the legend)[185] referred to the mother of Jesus who, as an adulteress אשת איש שזינתה, deserved and was sentenced to death, though the sentence was not exe-cuted. And they also heard that the name of the husband of that Mary was Joseph, shortened or corrupted into Pappos.[186]

[180] Laible, 28 and 18–19.

[181] Laible, 18.

[182] See Krauss, 275. It is assumed by some scholars that there is a con-fusion between Mary, the mother, and Mary Magdalene. In the name Mag-dalene some saw an allusion to the bad reputation with regard to sexual morality which the town of Magdala had — מגדלא מפני הזנות (Midrash Lam. r. II). It may be that women hair dressers did not have such a good reputa-tion. (See R. Hananel in Tosafot, Ḳid. 49a, *s. v.*, מאי מגודלת) and the name was given to Mary to reflect on her character.

[183] John 11.2.

[184] See the remark of R. Hananel in Tosafot, Ḳid., *loc. cit.*

[185] Hagigah, cited in Tosafot, *supra*.

[186] See Cassel, *loc. cit.*, and also Krauss, 187, reference to קשת ומן.

Looking around for such a man, they found Pappos b. Jehudah
who lived in the time of R. Akiba and who was so jealous of his
wife that whenever he left his home he would lock her up, but
here is the humor — to no avail, for "There is no guardian against
unchastity," אין אפטרופוס לעריות. The legend told in the later
Toledot, of how Mary was deceived by — or received — the
paramour, after her husband or betrothed, ארוס, had left the
house, may well have been current and so they decided it must
have referred to the same Pappos or Joseph, who was deceived
by his wife, no matter how he guarded her. That he lived more
than a hundred years later than the husband of Mary did not
bother them, as chronology was not their strong point. We thus
find that the amoraic identification of Jesus with Ben Satada is
based upon confusion of similar reports and on a mistaken identification of different persons by the same name, and there
is really no connection whatever between Jesus and Ben
Satada.

The other name בן פנדירא mentioned here by the Amoraim
in connection with Jesus seems actually to have been a designation for Jesus, though its meaning has not been correctly
understood and not sufficiently explained. This name occurs
already in tannaitic sources and in different spellings. In Tosefta
Ḥul. 2.22 and 24[187] we read: מעשה בר' אלעזר בן דמה שנשכו נחש ובא
יעקב איש כפר סמא לרפאותו משום ישוע בן פנטירא ולא הניחו ר' ישמעאל
אמרו לו אי אתה ראש בן דמה אמר לו אני אביא לך ראיה שירפאני ולא הספיק
להביא ראיה עד שמת .... מעשה בר' אליעזר שנתפס על דברי מינות והעלו
אותו לבמה לדון אמר לו אותו הגמון זקן כמותך יעסוק בדברים הללו אמר לו
נאמן דיין עלי כסבור אותו הגמון שלא אמר אלא לו ולא נתכוין אלא נגד אביו
שבשמים אמר לו הועיל והאמנתי עליך אף אני כך אמרתי אפשר שהסיבו הללו
טועים בדברים הללו דימוס דימוס הרי אתה פטור וכשנפטר מן הבמה היה מצטער
שנתפס על דברי מינות נכנסו תלמידיו לנחמו ולא קבל נכנס ר' עקיבה ואמר
לו ר' אומר לפיכך דבר שמא אין אתה מיצר אמר לו אמור אמר לו שמא אחד
מן המינין אמר לך דבר של מינות והנאך אמר השמים הזכרתני פעם אחת הייתי
מהלך באיסטרטיא של צפורי מצאתי יעקב איש כפר סכנין ואמר דבר של
מינות משום ישוע בן פנטירי והנאני ונתפסתי על דברי מינות שעברתי על דברי
תורה הרחק מעליה דרכך ואל תקרב אל פתח ביתה כי רבים חללים הפילה

[187] Zuckermandel, 503.

 וגו' שהיה ר' אליעזר אומר לעולם יהא אדם בורח מן הכיעור ומן הדומה לכיעור.[188]

First we must take notice of the fact that the reading is not certain. Tosefta already has two forms of the name פנטירא (22) and פנטירי (24). In the later works, the *Toledot Jeshu*, and in fragments, there are different forms and also different persons, owners or bearers of the name. There occurs ישו בן פנדירה[189] and ישו בן פנדרא.[190] Also יוסף בן פנדירא the paramour of Mary — and father of Jesus,[191] while the husband's name is given as Johanan, and contrariwise יוסף בן פנדירא is given as the name of the husband, while the name of the lover, and hence the real father of Jesus, is given as Johanan.[192] So Pandera, or Pantera, was either the name of Jesus' father, or of Joseph's father, hence the grandfather of Jesus or of Mary's husband's father and no relation at all to Jesus, or it may be a family name and not the name of any one person in particular.

Now, as to the meaning of this designation, if it was not simply the proper name of a person in which case it need not have special meaning. One interpretation is that פנתירי is corrupted from $\pi \alpha \rho \theta \acute{e} \nu o s$ which means the virgin, or young woman. Now, of course, the Jews did not believe Jesus to have been the son of a virgin. But, according to this interpretation of the word פנתירי[193] the Jews, already in very early times, sought to make fun of the claim that Jesus was the son of a virgin and therefore twisted the name to בן פנטרא, the son of the lustful panther. The panther was the animal sacred to Bacchus and also was believed to be descended from the lioness.[194] The Jews then meant by this designation to describe him as the son of the animal devoted to Bacchus, i. e., the result of heathenism . . . and also the illegitimate son of the unchaste panther or leopard. The church which also knew the name בן פנתירי for Jesus, did not

[188] Cf. b. 'Ab. Zarah 16b–17a and 27b.
[189] Krauss, 144.
[190] *Ibid.*, 146, 147.
[191] *Ibid.*, 38, 40, 118, 131, 140.
[192] *Ibid.*, 64.
[193] Cassel, *op. cit.*, 334 ff.
[194] See Cassel, *ibid.*, 337, note 19.

understand the insult and mockery intended by the Jews with this name, and hence adopted the name, but they first legitimatized, as it were, the panther. The panther is compared with Mary.[195] Perles, in *Die Namen Jesus im Talmud*[196] rejects this interpretation of P. Cassel on·the ground that he (Perles) did not find an allusion in Jewish literature to the belief that the panther is the type of unchastity.... In this Perles is wrong, as pointed out by Goldfahn[197] who says: "Dr. Perles hat b. Kiddushin 70a vergessen, wo R. Abbahu die Stelle in Nehemiah 7.61: אמר אדון ששמו..., wozu Raschi עצמו כנמר deutet כרוב אדון ואמר bemerkt: כחיה זו שאינו מקפדת בזוג חברתה. Das von Cassel (*loc. cit.*, S. 337, Anm. 191) erwähnte mittelalterliche zoologische Märchen, dass die Parden von dem unkeuschen Gelüste der Löwinen ableitet, kennt auch die rabbinische Literatur. R. Simon b. Zemaḥ Duran, der es in seinem Commentar מגן אבות zu Abot 5.20 (ed. Leipzig, 1855, S. 91a) mittheilt, macht aber keinen Unterschied zwischen Parden und Panther und sagt der נמר sei ein Mischling בן חזיר היער und בן לביאה. Dieses zoologische Märchen dürfte vielleicht auch einen geschichtlichen Sinn haben. Jecheskel 19.2 ist לביא Symbol des Judenthums, vgl. Sotah folio 11b; חזיר היער ist nach der Deutung der Midrashim zu Ps. 80.14 (vgl. Midrasch z. Ps. *loc. cit.*, ed. Buber § 6 nebst Parall.) Symbol Roms. Aus der Vermischung Roms mit dem Judenthume entspringt der ''נמר'' der kühne Panther, des Christentum, welches das Judentum u. seinen Gesetzgeber, Gott, schmäht (vgl. Pesikte dr. Kahana, ed. Buber, pagina 41a) אריה ist Symbol Gottes (vgl. Chullin 59b und Pesikta dr. Kahana, ed. Buber, pagina 116a, zu Amos 3.8). Auch der Midrasch zu den Psalmen 78.45 (ed. Buber § 11) sagt: Der Panther (פנתירין) sei ein Mischling (ערוב).'' While all this, ingenious though it is, may be correct and Perles' ground for rejecting Cassel's interpretation not sufficient, it does not make the interpretation correct. It is very unlikely that at such an early time, in the days of R. Eliezer, i. e., in the second half of the first Christian century, the Jews wanted to designate Jesus by a name

---

[195] See Cassel, *ibid.*, *loc. cit.*, note 20.
[196] In *Magyar Zsido Szemle*, (1889), 193–200.
[197] In Rahmer's *Literaturblatt* XX, (1891), No. 39, p. 151.

expressive of their appraisal of him, and that they would use
such a complicated allusion referring to the legendary nature of
the panther. Especially is it unlikely that the church should not
have recognized the intended insult, and that the Amoraim too
did not recognize its meaning and considered instead Pantera as
the name of the father אבי פנדירא הוה. So this interpretation of
Pantera is not acceptable. No more acceptable is the interpretation given by Perles[198] that Pandera is like ὕπανδρος.[199]

Another fanciful interpretation of this strange designation is
given by A. S. Kamenetzki in ספר יובל של הדואר[200] which reads as
follows: מוצא שם בן פנדירא: לדעתי נתחלף אז ליהודים ישו זה בישוע
בן סירא[201] והשם בן פנדירא הוא שם המשובש מ.בן סירא" ואפשר גם שאחרי
שנעשה החלוף הזה מצאו המחרפים עוד סימן מיוחד בשם בן תירא לאמור
בן החיה (תירא=חיה בלשון יוני) בנגוד לכנוי בן אלהים שהמציאו מכבדי
הנוצרי. וככה הלך השם הלוך והשתבש עד שהיה לפנתירא (=נמר, חיה רעה)
ולבסוף לפנדירא לפטירי ואולי גם ל(ס)טרא שנשתבש אחר כך לסטדא (בן
סירא). Previously Kamenetzki in *Hatekufah*[202]
had said quite differently:.... (פנתרי) "בן פנטירי" או "בן פנדירא" השם
הוא לדעתי שמסרס בכוונה משם בן אנתרופי בן האדם "מענשענזאהן" שהשתמש
בו ישו הרבה לפי דברי האוונגליונים. And in the same article[203] he also
says אפשר שבן פטירי (נ"א פטורי) הנזכר בתלמוד (ב"מ) הוא בן פנטירי.
In the latter point, the writer in Rahmer's Literaturblatt, to
be discussed below[204] anticipated him. Of course all these fanciful
interpretations involving a series of corruptions and misunderstandings are far fetched and far from plausible. I would add to
this, the interpretation of Strauss quoted by Hitzig[205] with some
modification and improvement of my own. According to this
interpretation פנטירי is the Greek πενθερός meaning "son in law"
חתן. Herford's argument: "But surely there is nothing distinctive

---

[198] *Ibid., loc. cit.*

[199] Consider the full implication of ὕπανδρος! Does it mean "a married
woman" and imply "the son of a married woman by a man other than her
husband?" — which might fit Mary, or does it mean, as it seemingly is used
by Plutarch "ein liederliches Weibsstück" — an unchaste woman?

[200] New York, (1927), 323.

[201] Cf. Brüll, *Jahrbücher*, V, 201 and VII, 95. See also above, p. 489.

[202] XVIII, (1923), 511–512.

[203] P. 511, note 1.

[204] Pp. 537 f.   [205] See Herford, 39.

in such an epithet to account for its being specially applied to Jesus" may be met in the following wise. The implication of the name is that Jesus was not a bastard, he was the legal and legitimate son of Joseph and Mary who were merely betrothed — which is legally married but not yet married in fact. Mary was an ארוסה but not a נשואה. Thus there was a good reason to apply the name בן החתן not בן הבעל to Jesus, for while this casts a little reflection on Jesus, it does not call him illegitimate. It seems that in Galilee they were more strict than in Judea as regards the relation between the betrothed and it was considered bad taste and the unusual thing for the חתן to have intercourse with the betrothed before the concluding marriage formalities or נשואין took place.[206] In general it was considered improper for the betrothed to live in the house of his father-in-law before marriage. In b. B. B. 98b there is quoted a saying of Ben Sira disparaging the חתן who does so: קל מסובין, חתן הדר בבית חמיו. And in b. Yeb. 52a and in Ḳid. 12b it is said that Rab (Abba Areka) would administer a punishment to a betrothed חתנא who dwelt in the house of his father-in-law: רב מנגיד על חתנא דדייר בבית חמוה.[207] The name בן פנתירי would then designate or point to Jesus as one merely conceived and born before the marriage was perfected (נשואין) but nonetheless legally and legitimately and not a bastard.[208]

I have cited all these fanciful interpretations of the name, although none of them is satisfactory.[209] *Perhaps, however, we need no interpretation beyond the simple interpretation that Panther was just a name or still better a family name.* Origen quoted by Epiphanius[210] says that Jacob the father of Joseph and grand-

---

[206] See Ket. 12a.

[207] Perhaps, however, this may apply in general even to a married son-in-law, because of suspicion about possible, indecent relations with his mother-in-law. Cf. the saying הוי זהיר באשתך מחתנה הראשון, Pes. 113a.

[208] Perhaps the saying in p. Pes. I (37b) האוכל מצה בערב פסח כבא על ארוסתו contains a subtle, veiled allusion to Jesus who, according to the Gospels, had his סדר with מצה etc. in the evening preceding the eve of Passover, or in the night preceding the 14th of Nisan, just as his father had intercourse with his betrothed before the proper time, and it hints that he acted in a manner like his father in doing things too soon!

[209] Cf. Krauss, 276, for the literature on other interpretations.

[210] See Herford, 39, note 2.

father of Jesus was called Panther. This would explain how in some of the later sources of the *Toledot Jeshu*, Joseph is called יוסף בן פנטירא. The Jews and the Christians had the same legend on this point, and when they speak of Jesus the son of Pandera, they either mean the grandson, for בני בנים הרי הם כבנים, "the sons of one's son are like one's sons"[211] or they mean Jesus of the family of Pandera. Furthermore, as Deismann showed[212] Πανθήρα was quite a common Greek proper name, and there were in Judea, Jews with Greek names. If, however, we want to indulge in speculations about possible corruptions and misunderstandings, we should consider also the name בן פטורי mentioned in b. B. M. 62a.

M. S. Rens (of Hamburg)[213] believes that he has found an allusion to Jesus and his teachings in the Baraita B. M. 62a which reads as follows: שנים שהיו מהלכין בדרך וביד אחד מהן קיתון של מים אם שותין שניהם מתים ואם שותה אחד מהן מגיע לישוב דרש בן פטורא מוטב שישתו שניהם וימותו אל יראה אחד מהם במיתתו של חברו עד שבא ר' עקיבא ולימד וחי עמך חייך חייך קודמין. Now Rens claims, though without any justification for his opinion, that the use of the term דרש when the verse expounded or used as the basis of the opinion is not cited, is unusual[214] and could have been used only by one who was not one of the Rabbis. Who, then, was this Ben Patura who employed terms not usually employed by the Rabbis? Rens suggests that Jesus is here designated by this name.[215] Jesus frequently refers to himself as "the son of the father"[216] so his disciples likewise referred to him as "the son of the father" in heaven, "filius patri" or Ben Patri, and quoted in his name

[211] b. Yeb. 62b.

[212] See Strack, *op. cit.*, 21.

[213] In Rahmer's *Literaturblatt* XIV, (1885), No. 42, p. 165.

[214] It occurs, however, in Giṭ. 43a; Pes. 42a; cf. also Ket. 49a זה מדרש דרש ראב"ע, and if it should be claimed that the Mishnah there may have omitted the verse which was the basis for the decision of R. Eleazer b. Azariah and which he cited when giving the decision, then one might as well assume that here, likewise, Ben Paturi cited the verse on which he based his decision but when quoting the decision the Baraita omitted the verse.

[215] He might have simply said that Ben Paturi, or as some readings have it, Ben Patiri, is corrupted from Ben Pantiri, just as we have seen above, it could be claimed that Ben Pantiri is a mistake for Ben Patiri.

[216] Matth. 15.13; John 13.17, etc.

this teaching. Although we do not find this teaching or saying in the Gospels, it may have been one of the Agrapha — though Resch does not mention it either — . At any rate it is in keeping with and in the spirit of the sermon on the Mount[217] and may have formed part of it, though subsequently omitted in the Gospel. It may have been preserved by one of his disciples who referred to him as "filius patri," and another, quoting it, misunderstood it to mean the son of a man named Patri, hence he gave it in Hebrew Ben Patri. This would explain the apparent irregularity of using one word — for son — in Hebrew, בן and the other — for father — in Latin, *patri*. And the term דרש which introduced this teaching may indicate that it originally formed part of the sermon — דרשה — on the mount. This is the theory of Rens slightly improved by me to increase the possibility of its being correct. There is one other difficulty in its way which we must and can remove, *viz.*, how could it happen that all the teachers up to the time of Akiba, should have accepted a teaching of Jesus. This difficulty can easily be explained away. It might have been an old Jewish teaching merely emphasized by Jesus, hence cited by some in his name; or, though it was believed to be his teaching, it was not rejected for this reason by the Rabbis, just as they did not cease to declare that "thou shalt love thy neighbour as thyself" is the great commandment of the Torah[218] although Jesus also declared it to be the greatest commandment. Furthermore, we have seen that R. Eliezer accepted or at least was pleased, as he admitted, with a teaching of Jesus quoted to him by Jacob of Kefar Sekarya. In this latter case it may have been made easier for the Rabbis to accept it for they did not recognize Jesus in Ben Patri, but took Patri to be the name of a person. Thus the teaching, even if it had come from Jesus, might have been circulated and accepted by the teachers until Akiba had recognized it as Christian or for other reasons disagreed with it and rejected it. All this is possible, but what reason have we to assume that it was so, especially when we find no difficulty at all in the name

217 Matth. 5.39–40.
218 p. Ned. 9.3 (41c); Sifra, *Kedoshim* IV, (Weiss, 89b).

Ben Patura or Patera? This whole Baraita here in B. M. is taken
from the Sifra, *Behar* VI[219] and there the teaching of Ben Paturi
is given together with the verse[220] on which he based it; it reads
as follows: וחי אחיך עמך זו דרש בן פטורי שנים שהיו הולכים במדבר
ואין ביד אחד אלא קיתון של מים אם שניהם שותהו אחד מגיע ליישוב ואם
שותים אותו שנים שניהם מתים דרש בן פטורי ישתו שתיהם וימותו שנאמר וחי
אחיך עמך אמר לו ר"ע וחי אחיך עמך חייך קודמים לחיי חבירך. Here,
not only is the verse on which it is based cited, so that there
is nothing unusual in the usage of the term[221] but Ben Paturi
discusses it with R. Akiba, so he was a contemporary of Akiba
and could not have been Jesus.[222]

Dr. Sidon[223] further disproves the theory of Rens by calling
attention to the fact that Ben Paturi is mentioned elsewhere
with his full name Jehudah b.[224] Paturi, as a contemporary of
Akiba, even a younger contemporary, in whose name he gives
an interpretation דרש ר' יהודה בן פטורי משום ר' עקיבא.[225] It is
strange though that R. Joshua quotes him there, but then this
Joshua may have been another Joshua, not Joshua b. Ḥananiah.
It is most likely that פטירי is a different form of בתירי (ב and פ
interchange as in הבקר for הפקר) and this Judah b. Patera is
none other than Judah b. Betera, and in B. M. בן פטורא is a
corrupt form of בן בתירה who is often mentioned without his
first name.

Another designation assumed by some to have been used in
the Talmud in referring to Jesus is פלוני "a certain one" or

---

[219] (Weiss, 109c).

[220] Lev. 25.35.

[221] Which, as we have seen above, occurs elsewhere even without the
verse. In addition to the instances cited above see b. Shab. 21b and 88;
Beẓah 33a; Shab. 14a and 39a.

[222] Cf. Goldfahn, in Rahmer's, *Literaturblatt* XIV, No. 42, 173 and No. 49,
193, where Rens answers Goldfahn, insisting that דרש without a verse is rarely
used and points to the reading פטירא instead of פטורא as found in some editions
of the Talmud, in En Jacob and in Yalkuṭ.

[223] *Ibid.*, 204.

[224] Of course one might argue that יהודה is a mistake for ישו and that it
came about by a mistaken resolution of the abbreviation ר"י בן פטורי — reading
ר' יהודה instead of ר' ישו! But the time element — his being a contemporary of
R. Akiba cannot be argued away.

[225] Tosefta Soṭah 5.13 and 6.1 (Zuckermandel, 307).

איש פלוני, "a certain man," but in all instances where this epithet פלוני is used it is very doubtful, to say the least, whether the reference is to Jesus. First among these is the passage in M. Yeb. 4.13 (b. Yeb. 49a,b) where Ben Azzai says מגלת יוחסין מצאו בירושלים וכתוב בה, איש פלוני ממזר מאשת איש, "They found a scroll of genealogies[226] in Jerusalem in which — among other entries — was written: 'a certain man was a bastard, the son of a married woman by a man not her legal husband.'" Of course, if we assume that Jesus was a *mamzer* and that the Rabbis believed him to have been one, then it is not *impossible* that when they cited a certain geneological list in which an entry was found about "a certain man," that he was a bastard, they had reference to the entry about Jesus whom they designated as פלוני "a certain man." But there is absolutely no positive reason for assuming this. Why should the Rabbis in the first half of the second century seek to shield Jesus in not exposing his name but merely referring to him as "a certain man." For this seems to be the original reading and not a substitute reading due to the fear of any censor, since in no MS or older text, or quotation, is there a passage reading ישו instead of פלוני.

In this connection we might discuss the passage in Masseket Kallah[227] about a certain child who passed by the elders with head uncovered, an act considered bold and disrespectful;[228] the teachers, judging by the disrespectful behavior of the child, declared that that child must be a bastard or one conceived by his mother during the period of her menstruation, בן הנדה and R. Akiba said it was both a ממזר ובן הנדה. The passage in מסכת כלה רבתי reads as follows: פעם אחת היו זקנים יושבים עברו לפניהם שני תינוקות, אחד גלה את ראשו ואחד כסה את ראשו, זה שגלה ראשו, ר' אליעזר אומר ממזר, ר' יהושע אומר בן נדה, ר' עקיבא אומר ממזר ובן נדה, אמרו לו, עקיבא, איך מלאך לבך לעבור על דברי רבותיך, אמר להם אני אקיימנו, הלך אצל אמו של אותו תינוק ומצאה שהיא יושבת ומוכרת קטנית בשוק. אמר

---

[226] On this passage and on the question of genealogical books, see my "The Three Books Found in the Temple at Jerusalem." See above note 129.

[227] Ed. Higger, (New York, 1936), 191–192.

[228] Women and children were expected to cover their heads but not grown-up men; see my responsum "Should one cover the Head when participating in Divine Worship?" in *CCAR Yearbook* XXXVIII, (1928).

לה, בתי אם תאמר לי דבר זה שאני שואליך, הריני מביאך לחיי עולם הבא,
אמרה לו השבע לי, היה ר' עקיבא נשבע בשפתיו ומבטל לו בלבו. אמר לה
בנך זה מה טיבו? אמרה לו כשנכנסתי לחופה נדה הייתי ופירש ממני בעלי
ובעלני שושביני ועברתי את זה, נמצא אותו תינוק ממזר ובן נדה. אמרו גדול
היה ר' עקיבא שהכחיש את חברו. באותה שעה אמרו ברוך שגלה סודו לעקיבא
בן יוסף. This passage has also been understood as referring to Jesus.
Thus Ibn Yarḥi in his commentary פרוש מסכת כלה רבתי[229] says:
נחלקו חכמים ז"ל על אותו הפריץ יש"ו שהולך לפניהם בקומה זקופה ובגלוי
הראש וכו'. The fact that Akiba spoke to the mother of that
child precludes the possibility of that child having been Jesus.
The mistake of taking that child for Jesus could have been
made by later people only on the basis of two other mistakes,
viz., the mistaken identification of Pappos b. Jehudah, a contemporary of Akiba, with the husband of Miriam, the women's
hairdresser, and the identification of the latter with the mother
of Jesus. The story told by the mother of the child of how the
friend of the husband or best man שושבין substituted for the
husband, resembles the story told in later *Toledot Jeshu* about
Mary mistaking her husband's friend for her husband and hence
yielding herself to him, and this resemblance in the stories
also helped to mislead some people into believing that both
deal with the same persons. Incidentally it may be noticed
that the Mishnah in Yebamot, citing the passage from מגלת יוחסין
in support of the opinion of R. Joshua that only a child conceived
in such sin for which the parents were liable to be punished
with death by human courts כל שחייבין עליו מיתת בית דין, could
be considered a bastard, could not have known the story of the
Tractate Kallah nor its interpretation as referring to Jesus, for in
the Mishnah, R. Joshua declared the child — presumed by some
to be Jesus — to have been merely a בן הנדה but not a ממזר.
But there is not the slightest reason for assuming that either
of the passages in מגלת יוחסין or in מסכת כלה refer to Jesus.[230]

---

[229] Ed. Toledano, p. 4. Quoted by Higger, *op. cit.*, Introduction 25.

[230] See also Chwolson, *Das Letzte Pessahmahl*, 100–102. Cf. also Hans
Leisegang, *Pneuma Hagion, Der Ursprung des Geistesbegriffs der synoptischen
Evangelien aus der Griechischen Mystic* (Leipzig, 1922), p. 18, who probably,
on the basis of the misunderstood and misinterpreted passage above which
he accepted from secondhand sources says: 'Auch die Stellungnahme zur

In another passage in the Talmud[231] where "a certain man" פלוני is mentioned, some scholars would discover Jesus. The passage reads: שאלו את ר' אליעזר פלוני מהו לעולם הבא, "What about so and so in the future world?" R. Eliezer who was suspected of heresy or leanings toward Christianity and who once enjoyed a teaching of Jesus reported to him by Jacob of Sakanya, is, according to the opinion of some scholars, here asked what his opinion of Jesus was; whether he will have a share in the world to come?[232] But why did neither the questioners nor R. Eliezer in his answers mention ישו by name? What reason was there to shield Jesus, especially since nothing definite was said about him, and the question was not decided in his disfavor. Rashi's explanation that Salomon is meant here and R. Ḥananel's interpretation that Absolom was meant make very good sense.[233] They wanted to spare Solomon or even Absolom the insult of recording that there was serious doubt as to either of them having a share in the future world. Even if it were not Solomon or Absolom but another person אדם אחר, someone whom they

---

Geburtsgeschichte Jesu innerhalb des Talmud, die stets darauf hinausläüft irgendeinen Ehebruch der Maria zu construiren und so die Geburt Jesu auf natürlichem Wege zu erklären, macht das vor allem deutlich." This is not correct, since with the exception of the reference of the Amoraim to בועל בן פנדירא the Talmud does not ("stets") seek to assume an act of adultery on the part of Mary. Leisegang refers to Hennecke, *Apocryphen* (1904) where he says, the passages from the Talmud are given. In the second edition of Hennecke, p. 21, Hennecke does not give the passages but merely refers to the literature. On one point, however, Leisegang is correct, namely: that in Jewish circles the idea or myth of God physically begetting a child could never have been accepted. Hence Mary was said to have conceived, not directly from God but through an agent of God, the Holy Ghost. Since שלוחו של אדם כמותו and the Holy Ghost merely acted as the agent of God, Jesus could still be called the son of God. Later on the Holy Ghost, the agent who impregnated Mary, was made identical with God and in the Trinity Mary was accounted as the third party, Father, Mother and Son, instead of Father, Holy Ghost and Son.

[231] b. Yoma 86b.

[232] Evidently the author of this Baraita or the Gemara here, as referring to Jesus, did not understand the Mishnah in Sanhedrin which included Balaam among the four commoners who were not to have a share in the world to come.

[233] Tosafot, *ad loc., s. v.* פלוני.

wanted to spare the insult, one can understand why they
designate him as פלוני. But there was no such reason for so
designating Jesus. The other question asked of R. Eliezer[234] about
a bastard, whether he can inherit from his father, ממזר מהו לירש,
is also understood by some as possibly referring to Jesus.[235] It
is argued that it may have been an ironical question. Jesus
boasted of having inherited and acquired from his father powers
like his own e. g., to forgive sins, etc.; but how could a bastard
inherit from his father? For even God has no right to beget a
child with a married woman. Or the question was, how could
Jesus who claimed to be the Messiah, inherit the messiahship from
David when he was not a real descendant from David, since
Joseph, the husband of his mother, was not his father? All these
interpretations are far-fetched and forced, and have no basis
whatever except the wish to find allusions, and disparaging allusions at that, to Jesus in the Talmud.

Some modern scholars are so eager to discover allusions to
Jesus, that at an allusion in the Talmud to any person in whose
history or character there is the slightest hint or a resemblance
to one feature or another in the life story of Jesus, they immediately jump to the conclusion that the person referred to was
Jesus presented under some disguise. To this class of misunderstood passages belongs the passage in M. Sanh. 7.5 (b. Sanh. 56a)
where it is said that in the case of a trial for blasphemy, to avoid
repetition in their testimony of the words of the blasphemy, the
witnesses use a circumlocution, כנוי, and do not recite the blasphemy as it was uttered by the accused, but substitute the
phrase יכה יוסי את יוסי in which phrase the second יוסי is a substitute for the Tetragrammaton. Now, why use Josi as a substitute for the name of God?[236] It is therefore suggested that Josi

---

[234] Loc. cit.

[235] But if פלוני was Jesus, why did they not ask in one question פלוני
ממזר מהו לירש חלק עוה'ב. Of course, it could be argued that the one question is
the logical sequel to the other. If a man of Jesus's character could merit a
share in the world to come, could he as a bastard whose father was said to be,
in Christian tradition, God, claim a share in the world to come, which God,
the Father, gives as an inheritance to his beloved and are we to derive from
this the general rule that a bastard can legally inherit?

[236] One could ask the counter question, why use the name Josi for the

is an allusion to Jesus.[237] But this is far from plausible. The Rabbis would not have substituted the name of Jesus for the name of God even in a blaspheming phrase, for such a substitution might be taken as an indication of a certain similarity between the two, and it would have suggested that Jesus had a somewhat divine character. It is simply a convenient substitute using names which frequently occur, just as when they wish to refer to a case of two people having the same name, they speak of שני יוסף בן שמעון. Perhaps the choice of this substitute was prompted by the desire of using a four-letter name.[238]

Another such forced allusion to Jesus under a disguised name is found by some in the saying of Rab in b. Sanh. 38b, which reads אמר רב אדם הראשון בלשון ארמי סיפר שנאמר ולי מה יקרו רעיך אל.[239] Duschak[240] assumes that אדם הראשון here is a name for Jesus who was called אדם קדמון "der zuerst ausgeflossene Grundquell der Dinge, die aus Gott emanirten, ist der erstgeborene Sohn Gottes . . . diesen angeblichen אדם קדמון nennt der Talmud zuweilen אדם ראשון." Hence in the saying of Rab, the reference is to Jesus who spoke Aramaic, for he said אלהי אלהי למא שבקתני[241] instead of the

---

smiter as well as for the smitten? The first Josi then must also stand for something else, unless we assume that the blasphemy consisted in the utterance: May God smite God or Himself?

[237] See Dr. A. Lewin in Rahmer's *Literaturblatt* VIII, (1879), No. 32, 127.

[238] There are many other theories about the meaning of the name יוסי in this phrase which we might as well mention here. M. S. Rens (*ibid.*, No. 39, 157), assumes that it is a somewhat inverted form of Jovis. This inverted form was used in order to avoid the mention of the heathen deity by name, on the ground ושם אלהים אחרים לא תזכירו. Another theory is that Josi here was pronounced as ὀυσια = הויה or היות i. e., a substitute for the שם הויה. But there is no reason for attaching any special significance to the choice of a substitute or circumlocution beyond the possible consideration that they may have looked for another four letter name. Cf. also Dr. Sidon, *ibid.*, Nos. 47, 186, who also favors the idea that the consideration was that Josi was a common name, just as in the case of שני יוסף בן שמעון.

[239] The quotation is Ps. 139.17. The entire psalm is supposed to refer to the creation of man — Adam. See Rashi, *ad loc.*

[240] Rahmer's *Literaturblatt* VI, (1877), No. 51, 203.

[241] Mark 15.34.

Hebrew.[242] Likewise the saying in Sanhedrin[243] אדם הראשון מושך
בערלתו, might — according to Duschak — fit Jesus, "da er am
liebsten mit dem schönen Geschlecht Umgang pflegte."[244] And,
of course, the saying אדם הראשון מין הוא and R. Naḥman's saying
כופר בעיקר הוה[245] would fit Jesus.[246] The arguments against Duschak's theory might be augmented as follows: First, Paul calls
Jesus the *second Adam*, "the second man is the Lord from
heaven."[247] Secondly, if this אדם ראשון who has some divine
character, as in Zohar עתיקא קדישא אדם קדמון[248] or אדם עילאה[249] or
in Philo[250] ὀυράνιος ἄνθρωπος had been meant in these passages, the Rabbis would not have applied it to Jesus, since it
would have given him divine character and especially since
saying "Adam spoke Aramaic" does not contain anything
disparaging.

I believe we have exhausted all the passages in the Talmud
in which Jesus actually or supposedly is referred to under any
name, surname, or disguised designation.

We shall now proceed to consider such passages in which
Jesus is, actually or supposedly, alluded to, not by any special
name but as one who claims, or is considered by his followers, to
be of unique or divine character, or to possess a special authority.
The first passage of this kind is the one in b. Sanh. 106b where
the verse in Num. 24.23 אוי מי יחיה משומו אל is interpreted by R.
Simon b. Laḳish, a Palestinian Amora of the second generation as
אוי מי שמחיה עצמו בשם אל. Rashi,[251] explains it to mean עושה עצמו אלוה,

[242] One could perhaps support this by the consideration that according to
the Rabbis העולם נברא בלשון הקודש (Gen. r., 18.6 and 31.9). Hence the Biblical
Adam must have spoken Hebrew and not Aramaic.

[243] *Loc. cit.*

[244] This is rather doubtful. If one accepts the suggestion that the reference
is to Jesus, then perhaps מושך בערלתו means the practice of covering up the
circumcision and ascribes to Jesus instead of Paul the abolition of מילה.

[245] Sanh., *loc. cit.*

[246] Against Duschak see Friedländer in Rahmer's *Literaturblatt, ibid.,* 208
and the note of the redaction.

[247] I Cor. 15.47.

[248] Idra r. 141b.

[249] Zohar II, 70b; II, 48.

[250] *De Allegoriis Legum* I, XII.   [251] *Ad loc.*

"one who declares himself to be God." Of course, Resh Laḳish's interpretation of the verse may simply mean, one who supports himself or makes a living by using or abusing the name of God, i. e., employing it in incantations and cures. In this sense it might well refer to Jesus, whose healing of people or driving out evil spirits was claimed to have been performed with, or in, the name of God.[252] But more likely Rashi's explanation is correct and it refers to Jesus who declared himself to be like God, or claimed to have arisen from the dead, שהחיה עצמו, as a god over whom death has no power. Of course, we have no proof that Jesus expressly declared himself to be God, though he claimed equal authority with God. He is reported as having said: "I and my father are one"[253] though in the earlier Gospels,[254] Jesus never declares himself to be God, but merely the son of God who is almost like his father. However, in Luke and John,[255] Jesus is referred to in the narrative portions as the Lord. Simon b. Laḳish in the third century may have heard or known that, according to some Gospels or Christian sources, Jesus was considered to have divine powers or to be God; and he assumed that these sources or Gospels had this idea from their master Jesus who himself made this claim. Simon b. Laḳish interpreted this utterance by Balaam as prophetically cursing Jesus for making such claims, for Balaam (so it was believed) was able to foresee Jesus' claims, just as, according to the passage in Yalḳuṭ to be discussed below, he is reported as having predicted the appearance of Jesus with his misleading doctrines. Furthermore, Simon b. Laḳish could have heard of Ignatius (70–150) and Polycarp (also 70–150) and others who considered Jesus as God and he assumed that they could not and would not have done so if Jesus himself had not declared himself as such.

The development of the idea that Jesus was God was a slow process. The origin of this idea may have been in Greek communities; then it was developed by Paul and then came into the younger Gospels. In the older Gospels, Mark and Matthew,

[252] See Matth. 12.24–28.
[253] John 10.10.
[254] Matth. 11.25 ff. is the crucial passage.
[255] Luke 6.46; 7.13; John 4.1.

Jesus is merely the Messiah, Christus, and the name Lord referring to Jesus in the sense of deification is rarely found there. The passage in Mark 12.36–37, "David himself called him Lord" is doubtful.[256] All the other passages where Jesus is spoken of as the Lord Κύριος are either doubtful, as Mark 16.19, or the term may be used merely in the sense of master, like רבון, אדון.[257]

In Paul, however, Jesus' title is no longer Christus. Only occasionally Paul uses the term Christus Jesus. Predominantly Paul uses the title Kyrios, the Lord, for Jesus. This title explicitly denotes Jesus' divine nature and identifies him with God.[258] This conception could not have originated in Palestine among the Jews. It originated among Gentile Christians in Hellenistic communities and Paul learned it from them. We find it, therefore, frequently in the younger Gospels, in Luke and especially in John.[259] The apostolic fathers identify Jesus with God. Ignatius in all his epistles and Polycarp in his epistle to the Philippians, and Barnabas not later than Hadrian, teach that Jesus was God; and Second Clement (about 140) opens with the words: "Brethren, we must think of Jesus Christ as of God . . . as of the Judge of the living and the dead."[260] Simon b. Laḳish as well as R. Abahu, a Palestinian Amora of the third generation (whose saying will be cited below) both living in Palestine in the third century, knew from Christians of their time that Jesus was considered to have been God and they believed that Jesus himself made this claim, and hence they, Resh Laḳish and Abahu, directed their respective sayings against him and his supposed claims. Of course, these are third century polemics and not contemporary reports about Jesus.

[256] See Bousset, *Kyrios Christos*, 2nd Edition (Göttingen, 1921), 78.
[257] See Bousset, *op. cit.*, 79.
[258] Cf. especially Romans 10.13 where he interprets the passage in Joel 3.5, כל אשר יקרא בשם ד' ימלט, as referring to Jesus. See Bousset, *op. cit.*, 99 ff.
[259] See e. g., Luke 2.11, "a saviour who is Christ the Lord;" 5.24, Jesus claims authority on earth to forgive sin (like God); 6.46, "why call ye me Lord and do not the things which I say?" In John there are many such passages, especially 20.28 where Thomas calls Jesus, my Lord, my God, and 21.7, 12 and 15.
[260] Cf. Edgar Hennecke, *Neutestamentliche Apocryphen*, 2nd ed., (Tübingen, 1924).

While thus considering the development of the belief that Jesus was God, we may, in this connection, also consider here the development of the doctrine of the Trinity, which will also help us in the discussion and understanding of some talmudic and midrashic passages. It is commonly assumed that the doctrine of the Trinity was formulated and accepted in Nicea in 325 and was merely confirmed in the Council at Constantinople in 381, though some scholars maintain that the *Holy Ghost* came into — and thus completed — the Trinity at Constantinople.[261] According to this theory, then, there was, up to 381, only a Dualism but not a Trinity. Robert Rainy[262] maintains that the Trinity was already formulated in the Athanasian Creed, or in the original Nicene Creed. At any rate, the Trinity is much later than the Gospels and was definitely accepted only in the fourth century. It is true a suggestion of the doctrine of the Trinity is already found in Matth. 28.18 in the baptism formula: "In the name of the Father and the Son and the Holy Ghost." Likewise, in Paul's words: "The grace of the Lord Jesus Christ and the love of God and the communion of the Holy Spirit be with you all"[263] there is a suggestion of the Trinity, but it was not formulated as a dogma. And in the third century there were many Christians who rejected the belief in the Trinity. Some, like Noetus, taught that the three are merely three aspects of God but not three entities.[264] At any rate, we may safely say that up to the beginning of the fourth century there was in Christianity — as far as generally accepted doctrines are concerned — merely a dualism — God and Jesus — and not a Trinity. If, therefore, we find in Talmud or Midrash an argument against dualism, it may possibly, dependent on other considerations such as content and context, be interpreted as an allusion to or argument against Christianity, and not as an argument against Persian dualism. Such a statement is, to my mind, the saying of Ḥiyya II bar

---

[261] See Reinach, *A Short History of Christianity*, (Putnam, 1922), 54, who decides in favor of this opinion.

[262] *The Ancient Catholic Church*, (Scribners, New York, 1902), 355 ff.

[263] Cor. 13–14.

[264] See M. Friedländer, *Synagoge und Kirche in ihren Anfängen*, (1905), 225 ff.

Abba, a Palestinian Amora of the third generation, contemporary of R. Abahu and pupil of R. Johanan.

In Pesiḳta Rabbati xxi (Friedmann, 100b–101a) we read as follows: אמר ר' חייה בר אבא אם יאמר לך ברא דזניתא תרין אלהים אינון אמר ליה אנא הוא דימא (על ים סוף) אנא הוא דסיני (שעל הר סיני). "If the *son of the harlot* will tell you that there are two gods [and in support of the doctrine point to the two different manifestations of God, on Sinai, as איש זקן ויושב בישיבה and on the Red Sea as איש מלחמה]²⁶⁵ you should tell him that I am the same God who manifested Himself at Sinai and at the Red Sea." Of course one could argue that there is no allusion here to Jesus' person, since Mary is nowhere else in Palestinian sources referred to as a harlot (even in the later amoraic description as סטת דא מבעלה she is not characterized as a זונה). Heresy or מינות is very often represented as a harlot.²⁶⁶ Hence ברא דזניתא here is like בן המינות — the heretic. One might interpret the saying of Ḥiyya II b. Abba as being directed against the heretic who argues in favor of dualism — i. e., Persian dualism. This, however, would not be correct. The Persian dualism consists of two *opposing* powers, the god of light and the god of darkness, while the dualism represented or favored by this heretic consists of two gods in harmony with one another, only manifesting themselves differently, as, at Sinai and the Red Sea, or as the father in heaven and Jesus, the son in human form on earth. Hence the heresy here is Christianity and the argument is against Jesus' claim to divinity. For, as we have seen, in the third century, Christianity had only a dualism of the father and the son. It is, however, possible that Ḥiyya II b. Abba, wishing to refer to Jesus who, by claiming to be God, asserted that there are two Gods, purposely chose the ambiguous designation ברא דזניתא which in a figurative sense means heretic and literally the son of an unfaithful wife. Since Ḥiyya knew that the Christians admit that Joseph, the

²⁶⁵ See the Midrashim *ad loc.* and expecially Mekilta, *Shirata* IV (ed. Lauterbach II, 31) and Lauterbach, מביאורי המכילתא in ספר קלוזנר (Tel Aviv, 1937), 181 ff.

²⁶⁶ See b. 'Ab. Zarah 7a where the passage in Prov. 5.8 referring to the harlot is interpreted זו מינות, as dealing with heresy, figuratively represented as a harlot.

husband of Mary, was not the father of the child, he drew his own conclusions, rejecting the Christian explanation that the child had been conceived of the Holy Ghost. Hence he calls Jesus ברא דזניתא both in a literal and in a figurative sense.[267] Another saying in which Jesus is alluded to as one who claims to be God is found in the passage preserved to us in the Yalkuṭ Shimeoni[268] to Numbers § 765,[269] which reads as follows:[270] דבר

אחר מברך רעהו בקול גדול כמה היה קולו של בלעם ר' יוחנן אמר ששים מילין ר' יהושע בן לוי אמר שבעים אומות שמעו קולו של בלעם ר' אלעזר הקפר אומר נתן אלהים כח בקולו והיה עולה (ט. הולך) מסוף העולם ועד סופו בשביל שהיה צופה וראה האומות (ט. את האומות) שמשתחוין לשמש ולירח ולכוכבים ולעץ ולאבן וצפה וראה שיש אדם בן אשה שעתיד לעמוד שמבקש לעשות עצמו אלוה ולהטעות (ט. להטעות) כל העולם כולו לפיכך נתן כח שקולו (ט. בקולו) שישמעו כל אומות העולם וכן היה (ט. הוא) אומר תנו דעתכם שלא לטעות אחרי אותו האיש שנאמר לא איש אל ויכזב ואם בן אומר (ט. יאמר) שהוא אל מכזב (ט. ועתיד הוא לומר שהוא בן אלהים ואינו אלא בן אדם שנאמר ובן אדם ויתנחם שהוא) והוא עתיד להטעות ולומר שהוא מסתלק ובא לקיצים ההוא אמר ולא יעשה ראה מה כתיב וישא משלו ויאמר אוי מי יחיה משומו אל אמר בלעם אוי מי יחיה מאותה אומה ששמעה אחרי אותו האיש שעשה עצמו אלוה. The source of this saying is not given. But since the passage preceding it in the Yalkuṭ is taken from ילמדנו, it is probable that this other interpretation is from Midrash Yelamdenu as well. In passing it should be noticed that this passage containing a condemnation of Rome or Edom אותו אומה ששמעה "that nation that listened to" and accepted Jesus who declared himself to be God. So the saying as given in this passage dates from the time after Rome became Christian, that is later than the beginning of the fourth century.

But this saying may be an elaboration of an older saying with

[267] Friedländer suggests that this interpretation of Ḥiyya II b. Abba, repeated in Midrash Tehillim 22.16 (ed. Buber) on the verse אלי אלי may have an illusion to Jesus who called on the cross אלי אלי למה שבקתני, as if he would have believed in two Gods and called on both to help him, when there is only one. This is farfetched. I cannot locate the reference to Friedländer, so I cannot examine it more carefully.

[268] Editio princeps, Saloniki, 1526.

[269] In the MS it is § 765. In the later edition, although it is missing, the paragraph in which it should occur is numbered 766.

[270] The variants found in the Oxford MS are indicated in parenthesis.

additions about the nation that followed Jesus. For the same reference to Jesus claiming to be God, or the same interpretation of the verse in Numbers is also found and even more clearly expressed in p. Ta'an. 2.1 (65b near bottom). No doubt Yelamdenu took it from the Yerushalmi and enlarged and developed it. The Yerushalmi passage also alludes to Jesus' claim that he would go up to heaven (= Yalḳuṭ שהוא מסתלק) and would come back after a certain period of time. The passage reads as follows אמר רבי אבהו אם יאמר לך אדם אל אני מכזב הוא בן אדם אני סופו לתחום (לתהות? לרדת שחת?) בו ויתנחם שאני עולה לשמים ההוא אמר ולא יקימנה , "If he says he is God he is lying. If he calls himself בן אדם [or בר נש in the technical sense], he will regret it."[271]

A reference to Jesus' claim to be the son of God בן אלהים may be that found in p. Shab. 6.9 end (8d). Commenting on the phrase דמי לבר אלהון, "like unto a son of God," in Dan. 3.25 it says: באותו שעה ירד מלאך וסטרו לההוא רשיעה (נבוכדנצר) על פיו אמר ליה תקין מיליך (correct your words!) ובר אית ליה? חזר (נבוכדנצר) ומר בריך אלההון די שדרך מישך ועבד נגו די שלח בריה לית כתיב כאן אלא די שלח מלאכיה ושזיב לעבדוהי די התרחיצו עלוהי. This is a protest against anyone speaking of God as if he had a son. And the author, while referring the rebuke to Nebuchadnezzar, no doubt had in mind Jesus and his followers.[272] In connection with this Yerushalmi passage, we may also refer to the passage in the Zohar *Vayaḳhel*:[273] בריך שמיה וכו', which was incorporated in the prayer-book at a late date, and in which the phrase occurs ולא על בר אלהין סמיכנא. This is probably also directed against Christianity, though Aptowitzer, cited by Zimels[274] would understand it to refer to the angel Gabriel or Michael and protesting against mediatorship.[275]

[271] This would be the sense of the reading in the Wilna edition לתהות בו which is explained in *Korban Edah* as להתחרט בו. It may, however, be that לתהות is corrupt from לתחית = לתחיה and refers to his claim that he would come to life again. It is also possible that something is missing in our text. Maybe it read לתחית לתחת, meaning "if he claims to come to life, he will go down to hell instead," and a copyist, considering it a dittography, omitted the one word.

[272] Cf. Zimels in *Oẓar ha-Ḥayyim* VI, (1930), 166.

[273] (Lublin, 1872), 411.   [274] *Loc. cit.*

[275] Cf. Anatoli, מלמד התלמידים, section יתרו, 67b, against the prayer מכניסי רחמים.

A similar protest against anyone claiming to be a son of God is to be found in Gen. r. 26.5 in the comment on the passage ויראו בני אלהים[276] which reads as follows: רשב"י קרא להון בני דייניא רשב"י מקלל לכל מאן דקרי להון בני אלהין. R. Simon b. Yoḥai, Tanna of the third generation, living in the middle of the second century knew that the followers of Jesus called him, as indeed he called himself, the son of God and R. Simon directed his attack against them. When, after having explained that בני אלהים means "sons of the judges" he proceeds to curse those who take the words to mean "sons of God," he meant all those who call anybody a son of God, including the Christians. Likewise the passage in Ex. r. 29.4 no doubt is aimed against the Christian claim.

The passage reads as follows: אמר ר' אבהו . . . . אמר הקב"ה אני איני בן אני ראשון שאין לי אב ואני אחרון שאין לי אח ומבלעדי אין אלהים שאין לי בן. Coming from Abahu who had disputes with Christians, this no doubt points to Jesus' claim to be the son of God.

Likewise the passage in Deut. r. 2.33 which reads as follows: „ועם שונים אל תתערב"[277] עם אלו שאומרים יש אלוה שני אל תתערב . . . . הפיות שאומרים שתי רשויות הן יכרתו וינועו . . . . א"ר אחא כעס הקב"ה על שלמה כשאמר הפסוק הזה אמר לו דבר של קידוש שמא (קידוש השם) היות אומרו בלשון נוטריקון[278] ועם שונים אל תתערב? מיד חזר (שלמה) ופירש את הדבר יש אחד ואין שני גם בן ואח אין לו[279] אין לו לא אח ולא בן אלא בן שמע ישראל . . . ה' אחד, is a protest against Christianity, not against Persian dualism as the middle statement הפיות שאומרים שתי רשויות might suggest. For it was just because of this ambiguity in the interpretation of the expression ועם שונים as "those who believe in two Gods" which might refer to Persian dualism as well as to Christianity, that God was angry with Solomon. For it might be understood that only Persian dualism in which the one god, Ahriman, is antagonistic to and an opponent of the other, Hormuzd, is objectionable, but not the Christian dualism in which the second god works in harmony with and claims to be a son of or associate to the One God. Hence Solomon had to expressly state that there is only one God who has no son or

[276] Gen. 6.2.
[277] Prov. 24.21.
[278] I. e., by indirection and not expressly.
[279] Eccl. 4.8.

brother who shares his divinity. This is expressly a reference to Jesus who claimed to be the son of God, sharing the rule with his father.

In this sense we must also understand the passage from Yelamdenu cited in *Or Zarua*[280] which reads as follows: אמרו בילמדנו פ' שמע ישראל רבינו הקדוש כשהיה כותב לאנטונינוס היה כותב לו יהודה עבדך שואל בשלומך הוה ירא את השם ועם שונים אל תתערב מהו עם שונים ר' נתן בשם ר' אחא עם אותם שהם אומרים שהם שני אלהות. Here likewise the reference is to Christianity which at the time of Judah Hanasi had not yet accepted the trinity but believed in a dualism of Jesus and God. Wohlman in *Hatekufah* XIX is mistaken when he assumes that it refers to Gnostics or Judeo-Christians only. Why mix up Gnostics with Christians and limit this belief in dualism to Judeo-Christians only, when Christians in general believed that Jesus was like God, so that they practically believed in two gods.

Perhaps we ought to mention here a possible, though very doubtful, reference to Jesus in Tractate Semaḥot.[281] The passage reads: ראוין היו ישראל ליפול בחרב אילולי עמד בלעם.[282] Brüll[283] commenting on this passage, says: "Es scheint, dass hier eine antichristliche Stelle unterdrückt wurde." And on pages 240–241 Brüll refers to Galatinus who quotes a passage from Tractate Soferim, as follows: ישו הנוצרי נראה משיח ונהרג בבית דין והיה סְבָּה שישראל נהרג בחרב. This passage is not found in any of our editions of מסכת סופרים. S. Liberman[284] suggests that סופרים in Galatinus is a mistake for שופטים and the passage is a quotation not from Tractate Soferim but from Maimonides' *Yad*, ספר שופטים, where in Chapter XI of הלכות מלכים the passage is actually found in the Constantinople edition and reads: אף אותו האיש שדמה שיהיה משיח ונהרג בבית דין וכו' וזה גרם לאבד ישראל בחרב.

Perhaps the passage in Mishnah Soṭah 9.15 בעקבות משיחא חוצפא יסגא . . . והמלכות תהפך למינות is a later insertion referring

---

[280] (Zitomir, 1862), p. 7, 20 דף ד' אלפא ביתא.

[281] Ed. Higger, (New York, 1931), Chap. VIII, p. 163.

[282] Our text has פלוני hence it has been assumed that בלעם or פלוני is a surname for Jesus. See however above.

[283] *Jahrbücher* I, 53.

[284] In קרית ספר XV (1938), 60.

to the conversion of Constantine to Christianity and the meaning
of בעקבות משיחא is: As the result of that *would be* Messiah,"
referring to Jesus, who claimed to be the Messiah.

This, to my knowledge, concludes the list of all passages
in Talmud and Midrashim where a reference or an allusion to
Jesus himself can be found or read into.

We shall now proceed to a consideration of passages in which
an express reference or a veiled allusion may be found to the
disciples or followers of Jesus, or to Christians in general. The
first such passage to be considered is the one cited in the form
of a Baraita in b. Sanh. 43a (omitted in our editions but found
in חסרונות) which reads as follows:[285] תני רבנן חמשה תלמידים היו לו
לישו (מ. לישו הנוצרי) מתאי נקאי (מ. נקי מתי) נצר (מ. >) ובונה (מ. בוני)
ותודה איתוהי למתי אמר להו מתי יהרג הכתיב (מ. והא כתיב) מתי אבוא
ואראה פני אלקים? אמרו לו (מ. ליה) אין מתי יהרג (מ. >) דכתיב מתי
ימות ואבד שמו. אתיוהו לנקאי אמר להו נקאי יהרג הכתיב ונקי וצדיק אל
תהרוג? אמרו לו אין נקאי יהרג דכתיב במסתרים יהרג נקי אתיוהו לנצר אמר
להו נצר יהרג הכתיב ונצר משרשיו יפרח?[286] אמרו ליה אין נצר יהרג דכתיב
ואתה השלכת מקברך כנצר נתעב. אתיוהו לבוני אמר להו בוני יהרג הכתיב
בני בכורי ישראל? אמרו ליה אין בוני יהרג (מ. >) דכתיב הנה אנכי הורג
את בנך בכורך. אתיוהו לתודה אמר להו תודה יהרג הכתיב מזמור לתודה?
אמרו ליה אין תודה יהרג דכתיב זובח תודה יכבדני.

That this whole account, though stated in form of a Baraita
is of a later date and peculiarly legendary in character is evident
from the artificial meaning assumed for the proper names and
from the twisted childish interpretation given to the verse cited
by the opposing parties. The first strange feature to be noticed
in this legendary account is that it mentions only five names
and says that Jesus had five, not twelve disciples.[287] This, however, may be explained by assuming that the author or authors
of this legend may not have heard or known of more than five.
More likely, however, it is to be assumed that the author mentions only these five because he had clever interpretations of

[285] This passage is quoted in Yalkuṭ Makiri to Isa. 11, p. 84, with a few
different readings. The variants are indicated here in the text in parenthesis.

[286] מ has only the defense verse of נצר. All the rest referring to him is
omitted.

[287] Cf. also Laible, *op. cit.*, 68.

verses, suggesting that people by these names, who claimed special distinctions or privileges because of their significant names, actually should be punished by death. It is also possible that these five disciples were regarded as the most prominent, hence these alone are mentioned without in any way implying that Jesus had only five disciples. In the same manner Ab. 2.8 mentions that Joḥanan b. Zakkai had five disciples, but this certainly does not mean that he had only these five disciples.[288] These five are mentioned because they were outstanding and because the Mishnah wants to record the characterizing remarks the master made about each one of them.

It may also be that in Jewish circles they would purposely avoid speaking of the twelve apostles or disciples of Jesus, in order not to support the claim made, or at any rate implied, in the N. T. that the number of the disciples of Jesus corresponded to the number of the tribes of Israel, all of whom were expected to be restored by the Messiah. The apostles themselves were very eager to have this number of their group complete.[289] The purpose of having twelve apostles was to make them correspond to and represent the twelve tribes of Israel, each tribe to have one apostle.[290] The idea, no doubt, was that if Jesus was the Messiah he would bring home the lost ten tribes and restore the ancient Kingdom of David.[291] It may also be that the number twelve was chosen to provide a resemblance between Jesus and his twelve disciples and Moses and the twelve princes שנים עשר נשיאים. In the same manner that Moses was commanded by God: "Gather unto me seventy men . . . . . and they shall bear the burden of the people with thee,"[292] Jesus was declared to have

[288] Cf. also the number "five" in the account of the 5 pupils of R. Akiba ordained by Judah b. Baba, (Sanh. 14a).

[289] See Acts 1.26 where it is reported that Matthias was substituted for Judas Iscariot "and he was numbered with the 11 apostles," that is he completed the number 12, of which the apostles should consist.

[290] See Matth. 19.28 "Ye also shall sit upon 12 thrones, judging the 12 tribes of Israel," and likewise Luke 22.30 "that ye may eat and drink at my table in my kingdom and ye shall sit on thrones judging the 12 tribes of Israel."

[291] Cf. also the superscription of the Epistle of James, saying it was addressed "to the twelve tribes which are of the dispersion."

[292] Num. 11.16–17.

had seventy disciples, thus having a Sanhedrin like Moses.[293] The Jews, of course, would not regard Jesus as being in any way like Moses and they would, therefore, not refer to the twelve and the seventy, which would emphasize the parallel to Moses.

Now let us see whether we can identify any or all of the five disciples, mentioned in the Baraita, with some of the disciples or apostles known to us from the N. T. First, we must ascertain the names of the twelve apostles, as given in the N. T. records. According to Matth. 10, they were (1) Peter-Simon; (2) Andrew; (3) James (Jacobus) the son of Zebedee; (4) John, the son of Zebedee; (5) Philip; (6) Bartholomew; (7) Thomas; (8) Matthew the publican; (9) James (Jacobus) the son of Alpheus; (10) Thaddeus; (11) Simon the Cananaean;[294] (12) Judas Iscariot. In Mark 3.17 the two sons of Zebedee, James and John were "surnamed Boanerges which is Sons of Thunder."[295] In Luke 6.16 and Acts 1.13 Thaddeus is called Judas, the son of James. In John 1.42 Simon is called Cephas כיפא meaning "rock" which is the same as Peter.[296] In John 21.2, Thomas is called Didymus, (the twin) and Nathanael of Cana in Galilee is mentioned as the name of the person known in Matthew as Bartholomew. According to Acts 1.26 the twelfth was Matthias who took the place of Judas Iscariot. These are all the names of the Apostles known from the N. T. records. Now of all these names we can definitely recognize and identify among the five mentioned in our Baraita, only two, i. e., Matthew מתי, which may be either Matthew the Publican or Matthias, the successor or substitute of Judas Iscariot, and Thaddeus here called תודה. The other names mentioned in our Baraita are difficult, if not impossible, to identify with any of the names known from the N. T. records,

---

[293] See Luke 10.1: "The Lord appointed 70 others (besides the 12) and sent them two by two before his face." Also "and the 70 returned with joy" (*ibid.*, 17). Cf. also Eusebius, *Church History*, Book I, ch. 28, English translation by C. F. Cruse, (London, 1851), p. 28.

[294] Of Cana? or קנא =Zealot, as in Acts 1.13.

[295] Is there a possibility in "Boni" בוני, an echo of בני רוגז? Our author would hardly have left out an allusion to the second part of the name רוגז!

[296] See John 21.2.

or in the case of some even with proper names current among the Jews of N. T. times.

Buni or Boni בוני is a name mentioned in b. Ta'an. 19b–20a as having been the proper name of Naḳdimon b. Gorion נקדימון בן גוריון. This latter name is explained as having been a nickname, recalling the miracle that happened to and through him נקדימון שנקדרה לו חמה, "he was called Naḳdimon because the sun broke through on his behalf." This בוני־נקדימון lived around the year 70 C. E. and, considering the high regard in which he was held by the Jews, he cannot be identified with the Boni in our Baraita who was reprted to have been killed for being one of the disciples of Jesus.[297] Of course, as has already been suggested above בוני may be an echo of the name of one of the בני רוגז, a designation of the sons of Zebedee.[298] But it would be strange to assume that a Jewish author, mentioning one of the sons of Zebedee by his surname, Boanerges, should leave out that part of the surname, the word רוגז, which would have lent itself to an exchange of fancifully applied verses advocating his acquittal, e. g., ברוגז רחם תזכור[299] as well as his condemnation, e. g., וברוגז ינמא ארץ[300]

The name נקאי Nakai or Naki or Niki is peculiar and difficult. It may be a shorter form of Nicolaus, Nicodemus, or Nikanor. All these names in their full form occur in N. T. records, though not as a name of one of the apostles. Nicanor and Nicolaus are mentioned in Acts 6.5 as followers of Jesus, having been chosen and ordained (?) by the apostles. Nikai shortened from Nicolaus may be an allusion to the founder or leader of the Nicolaitans.[301] Again, Nikai, a short form of Nicodemus may refer to the Nicodemus in John 3, referred to above, or to another Nicodemus known in Christian circles. There is an Evangelium of Nicodemus

---

[297] Some scholars have indeed identified our Buni with Nicodemus of the Gospel of John, (3.1, 4, 9). See Laible, *op. cit.*, 70.

[298] Klausner, p. 20, assumes indeed that בוני is a corrupted form from יואני or יוחנן, the son of Zebedee. See against him A. S. Kaminetzki in *Hatekufah* XVIII, 512. Might not בוני be a corrupted form of אביוני?

[299] Hab. 3.2.

[300] Job 39.24.

[301] Revelations 2.6 and 15. See Laible, *op. cit.*, 71.

also called *Acta Pilati*.[302] This Gospel of Nicodemus is said to have been written originally in Hebrew. The Jews may have heard of this author of a gospel; hence they took him to have been one of the disciples of Jesus and mentioned him by a shortened form of his name, Niki, together with Mattai, another disciple credited with the authorship of a gospel.

Nakai or Niki as a proper name is mentioned in p. Ma'as. Sh. 5.2 (56a). A man by that name, said to have been warden שמש, or scribe and teacher ואית דאמרין ספר הוה in Magdala Zabuaya, is reported to have gone up to the Temple לבית המקדש (in a miraculous way?) on every Friday and to have returned to his home before the beginning of the Sabbath. According to this story, this Nakai lived in Temple times. In Gen. r. 79.6 a teacher by the name of Nakai also of מגדלא דצבועיא is said to have lived in the time of Simon b. Yoḥai, around 150 C. E., so he could not have been the same as the one mentioned in p. Ma'aser Sheni who lived in Temple times. There is something strange and legendary about this man Nakai. Is מגדלא identical with the town or village Magdala and דצבועיא a surname characterizing a certain class of people, either hypocrites צבועים or Baptists צבע? Or is מגדלא merely a "tower," designating the seat of these people, which may have been not far from the Temple and one could easily go from this tower to Temple in a short time, or is it identical with אנשי הר צבועים.[303]

Of course, it is also possible, since the letters ל and נ are interchangeable, that Nakai is here read for לקי and Luke is meant.[304] Of course, in this case it need not nor can it be a textual mistake, since in the Baraita the verses cited contain the word נקי. It is possible that the writer had heard of a Luke, the author of a Gospel, whom he believed to have been, like Matthew, a disciple of Jesus, and he pronounced his name נקי. It is strange though

---

[302] See Hennecke, *N. T. Apocryphen*, 77. It is printed as "The Gospel of Nicodemus" in *Excluded Books of the New Testament*, (New York, 1927), 51 ff.

[303] See Hirschenson, שבע חכמות, 152.

[304] Krauss, *op. cit.*, 57, note 3: Klausner, *op. cit.*, 4th ed. (1933), 20; also Grünwald in his "Eine neue Ethymologie des Wortes נצר = Naza er" in Rahmer's *Literaturblatt* XXII, (1893), No. 9, 35. Anm. 2, where he says: "Statt נקי wird wohl לקי zu lesen u. Lucas gemeint sein."

that they did not make a pun on his name Luke, like לוקה, i. e., should receive punishment.

The name נצר is probably merely an allusion to the name Nazarene = Christian, not a corrupted form from Andrew as assumed by Klausner.[305] But it is strange that the verse ונצר משרשיו should be applied to or claimed by a disciple, when it was understood to refer to the Master. Considering that in Makiri the whole passage about נצר is missing and the verse is cited in connection with נקי it is perhaps possible that נצר = Nacar is identical with Nakai, the "c" being pronounced and written as a ק, as in Caesar, קיסר. And the ר at the end is merely an enlarged י. This would remove the difficulty of a disciple being called נצר which designation belongs to Jesus himself, either because he came from Nazareth or because he was believed to have been referred to in the verse ונצר משרשיו יפרח.

It should be added, that according to Laible[306] our Baraita has no reference to the apostles but to some followers of Jesus, i. e., Christians who were persecuted and killed in the time of Akiba and Bar Kochba.[307]

A disciple of Jesus by the name of Jacobus of the village of Sekanya[308] is reported to have had a discussion with R. Eliezer b. Hyrcanus in which he repeated halakic teaching he had learned from his master Jesus. Whether this Jacob of Kefar Sekanya is identical with Jacob of Kefar Sama and whether he was a disciple of Jesus himself or merely a disciple's disciple cannot be definitely decided, though Klausner[309] assumes that Jacob of Sekanya was a disciple of Jesus and is perhaps identical with James, the brother of Jesus.

Disciples or apostles are believed by some scholars to be found mentioned in the Talmud under disguised names. Thus A. S. Weissman[310] would identify the "other person" איש אחרינא

---

[305] *Loc. cit.* See against him A. S. Kaminetzki in *HaTekufah* XVIII, 512.
[306] *Op. cit.*, 68, 69.

[307] See against this Klausner, *op. cit.*, 20, and cf. Herford, *op. cit.*, 91–95.

[308] b. 'Ab. Zarah 17a, see reading in דקדוקי סופרים; also 27a and Tosefta Ḥul. 2.24. For a fuller discussion of this person see below p. 563.

[309] See below p. 563, note 329.

[310] Rahmer's *Litteraturblatt* VII, (1879), No. 28, 109–110.

mentioned in b. Sanh. 11a as having intruded into the meeting
called by R. Gamaliel, with Saul-Paul who, after having changed,
was designated as "another person" אינש אחרינא or אחר. But this
is a mistake. Saul-Paul was, or claimed to have been, a disciple
of R. Gamaliel the elder in the time of the Temple, while the
אינש אחרינא mentioned in Sanhedrin intruded into a meeting
called by Gamaliel II of Jabneh.

Some scholars would see in the names אחיתופל, גיחזי, דואג mentioned in the Mishnah Sanhedrin 9 (90a) designations, or epi-
thets, for some of the disciples of Jesus. If Balaam mentioned
there in the Mishnah refers to Jesus, as assumed by some
scholars, then the other three הדיוטות mentioned with him must
likewise be assumed to be, not the Biblical persons by these
names, but disguised references to associates or disciples of
Jesus. Of course, there is no reason for not taking these names
as actually designating the Biblical persons. These men, Ahitophel and Gehazi and Doeg were Jews and could well be discussed
in the Mishnah as exceptions to the כל ישראל who have a share in
the world to come. But the company of Balaam with whom these
three men are mentioned caused some scholars to see in them
not Biblical persons but associates of Jesus. I shall quote and
discuss these theories, incorrect though they may be, and I shall
take up these names in the historical order and in the order in
which they are mentioned in the Mishnah: (1) Doeg, (2) Ahitophel, (3) Gehazi. These three names are assumed to refer to
(1) Peter, (2) James, and (3) John.[311]

1. Doeg. Some people[312] suggest that Doeg is a surname of
Peter who was a fisherman and whom Jesus promised to make
a "fisher of men."[313] This implies the pronounciation of דואג like
צייד דגים = דויג. To this I could add that perhaps האדומי suggests,
not the Edomite but אדם man, thus specifying the "fisher of
men." But on the same ground Andrew, the brother of Peter,

311 See Gustav Rösch in *Theologische Studien und Kritiken*, (1878), 516-
521, as to the reasons given for these identifications. See also Laible, *op. cit.*, 54.

312 See Jacob Ezekiel Löwy, *Kritisch-Talmudisches Lexicon*, (Wien, 1863),
112. Perhaps Rosch, *loc. cit.*, has the same reason for identifying Doeg with
Peter.

313 Matth. 4.18–22.

who also was a fisherman and whom Jesus likewise promised to make a "fisher of men"[314] could also be designated as דוינ האדומי. And Doeg could also refer to either John or James, the sons of Zebedee who likewise were "fishermen." Herford[315] suggests that Doeg designates Judas Iscariot who betrayed the Messiah Jesus, just as Doeg betrayed David.[316] But the comparison is lame. David escaped the danger involved in the betrayal while Jesus succumbed to or was the victim of the betrayal by Judas. Furthermore, as Herford himself asks, why should Judas have been so strongly condemned by the Rabbis for his act, so as to declare him to be deprived of a share in the world to come. Did the Rabbis of the second century (time of the Mishnah) already feel that the betrayal which caused the death of Jesus and hence subsequently all the accusations against the Jews, entailing so much suffering, was a sin to deprive one of his share in the world to come? We could just as well suggest that Ahitophel who betrayed David and joined his enemy Absalom and later committed suicide[317] designates Judas Iscariot who betrayed Jesus and then committed suicide. The dissimilarity between the two betrayers, however, is that Ahitophel failed and committed suicide because of the failure of his plot while Judas succeeded in his plot and committed suicide out of remorse, not because of failure. Herford[318] also thinks that Doeg may be identical with James who was a fisherman, and Ahitophel designates Peter, because the high position held by Ahitophel resembles the position held by Peter, and Gehazi may be a designation of Paul, the renegade. But Herford concludes that Ahitophel is Peter; Doeg, Judas Iscariot; and Gehazi, Paul.[319]

2. Ahitophel. As already mentioned above, it could be Judas Iscariot who is so designated, though Herford would

---

[314] *Ibid.*   [315] *Op. cit.*

[316] I Sam. 22.9.

[317] II Sam. 17.23.

[318] *Ibid.*

[319] On Paul see Gerhard Kittel in *Arbeiten zur Religionsgeschichte des Urchristentums*, Bd. I, Heft 3, (Leipzig, 1920), under the heading "Rabbinica, Paulus im Talmud, etc." Kittel also discusses there the Mishnah 'Ab. 3.2, ... המפר בריתו, see also Weiss, *Dor*, I, 232.

identify him with Peter. But Löwy[320] also Rösch[321] who perhaps read Löwy though he does not mention it, takes him to be James, the brother of Jesus. The name Ahitophel is taken to be a com posite of אחי "brother" and תופל which is assumed to be *theofilius*, i. e., בן אלהים so that the name means "the brother of [him who calls himself] the son of God." But in the first place why should James be so condemned? Secondly, the Rabbis would not even thus indirectly acknowledge Jesus as the son of God or even refer to him as such. Against this, however, it could be argued that the Rabbis may have taken תופל to be like תיפלה, "frivolity" or "unseemliness," a fault of the false prophets of Samaria[322] or תָּפֵל, "delusion," which the false prophets are accused of having seen,[323] thus referring to James as the brother of the false prophet or of the prophet of delusions. But any such interpretation of the name Ahitophel, though ingenious, is far fetched and incorrect, although Löwy cleverly interprets the Baraita in B. B. 147a as fitting James the brother of Jesus who was the head of the church of Jerusalem.

The Baraita reads as follows: שלשה דברים צוה אחיתופל לבניו אל תהיו במחלוקת ואל תמרדו במלכות בית דוד וכשעצרת ברור זרעו חטים. The meaning according to Löwy is this: he told his spiritual sons, the members of the church, (1) keep united; (2) believe in the Davidic kingdom, i. e., in Jesus' messiahship and that his kingdom is not of this world; (3) when Pentecost is clear sow your seeds . . . . i. e., accept proselytes or confirmants by baptism on Whitsunday. This would be an allusion to what is recorded in Acts 2.1–12. This would also explain the remark of Mar Zuṭra[324] בלול איתמר which echoes what is recorded in Acts 2.13: "But others mocking said, 'They are filled with new wine.'" That is, the disciples who talked in different tongues were not filled with the spirit, but were plain drunk, full of spirits and confused. All this is clever but most improbable.

3. Gehazi. We have already mentioned above that this name

[320] *Op. cit.*, 112.
[321] *Loc. cit.*
[322] Jer. 23.13.
[323] Lam. 2.14. See Midrash Lam. r. 2.23.
[324] B. B. 147a.

is regarded by some as an allusion to Paul, the renegade, but there is no reason or justification for this identification.

In. b. 'Ab. Zarah 17a and 27b there is mentioned a certain Jacob of the village of Siknin or *Sekanya*.[325] In *Dıkduke Soferim* to 'Ab. Zarah 17a and in הגדות התלמוד Constantinople, 1511[326] there are added the words אחד מתלמידי ישו הנוצרי.[327] In הגדות התלמוד, this Jacob quotes his teaching as having received it from Jesus כך לימדני ישו הנוצרי and in En Jacob[328] it reads כך אמר לי ישוע. From this it would seem that Jacob was a disciple of Jesus.[329] But since the encounter of this Jacob with R. Eliezer b. Hyrcanus and also with Ben Doma, the nephew of R. Ishmael must have been around the year 100, this Jacob must have attained an exceptionally old age, if he had been a direct disciple of Jesus. Most likely, however, the words אחד מתלמידי means, one of the followers, not a direct disciple, and the reading in the Tosefta, משום ישוע, suggests that Jacob did not receive the teaching directly from Jesus. The words כך לימדני need not mean "taught me personally." And כך אמר לי is but a later change from כך לימדני.

A follower of Jesus, though by no means a direct disciple is mentioned in p. Shab. 14.4 (14d) and Kohelet r. to 10.5 in the story of the grandchild of Joshua b. Levi who choked on something he had swallowed. According to the story, they brought in one of the followers of Bar Pandera to assist them, אזל ואייתי חד מן אילין דבר פנדירא לאפקא בלעיה. This Christian was probably called in as a physician to pull out what the child had swallowed, but instead he used magic or recited certain verses, which displeased Joshua b. Levi so much that he would have preferred to have the child die rather than have such a verse recited over him, אמר והוה נייח ליה דקברריה ולא הוה אמר עלוי הדין פסוקה. This whole question of performing *cures* by reciting verses or incan-

---

[325] See above.

[326] Cited by Chwolson, *Das Letzte Passahmahl*, 100, note 1.

[327] Probably this disciple or follower is identical with Jacob of Kefar Sekanya mentioned in in Ḥul. 2.22 and p. 'Ab. Zarah 2 (40d).

[328] Ed. Saloniki.

[329] Klausner 30–31 assumes that he is identical with James the brother of Jesus. But James was killed and it is now here mentioned that he reached an exceptionally old age.

tations requires a careful study into which I cannot enter here. But it certainly has some connection with the attitude toward the early Christians who apparently pursued such practices. Thus it may be that the saying in the M. Sanh. 10.1 that הלוחש על המכה ואומר כל המחלה אשר שמתי במצרים לא אשים עליך כי אני יי רופאך[330] is also among those who have no share in the world to come, may have reference to Christians, who may have applied the words "I the Lord am thy healer" to their Lord Jesus in whose name they were performing the alleged cures. The comment of R. Joḥanan[331] וברוקק בה לפי שאין מזכירין שם שמים על הרקיקה may be an allusion to the baptism or "sprinkling," רקיקה being a derogatory or contemptuous circumlocution of זריקה. Such an explanation would remove the conflict with the practice of Joshua b. Levi to recite Ps. 91[332] though he strongly objected to the לוחש על המכה even though it consisted in reciting Scriptural verses[333] and with the saying of R. Joḥanan in b. Shab. 67a permitting the recitation of verses over a fever sickness, since, of course, as R. Joḥanan said, the objection was only to those who combine רקיקה or זריקה with the recitation. People not suspected of Christianity could well have recited verses over sickness.

An allusion to Christians may be found in the Midrash Kohelet r. to 1.8 in the story of Ḥananiah the nephew of R. Joshua b. Ḥananiah who went to Kefar Naḥum where the מינאי = Heretics did something to him and led him openly to violate the Sabbath laws. Then there follows in the Midrash a story of a pupil of R. Jonathan who ran away from his teacher and went to the מינאי and when R. Jonathan went after him to bring him back he found him (or them?) engaged in some evil practice or immoral doings. The passage reads as follows: חנינה בן אחי ר' יהושע אזל להדיה כפר נחום ועבדון ליה מינאי מלה ועלון יתיה רכיב חמרא בשבתא....ר' יונתן ערק חד מן תלמידיו לגביהון אזל ואשכחיה עבד בן אפטוניות שלחון מיניא שתריה כך אמרין ליה ולא כך כתיב גורלך תפיל בתוכנו כיס אחר יהיה לכולנו והוה פרח ואינון פרחין בתריהון אמרין ליה

[330] This is the continuation of the saying of R. Akiba אף הקורא בספרים החיצונים which suggests that it was directed against heretics or the Christians.

[331] Sanh. 101a.

[332] b. Shebu. 15b.

[333] See p. Sanh. 10.1 (28b)

ר' איתא גמול חסדא להדא כלתא הלך ומצאן עסוקין בריבה אחת אמר לון
כן ארחיהון דיהודאי עבדין. אמרי ליה ולא כן כתיב בתורה גורלך תפיל
בתוכנו כיס וגו' והוה פרח ואינון פרחין בתריה עד דמטא לתרע וטרד באפיהון.
אמרין ר' יונתן אזיל נלוג לאמך דלא הפכת ולא איסתכלת בן דאילו הפכת
ואיסתכלת בן יותר מן מה דהוינן פרחין בתרך הוית פריח בתרן. ר' יהודה
בן נקוסה היו המינים מתעסקים עמו היו שואלים אותו ומשיב שואלין אותו
ומשיב. אמר לון על מגן אתון מגיבין אתון נעביד בינינן דכל בר נש דנצח
חבריה יהא פצע מוחיה דחבריה בקורנס והוא נצח לון ופצע מוחיהון עד
דאתמלאון פיצעין פיצעין. וכיון דאתא אמרין ליה תלמידוי רמי סייעוך מן
השמים ונצחת. אמר לון ועל מגן לכו והתפללו על אותו האיש ועל אותה החמת
שהיתה מלאה אבנים טובות ומרגליות אבל עכשיו מלאה פחמין . . .

This passage is the subject of much discussion among scholars
and the commentators give many different interpretations, some
of which I will cite here though none, however, is completely
satisfactory. I will cite and consider here some of these.

Graetz[334] identifies these מינאי with the Nicolaitans. He seems
to understand the phrase איתא גמול חסדא לחדא כלתא with which
these heretics invited R. Jonathan, to mean, that he should
make love to the bride, and like them have intercourse with her.
And the phrase עסוקין בריבה אחת, then, means they were engaged
in immoral practices with a certain girl. The phrase כיס אחד
לכולנו possibly would also have an allusion to the fact that this
bride or girl was the common possession of all of them.[335] Against
Graetz see Chwolson[336] who thinks that it was simply an invi-
tation to perform a charitable deed מצות הכנסת כלה. They sought
to deceive R. Jonathan and cause him to come to them, by
pretending that they wanted him to help in some wedding
ceremonies. The most obscure and difficult expression in this
passage is עבד בן אפטוניות. Perles[337] says: "Ich denke an *optio*,
ὀπτίων — Leutnant, Verpflegungsofficier."[338] It may also mean,
assistant to or vice-general, the one who takes the place of the
general commander. The meaning then here might be: He made
or recognized the son, עבד בן or a son, as an assistant or associate

[334] *Geschichte* IV, 4th ed., (1908), 92.
[335] See also the commentaries מתנת כהנים and יפה תואר, *ad loc.*
[336] *Das Letzte Passahmahl*, 104, note.
[337] *Ethymologische Studien*, 103, *s. v.*, אבטיונא.
[338] Cf. *Aruk, s. v.*, אָבטיונס.

to God, that is, he believed Jesus to be the son of God, sharing authority with or substituting for the father. But elsewhere Perles[339] gives a different explanation, taking אפטוניות to be like πουτάνα = harlot. Accordingly it would mean, he practiced harlotry with them (בהן = בן בן), or he committed sodomy with them. Possibly the meaning of the passage would be, "he found him worshipping the son of the harlot," עובד (ל) בן אפטוניות. This then would be a reference to Jesus by the name of בברא דזניתא[340] and it would practically result the same as the interpretation of the word as *optio*. I might also suggest that אפטוניות is identical with πιθανός, i. e., persuading, convincing, and the sense would be that R. Jonathan found the pupil among the heretics, and he, Jonathan, then did some arguing, or attempted to persuade them. This would explain why they again tried to entice Jonathan to come to them for at their first meeting he was successful in his arguments with them.

Dr. Adolph Honig[341] explains the phrase עבד בן אפטוניות to mean he practiced with or among them "ophitische Orgien," excesses of the Ophites. Im. Deutsch[342] assumes the word אפטוניות to be like πύθωνες, ventriloquist. He says: "Es ist möglich dass man bei Orgien und wüsten Ausschreitungen zur Tauschung der unschuldingen Opfer, die man anlocken wollte, das verfahren der πύθωνες, Bauchredner einschlug." Goldfahn in Rahmer's *Literaturblatt*,[343] argues against Perles' interpretation of the word אפטוניות as πουτάνα = harlot. He takes the word to be like ἀπείθεια rebellion, disobedience so that עבד בן אפטוניות would mean he becomes υἱος τῆς ἀπείθειας i. e., נעשה בן מְרִי or ἀπειθούντες rebellious, denying, ungehorsam = מאין = מין, den Gehorsam verweigern בן מְרִי.[344] Kohut[345] identifies it with the Greek υπευθυνος, responsible or accountable and translates our passage "zog ihn zur Rechenschaft," "he made him account for

339 *MGWJ*, (1892), 272.
340 See above.
341 *Die Ophiten*, (Berlin, 1899), 79 ff.
342 Rahmer's *Literaturblatt* XIX, (1890), No. 28.
343 *Ibid.*, 162.
344 Cf. also Sachs, *Beiträge*, I, 168 and II, 140.
345 *Aruk Completum* I, 211, *s. v.* אַפְּטוֹנִיּוּת.

his conduct" (or if we read בהן = בָּן not בָּן made *them* responsible). He also suggests, without quoting Perles, that it may mean πουτάνα (late Greek) = harlot, and he translates it, בן הזונות i. e., he became a רועה זונות.[346]

We now come to a consideration of the name מין, pl., מינים which in some instances may designate Christians and in some passages may simply refer to heretics of any kind.[347] As to the meaning or etymology of the word מין, it may simply mean genus, species or kind, and may designate any group or class of people within the larger group of the people i. e., among the Jews, and would then designate one who belongs to any Jewish sect, or special group of the Jewish people different or separate from כלל ישראל. Hence, in later times, when the whole Jewish people followed the Pharisees, a Sadducean was considered as one who did not belong to כלל ישראל, and therefore was designated as a מין. Perhaps the saying in Ḥullin 13b אין מינים באומות originally meant that among non-Jews we cannot distinguish one from the other and cannot designate one small group as being separated or different from the larger group. Since the larger group likewise has no correct beliefs, we cannot characterize one group with different beliefs as heretic. Among the Gentiles those with correct beliefs are rather the exception and are designated as צדיקי (חסידי) אומות העולם. The Gemara in Ḥullin[348] however misunderstood the original meaning of this statement.

Some scholars, however, take the word מין to be like מאין, denier, one who refuses to accept the correct beliefs. Others consider the word as shortened from מאמין "believer." Since the heretics called themselves true believers מאמינים the Rabbis shortened the term and referred to them as מינין.[349]

The name נוצרים occurs in b. Ta‘an. 27b where it designates the Christians who observe Sunday.[350]

---

[346] Cf. further Lewy, Jastrow, Krauss' *Lehnwörter*, and Fürst.

[347] See especially Graetz, *Geschichte* IV, 4th ed., 400, note 11.

[348] *Loc. cit.*

[349] Cf. Kohut, in *Aruk Completum* V, 168–169, *s. v.*, מן חסרונות.

[350] See Rashi *ad loc.* מפני הנוצרים שעושין אותו (יום א') יום טוב שלהם, as to the derivation of his name, whether from Nazareth or from שומר = נוטר = נוצר, see above.

Another possible reference to the Christians who keep the Sunday as their Sabbath may be found in b. Ab. Zarah 6a and also 7b in the saying of Samuel: אמר שמואל יום נוצרי (חסרונות בהוצאות שלנו אחד) לדברי ר' ישמעאל לעולם אסור. In the Munich manuscript the word יום is omitted. Perhaps we ought to read עם instead of יום, the meaning being that in the case of Christians who observe the first day of the week, were we to prohibit three additional days before and three after the Holiday, it would always be forbidden to do business with them. Further, the passage may originally have been meant as a question: עם נוצרים לעולם אסור? Is it forbidden to do business with a Christian at any time? That the reference is to Sunday, even with this emendation is evident from the rest of the Gemara והאיכא ארבעה וחמישה דשרי. As a curiosum we may cite here an apologetic etymology of this name, probably intended to fool the censor. Grunwald in his article in Rahmer's *Literaturblatt* referred to above, quotes from a התנצלות contained in an old מחזור printed in Prague in 1680 which explains נוצרים as referring to the followers of Nebuchadnezar i. e., ancient Babylonians. It says: והם אשר נקראים מקדם דרך כלל הנוצרים כי מלכם בראשם נקרא נבוכדנצר ועל שמו נקראו נוצרים.

Probably the philosopher mentioned in b. Shab. 116b as an arbiter between R. Gamaliel and his sister in a dispute about their inheritance was a Christian, since he seems to refer to the New Testament or quotes a passage from one of the original Gospels, for the אורייתא אחריתא no doubt means the new covenant or N. T. even though the passage quoted from that "other law" is not found in our version of the Gospels.[351] The question as to whether a daughter may inherit may have been a veiled attack on Jesus who could trace his descent from David through his mother only. Hence if a daughter cannot inherit, Jesus could not be the heir of David and had no claim to the Messiaship.[352]

A reference to Christians is seen by some scholars in the two

[351] See M. Güdeman, *Religionsgeschichtliche Studien*, (Leipzig, 1876), 65 ff.

[352] The N. T. genealogies trace the descent through Joseph, but of course since he was not Jesus's father, Jesus could not claim Davidic descent through him.

names for groups or assemblies of heretics בי נצרפי and בי אבידן mentioned in the Talmud. I quote here these three passages in full. The first passage is the one in b. Shab. 152a which reads as follows: אמר ליה קיסר לר' יהושע בן חנניה מ"ט לא אתית לבי אבידן אמר ליה טור תלג מחרוני גלידין כלבוהי לא נבחין טחנוהי לא טוחנין. This then was about 100 C. E. when the emperor referred to this institution.

When Eleazar b. Perata, a Tanna of the younger group of the second generation, in first half of the second century, was arrested together with Ḥananiah ben Tradyon and charged with disregarding the Roman decreees, one of the questions asked of him or one of the charges against him was that he neglected to attend the meetings at the בי אבידן. The passage reads: אמרו לו ומאי טעמא לא אתית לבי אבידן אמר להו זקן הייתי ומתיירא אני שמא תרמסוני ברגליכם.[353]

The third passage is found in b. Shab. 116a and reads as follows: בעי מיניה יוסף בר חנין מר' אבהו הני ספרי דבי אבידן מצילין אותן מפני הדליקה או אין מצילין אין ולאו ורפיא בידיה רב לא אזיל לבי אבידן וכ"ש לבי נצרפי שמואל לבי נצרפי לא אזיל לבי אבידן אזיל אמרו ליה לרבא מ"ט לא אתית לבי נצרפי אמר להו דיקלא פלניא איכא באורחא וקשי לי ניעקריה דוכתיה קשי לי מר בר יוסף אמר אנא מינייהו אנא ולא מסתפינא מינייהו זימנא חדא אזיל בעו לסכוניה... Here there is mentioned besides the בי אבידן also the בי נצרפי which latter may have been only in Babylon in the time of Rab and Samuel, i. e., the first half of the third century. But the בי אבידן must have been an institution, both in Babylon during first half of the third century as well as in Palestine during the first half of the second century. We must keep this fact in mind, for any explanation of the term must fit an institution that existed in both countries and in the different periods of time from about 100 to 250 C. E.[354] Of all the interpretations only one, that of Löw[355] who takes

---

[353] b. 'Ab. Zarah 17b.

[354] For the various interpretations see among others: S. J. Rappoport in ערך מלים (ed. חכונה, Warsaw, 1914), 6; L. Ginzberg, *MGWJ*, LXXVIII, 28; Scheftelowitz, *Die Entstehung der Manichäischen Religion*, (Giessen, 1922), 3; Kohut, *Aruk Completum*, *s. v.*; B. Geiger in תוספות הערוך השלם (Wien, 1937), 84; *Hamburger Realencyclopädie*, II, 95–96; Israel Horowitz, ארץ ישראל ושכנותיה (Wien, 1923), 111, *s. v.*, בי אבידן, and 112, *s. v.*, בי נצרפי; Krauss, *op. cit.*, 255; Herford, *op. cit.*, 165–166.

[355] *HeḤalutz* II, 100–101.

נצרפי as a corrupt form of נצרני, i. e., Christians and אבידן as a corrupt form of אביון designating the Ebionites, also Christians, brings the discussion of these names within the scope of our study.[356] I personally think that these names are deprecatory or cacophemistic forms, substituting for the real names, so as to indicate that those who frequent them are headed for hell אבדון, or most certainly should perish, or in the case of נצרפי, those who should go to purgatory, or who need to be purged. They may have referred to Christians and also to other heretic groups or sects whom we can no longer identify, as their real names are hidden under these ill-wishing disguised designations.

A reference to the Gospels may be found in b. Shab. 116a according to the reading of Diḳduke Soferim[357] רבי מאיר קרי ליה און גליון ר' יוחנן קרי ליה עון גליון, and hence the הגליונין mentioned in the Baraita there and Tosefta Shab. 13.5 together with ספרי צדוקים which stands for ספרי מינין may also refer to the *evangelium*, i. e., Gospel, and other Christian writings. The phrase ועליהם הוא אומר ואחרי הדלת והמזוזה שמת זכרונך[358] may refer to the secret meetings held by the Judeo Christians!

---

[356] Is the reference in B. Ḳ. 117a לבי אביוני also a reference to the Ebionites?

[357] See חסרונות, *ad loc.*

[358] *Ibid., loc. cit.*

The Historical Jesus

By Samuel Sandmel

ABOUT THE TIME of the American Revolution, a leading intellectual doctrine called Rationalism emerged in Western thinking. The movement, which exalted man's reason and common sense and looked askance at the supernatural and the miraculous, has persisted as a dominant trend into recent times. It was under the impact of Rationalism that the beginning was made in the historical study of the Gospels.

It was inevitable within this framework of thought that the view became crystallized that much of the New Testament had lost its authority. The Epistles of Paul bore the brunt of an attack on mysticism, and ultimately a Christian scholar was to declare that Paul had substituted a religion about Jesus for the religion of Jesus. The Gospels, it was then averred, were irrational accounts, with incredible details; but there were some fine ethical teachings by Jesus, which were valid, even if the framework in which they were preserved was not. If only the Gospels could be stripped of the legendary and the supernatural, so the argument ran, then the ethics of Jesus would emerge more clearly, and the historical Jesus would be discernible as a man whom rational men could imitate. The need, accordingly, was to "recover" this "historical Jesus."

What manner of man was Jesus? Was he a Jewish Messiah? A great teacher? A prophet? The end of virtually all scholarly Gospel study was directed to the goal of answering this most insistent question. The Gospels had to be studied for themselves and for their relationship to each other; their broad background needed minute investigation. It is no exaggeration to say that virtually every phrase, or even every word in the Gospels, was scrutinized with exacting care. No stone was left unturned in the great quest.

Along the way, a number of efforts were made to answer the question, "What manner of man?" The answer almost invariably was influenced by some special interest of the answerer. The man who learned rabbinic literature quickly noted Jesus' resemblance to the rabbis, and the answer was given simply, Jesus was a rabbi. Or, another who drew together some clews from here and there answered that the historical Jesus, like a more typical Jewish messianic claimant, had been a political rebel against Rome. Christian Old Testament scholars saw him as the last and greatest of the prophets. For several decades men interested in social problems were sure that Jesus was a social reformer. Then, later, a school of mythologists used the term Christ-myth to express the conviction that there had never been a historical Jesus at all. More recently, some popular authors have indirectly depicted Jesus as a liberal rabbi, a Quaker, a Unitarian, or, in one atrocity, an advertising expert.

It is quite easy to be glib about the historical Jesus. Some popular novelists who have written about the life and times of Jesus are able to speak with a facility that an earnest student lacks. Their works give us not history, but imaginative portraits. The insistent question remains, What manner of man was the historical Jesus?

Jesus is mentioned in the rabbinic literature, but the passages are rather late retorts to post-New Testament Christian claims. They are of no value for the history of Jesus. A mention of Jesus in Josephus is regarded by most scholars as an interpolation; and the handful of conservatives who do not declare in favor of the interpolation concede that the passage is so reworked as to be of no historical value. Jesus is not mentioned in

194

Greek or Latin histories of the period. Only one bit of writing that purports to be in his hand is extant, contained in a legend, of no historical relevance, of his having written in Greek to a certain king, Abgar.

The Gospels, then, are our only real source. But, we have said, they came at least two or three generations after Jesus; not from Palestine, but from the Diaspora; and they were written in Greek, not in Aramaic. Some pericopes, we have said, were shaped by the church, while others were created by it. Within almost every pericope the hand of the growing church can be discerned. It is only within the narrowest limits that one can discern readily separable layers of traditions. The Gospels do not in reality tell us about Jesus; they tell us about the faith, the problems, and the interests of the church which created them.

If the hand of the church is so clearly discernible, is it not possible to remove later accretions and get back to a historical kernel? Scholars have found it partly possible. Even the most skeptical scholars of our day do not deny that some materials in the Gospels go back to Jesus. For example, it is unlikely that the church, forming the Gospels generations after Jesus, would have deliberately ascribed to him a prediction of the early End which by their time was so clearly wrong, unless it was part of an authentic tradition. Thus many scholars consider the Gospel materials to have a large measure of historical reliability about Jesus, though they would not insist on the historicity of every detail, and they would concede that the historical materials are shaped considerably by the developing church. Other scholars, perhaps fewer in number, find that the accretions in the pericopes are so thoroughly blended with what may have been authentic materials that to remove the accretions leaves a formless remainder; and to retain them yields a totality so obviously comporting with the later church of the dispersion that it

195

supplies no great illumination for the historical Jesus. Perhaps we might call the first group of scholars the moderates and the second group the extremists.

There appears to be among moderates no thorough agreement as to what sections of the Gospels can yield historical data about Jesus, and two moderates can often be quite far apart from each other. What the moderates have in common is not an agreement on what is historical, but rather the conviction that there is much historical material about Jesus in the Gospels. The moderates, accordingly, go in the direction of the extremists, but not nearly so far. Indeed, among the moderates there are perceptible differences in the distances which now one and now another travels.

Most moderates would probably conclude that no secure biography of Jesus can be written. But not even the extremists would permit this circumstance to lead to a denial that Jesus is a historical character. In the 1910's a few scholars did argue that Jesus never existed and was simply the figment of speculative imagination. This denial of the historicity of Jesus does not commend itself to scholars, moderates or extremists, any more. On the basis of simple human experience, it seems to most scholars more likely that a historical personality was elevated into divine rank, than that a speculative abstraction was turned into some fictitious person. To believe the latter would raise the problem of why a Jew, of Galilean origin, would have been hit upon as the fictitious embodiment of a divine being. Why not a Roman, of noble birth, of great education and wealth? The obscurity and humbleness of the background of Jesus, preserved by the church even in the face of its deification of him, form a compelling argument that he was a historical character.

While the liberal scholar will concede that some, or much, or even most, of the data which the New Testament reports about Jesus is unhistorical, he concludes that to deny his historicity

196

entirely is neither necessary nor reasonable. It seems perfectly natural that behind the accrued beliefs there was a historical person; and the burden of proving a case would today seem to fall upon those who would deny that Jesus ever existed, not upon those who affirm it. Indeed, when resort is made to tolerably reasonable proofs, the weight seems in the direction of affirming that Jesus lived, even though Jewish and Roman sources of his day fail to mention him. The mention of a mother and of brothers and sisters of Jesus in the Gospels, and the mention of James in Paul's First Epistle to the Corinthians, are understandable only as genuine historical reminiscences, but not as possible by-products of speculation, since their very nature would tend to be refuted by the speculative deification. In short, the New Testament has so many overtones about Jesus which point to a historical person that it is excessive skepticism to doubt the direct statement that he was a historical person who was born, lived, and died. The "Christ-myth" theories are not accepted or even discussed by scholars today.

The quest for the historical Jesus, that is, for the precise biography of the man, began with optimistic certainty that it would be successful in all details, and more than one premature cry of "eureka" has echoed through the scholarly world. But modern scholarship appears to be skeptical of the long expected success. Indeed, some of the extremist scholarship even concludes that we cannot be certain that any single incident about Jesus, or any word attributed to him, is genuine. More moderately, others would hold that a general portrait of Jesus is discernible; a portrait perhaps like one painted in oil which must be viewed from some distance.

The political rebel, or the social reformer, or the teacher par excellence, or the rabbi, or the prophet was never the center of the New Testament faith. Sentimentality may invest parables

197

attributed to Jesus with a value far beyond what the words carry, or obscure statements may be considered to be pertinent to a given cause. Yet it must be insisted that the church did not worship the Christ as a master of parable, nor as a climax in the line of Amos or Hosea, nor as a precursor of Thomas Jefferson or of Abraham Lincoln. The church worshiped him as the Christ in whom God was revealed. Whatever it preserved or created in the Gospels was retained because it had some direct or indirect relationship to God's revelation and to the need of the church. The church insisted that the revelation of God in Christ was in the historical Jesus, but the New Testament faith is centered in the divinity of the Christ, not in the historical man Jesus.

The quest for the precise, human Jesus has not been successful. Indeed, we can see now that it was foredoomed to failure since it essayed something impossible, on an attractive but deceptive premise, that literary materials created out of supernatural beliefs would submit to scholarly sifting and yield a naturalistic residuum.

A single, unified catalogue of the teachings of Jesus proves to be as impossible to extract from the Gospels as is the historical impression of Jesus himself. To a question such as, What was Jesus' view of sin?, three varying answers, according to Matthew, Mark, and Luke, present themselves. Did Jesus prohibit divorce? The precise answers to such questions cannot be direct, but must be conditioned by the fact that Mark and Luke may say one thing, but Matthew another. Or, each evangelist may give a different answer. Or one or two may be silent on the matter.

Only if one wants a semi-historical answer, or an unconsciously or deliberately mendacious one, or a careless summary, can one stop at the statement, Jesus said this, or Jesus taught that. It

198

is possible to report on Jesus only as the evangelists report on him.

Many of the statements attributed to Jesus are paralleled in the ancient Jewish literature. Some Jewish scholars have used this circumstance to deny originality to Jesus, while others have used it to show the "essential Jewishness" of Jesus.

One needs to note that the parallels have usually been scrutinized for facets of similarity, and not nearly so often for facets of difference. Moreover, the rabbinic literature has been used with considerable carelessness, not only by Jewish scholars, but also by Christians. Not alone has the motive existed either to glorify Jesus at the expense of the rabbis or the rabbis at the expense of Jesus, but ordinary cautions of primary concern in the historians' method have been tossed aside. Excerpts from the difficult rabbinic literature, available in convenient translation, especially in a highly commendable five-volume German commentary (known as *Strack and Billerbeck*), have encouraged both the imprudent and, one must say, the impudent.

Even when bias and partisanship are absent from the hearts and minds of scholars, the comparisons are seldom capable of realization. This is true not only because the Jesus of the Gospels, as we have seen, is not completely the "original" Jesus but has been enriched with additions by the church, but also because of significant factors in the rabbinic literature.

Rabbinic traditions, parables, and statements are older than the time of Jesus. Some of these appear in non-canonical works, such as the Book of Jubilees; some appear in Josephus. But the earliest rabbinic collections, which contain the oldest material, were written down two centuries after Jesus. The material in the collections includes some which undoubtedly antedates Jesus — but to separate the layers in the rabbinic literature is a task of

199

great delicacy, and one which has yielded, for the few who have tried it, no abundant agreement. Much of the parallel material comes from rabbinic collections, which were made in Babylonia, and not in Palestine, in even later centuries; these later collections admittedly also contain very old material, but again the uncertainty exists about the age of relevant passages. Some Jewish scholars seem to believe that since some of this material is demonstrably older than Jesus, potentially all of it is; and some Christian scholars, overlooking the fact that late collections contain quite ancient materials, declare that the true priority and hence the inherent virtue of originality belong to Jesus. But since controlling criteria are absent, these quarrels about priority are as useful, and truly as relevant, as that about the chicken and the egg.

Even when the rabbinic literature is used in a non-partisan manner, it does not furnish a full and exact understanding of the time of Jesus. Just as the Gospels reflect, in their presentation of older material, the newer times in which they were recorded, so, in their own peculiar way, the rabbinic collections reflect the interests of the editors. Pharisaic in its outlook, rabbinic literature has little that is charitable to say about the Sadducees. So selective is it in what it offers that it mentions neither Philo nor Josephus; we should not know from the rabbinic literature about the mere existence of most of the other preserved Jewish writings called Apocrypha and Pseudepigrapha. Traditions older than the year 70 are to be found in the rabbinic literature, but only in the form of stray bits.

It is to be remembered that between the time of Jesus and the time of the recording of rabbinic literature, the tremendous upheavals of 70 swept the Pharisees into the ascendancy. The destruction of the Temple in 70 ended the Temple cult and the Sadducean movement which presided over it. The Pharisees,

200

who had been until then an active but possibly small minority among many minorities, rose with their institution, the synagogue, to become practically synonymous with Judaism.

Is the historical Jesus to be reckoned as close to the Pharisees, despite the anti-Pharisaic tone of the Gospels? Or is he, a Galilean, more aptly to be joined with some now obscure sectarian group, possibly the Essenes or the Fourth Philosophy? Was he an *am ha-aretz*,* as some scholars have suggested (though they have not agreed on the meaning of the term) on the basis of the contempt expressed in the Pharisaic literature?

Since the period before 70 in Palestine is not readily to be recovered from rabbinic literature because of its Pharisaic one-sidedness, these variables tantalize the historian. (The Dead Sea Scrolls serve most conspicuously in underlining the limitations on, and the uncertainties in, our knowledge; they do not materially increase our specific knowledge, but only offer some corroboration of what was already known.)

The end result is that the more closely we look for exactness in details, the more elusive it is. The reluctant conclusion seems to me this, that to attempt to fit the historical Jesus into his Jewish setting is to put a somewhat uncertain figure into an uncertain background. We are on the safest ground when we are the most general; when we proceed to specific matters, definiteness eludes us.

Moreover, respecting the comparison of Jesus and the rabbis, there would seem to be little gained from contrasting a single individual with a host of individuals. It needs to be said, again if necessary, that the motives in such comparisons, even when they are unconscious, are not without some impetus to exalt the one party at the expense of the other. Some writers, especially

---

*It seems to me that this variously explained term means simply a rural person.

201

107

Jews, taking their cue from the Fourth Gospel, speak of Jesus as a "rabbi," even though that title was not used by Jews until after the time of Jesus. This title would, from one aspect, "raise" Jesus from the supposedly low level of a political rebel, or, from another, it would lower him from a supposedly loftier one of uniqueness. For many Protestants the role of rabbi seems understandably insufficient; their tradition, having broken with priestly Catholicism, puts great store on the laymen. Some Protestants, accordingly, insist that Jesus was not a rabbi but a "lay" prophet who broke with the priesthood of his day — and some such Protestants seem mistakenly to equate the rabbinate — a thoroughly lay institution — with the priesthood! The motive in terming Jesus a prophet is to counter the priestly claims of Catholicism; in Catholicism, Jesus is the prototype of the priest, a view derived from its explicit formulation in the Epistle to the Hebrews.

Since motive, of aggrandizement or of reduction, enters into the comparisons, objectivity fades and even disappears. This is as true of comparisons made by partisans of Protestantism and Catholicism as it is true of Christian and Jewish partisans.

The viewpoint advanced here is not that the comparisons should not be made between the rabbis and Jesus, and not that the effort to set Jesus in his Jewish background is unworthy. On the contrary. But scholarship has tried, even desperately, to do exactly that and on substantial basis; but when more than generalities have been considered, the effort has failed. Because the tools for an objective comparison are lacking, whatever comparisons emerge are the result of predisposition and partisanship.

Since in the past, and even in the present, the epithet of "Christ-killer" has been directed by some Christians at Jews,

202

and the epithet has often been accompanied by physical on-slaught — and this may well continue in the future, too — the search for the historical facts relating to the crucifixion has long been a Jewish concern. Jews have written abundantly, and feelingly, to show that the epithet does not rest on sound histor-ical bases. Crucifixion was a Roman form of punishment; hence, it is argued, the Romans, and not the Jews, crucified Jesus; secondly, the judicial procedures described in the Gospels do not accord with Jewish practices, and therefore the Gospel accounts are not historical. To the first point, the reply has been made that while the Romans, indeed, did the actual crucifying, it was at the behest of the Jews; on the second point, there exists a huge literature elaborately defending the supposed authenticity of the Gospel record by demonstrating that the trial was in conformity with such irrelevant judicial processes as those, for example, of British Common Law. The Jewish retort may be just, but it has hardly been widely effective.

For those Christians for whom there is meaning or satisfaction in blaming Jews of two thousand years ago for something which transpired, and who enjoy exacting from Jews of our day, or from their children, some penalty for the transmitted guilt, the recourse to historical scholarship is totally useless. So, too, is the appeal to conscience or to Jesus' summary of the Golden Rule, or to any standard of ethics or justice. There have been, are, and probably will be forever some Christians to whom this single item of New Testament tradition is more vivid than anything else, and Jews must face the reality of the fact. Especially in the week before Easter, Jews need not be surprised to read in their daily newspaper abstracts from sermons derived from the crucifixion account which may upset them.

There are many Christians for whom a distinction between the Jews of two thousand years ago and those of our day still

203

seems possible, yet whose fidelity to their training conditions them to affirm and transmit the blame of the ancient Jews for the crucifixion. Such Christians can wholeheartedly oppose discriminations against the Jews of our day — which are often abetted unconsciously by the words and phrases which these people use.

There are, however, Christians in abundance who recognize the circumstance that the anti-Jewish tone of the New Testament is the product of an age and of a set of conditions. They point out that the progressive shift of blame from the Romans to the Jews in the developing Christian literature, both within the New Testament and beyond it, is a result of the need to appease the Romans, and, further, that the church conviction that it had taken the place of the Jews in God's favor made concrete the blindness attributed to the Jews by extending it to the point of malicious, premeditated responsibility for the death of Jesus. These Christians deny that anti-Jewish sentiment is a necessity for the Christian faith. There is quite an extensive literature, written by Christians for Christians, deploring the intrusion of anti-Jewish feeling into the New Testament. Such Christians have recognized that the New Testament can be, for those who wish it, the source and the justification for hatred of Jews; they have made sincere efforts to forfend against a use of this kind in the preparation of the textbooks which they use in their religious schools.

Among such Christians, the crucifixion narrative is handled in such a way that the virulent hatred of certain of its passages is neutralized. The opponents of Jesus cease to be simply "Jews," but are interpreted as the wayward universally found in every land or religious communion; the Pharisees cease to be typical of all Jews, and become a type of communicant recognizable within any Christian denomination. And the telling questions are asked, If the crucifixion brought a benefit, atonement, to

204

mankind, then why should hatred be expressed against those who were involved in the incident? And if the crucifixion was divinely ordained, then was not the role of the crucifiers fixed by God, rather than capriciously chosen by man?

Just as there are both Jews with prejudice and without it towards Christians, so, too, despite the anti-Jewish bias of the New Testament, there are many such Christians without prejudice against Jews. Their approach to the crucifixion narrative is constructively gratifying. Yet it, too, cannot be called historical, for it is commendable interpretation, but still interpretation.

The historical circumstances which led to the crucifixion of Jesus, in my judgment, are beyond recovery.

The scholarly conclusion that the "historical" Jesus is not to be "recovered" emerged shortly after World War I. Since that time, as we know, mankind has been in the most serious straits in the recorded history of humanity.

Rationalism, and optimism about man's potentialities, had led in the nineteenth century to a view of man directly the opposite, we may say, of Paul's view. Paul believed that man needed God's redemption; nineteenth-century liberalism believed that man could redeem himself.

Since World War I Paul has been, as it were, rediscovered, as many theologians have seen in contemporary history the confirmation of Paul's view of man. The older premise that Paul might well be discarded has been supplanted by a growing conviction in exactly the opposite direction, with the result that Pauline doctrine has been extolled with refreshed approbation. The unavailability of the historical Jesus has promoted an ascendancy of the Pauline Epistles; and if Paul has not quite supplanted Jesus in contemporary thought, it is little exaggeration to report that the Epistles have been more emphasized than the Gospels in much of current Protestant theological concern.

205

For some such theologians the authority of Paul is, under-standably, insufficient, and, naturally, they turn to Jesus. But here such theologians run headlong into the conclusions of the scholarship which this volume tries to mirror, that the historical Jesus is not readily to be recovered. It is not surprising that these theologians have been considerably dismayed at failing to elicit from specialists in the Bible the desired confirming word. Some have been understandably incensed, and they have not hesitated to express their displeasure at the tone of Biblical scholarship. From such circles there has emanated a repeated disparagement of Biblical scholarship, on the grounds that the career of Jesus was "suprahistorical," and therefore historical scholarship is a wrong and useless tool. An outsider suspects that the efforts to discredit the historical approach would be less arduous if the historical approach were not so inconvenient to the discreditors. There are a perceptible number of theologians who, bypassing the scholarship of the New Testament, go on to affirm conclu-sions more congenial to their own dispositions. Such theologians appear to be in the minority, and do not seem to include the leading theological figures of the day.

The leading theologians seem to feel, on the contrary, that to disparage Biblical scholarship is to be guilty of intellectual blindness or dishonesty. These would not only not. discourage such scholarship, but even encourage it, however extreme its conclusions. But they are also critical of "liberal scholarship," yet in a completely different way; the Bible specialist among these would reject the label "liberal" in favor of the term "radical." The inadequacy which these theologians note in the liberal scholarship is an alleged failure to proceed beyond histor-ical study into an assessment of the meaning of the history studies. The "radical" will confirm the "liberal" conclusion that no satisfactory life of Jesus can be written. But for the "radical" the "truth" of the Gospel is not the accurate records of events,

206

but the way in which the events illustrate or elucidate the fulfillment of divine purposes in history. For such theologians the
traditional terms of the Christian faith, even when abundantly
reinterpreted, are still: "creation," "the redemption of man,"
and the "events of the End"; accordingly, they contend, the
results of modern Biblical scholarship must be shown in some
positive relationship to the traditional terms.

The distinction to be drawn between the two groups is that
the former disparages the liberal scholarship and dismisses it as
wrong; the latter is, indeed, critical of the uses of the scholarship,
but endorses it as right as far as it goes, insisting that it must go
farther.

But since out of the theological discussions there emanate from
time to time random phrases and sentiments in criticism of the
liberal scholarship, it has seemed to me desirable to digress for
the brief mention of these movements for the purpose of making
the conclusion unmistakable.

Though a voice here and there questions the validity of the
liberal scholarship, the prevailing view is this: the evangelists
disclose Jesus to us only after the church has meditated on his
significance as the Christ. The form of the Gospel writings is
such that it is not always possible to penetrate effectively beyond
the Gospel portraits of Jesus to Jesus himself. We can know what
the evangelists saw in Jesus the Christ. We can know what the
evangelists report of his teaching; we can be sure that however
the Gospels have shaped his words, some echo of them is discernible. But we cannot describe with exactness and precision
the details of the life and career of Jesus.

It certainly does not follow, since the "historical" Jesus is not
"recoverable," that the place of Jesus in the liberal Protestant
mind has therefore given way to a vacuum. On the contrary.
It means only that glibness and careless pigeonholing are re-

207

placed by some sturdy efforts to conceive of Jesus in more tenable ways. Perhaps this is more often implicit than articulate among liberals. But, to begin with negatives, the liberal scholar would avoid "modernizing" Jesus; that is to say, he would not describe Jesus in some category in which the modern age is interested and which would ill suit the Jewish world of almost two thousand years ago. The liberal might use a term—how can he speak without using terms? — such as prophet, or teacher, but always with the sense that the term is only an approximation. For him the figure of Jesus is beyond whatever description he can accord it; therefore he necessarily has both reservations and also implied overtones in his mind as inevitably his wish to communicate leads him to use specific terms in his description.

Such a person is likely, also, to see in the words of the Gospels not a literal truth, but symbolic or ineffable truth. He would not insist necessarily that Jesus did or said some particular thing recorded in the Gospels, but he would proclaim himself attuned to what the intent of the Gospel is in attributing that detail to Jesus. In illustration, such a person might, as many do, deny the virgin birth; or else he might deny the physical aspect involved; and he might aver that he sees in Jesus an exalted person whose essence the First and Third evangelists try to portray through the medium of the virgin birth. He would focus not on the virgin birth, but on the implicit exaltation.

Obviously, variety exists among such New Testament scholars, and no single description can fit all. But however negative the results from pure historical study, they have not been accompanied in liberal Christianity by negative approaches to the significance of Jesus. The usual liberal Christian has a positive conception of Jesus, difficult as it may be to contain it within definitions. It may be said, in general, that Jesus, as a man, serves the liberal as the model for those things which he con-

208

siders the most cherished human ideals. Uncertain as he may be about details of the career of Jesus, even to the point of rejecting this or that item of the traditional faith as unreasonable, or as untenable, he sees in that career the supreme idealism which he considers worthy of imitation. In this, at least, he concurs in the faith of the evangelists, who saw in Jesus the pinnacle of human achievement, love, and solicitude. To an outsider, it may appear that an idealized man, not a real man, has been accepted as the model to emulate; to the liberal Christian, Jesus seems to be not an idealized man, but the ideal man of history.

From this conception, the liberal can derive inspiration, and also an imperative which influences or guides his conduct. His actions and his attitudes can therefore be self-effacing, noble, and exalted. There are Christians whom I know to be such persons. They would attribute their attainments not to their own merit, but, in humility, to him whom they call their Master.

In the Jewish tradition there have been many men who have inspired in modern Jews ideals such as self-effacement, nobility, and exaltation, yet neither the Old Testament nor rabbinic literature depicts the ancient worthies — Abraham, Moses, David — as perfect. Not perfection, but goodness, has been the Jewish demand from the individual, a goodness which we Jews have urged upon ourselves as a personal responsibility to be as nearly perfect as possible. But we Jews have not equated strict perfection and goodness as interchangeable. If this standard seems deceptively to be lower than Christian perfectionism, we Jews would reply that the standard is not less exacting, but only more humanly tolerable. In the Jewish view, there have been many great men, but not any perfect man to be exalted above all others.

The Career of Jesus

By Solomon Zeitlin

The Sources

It has been said correctly of the life of Jesus, "We do not have enough material to write a respectable obituary."[1] The reason is simple; there are no sources that can be called historical. The authors of the Gospels were not primarily interested in recording reliable historical data, but in presenting him as seen through the eyes of faith. What is historical in their accounts they swathed so completely in theological wrappings that it almost cannot be laid bare. Moreover, there are no other nearly contemporaneous accounts of him. No mention is made of the name of Jesus outside of Christian records. The well-known Christ passage in Josephus was interpolated in the fourth century by the Church historian Eusebius.[2] It reads as follows:

Now there arose about this time Jesus, a wise man, if indeed one ought to call him a man. For he was a doer of wonderful works, a teacher of such people as accepted the truth gladly. He drew over to him both many of the Judaeans and many of the Hellenes. He was the Christ. When Pilate, at the suggestion of the principal men among us, condemned him to the cross, those that loved him at the first did not give up their affection for him. On the third day he appeared to them, as

152

the divine prophets had foretold this and ten thousand other wonderful things concerning him. And the tribe of Christians, so named from him, is not extinct.

The name of Jesus in connection with the death of James in Josephus is also a later interpolation.[3] The Roman historian Tacitus does make reference to Christus who was put to death by Pontius Pilate,[4] but he wrote his history during the close of the first and the beginning of the second centuries. Even then he does not mention Jesus by name. There are a few references to Jesus in the Talmud, but they are not earlier than the fourth century.[5]

Thus, to present a sketch of the life of Jesus one can draw only on the Gospels. Mark, Matthew and Luke are called the synoptic Gospels, since they are more or less in agreement. John is unsynoptic, for his narrative of events in the life of Jesus and his theology often manifest a distinctly different approach. The earliest Gospel is the one "according to Mark." Papias, who lived in the first part of the second century, said that Mark, a disciple of Peter, composed the Gospel from stories related to him by Peter.[6] The authorship of the Gospel according to Mark should consequently be placed in the period shortly after the destruction of the Temple, during the last quarter of the first century, or more than one generation after the death of Jesus.[7] Matthew, in writing his Gospel, made use of Mark and also of collections of the sayings of Jesus, *logia*.[8] The author of the third Gospel, Luke, was a disciple of Paul according to tradition. He was a physician and at the same time a man of culture who had genuine literary skill.[9] He endeavored to present an historical narrative of the life of Jesus and utilized the writings of Mark and possibly Matthew. John did not intend to present a biography of Jesus, but an essentially theological interpretation of his existence. Thus, he did not stress Jesus' descent from David, as the synoptics did, but that he was the Messiah, the Son of God, the Lamb of God which takes away the sins of the world. The book of John was probably written in the middle of the second century for Gentile Christians.[10]

His Birth

A biography usually begins with the date of birth, but in Jesus' case that is not known. Mark passes the birth of Jesus by in silence. Matthew says it occurred during the reign of Herod.[11] Herod died at the end of March, 4 B.C.E.[12] Luke says that Jesus was born when Quirinius (Cyrinius) took his census of Judaea, which was 6 C.E.[13] John says nothing on this score, and the early Church Fathers record different dates for the birth of Jesus.[14] It may be said that Jesus was born some time between the years 6 B.C.E. and 6 C.E. The exact month is more problematic. The Gospels did not record it and, while some Church Fathers placed it as early as November, others said it was March or April.[15]

Matthew and Luke identify the birthplace of Jesus as Bethlehem, which is south of Jerusalem, but still in Judaea, and state that the family moved from there to Nazareth which is not in Judaea proper but in Galilee.[16] Mark, on the other hand, does not mention that Bethlehem was the birthplace of Jesus. He always designates Jesus as "Jesus of Nazareth."[17] John, too, was not aware that Jesus was born in Bethlehem, but considered him a Galilean, as he wrote, "Others said: 'This is the Christ.' But some said, 'Shall Christ come out of Galilee'?"[18] Luke records the virgin birth and the manger scene in detail.[19] Matthew adds the homage of the Magi, the flight to Egypt and Herod's slaughter of the innocents.[20] After the death of Herod, Joseph and his family returned to the land of Israel but went to Nazareth, not Bethlehem, for fear of Archelaus. Matthew's explanation is unconvincing. If Joseph did not return to Bethlehem because of Archelaus, why did he return to Nazareth which was ruled by Herod (Antipas), called "the fox" in the Gospels?[21] The birth of Jesus in Bethlehem arose out of theological speculation, as further proof that Jesus was the messiah, the son of David. (David's family was from Bethlehem, and both Matthew and Luke take pains to trace the genealogy of Jesus back to King David.) Thus, Matthew quotes Micah as referring to the birth of Jesus, "And thou Bethlehem, in the land of Judaea . . . for out of thee shall come a ruler that shall rule my people Israel."[22] Matthew is likewise suspect, because his tale of the slaughter of the innocent babes has no historical foundation. Josephus, who was inclined to dramatize the cruelties committed by Herod, does not refer to a massacre of infants which he surely would not have failed to mention had there been one—a supposition confirmed by the silence of the early Church Fathers. Neither Mark nor John know that Jesus was born in Bethlehem, but regularly refer to him as Jesus of Nazareth, indicating that he was born there.[23]

Mariamme's son was circumcised on the eighth day and named Yeshu'a, Jesus in Greek.[24] His mother took him to Jerusalem to be redeemed, as he was her first born, and brought a sacrifice as prescribed by the Pentateuch.[25] That she brought two doves instead of a lamb shows that the family was poor. Mariamme bore four more sons, named Jacob (James), Joseph, Simon and Judas, and daughters[26]—at least two. Thus the family was of considerable size. Joseph, a carpenter, was the provider.[27]

According to Luke, Joseph and Mariamme went on a pilgrimage every year to Jerusalem for the Festival of Passover. They took Jesus along when he was twelve years of age.[28] According to the same Gospel, Jesus was enchanted by the discourse of the teachers in the Temple and had the intelligence to ask them various questions. It must be assumed that Jesus had received some kind of Judaean education in the small town of Nazareth. On the Sabbath he most likely attended the synagogue where the Torah was read and he listened to the discourses of the sages.

No further mention is made of Joseph after these stories of Jesus' youth. It is less likely that he was ignored than that he died early. Since it is recorded that Jesus pursued the trade of carpentry,[29] he probably took up the burden of supporting the family.

Jesus' Active Career

Nothing more is known of the life of Jesus[30] until he arrived at about the age of thirty when he met John the Baptist.[31] John began his ministry in the fifteenth year of Tiberius Caesar, that is, in 29 C.E.[32] Garbed in haircloth and with a girdle around his loins, John lived on dried locusts and honey. He besought the people to repent and be baptized in the Jordan.[33] The adult Jesus appears after his "hidden years," when he comes to John to be baptized. The various Gospels believe that John was the forerunner of Jesus the Messiah, or the Christ.[34]

The relationship between John and Jesus raises many problems. Jesus was not garbed like John the Baptist, nor did he subsist on dried locusts and honey. He was not an ascetic whose home was in the wilderness. He lived the same life that others did in Judaea, mingling with the people and visiting their synagogues.[35] While John appealed to the people to be baptized, Jesus never did so. John, the evangelist, says only that the disciples of Jesus practiced baptism.[36] Matthew's account of Jesus directing his eleven disciples to go and baptize in the name of the Father, the Son, and the Holy Ghost, places this after the resurrection.[37] According to Acts, Peter called for baptism in the name of Jesus Christ, and it is noted that Philip's converts were baptized.[38] Thus the evidence for baptism becomes clear later than the time of Jesus.[39]

Historically, therefore, the view that Jesus was not baptized by John carries great weight.[40] They ministered independently and there were even disputes between their disciples. The Gospel according to John records a sort of animosity against the disciples of John the Baptist.[41] The tale that Jesus was baptized is of theological origin, arising in the days when baptism became a fundamental symbol of the new faith. Since Jesus never practiced baptism, it was necessary for the early Christians to connect Jesus with John, who was regarded as his herald, and to assert that Jesus was baptized by him.[42]

According to Mark, Jesus began his ministry after the imprisonment of John the Baptist.[43] How long his ministry lasted is a matter of conjecture. It appears from the synoptic Gospels that it lasted less than a year.[44] According to John, it lasted several years. John says that during his ministry Jesus was in Jerusalem several times at the time of Passover. He also made a pilgrimage for the festival of Tabernacles, and visited during the days of Hanukkah.[45] According to the synoptic Gospels, however, he was in Jerusalem only once—during the festival of Passover, when he was tried and put to death by Pilate. The early Church Fathers had no definite tradition as to the length of Jesus' ministry, some following the synoptics,[46] others following John.[47]

There may be no contradiction between the accounts. John dates some of the events of Jesus' activity from the time when John the Baptist was still preaching, while the synoptic Gospels record them after the termination of John the Baptist's imprisonment (which lasted not quite one year). It seems likely that the ministry of Jesus did coincide for a few years with that of John the Baptist.

The synagogue of that day was not a house of prayer, with formal services, but a house of study and preaching, where the Torah and the Prophets were read and expounded. Both the reading and the preaching must have impressed Jesus deeply, and he followed this same method in his ministry. According to Mark, he entered upon his mission with an appeal to the people that, "The time is fulfilled and the kingdom of God is at hand; repent ye and believe the good tidings."[48] The Judaeans were suffering severly under Pontius Pilate. Some of them were eager to believe the good tidings proclaimed by Jesus that the kingdom of God was approaching. Jesus preached this gospel on the Sabbath day in various communities in Galilee. His preaching did not impress the people of Nazareth, who knew him as a carpenter's son. Thus he was led to exclaim, "a prophet has no honor in

his own country."[49] His followers were mainly women,
who were deeply impressed with his sincerity and
simplicity. He mingled with the lower classes of society,
publicans and sinners. When questioned as to why a man
of piety should associate with such social outcasts, his
answer was simple and to the point—the sick people, not
the healthy, needed a physician.[50]

The Gospels attribute many miracles to Jesus; but
such matters fall outside the historian's domain. Jesus
is also said to have driven out evil spirits, particularly
from women. Many people at that difficult time were
distraught, psychically ill, and Jesus with his deep understanding and compassion was able to cure them because
of their great faith. A similar power has been attributed
to many great religious leaders and operates today in a
different guise in psychotherapy. The followers of Jesus
addressed him as "teacher," or "master."[51] It is recorded
in the Gospels, particularly that of John, that Jesus was
also addressed as "rabbi."[52] This is an anachronism, since
that title was not introduced among the Judaeans until
after the destruction of the Temple. Some of Jesus'
enthusiastic followers who were cured, or expected to be
cured of their ills, addressed him as "son of God."[53] Jesus,
however, referred to himself only as *ben adam*, or in
Aramaic *bar nasha*. Its original connotation is simply "a
man," not the literal "son of man" as it was rendered in
the Greek.[54] When Jesus acquired a considerable following, he appointed twelve men to whom he delegated his
power of casting out evil spirits and healing the sick.[55]
Twelve were required to symbolize all the tribes of Israel
restored to their primal fullness. Jesus instructed his
disciples to carry his message to the Judaeans. He ordered
them, "Go not into the way of the Gentiles, and into the
city of the Samaritans enter ye not."[56] However, he himself went to Samaria and to the cities of the Gentiles,
Tyre and Sidon.[57]

There are numerous such contradictions and complications in the character of Jesus as recorded in the Gospels.
Jesus preached love. According to Matthew, Jesus said

JESUS OF NAZARETH : 159

in his sermon on the Mount, "Whosoever shall smite thee on thy right cheek turn to him the other also."[58] Yet Jesus bitterly upbraided the people of the cities who rejected his teachings. He was especially incensed against the people of Capernaum and said, "But I say unto you that it shall be more tolerable for the land of Sodom in the day of judgment than for thee [Capernaum]."[59] He also said that anyone who was not with him was against him.[60] He generally considered himself a Judaean, and felt deep concern for his own people. He said, "Think not that I am come to destroy the Torah or the prophets; I am not come to destroy, but to fulfill. For verily I say unto you, till heaven and earth pass, not an iota or one tittle shall in all wise pass from the Torah until all be fulfilled."[61] A similar patriotism is found in the story of the Canaanite[62] woman who besought him to cast out the evil spirit from her daughter. At first he declined and said, "For it is not meet to take the children's bread and to cast it unto the dogs."[63] Although Jesus believed it almost impossible for a man of wealth to enter heaven, and he associated with publicans and sinners, he did not hesitate to dine with the wealthy[64] or even with the Pharisees, whom he is alleged to have despised.[65] He was so obsessed with his mission that, when he was told his mother and brothers were outside waiting to see him, he said, "Who is my mother or my brethren? . . . For whosoever shall do the will of God the same is my brother and my sister and my mother."[66] Jesus thus ignored the presence of his mother and brothers; yet the law of Moses, the Torah, says, "Honor thy father and thy mother."[67]

It must therefore be emphasized: the sayings of Jesus as reported in the Gospels were not recorded during his lifetime. His disciples and followers had different traditions of his sayings and acts and these were not consciously collected until two generations after his death. Then the various accounts were incorporated into the Gospels and thus the contradictions. The historical Jesus is still an enigma.

The Messianic Claim

Did Jesus consider himself to be the Messiah, the Christ? Mark relates that when Jesus was with his disciples near Casarea Philippi, he asked them, "Whom say ye that I am?" and Peter answered and said unto him, "Thou art the Christ (Matthew adds, 'the son of the living God') and he charged them that they should tell no man of him."[68] According to Mark, there must have been some sort of discussion between Jesus and Peter, for Jesus rebuked him saying, "Get thee behind me Satan."[69] Matthew records the story differently. When Peter told Jesus he was the Messiah, Jesus praised him saying, "Blessed art thou, Simon bar-Jona, for man hath not revealed it unto thee, but my Father which is in heaven. And I say also unto thee that thou art Peter (rock) and upon this rock I will build my *ecclesia* (Church) and the gates of hell shall not prevail against it. And I will give unto thee the keys of the kingdom of heaven; and whatsoever thou shalt bind on earth shall be bound in heaven; and whatsoever thou shalt loose on earth shall be loosed in heaven."[70] Then he charged his disciples that they should tell no man that he was the Messiah (Christ). What was the underlying reason for Jesus to tell Peter not to divulge that he was the Messiah? Was this because Jesus himself did not think that he was the Messiah or only that it was premature to proclaim it lest he be persecuted by the authorities? No historical explanation can be advanced. His motives remain a mystery.[71]

Matthew relates that, when Jesus was in Capernaum, those who collected the half-drachma (half-shekel), the annual Temple levy, came to Peter and said, "Doth not your master pay the half-drachma?" Peter said, "Yes." Then Jesus said to Peter, "What thinkest thou Simon? Of whom do the kings of the earth take custom or tribute? Of their own children or of foreigners?" Peter answered, "Of foreigners." Jesus said to him, "Then are the children free."[72] This passage is ambiguous. The half-shekel had to be paid by all who embraced the Judaean religion regardless of where they resided. It was collected for the Temple and had no connection with earthly powers. Therefore Jesus is not understandable when he stated, "Then are the children free." In order not to give offense, however, Jesus said to Peter, "Go thou to the sea and cast an hook and take up the fish that first cometh up; and when thou hast opened his mouth thou shalt find money (shekel); that take and give unto them for me and thee." Although Jesus maintained that he was free from paying the half-shekel (he was not free), he did pay it in order not to offend the authorities.

Jesus' disposition to compromise in order not to antagonize the authorities is manifested in another, more famous, instance. When asked, "Is it lawful to give tribute unto Caesar, or not?" Jesus perceived that the questioners were trying to place him in a difficult position. "No," would make him a rebel against Rome; "Yes," would discredit him among the nationalists. To escape the net spread out for him Jesus said, " 'Show me the tribute money.' And they brought unto him a dinar. And he said unto them, 'Whose is this image and inscription?' They said to him, 'Caesar's.' Then said he unto them, 'Render therefore unto Caesar the things which are Caesar's; and unto God the things that are God's' "[73]

In the spring of 34, Jesus and his disciples went from Capernaum to Jerusalem. They did not go through Samaria, but crossed the Jordan and traveled by the east coast.[74] His disciples sensed that the trip to Jerusalem would be fatal. Again crossing the Jordan, they arrived in Jericho. From there they went to Jerusalem.[75] As they approached the city they stopped at Bethphage at the Mount of Olives.[76] From there Jesus rode on an ass to Jerusalem to demonstrate his humility or, more probably, to fulfill the prophecy of Zachariah who said, "Behold, thy king cometh unto thee, sitting upon an ass."[77] Thus Jesus' entry into Jerusalem may have been symbolic of

125

his claim to kingship. According to the Gospels, when Jesus entered Jerusalem, many of the people spread their garments on the ground before him proclaiming, "Hosanna. Blessed is he that cometh in the name of the Lord."[78] John adds that the people took branches from the palm trees (an expression of victory and thankfulness) and called him "the king of Israel."[79] That night Jesus went with his disciples to Bethany.[80] Apparently he feared to remain in Jerusalem at night, feeling that a conspiracy was being fomented against him. Hence he spent every night away from Jerusalem.

On the following day Jesus went to the Temple. According to both Mark and Matthew, Jesus cast out the people that·"sold and bought in the Temple and overthrew the tables of the moneychangers and the seats of them that sold doves."[81] The moneychangers, known in Hebrew literature as *shulhanim*, were a well-established and very useful institution. During the festivals many Judaeans from the Diaspora came on pilgrimage to the Temple. There they purchased from local farmers livestock for the sacrifices. This sale had to be transacted in Judaean currency, as the farmers would accept no other. Foreign money had therefore continually to be exchanged for the money of Judaea. The *shulhanim* served this purpose and charged a small percentage for their services. Most likely some of them occasionally made an excessive charge for the exchange of the various foreign moneys, the values of which were not well known to the average men of Judaea. It is doubtful, however, that Jesus could have thrown them out of the Temple area. They were well-entrenched and protected by the Temple guards. Luke and John do not mention moneychangers, but they do refer to the expulsion of those engaged in buying and selling—apparently the dealers in animals for the sacrifices.[82]

ARREST, TRIAL, AND CRUCIFIXION

The Course of the Arrest

The coming of Jesus to Jerusalem disturbed the Judaean leaders in Jerusalem. But a short while previously, Herod Antipas had put John the Baptist to death because he considered him a potential political problem—and some now believed Jesus was John, arisen from the dead to come to Jerusalem to preach his doctrine. Any disturbance was a peril to the Judaean authorities, who could maintain their status only if complete tranquility prevailed. The high priest in particular—then Caiaphas—was really a servant, or lackey, of Rome, appointed by the legate or procurator to ensure local control of malcontents. His sensitivity to the Galilean preacher is not difficult to imagine. Nor is Pilate's. As described above, Pilate was vicious to the people and hostile to their religion. He was cunning and treacherous. Due to his provocations, Judaea was on the brink of rebellion. The leaders of the people and High Priest Caiaphas, knowing his cunning and treachery, were fearful that if anything should happen Pilate would hold them responsible and wreak vengeance on the entire people. Thus John tells how even before the Passion week began a *synedrion* was called and it was argued that if Jesus continued his preaching, the Romans would come and "take away both our place and nation." High Priest Caiaphas elaborated on this and said, "It is expedient for us that one man should die for the people, and that the whole not perish."[83] Thus, the complex and stormy background of Judaea under the tyranny of Roman rule brought about Jesus' preaching and also his tragic death.

There is a fundamental discrepancy between the Passion narrative in the synoptic Gospels and John; but there are also contradictions, inconsistencies, and obscurities in the synoptics themselves. The problems of historical analysis would thus already be great. They are

further compounded by the intense theological significance of the events for the earliest witnesses and trans-
mitters of the traditions and for modern interpreters as
well. The historian who approaches this topic must call
upon all his resources of open-mindedness and objectivity.

Mark tells this story: Two days before the slaughtering of the paschal lamb and the Festival (of Passover),
the chief priest and the scribes sought to take Jesus and
to destroy him, "but they said, not on the feast day, lest
there be an uproar of the people."[84] Matthew says they
assembled in the house of High Priest Caiaphas, "and
consulted that they might take Jesus by subtility and
kill him. But they said, not on the feast day, lest there
be an uproar among the people."[85] Luke relates: "Now
the feast of unleavened bread drew nigh, which is called
the Passover, and the chief priest and the scribes sought
how they might destroy Jesus, for they feared the
people."[86] John knows of no plot among the high priest,
scribes and elders to kill Jesus—a departure of important
historical significance.

The synoptic Gospels describe the betrayal by Judas
Iscariot as follows: Judas went to the high priest and
offered to betray Jesus and in return was either promised
money or paid in advance.[87] John, on the other hand, does
not connect the betrayal by Judas Iscariot with the high
priest nor mention that he received money, but says that
he decided to betray Jesus because Satan had entered
into him after he had supped with Jesus. He writes, "And
after the sop Satan entered into him. Then said Jesus
unto him, 'That thou doest, do quickly.' "[88] This is another meaningful variation from the synoptic Gospels.

Jesus' betrayal by Judas Iscariot raises many perplex-
ing problems. Jesus trusted his disciples implicitly and
gave them the powers which he possessed. What then
prompted Judas to betray his master? The money, thirty
shekels, was of no significance. Only one other motive can
be substantiated by the sources, the Gospels, and that is
John's assertion that Judas became possessed. In other

words, John says that Judas was impelled to his conduct
by a supernatural demonic force, over which he had no
control. Where antiquity said Satan entered him, a
modern would say he was not of sound mind. But why
was Judas needed at all? Jesus could have been arrested
without being betrayed. He was well-known and preached
in the Temple every day. This enigmatic story may have
been inspired by some theological speculation which is
no longer known.

The Time of the Arrest

The synoptic Gospels say that on the fourteenth day of
Nisan, when the paschal lamb was slaughtered, Jesus and
the twelve apostles ate dinner together. He took the unleavened bread, broke and blessed it, and gave it to the
apostles. He then took a cup of wine, drank of it, and
passed it among his disciples. They sang a hymn, *hallel*,
and went out on the Mount of Olives.[89]

John says that Jesus supped with his disciples, but does
not make reference to the breaking of bread, the drinking
of wine, or the chanting of the *hallel*.[90] According to the
synoptic Gospels, Jesus was arrested on that night (according to the Judaean calendar, already 15 Nisan) and
crucified on the following day,[91] the first day of the Feast
of Unleavened Bread. Thus the last supper was on the
first night of the festival, now known as the *seder*. That
is not John's understanding. He relates that Jesus was
arrested on the night of 14 Nisan and crucified on the
following day (still 14 Nisan) when the paschal lamb was
to be slaughtered.[92] Thus the last supper that Jesus
shared with his disciples was an ordinary meal.

The discrepancy led to schism in the early days of
Christianity regarding the fixing of the day of the *pascha*
(called Easter in English-speaking countries): between
the Quatrodecimans and the anti-Quatrodecimans.[93]
Some churches, following the date given by the Gospel
according to John—that Jesus was crucified on the eve
of the Passover festival, when the paschal lamb was

slaughtered—celebrated *pascha* on the fourteenth day of
Nisan. They were the Quatrodecimans. Other churches,
holding that Jesus ate the paschal lamb and was crucified
on the first day of the festival, as the synoptic Gospels
say, celebrated *pascha* on the fifteenth day of Nisan.
These were the anti-Quatrodecimans.[94]

The Investigation Before the High Priest

Although the Gospels are based upon common oral
traditions, there are some discrepancies in their accounts
of the arrest and trial of Jesus which cannot be explained.
According to Mark, Judas came with a great, armed
multitude from the high priest, scribes, and the elders,
and he betrayed his master with a kiss. Jesus complained
against them for coming with swords as if he were a
lestes, a robber. Further, he said that he was in the
Temple teaching and no one had ever molested him. He
was then led away to the house of the high priest where
all the chief priests, the elders and the scribes were assembled. All the disciples fled, except Peter, who followed
his master. While Peter was in the courtyard, he was
asked whether he was associated with Jesus of Nazareth.
He denied that he was. They recognized him as a
Galilean and therefore concluded that he must have
known Jesus. He said, "I know not this man of whom you
speak."

The high priests and all the members of the *synedrion*
sought testimony against Jesus to put him to death,
but found none. Some men testified falsely that they
heard Jesus say that he would destroy the Temple
that was made by human hands, and that he would
within three days build another not made by human
hands. The high priest asked Jesus what he had to say,
but Jesus did not answer. Then the high priest asked him,
"Art thou the messiah (Christ) the son of the Blest?"
And Jesus said, "I am, and ye shall see the Son of Man
sitting on the right hand of Power (God) and coming in
the clouds of heaven." The high priest, on hearing these

words, rent his clothes and exclaimed, "What need we any further witnesses? You have heard the blasphemy: What think ye?" And they all condemned him, as guilty of death. The following morning the chief priests held a consultation with the elders, the scribes and the whole *synedrion*, and delivered Jesus over to Pilate.[95]

Matthew gives the same account with slight variations.[96] Luke presents a different picture of the arrest. He does not say that the elders and the scribes were assembled in the house of the high priest when Jesus was arrested. He states that the morning after Jesus' arrest, "The elders of the people, the chief priests and the scribes came together and led him into their *synedrion* (their council)."[97] He was then asked, "Art thou the Messiah (Christ)? Tell us." Jesus answered, "If I tell thee, thou will not believe." This Gospel makes no mention of the high priest's accusation of blasphemy against Jesus. It says that when Jesus was delivered to Pilate he was accused of "perverting the people and forbidding giving tribute to Caesar, saying that he himself is a Messiah, a king."

There is a sharp disagreement among the synoptic Gospels themselves. According to Mark and Matthew, the scribes and the elders were assembled in the house of High Priest Caiaphas, and Jesus was examined and charged with blasphemy.[98] Jesus did not use abusive language against God. Even had he used such language, a person who does so cannot be condemned to death by a court according to Judaean law; he would be punished only by divine visitation.[99] Only a person "cursing God by the name of God" was liable to capital punishment.[100] Jesus did not curse God. His declaration that he would sit on the right hand of Power (God)[101] and come on the clouds of heaven cannot be considered blasphemy under Judaean law or even custom. Many a pious Jew then confidently anticipated a future world where they would sit in the company of God and enjoy the divine glory.

According to Luke, Jesus was interrogated on the first day of Passover, and was asked only whether he was the

Messiah. When the multitude delivered him over to Pilate, they accused him of perverting the nation, of forbidding the people to pay tribute to Caesar, and of saying that he was the Messiah (Christ), the King.[102] Luke does not mention that he was condemned to death by the high priest and his council on religious grounds. The accusation against him was political; he was accused of subversion and charged with being a rebel.

The Trial Before Pilate

To continue Mark's account, when Jesus was brought before Pilate, the procurator phrased his inquiry in this way: "Art thou the king of the Judaeans?"[103] Mark says, and the synoptics agree, that it was customary to release a prisoner on the Festival of Unleavened Bread.[104] Pilate asked the Judaeans, "Shall I release unto you the king of the Judaeans?" But, the Gospels continue, the chief priest instigated the populace to ask for the release of Barabbas who, according to Mark, had stirred up insurrection and had committed murder. Pilate then asked them, "What shall I do to him whom you call King of the Judaeans?" They cried out "Crucify him." Pilate then released Barabbas. He scourged Jesus and ordered that he be crucified.[105]

The other two synoptic Gospels give the same account, but again with some variations. Matthew says that when the procurator asked Jesus, "Art thou the King of the Judaeans?" Jesus answered, "Thou sayest." Pilate asked, "What shall I do with Jesus who is called Messiah (Christ)?" When Pilate pronounced sentence, he washed his hands and said, "I am innocent of the blood of this just man." To this the people replied, "His blood be on us and on our children."[106] This account is not recorded in any other Gospel. It must be added that the washing of the hands, symbolizing guiltlessness, was not a Roman custom, but a Judaean one. By no stretch of the imagination can it be supposed that Pilate, who

132

despised Judaean customs, would at such a time have mocked one of their customs.

Luke remains political: When Jesus was delivered over to Pilate he called the chief priests, the leaders and the people and said to them, "You have brought this man unto me as one that perverteth the people; and behold I have examined him before you, have found no fault in this man touching those things whereof ye accused him."[107]

The Theological Interpretations

John's narrative presents a rather different picture. He states that Judas Iscariot had with him a cohort which he received from the chief priests and the Pharisees. When he arrived with the cohort, Jesus said, "Whom seek ye?" They answered that they were looking for Jesus of Nazareth. Then Jesus said, "I am he."[108] They arrested him and led him to the house of Ananus, the father-in-law of Caiaphas. John adds that this was the same Caiaphas who had counseled that it was better that one man should die than that all the Judaeans should die for one man.

Jesus was taken from the house of Annas to the house of the Caiaphas, and the following morning to the judgment hall (*Praeatrium*). The priests and the leaders did not enter it lest "They should be defiled, but that they might eat of the paschal lamb (Passover)."[109] On (for John it is clearly the morning of) the 14th day of Nisan the paschal lamb was slaughtered. This discrepancy as to the correct date cannot be explained as due to different oral tradition. The eve (more precisely, the afternoon before) of the Festival of Unleavened Bread was then a very significant day in the Judaean calendar; people made pilgrimages to Jerusalem from far distant countries for the solemn slaughtering of the paschal lamb. After the sacrifice, as darkness fell, the families gathered to eat of the paschal lamb and chanted hymns in commemoration of the deliverance from Egypt. That night and the following day was the first day of the Festival of Unleavened Bread. No one could have confused slaughtering day with the festival day. If Jesus had been crucified on the day and just at the hours when the paschal lamb was slaughtered, his followers would have been so impressed that no tradition could have arisen to place the crucifixion one day later, on the first day of the Festival of Passover. And the opposite is also true: If Jesus had been crucified on the first day of the Festival of Unleavened Bread, no tradition would place the crucifixion on the day the paschal lamb was slaughtered.

The explanation of this confusion of dates lies in a different direction entirely: it is not a confusion of dates, but a difference of theological accent. The synoptic Gospels conceived of Jesus as the savior, personifying the idea of salvation in the Passover festival.[110] He suffered death for the sins of the people and, in his death and resurrection, fulfilled the words of the prophet of Israel. Just as the Israelites were saved from Egyptian slavery on the first day of Passover, having smeared the blood of the paschal lamb on their doors as a symbol of unity between God and Israel, so the blood of Jesus served as a symbol of unity between God and the followers of Jesus. The Gospel according to John, on the other hand, presented the view of Jesus as the redeemer, personifying the paschal lamb. Just as the paschal lamb was sacrificed on the eve of Passover, so Jesus the Redeemer was crucified on the fourteenth day of Nisan to redeem the world from original sin. So the evangelist said, "Behold the Lamb of God which taketh away the sin of the world."[111] In his narrative of the crucifixion, John says that "when they came to Jesus and saw that he was dead already, they brake not his legs."[112] He was alluding to the paschal lamb, of which the Pentateuch says, "a bone of him shall not be broken."[113]

While there is a discrepancy between the synoptic Gospels and the Fourth Gospel as to the date of the crucifixion, they agree on the day of the week; both say that it was a Friday. Again, this has a theological meaning. According to tradition, Friday saw the creation of Adam; on Friday he committed the original sin and was condemned to death.[114] He also died on Friday. So Jesus, the redeemer from the original sin, had to be tried and put to death on Friday.[115] It all had a theological rather than a historical meaning.

John continues: since the chief priests would not enter the judgment hall, Pilate himself went there. He called Jesus in and questioned him, "Art thou the king of the Judaeans?" Jesus asked Pilate if someone had told him this or whether this was his own thought. Pilate retorted, "Am I a Judaean?" and stated that the Judaeans and the chief priests had delivered him. Then Pilate asked, "What hast thou done?" Jesus answered, "My kingdom is not of this world." Pilate did not comprehend this and asked Jesus, "Art thou king then?" To this Jesus replied, "Thou sayest that I am king."[116]

John then gives the same account as to the release of Barabbas or the King of the Jews. After Barabbas is chosen, he asked them concerning Jesus, and the chief priests and their subordinates cried out, "Crucify him!"[117] Pilate then told them to take Jesus and crucify him themselves, since he found no fault with him. The Judaeans answered that according to the Torah, he ought to die because he had proclaimed himself "the Son of God."[118] When Pilate heard this he was frightened and again examined Jesus, but this time Jesus gave him no answer. John states that Pilate again wanted to release Jesus, but the Judaeans asserted, "If thou let this man go thou art not Ceasar's friend." John adds that it was on the day of preparation (Friday), on the sixth hour (noon), that Pilate brought Jesus forth a last time and said to the Judaeans, "Behold your king!" The people cried out, "Crucify him!" Pilate again asked the Judaeans, "Shall I crucify your king?" The chief priest answered, "We have no king but Caesar."[119]

Pilate delivered Jesus to be crucified. He was crucified between two other men, *lestaie*, robbers, one on each side.[120] For the *titulus* which was put on the crucifix to

135

indicate the victim's crime, Pilate ordered inscribed in Hebrew, Greek and Latin the words "Jesus of Nazareth, King of the Judaeans."[121] The chief priest urged Pilate not to put this inscription up. Pilate answered, "What I have written I have written." After Jesus was crucified the soldiers divided his garments into four parts among themselves.[122]

The Course of Events

A historical reconstruction of the ministry of Jesus may now be given: During the reign of Tiberius Caesar, in the year 29, Jesus of Nazareth began his ministry. It was concurrent with that of John the Baptist. Jesus had a following in Galilee while John the Baptist was still actively occupied with his mission. The followers of Jesus believed him to be the Messiah, the Son of God and King of Israel; some of them wanted to proclaim him king.[123] Jesus felt that the time for this had not yet come and resisted their importunities.

During those years Jesus went to Jerusalem several times, particularly on the Festivals of Passover and Tabernacles. While Jesus visited Jerusalem he attended the Temple and preached his gospel of the imminent coming of God's kingdom. Undoubtedly he mingled with the Apocalyptists who actively awaited the advent of a messiah, a scion of David. These activities brought him into conflict with the effective civil leaders, the high priests and their followers. Moreover, his association with sinners, publicans, and women of low repute, and his laxness in the observance of traditional laws, antagonized the Sadducees and Essenes and brought about clashes between him and the Pharisees. Those who embraced the Fourth Philosophy, the followers of Judas of Galilee, looked upon him with contempt, as a dreamer and deceiver.

After the execution of John the Baptist, many of the disciples of Jesus wanted him to go to Jerusalem. Others were opposed to his going there as they feared that he would be imprisoned or executed. Nevertheless, Jesus decided to go to Jerusalem even though he felt certain he would share John's fate. With the approach of the Festival of Passover, in the spring of the year 34, Jesus went to Jerusalem.

At that time Judaea was ruled like a conquered country by a Roman procurator. The Romans punished severely anyone who incited the people against Rome's authority. They held the local Judaean leaders responsible—hostages, as it were—for the submissiveness of the entire populace. Under such oppressive circumstances many informed on the dissenters among their own people, thus saving their own positions and even their lives, hoping, at best, to have prevented more punitive measures against Judaea as a whole.

When Jesus arrived in Jerusalem his followers acclaimed him as the Son of David and King of Israel. The high priest and his associates, in order to save themselves and the country, thought it best to deliver Jesus to Pilate as a rebel. The chief priest assembled a *synedrion* of his associates, friends and retainers. (The term *synedrion* should not be confused with *sanhedrin*, which denotes a religious court. The latter term came into use only after the destruction of the Temple. During the time of Jesus the religious court was called *Bet Din*).

When Jesus was brought before the *synedrion*, he was interrogated about his teachings, especially whether he had claimed to be the messiah, and therefore King of the Judaeans, and he was asked if he was the messiah. The Judaean leaders were highly sensitive on this score. Judaeans from all over the country had come on pilgrimage to Jerusalem, and the civil authorities were fearful that if Jesus claimed to be the messiah he might trigger a rebellion against Rome.

The following morning, Jesus was delivered to Pilate. The *synedrion* charged him with perverting the people by prohibiting them from paying tribute to Caesar, and by claiming to be the messiah, the King of the Judaeans. It seems reasonable that Pilate did not think Jesus would

be a source of danger to Roman rule and so tried to
turn the accusation into one of religious character. The
Judaeans claimed that Jesus was a political offender and
thus they had no jurisdiction. Then Pilate took advantage of the custom of releasing a prisoner for the festival, and asked the Judaeans whether they wanted
freedom for Barabbas, who was a murderer, or Jesus,
their king. The Judaeans asked for the release of Barabbas, being fearful that Pilate was scheming to involve
them as accomplices of Jesus in his claim to be king of
the Judaeans. Again and again the term king occurs
in the sources. Knowing the political situation, this cannot be a religious euphemism. Finally when Pilate again
asked the Judaeans, "Shall I crucify your King?" the
chief priest answered, "We have no king but Caesar."
Then Pilate was satisfied and ordered the crucifixion of
Jesus. Jesus was crucified in the Spring of the year 34.[124]
In that year neither the 14th of Nisan, when the paschal
lamb was slaughtered, nor the 15th of Nisan, the first
day of Passover, fell on Friday or on Saturday.[125] However, if the year 34 was intercalated, that is, another
month of Adar was added, the first day of the festival of
unleavened bread did fall on Saturday. Thus, in accordance with the Fourth Gospel, Jesus was crucified on
Friday, the eve of Passover.

Crucifixion was a regular, hideous, Roman punishment
for political offenders accused of subversion.[126] The two
men crucified with Jesus were executed by the Romans
as *lestai*, or brigands. But this term also has a political
connotation. They were almost certainly *not* common
thieves, but rebels against Roman rule, probably of the
group known as the Fourth Philosophy. They died for
political reasons, and so did Jesus. His *titulus* described
his crime. It should be taken in full literalness: *Iesus
Nazarenus, Rex Iudaeorum*, "Jesus of Nazareth, King
of the Judaeans." No wonder the chief priests requested
Pilate to alter it to read, "He (Jesus) said, 'I am the
king of the Judaeans.'" They feared that Pilate might
even use a dead man's dreams as a pretext by which to

oppress them. The Gospels further state that the soldiers divided the garments of Jesus. This need not be another effort to have the story fulfill Scripture. Since Jesus was executed as a political offender, his clothing belonged to the State.[127] Its minions took what they could.

One more fact deserves notice. Not all the Judaeans present at the trial approved of the execution of Jesus. When he was led to be crucified, Luke states, "There followed him a great company of people and women who bewailed and lamented him."[128] There is no good reason not to give credence to this testimony that many God and freedom-loving Judaeans were in distress on seeing Jesus led to Golgotha.

The historical Jesus died in the Spring of the year 34. He was born a humble Judaean and was crucified as a political offender against Rome for claiming, messianically, to be king of the Judaeans. The ideological Jesus, who revolutionized a large part of the world's thinking and changed the course of civilization, began with the crucifixion.[129]

1. See M.S. Enslin, *The Prophet from Nazareth* (1951); cf. also C.H. Guignebert, *Jesus*, p. 230: "Of facts which can be utilized by the historians, which really bring us near the true Jesus, there are none, or very few, even for those who are not hampered by critical scruples."
2. Cf. S. Zeitlin, "The Christ Passage in Josephus," *JQR*, XVIII (1928), 230-255; *idem, Josephus on Jesus* (1931), pp. 61-70. See Appendix IV.
3. *Ant.*, 20.9.1 (200). Cf. S. Zeitlin, *op. cit.*
4. *Ann.*, 15.44. *Ergo abolendo rumori Nero subdidit reos et quaesitissimis poenis adfecit, quos per flagitia invisos vulgus Christianos appellabat. Auctor nominis eius Christus Tiberio imperitante per procuratorem Pontium Pilatum supplicio adfectus erat; repressaque in praesens exitiabilis superstitio rursum erumpebat, non modo per Iudaeam, originem eius mali, sed per urbem etiam quo cuncta undique atrocia aut pudenda confluunt celebranturque.* "In order to destroy the rumor (Nero was accused of having set fire to Rome), Nero invented a charge of guilt and punished with the utmost cruelty a class of men hated for their vices whom the crowd called Christians. Christus, the founder of the name, had undergone the death penalty in the reign of Tiberius, by sentence of the procurator Pontius Pilatus; but the pernicious superstition was checked only for a moment, only to break out once more, not only in Judaea, the home of the disease, but in the capital itself, where all things horrible or shameful in the world collect and find a vogue."
5. Cf. S. Zeitlin, "Jesus in the Early Tannaitic Literature," *Abhandlungen zur Erinnerung an Hirsch Perez Chajes* (Vienna, 1933), pp. 295-308; *idem*, "Talmud," *Encyclopædia Britannica* (1963).
6. Cf. Eusebius, *Ecclesiastical History*, 2.15; 3.39.
7. Cf. S. Zeitlin, "The Crucifixion of Jesus Re-examined," *JQR*, XXXI (1941), 47-48; M.S. Enslin, *Christian Beginnings* (1938), pp. 386-387; E. Gould, *The Gospel According to St. Mark*.
8. Cf. Enslin, *op. cit.*; Guignebert, *op. cit.*, pp. 35-42, 50-57.
9. Eusebius, *op. cit.*, 3.4. See A. Harnack, *The Date of the Acts and the Synoptic Gospels* (1911); H.J. Cadbury, *The Making of Luke-Acts* (London, 1927).
10. Cf. S. Zeitlin, *Who Crucified Jesus?*, pp. 110-113; A. Loisy, *Le Quatrième Evangile* (Paris, 1921); S.W. Bacon, *The Fourth Gospel in Research and Debate* (1918); H.L. Jackson, *The Problem of the Fourth Gospel* (Cambridge, 1918).
11. Cf. Matt. 2.1.
12. See above, pp. 92-95.

13. Luke 2.1-5. See above, p. 137. Cf. also H.F. Clinton, *Fasti Hellenice* (Oxford, 1830), p. 256; E. Schürer, *Geschichte*, I, 524-527.

14. Tertullian, in his treatise *Against Marcion* (4.19) states that in the time of Jesus a census was taken in Judaea by Sentius Saturninus: *Sed et cenus constat actos sub augusto nunc in Iudaea per Sentium Saturninum aput quos genus eius inquirere potuissent.* Saturninus was the legate of Syria during the years 9-6 B.C.E. It can be seen from another treatise by Tertullian that he erred in his statement. In his treatise *Adversus Iudaeos* 8: *Videamus autem quoniam quadragesimo et primo anno imperii Augusti, quo post mortem Cleopatrae XX et VIII annos imperavit nascitur Christus.* "Let us see, moreover, how in the forty-first year of the Empire of Augustus, when he had been reigning XX and· VIII years after the death of Cleopatra, Christ was born." Thus Tertullian placed the date of the birth of Jesus in the twenty-eighth year after Cleopatra's death. She died in the first day of the seventh month, later renamed Augustus, in the year 30 B.C.E. Twenty-eight years after the death of Cleopatra would be the year 2 B.C.E. Thus Jesus could not have been living during the time of Saturninus, who was a legate in Syria between the years 745-748 A.U.C., 9-6 B.C.E. Cf. also *The Stromata* of Clement of Alexandria (d.c. 217 C.E.). "From the time of the birth of the Lord to the death of Commodus are, in all C and XCIV years, one month thirteen days." Emperor Commodus was slain on the thirty-first of December 192 C.E., which would make the date of the birth of Jesus 2 B.C.E. Cf. also Eusebius, *Ecclesiastical History* 1.5.1-3. Cf. further Clinton, *op. cit.*; Zeitlin, "The Dates of the Birth and the Crucifixion of Jesus," in *JQR*, LV (July 1964), 1-6.

15. Cf. *Stromata*, 1.21. "Others say that he (Jesus) was born on the twenty-fourth or twenty-fifth of Pharmuthe." According to Josephus the Egyptian month Pharmuthe corresponds to the Hebrew month Nisan. Cf. further, S. Zeitlin, *op. cit.*

16. Cf. Matt. 2.5, 22; Luke 2.4.7, 39.

17. Mark 1.9, 24; 10.47.

18. John 7.41.

19. Luke 2.1-20.

20. Matt. 2.9-16; 18-23.

21. Luke 13.32. The fox was regarded as the sliest among the beasts. See Talmud Ber. 61.

22. Matt. 2.6. In giving the genealogy of Jesus as the son of David, the Gospels record two lists. Matthew traces the descent of Jesus from David through his son Solomon. Luke, however, traces Jesus as a descendant of David's other son, Nathan. This is an impressive discrepancy between the synoptics.

One reason advanced for these two different genealogies of Matthew and Luke is that each had a different record.

Even if this were so, the question still remains why did Luke ignore Solomon and his descendants, the kings of Judaea, whose names are recorded in the Bible? Why should Luke record the names of the descendants of Nathan, names which are not recorded in the Bible?

Is not the true reason for these variations in the genealogy of Jesus to be found in this: that Luke had a theological reason for not giving Jesus' genealogical tree through Solomon. Solomon was the son of Bathsheba, who had committed an adulterous act. The Gospel of Luke, therefore, chose rather Nathan, another son of David, as the line of descent through which Jesus' ancestry was to be traced.

23. The modern city of Nazareth is situated S.E. of Sepphoris and S.W. of Tiberias. The name of the city of Nazareth is not found either in the Bible or in the Talmud, nor in the writings of Josephus. Neither the names Nazareth nor Nazarene are mentioned in the Epistles or in the Apostolic Fathers. Therefore some scholars are of the opinion that Nazareth does not designate a city, that Jesus was not born in Nazareth. An attempt was made to explain that the surname of Jesus was derived from the word *netzer*, meaning branch, and that it signifies that Jesus was the offshoot of the stem of Jesse, the father of David. (Cf. Isa. 11.1.) Some suggested that the surname of Jesus was derived from the word *nazir*, which may be translated as "holy," "consecrated." Cf. Matt. 2.23, "And he came and dwelt in a city called Nazareth, that it might be fulfilled, which was spoken by the prophets, he shall be called a Nazarene." See further Ch. Guignebert, *Jesus*, pp. 78-89.

24. Luke 2.21.

25. *Ibid.*, 24. Cf. Lev. 12.6-8.

26. Matt. 13.55.

27. *Ibid.*

28. Luke 2.41-42.

29. Mark 6.3. "Is this the carpenter, the son of Mary, the brother of James and Joses, and of Judah and Simon?"

30. See A. Loisy, *L'Evangile selon Mark* (Paris, 1912); Ch. Guignebert, *La Vie Cachée de Jésus* (Paris, 1924).

31. Luke 3.23.

32. *Ibid.*, 3.1-3. Tiberius became Emperor in the year 14 C.E. Cf. Suetonius, *Tiberius;* Dio, 57.

33. Matt. 3.4, 6; Mark 1.4, 6; Luke 3.3.

34. Mark 9.11-13; Matt. 17.11-13; John 1.20-28.

35. Cf. Mark 1.21, 6.2; Matt. 12.9; Luke 4.15-16.

36. John 4.2.

37. Cf. Matt. 28.19.

38. Acts 2.38; 8.12-13.

39. Cf. S. Zeitlin, "L'Origine de L'Institution du Baptême pour les Proselytes," *REJ* (1934), pp. 61-68.

40. Cf. M.S. Enslin, *Christian Beginnings*, ch. 10, pp. 149-153; S. Zeitlin, "The Duration of Jesus' Ministry," *JQR*, LV (1965), pp. 187-191.

41. Cf. John 3.25-26; Matt. 9.14; Mark 2.18; Luke 7.19-20.
42. Cf. M.S. Enslin, *op. cit.;* S. Zeitlin, *op. cit.;* M. Goguel, *The Life of Jesus.*
43. 1.14. "Now after that John was put in prison, Jesus came into Galilee preaching the gospel of the Kingdom of God." According to John, Jesus went to Judaea with his disciples at the same time that John was baptizing in Enon near Salim. The evangelist added, "for John was not yet cast into prison." (3.20-24.)
44. Ch. Guignebert, *op. cit.,* ch. 9.
45. John 2.13, 23; 5.1; 6.3-4; 7.1-2; 10.22-23.
46. Cf. Clement of Alexandria, *Stromata,* 1.21; Tertullian also states that Jesus' ministry lasted one year, and that he was crucified in the consulate of Rubellius Geminus and Fufius Geminus. *Quae passio huius exterminii intra tempora LXX hebdomadarum perfecta est sub Tiberio Caesare, consulibus Rubellio Gemino et Fufio Gemino. Adversus Iudaeos,* 8.
47. Irenaeus, who lived in the second half of the second century, opposed the view of those who maintained that Jesus' ministry lasted only one year. He asserted that it lasted much longer ... *affirment, dicunt uno anno eum praedicasse, et duodecimo mense passum. Contra Haereses,* 2.22.5. The Church historian Eusebius also maintained that Jesus' ministry lasted not a full four years. *Ecclesiastical History,* 1.10.
48. 1.15. The word gospel has the connotation "good news," a translation of the Greek word *euangelion.* With this word Mark opened his narration bringing good tidings that Jesus, the Messiah, the Son of God, had come.
49. Matt. 13.52-56; Mark 6.4; Luke 4.24.
50. Matt. 9.12.
51. Cf. Mark 9.17; 10.17, 20; 12.14; Matt. 8.19; 19.16; Luke 8.49; 9.38; 10.25; Luke 10.39; 11.1.
52. John 3.2; 1.38, "Rabbi (which is to say teacher)." It is possible that John, writing for the pagans, who were unacquainted with the term rabbi, interpreted it as meaning teacher. The connotation of the term rabbi as teacher came into vogue after the destruction of the Second Temple. John, in describing the controversies between Jesus and the Judaeans and the Pharisees, put into the mouth of Jesus the expression, "your Torah, your law." Cf. John 8.17, "It is written in your law that the testimony of two men is true." Cf. also 10.34; 15.25. The Gospel according to John, by its use of "your" in connection with the Torah, reveals that its message was directed to gentile Christians.

Another example that might well demonstrate the nature of the people to whom the Gospel according to John was written can be found in such phrases "Judaean Passover" and the "Judaean Feast of Tabernacles." This implies that this gospel was intended for gentile Christians to whom such a descriptive adjective as "Judaean" might be necessary. The names "Passover" and "The Feast of Unleavened Bread" are mentioned in the synoptic Gospels but never with the word "Judaean." Since they were written for Judaean Christians, the term "Judaean" would have been superfluous. Cf. S. Zeitlin, *JQR*, XXVIII (1937), 392-394; *idem*, *JQR*, LIII (1963), 345-349. *Idem*, *Who Crucified Jesus?*, pp. 110-112.

53. Cf. Mark 3.11; cf. also Matt. 16.16; Luke 4.3.
54. Mark 2.10, 27; Matt. 16.13. Cf. M.S. Enslin, *op. cit.*, pp. 162 f.
55. Mark 3.14-18; Matt. 10.1-4; Luke 6.13-16. The disciples were Simon (called Peter, meaning rock in Greek), his brother Andrew, both fishermen; James, the son of Zebedee; John and his brother James, whom Jesus surnamed Boanerges (meaning the sons of thunder—they were impulsive and quick to anger); Philip; Bartholomew; Thomas Mark, the publican; James, son of Alphaeus; Thaddaeus; Simon, the Canaanite (the zealot); and Judas Iscariot.
56. Matt. 10.5. According to Luke 10.1, Jesus appointed seventy (two) and sent them out to preach his gospel. Cf. Ex. 24.1; Num. 11.16.
57. Cf. Luke 17.11-16; John 4.40; Mark 7.24.
58. Matt. 5.39-44.
59. Matt. 11.23-24.
60. Matt. 12.30; Luke 11.23. Cf. also Mark 9.40, "For he that is not against us is on our part."
61. Matt. 5.12.
62. Some manuscripts have "a Greek woman."
63. Mark 7.27; Matt. 15.22-26.
64. Cf. Matt. 9.23; Luke 5.29.
65. Luke 7.36.
66. Cf. Mark 3.31-33; Matt. 12.46-47; Luke 8.19-21.
67. Ex. 20.12.
68. Mark 8.29-30; Matt. 16.16.
69. Mark 8.33.
70. Matt. 16.15-20.
71. Cf. M.S. Enslin, *The Prophet of Nazareth* (New York, 1961); M. Goguel, *The Life of Jesus* (New York, 1933); Ch. Guignebert, *Jesus* (New York, 1956).
72. Matt. 17.24-27. Josephus states in *War*, 7.6.6(218), "On all Judaeans, wheresoever resident, he (Vespasian) imposed a poll-tax of two drachmas, to be paid annually into the capitol as formerly contributed by them to the Temple at Jerusalem." This tax was called *fiscus Judaicus*. It was not levied on the Judaeans as an ethnic group, but was rather a religious tax upon those who professed the Judaean faith. According to the Roman historians, Suetonius (*Domitian* 12) wrote, "Besides other taxes, that on the Judaeans was levied with utmost rigor, and those were prosecuted who, without publicly acknowledging that

faith, yet lived as Judaeans." *Praeter ceteros Iudaicus fiscus acerbissime actus est ad quem deferebantur, qui vel improfessi.* . . . Dio also wrote that the tax had to be paid by "all who observed their ancestral customs." It seems that the story recorded in Matthew connecting the payment of the tribute to the Temple with temporal power is an anachronism.

73. Mark 12.13-17; Matt. 22.17-21; Luke 20.22-25.
74. Cf. John 10.40; 11.7.
75. Mark 10.32-33; John 11.8.
76. That Jesus took this road instead of the usual way through Samaria and Judaea may indicate that Jesus and his disciples wanted to avoid the populated country where most of the inhabitants were hostile and the Roman authorities had many spies to keep surveillance over any manifestation that might lead to a disturbance.

There has been considerable debate as to the historical value of the Gospel according to John. Many scholars maintain that this gospel is a work of theology devoid of historical value. On the other hand, New Testament scholars are of the opinion that the Gospel according to John presents reliable historical information about Jesus, Cf. A.J.B. Higgens, *The Historicity of the Four Gospels* (London, 1960); R. E. Brown, *The Gospel According to John*, The Anchor Bible (New York, 1966).

The synoptic Gospels, as well as the Gospel according to John, are based on tradition which the authors had either in writing, or, most probably, by oral transmission. To present the life of Jesus, a historian must carefully examine all the sources available. It seems that the duration of Jesus' ministry as well as his visits to Jerusalem as given by John offer the correct historical information and are supported by some of the early Church Fathers.

77. Mark 11.1; Matt. 21.1-2; Luke 19.29-30.
78. Mark 11.8-9; Matt. 21.9.
79. John 12.13.
80. Mark 14.3.
81. Mark 11.15; Matt. 21.12.
82. Luke 19.45; cf. also John 2.13-16.
83. John 11.47-50.
84. Mark 14.1.
85. Matt. 26.3.
86. Luke 22.1.
87. Mark 14.10-11; Matt. 26.14-16; Luke 22.3-6.
88. John 13.27-30.
89. Mark 14.12-26; Matt. 26.19-29; Luke 22.7-20.
90. Cf. John 13.21-30.
91. Mark 14.43-65; 15.1; Matt. 26.47-75; 27.1; Luke 22.47-71.
92. John 18.26.

93. On the schism, cf. Eusebius, *The Ecclesiastical History*, 5.23-24; Ch. Guignebert, *Jesus*, p. 426, and the literature there quoted.

94. Many New Testament scholars have tried in various ways to reconcile this contradiction. All critical, objective scholars of the New Testament have held that this contradiction is irreconcilable. See C.S. Davidson, *An Introduction to the Story of the New Testament*, vol. II; C. Torrey, "The Date of the Crucifixion According to the Fourth Gospel," *JBL* (1931), pp. 227-241; S. Zeitlin, "The Date of the Crucifixion According to the Fourth Gospel," *ibid.* (1932), pp. 263-271; Guignebert, *op. cit.*, pp. 429-431.

95. Cf. Mark 14.43-72; 15.1.

96. Cf. Matt. 26.47-75; 27.1-26.

97. Cf. Luke 22.66, 67; 23.2.

98. Mark 14.53, 65; Matt. 26.57-68.

99. Talmud Kerit. 7.

100. M. Sanh. 7.5.

101. The term "Power" was one of the circumlocutions for God.

102. Luke 23.2.

103. Mark 15.2; Matt. 27.11; Luke 23.3; John 18.33.

104. This custom is recorded only in the Gospels. There is no mention of it in rabbinic literature.

105. Mark 15.9-15.

106. Matt. 27.11-26.

107. Luke 23.13-25.

108. John 18.2-5, 12-14.

109. *Ibid.*, 18-28.

110. Cf. Justin Martyr, *Dialogue with Trypho*, 72. "This Passover is our Saviour and our refuge." Cf. also *ibid.*, 111, "And as the blood of the Passover saved those who were in Egypt, so also the blood of Christ will deliver from death those who have belief."

111. John 1.29.

112. *Ibid.*, 19.33.

113. Num. 9.12.

114. Cf. II Baruch 23.4-7.

115. Cf. Irenaeus, *Contra Haereses* 5.23. *Manifestum est itaque, quoniam in illa die mortem sustinuit Dominus, obediens Patri, in qua mortuus est Adam inobediens Deo. In qua autem mortuus est, in ipsa et manducavit. Dixit enim Deus: "In qua die manducabitis ex eo, morte moriemini. Hunc itaque diem recapitulans in semetipsum Dominus, venit ad passionem pridie ante sabbatum, quae est sexta conditionis dies, in qua homo plasmatus est.* "It is clear that the Lord suffered death, in obedience to His Father, upon that day on which Adam died while he disobeyed God. Now he died on the same day in which he did eat. For God said, 'On that day on which ye shall eat of it, ye shall die by death.' The Lord, therefore, capitulating in Himself this day, underwent his suffering upon the day proceeding the

Sabbath, that is the sixth day of the creation, on which day man was created; thus granting him a second creation by means of his passing, which is that [creation] out of death."

116. John 18.33-37.
117. *Ibid.*, 19.6.
118. There is no Jewish law, either in the Bible or in the Talmud, to the effect that a person who claimed to be the "Son of God" is liable to capital punishment. The use of the expression "Son of God" was common among the Apocalyptists. In the book of Enoch 105.2, the expression is found "And I and My Son."
119. John 19.12-15.
120. Cf. Mark 15.24.
121. John 19.19. Cf. Suetonius, *Caligula*, 32.
122. John 19.22-23. According to the Roman law, at the time of Jesus, the executioners took the minor spoils of those whom they crucified. This confirms the opinion that Jesus was put to death as a political offender, for in the case of anyone put to death by the religious Sanhedrin, his property belongs to his heirs; but the property of anyone put to death for political reasons belongs to the state. Cf. Sanh. Tosefta, *ibid.*, 4.
123. John 6.15.
124. Cf. S. Zeitlin, "The Duration of Jesus' Ministry," *JQR*, LV (1965), 200.
125. Cf. Ch. Guignebert, *Jesus*, p. 432. "It is possible that the tradition knew that Jesus died about the time of Passover. This fact, together with the desire to connect the institution of the Eucharist with the Last Supper, brought about the transformation of the Supper into the paschal meal."
126. In the opinion of Cicero, crucifixion is *crudelissimum teterrimumque supplicium.*
127. Cf. note 122.
128. Cf. Luke 23.27.
129. See further below, pp. 323-331.

Jesus and the Pharisees

By Solomon Zeitlin

It is understandable, therefore, that Jesus had disputations with the Pharisees. The synoptic Gospels record only one controversy with the Sadducees, in reference to resurrection,[83] since the Sadducees denied this belief entirely, spiritually as well as physically. No reference to the Essenes is found in the synoptic Gospels, since they were not interested in the destiny of the people as a whole. Thus it was with the Pharisees that Jesus had his collisions, for though the fundamental principles of the Apocalyptists were Pharasaic, their extension by the Apocalyptists, and their actions and attitude towards the law, were vehemently opposed by the Pharisees. A wide gulf developed between them.

This is reflected in the controversies between Jesus and the Pharisees, as recorded in the synoptic Gospels. The Gospels record that Jesus went to the cornfields on the Sabbath, and his disciples plucked the ears of corn:[84]

The Pharisees said unto him; Behold, why do they on the Sabbath day that which is unlawful? And he said unto them, Have ye not read what David did when he was hungered, and they that were with him? How he went into the house of God, and did eat the shewbread which was not lawful for him to eat, neither for them which were with him, but only for the priests? Or have ye not read in the Torah how on the Sabbath day the priests in the Temple profaned the Sabbath

148

and are blameless? And he said unto them, the Sabbath
was made for man, and not man for the Sabbath. For the
(son of) man is lord even of the Sabbath day.

According to the Pentateuch, no work can be done on
the Sabbath day. Sacrifices, however, were brought to
the Temple on the Sabbath, and the priests performed
their duties on this day. This work was not considered a
profanation of the Sabbath, in pentateuchal or Pharisaic
eyes, since it was connected with the Temple. The
Pharisees also allowed the profanation of the Sabbath in
order to save a man's life.[85] Jesus claimed dispensation
from the Sabbath law on the ground that he was the
(son of) man, hence a priest, and thus "lord even of the
Sabbath day." Jesus further argued his rights by stating
that David, with whom he associated himself, once ate the
consecrated shewbread, which was the bread of the
priests, thus demonstrating man's right against the law.
The Pharisees contested Jesus, saying that David ate of
the shewbread properly because it was a matter of life or
death; but that was not true of Jesus' disciples. Since
they rejected him as (the son of) man, or the Anointed
of Adonai, he was not a priest, nor was his work connected with the Temple, nor could he be called the "Lord
of the Sabbath."[86]

Some of the disputations between Jesus and the
Pharisees that are given in the Gospels are anachronistic.
Both Mark and Matthew record a controversy between
Jesus and the Pharisees regarding the washing of hands
before meals. However the institution of the washing of
hands before meals took place only after the year 65
C.E. to ease the burden of the laws of purity and impurity
upon the people.[87] The Pharisees could not, therefore,
have complained to Jesus, at a much earlier date, that his
disciples did not wash their hands before meals. Jesus
countercharged that the Pharisees rejected the commandment of God in order to keep their own traditions,
"For Moses said, honor thy father and thy mother, and
who so curseth father or mother, let him die the death.

But yé say, if a man shall say to his father or mother that by whatsoever thou mightest be profited by me is corban, [a vow], ye shall be free and ye suffer him no more to do aught for his father or his mother; making the word of God of none effect through your tradition, which ye had delivered."[88]

This dispute, like some others, shows their different attitudes toward man and society. According to the tannaitic law, based on the pentateuchal provision that a man shall not break his word, a vow has high sanctity and must be kept.[89] If, therefore, a man took a vow against a pentateuchal precept, he must still keep his vow and not observe the precept, though he makes himself liable to God's punishment for not fulfilling it. Thus the interpretation of the problem by Jesus is correct. However, to avoid a clash between two commandments in the Pentateuch—namely, "Honor thy father and thy mother," and "He shall not break his word"—the sages introduced a legal fiction to circumvent their own ruling on the stringency of vows. If a man vowed not to honor his father and his mother, he could in such a case absolve himself of his vow. This is called in tannaitic literature the "invalidation of vows."[90] The dispute reflects the differing concerns and interests of the Pharisees and Jesus. The Pharisees, as men of law and counsel. took cognizance of human weakness and knew that a person might transgress a precept. A son, on the impulse of anger, might vow not to honor his father and mother and the Pharisees, by their ruling, sought to find a way to give him the opportunity for readjustment. Jesus, as an ethical teacher, was so concerned to reach a utopian society that, disregarding man's frailty, he could not tolerate a person's ever transgressing God's laws.

This basic difference of outlook becomes evident when one contrasts the views of the Pharisees with those reflected in the Sermon on the Mount. This magnificent collection of ethical sayings which, according to tradtion, Jesus delivered somewhere in Galilee is the heart of Christianity's ethical and religious message to mankind.

In 'scrutinizing both versions of the Sermon on the Mount,[91] one finds the utopian ethical tone reminiscent of Apocalyptist writings. To take a famous example, Jesus says:

> Ye have heard that it hath been said: An eye for an eye, and a tooth for a tooth; but I say unto you that ye resist not evil; but whosoever shall smite thee on the right cheek, turn to him the other also. And if any man will sue thee at law and take away thy coat, let him have thy cloak also.

The pentateuchal law cited is called the *lex talionis,* or the law of *talio.* To understand this regulation one must bear in mind that the ancients had conceptions of the nature of crime and wrongdoing different from the moderns. Many wrongs which today are considered crimes against the state, and which the state is empowered to punish, were not so regarded in ancient times. They were held to be crimes and wrongs done by individuals against individuals, so that punishment rested in the hands of the individual wronged, or in the hands of his family or the tribe to which he belonged. The state actually had no power to interfere; it was purely a matter between the offender and the man who had suffered the loss. He could absolve the man who caused the injury from punishment entirely, or he could demand satisfaction, such as money, or even take out the eye of the man who caused the loss of his eye. The *talio* was therefore the ultimate limit the injured man could exact.[92]

The attitude of the Pharisees and of Jesus towards the law of *talio* reveals the essential difference between them in many of their controversies over Jewish laws and customs. In the early days of the Second Jewish Commonwealth, the Pharisees also felt the need of limiting the alternatives available under the *lex talionis.* This they did by a legal fiction, limiting the right of the man who suffered the loss of an eye to take out only an eye exactly like his own in size and color. Since it was impossible for two men to have organs exactly the same in every respect,

the injured could not make use of the law of *talio* to effect
bodily injury to his assailant. The injured man had the
right only to demand monetary satisfaction for the loss
of his eye, that is, for the pain, medical care, disability,
and humiliation he had suffered. The law of *talio* was in
reality replaced by a law of monetary compensation.[93]

Jesus, on the other hand, speaks as a utopian moralist
when he says, "resist no evil." He asks them not only to
refrain from demanding satisfaction by *talio*, but not to
resist evil at all. Note that neither by his attitude nor by
his exhortations did Jesus preach against the pentateuchal laws, for he declares:[94] "Think not that I am
come to destroy the Torah or the prophets; I am not come
to destroy but to fulfill." He apparently respected the law
of *talio* as stated in the Pentateuch, but appealed to the
conscience of the individual to rise to such a height that
he would not only not exercise his rights against the
evildoer, but not even resist the evil he was bent on doing.

Jesus approached the problems of his day purely as an
ethical teacher. He disregarded state and society in his
preaching, and addressed himself to the individual and
his needs. He made ethical appeals, seeking the reconstruction of innate human nature. The Pharisees, on the
other hand, sought ethical goals by means of the social
controls provided by the law and its interpretation.

This difference recurs continually. In relation to
divorce, Jesus says,[95] "It hath been said, Whosoever shall
put away his wife, let him give her a writ of divorcement.
But I say unto you, Whosoever shall put away his wife,
saving for the cause of fornication, causes her to commit
adultery; and whosoever shall marry her that is divorced
committeth adultery." Jesus again was not opposed to
the pentateuchal law of divorce, but his opinion was that
Moses permitted divorce only because of the hardness of
men's hearts, marriage being part of the original plan
of man's creation, according to which man and wife
should become one flesh, inseparable, except in the case
of adultery.

On the other hand, though the Pharisees had the same view of the original intention, they maintained that "one flesh" was no longer a reality when the husband ceased caring for his wife. Under such circumstances they believed it better that husband and wife separate; and they permitted either to remarry, both steps being guided by appropriate regulation.[96] The Pharisees thus resorted to legal interpretation to reflect reality and to enhance the possibilities of marital relationships. Jesus, attributing marital discord to sin, sought rather to reconstruct sinning human nature.

Jesus further declared,[97] "Ye have heard it was said by them in old time: Thou shalt not commit adultery. But I say unto you, that whosoever looketh on a woman to lust after her hath already committed adultery with her in his heart. And if thy right eye offend thee, pluck it out and cast it from thee; for it is profitable for thee that one of thy members should perish, and not that thy whole body would be cast into Gehenna."[97a]

The Pharisees, as members of the *Bet Din*, would punish a person only when he had committed an actual act of adultery, but not for his mere intention. They did consider the coveting of a married woman a sin, but this sin could not be punished by a court, only by God. Jesus did not reject the law. He sought to surpass it by stressing the inner significance of one's motives.

The tension between law and ethics is again revealed by Jesus when he said:[98] "Again ye have heard that it was said of them of old time, ye shall not forswear thyself, but shalt perform unto the Lord thy oaths. But I say unto you swear not at all." The Pentateuch records two types of oath; in one, a man makes a solemn vow to God concerning what he will do. In the other, he makes a solemn affirmation before God that his testimony before the court is true. The Pharisees, with their interest in creating a just social order, made one's responsibility when he had sworn an oath a matter of great legal concern. Jesus, whose ethical idealism wanted man's intentions to be trustworthy beyond doubt was therefore against the taking of any oaths.

The same approach is evident in the saying:[99] "Ye have heard it was said to the ancients, thou shalt not commit murder, and whosoever shall do so shall be in danger of the judgment. But I say unto you that everyone who is angry with his brother shall be liable to the judgment, and whosoever shall say to his brother Raca, shall be liable to the Sanhedrin, but whosoever shall say thou fool, shall be liable to the Gehenna of fire." According to Pharisaic law a court could not indict a person for his intent to commit a crime or for harboring feelings of violence. Jesus once again goes beyond the pentateuchal requirement and makes motive and not action the standard of judgment.

The apogee of Jesus' ethics is reached in the statement:[100]

Ye have heard that it hath been said, thou shalt love thy neighbor and hate thine enemy. But I say unto you, love your enemies, bless them that curse you, do good to them that hate you, and pray for them which despitefully use you and persecute you.

It must be pointed out that the saying, "hate thine enemy," does not occur either in the Bible or in the tannaitic literature. Nonetheless, according to Jesus, a man is supposed to love not only his neighbor but also his enemy. The need to desist from acts of revenge can easily be understood. It is conceivable that a man who was wronged should be enjoined not to hate a culprit who was mentally unbalanced or might have committed the crime unintentionally. But if a man deliberately breaks into the home of his fellow-man and callously kills his children, as has happened repeatedly, shall he love that murderer? To ask the victim to love his torturer approaches the humanly impossible.[101]

Jesus either did not fully comprehend the nature of human beings or else wanted his teachings to be a utopian standard to which mankind should strive. His apocalyptic vision may be seen in his concern for the coming kingdom as contrasted to this world. Thus, other Apocalyptists, the authors of the Twelve Patriarchs, could say,[102] "If any man seek to do evil unto you, do him a good turn and pray for him." Judging human nature by the history of the last two millennia, it may be said that it is possible for a man to love his neighbor, that it may even be possible not to despise his enemy, but it is impossible for a man to love his enemy. Men are not only not ready for the millennium, but bitter and deep hatred still exists in the hearts of men, even among Jesus' followers. Seneca rightly said,[103] "We are mad, not only individually but nationally. We check homicide and isolate murderers; but what of war and the much vaunted crime of slaughtering whole peoples?" Utopian ethics can be practiced only in a utopian world.

83. Mark 12.18-27; Matt. 22.23-33; Luke 20.27-40.
84. Mark 2.23-28; Matt. 12.1-8; Luke 6.1-5.
85. Ex. 20.10. Cf. Talmud Yoma 85.
86. Cf. S. Zeitlin, *The Pharisees and the Gospels* (1938).
87. Mark 7.1-5; Matt. 15.1-6. S. Zeitlin, "The Hakala in the Gospels," in *HUCA*, I.
88. Mark 7.10-11; Matt. 15.4-6. Cf. S. Zeitlin, *Who Crucified Jesus?*, pp. 132-135. The word *corban* does not have the meaning of a gift, but of a vow. See S. Zeitlin, *The Pharisees and the Gospels*, ad loc.
89. Deut. 23.24; Num. 30.8.
90. Cf. M. Ned. 11.11; cf. S. Zeitlin, *op. cit.*
91. Matt. 5.3-48; Luke 6.20-49.
92. The *actio furti* can be brought by the person who was injured.
93. Josephus, *Ant.*, 4.8.35 (280): "He that maimeth a man shall undergo the like, being deprived of that limb whereof he deprived the other, unless indeed the maimed man be willing to accept money; for the law empowers the victim himself to assess the damage that has befallen him and makes this concession, unless he would show himself too severe." Cf. also S. Zeitlin, *Who Crucified Jesus?*, pp. 119-121.
94. Matt. 5.17.
95. Mark 10.2-12; Matt. 5.31-32, 19.3-9; Luke 16.18.
96. Cf. M. Gitin 9.10.
97. Matt. 5.27-30.
97a. On the term Gehenna, see below p. 342.
98. Matt. 5.33-34.
99. Matt., *ibid.*, 20-22.
100. Matt., *ibid.*, 43-44. Cf. Luke 6.27-29.
101. The ethical teachings of the sages are far more practical than those of Jesus. Hillel laid down the golden rule when he said, "What thou hatest for thyself, do not do to thy fellow man." Hillel's golden rule may not be superior to the saying of Jesus, but is more in accord with the realities of human nature, and lies within the realm of possibilities.
102. The Testament of Joseph (18.2). Cf. Tobit 4.15.
103. *Epistle*, 95. *Non privatim solum sed publice furimus. Homicidia compescimus et singulas caedes; quid bella et occisarum gentium gloriosum scelus?*

The Teaching of Jesus

By Joseph Klausner

I. GENERAL NOTE

Jesus was not a philosopher who devised a new theoretical system of thought. Like the Hebrew Prophets, and like the Jewish sages from *Talmud* times till the close of the Spanish period, he put forward religious and ethical ideas which closely concerned the conduct of ordinary, daily life; and he did this whenever the occasion warranted it. Something might happen: Jesus utilizes the opportunity to draw some religious or moral lesson. Only rarely did he practise instruction for instruction's sake and piece together thoughts, sayings and proverbs, unconnected with any specific incident, like the "Proverbs of Ben Sira" or the incidental homilies given in the *Talmud* and *Midrash*.

Mark, for example, gives scarcely any sayings except those bound up with specific events. Yet there existed, prior to the Gospel of Matthew, a collection of sayings (*Logia*) which this Gospel transmits, in longer or shorter selections, as items of independent interest (*e.g.*, the Sermon on the Mount, and the harangue against the Pharisees). Luke follows in part the usage of Mark, and in part the usage of Matthew. It follows from this that where we have treated the life of Jesus in detail in the course of the present work, we have, necessarily, introduced the bulk of his teaching as well.

It is not necessary, therefore, to include in the present section *all* that Jesus taught: it will be enough to make a brief study of the principles of the teaching already given and to supplement it with points not hitherto dealt with. It need, then, be no matter of surprise if our treatment of Jesus' teaching appears scanty as compared with the detailed biography, or if it repeats many matters already touched upon. This is inevitable in view of the nature of the subject and of Jesus' manner of instruction, and the same fact has compelled most of those who have written on the life of Jesus to dovetail the teaching into the life, and not allot to it a special section.

The aim of this book (which is not only to give the life of Jesus but also to explain why his teaching has not proved acceptable to the nation from which he sprang) necessitates a special section devoted to this teaching: but this need not be lengthy after our minute treatment of the life which has included most of the teaching. It is,

361

unfortunately, impossible in this section to keep within the limits of pure, objective scholarship (as has been the aim in the preceding pages); argument and theorizing is inevitable—not from love of argument but from the very nature of the case.

II. THE JEWISHNESS OF JESUS

Despite the animus which Julius Wellhausen usually showed in treating of Pharisaic, *Tannaitic* and even Prophetic Judaism, he was responsible for the following bold estimate: *"Jesus was not a Christian: he was a Jew.* He did not preach a new faith, but taught men to do the will of God; and, in his opinion, as also in that of the Jews, the will of God was to be found in the Law of Moses and in the other books of Scripture." [1] How could it have been otherwise? Jesus derived his entire knowledge and point of view from the Scriptures and from a few, at most, of the Palestinian *apocryphal* and *pseudepigraphical* writings and from the Palestinian *Haggada* and *Midrash* in the primitive form in which they were then current among the Jews. *Christianity*, it must always be remembered, is the result of a combination of Jewish religion and Greek philosophy; it cannot be understood without a knowledge of Jewish-Greek (Alexandrine) literature and of contemporary Græco-Roman culture.

Jesus of Nazareth, however, was a product of Palestine alone, a product of Judaism unaffected by any foreign admixture. There were many Gentiles in Galilee, but Jesus was in no way influenced by them. In his days Galilee was the stronghold of the most enthusiastic Jewish patriotism. Jesus spoke Aramaic and there is no hint that he knew Greek—none of his sayings shows any clear mark of Greek literary influence. Without any exception he is wholly explainable by the scriptural and Pharisaic Judaism of his time.

Although our present Gospels, even the earliest of them, were composed at a time when the Christian Church was replete with religious ideas derived from the neighbouring races, the fact nevertheless emerges that Jesus never even dreamed of being a Prophet or a Messiah to the non-Jews. He has the same national pride and aloofness (*Thou hast chosen us*)[2] for which many Christians now and in the Middle Ages have blamed the Jews. Jesus commands the leper whom he cleansed to show himself to the priest and bring the offering to the Temple as Moses ordained.[3] He also enjoins that a man should bring the offering due from him, but that if he have offended his fellow he may not offer his gift until he first become reconciled.[4]

[1] *Einleitung in die drei ersten Evangelien*, Berlin, 1905, p. 113.
[2] See the *Authorised* [Jewish] *Daily Prayer Book*, ed. Singer, London, 1908, p. 4: "Blessed art thou, O Lord our God, King of the universe, who hast chosen us from all nations."
[3] Mark i. 44; Matt. viii. 4; Luke v. 4.
[4] Matt. v. 23-4.

363

He does not oppose fasting and prayer: he only requires that it be done without pride or display.[5] When he opposes divorce in general and his disciples ask, "Why did Moses command them to give the woman a bill of divorcement and put her away?"—he did not reply that he was come to take aught away from the Law of Moses, but, "Because of the hardness of your heart Moses wrote you this commandment"[6] (precisely as Maimonides interpreted the sacrificial system). He keeps the ceremonial laws like an observing Jew: he wears "fringes;"[7] he goes up to Jerusalem to keep the feast of Unleavened Bread, he celebrates the "Seder," blesses the bread and the unleavened cakes and breaks them and says the blessing over the wine; he dips the various herbs into the *haroseth*, drinks the "four cups" of wine and concludes with the *Hallel*.

It was against his *disciples* that the complaint was made that they did not strictly observe the Sabbath and despised the washing of hands: he himself appears to have been observant in these matters. When he sends out the disciples to preach the coming of the Messiah and the near approach of the kingdom of heaven, he tells them: "Go not the way of the *Gentiles*, neither enter into any city of the Samaritans; but go unto the lost sheep of the house of Israel."[8]

Once only does he heal a non-Jew—the daughter of the Canaanitish woman;[9] but to the Canaanitish woman he uses such harsh words that the ears of the most chauvinistic Jew must burn at them: "It is wrong to take the children's bread and throw it to the little dogs"—adding, according to Matthew,[10] words which he elsewhere addresses to the Apostles: "I was not sent except to the lost sheep of the house of Israel." "As a Gentile and as a publican" is with him the strongest term of contempt,[11] and he speaks of the Gentiles as not praying but as using "vain repetitions" ("babbling").[12] So "chauvinistic" was Jesus the Jew!

So far was Jesus from teaching the dogma which later arose— that he was the Son of God and one of the three Persons in the Godhead—that when someone hailed him as "Good master," Jesus replied, "Why callest thou me good? There is none good save one: God."[13] Matthew alone perceived the contradiction between this and the

[5] Matt. vi. 5-7, 16-18.
[6] Mark x. 5; Matt. xix. 8.
[7] The woman with the issue of blood takes hold of the "kraspedon" (hem) of his garment (Mark vi. 56; Matt. ix. 20; Luke viii. 44), but in Aramaic and Greek "kraspedon" is a stereotyped rendering of both "tsitsith" and "kanaf" (see Kohut, *Arukh ha-Shalem*, IV 364, s.v. "Kraspeda").
[8] Matt. x. 5-6.
[9] Mark vii. 24-30. The healing of the centurion's servant at Capernaum (Matt. viii. 5-13; Luke vii. 2-10) does not occur in Mark and is therefore of dubious authenticity.
[10] Matt. xv. 24.
[11] Matt. xviii. 17.
[12] Matt. vi. 7.
[13] Mark x. 18; Luke xvii. 19.

Christian doctrine of his own time: he changed the question and answer to: "Master, what good thing shall I do? . . . and he said unto him, Why askest thou me concerning what is good? There is none good save one: God." The end of the answer does not here correspond with the beginning.

When the same man asks how he shall inherit eternal life, Jesus answers: "Thou knowest the commandments: Thou shalt not commit adultery, Thou shalt not kill, Thou shalt not steal, Thou shalt not bear false witness, Thou shalt not defraud, and, Honour thy father and thy mother."

It is noticeable that Jesus here omits the commandments dealing with man's duty to God (the first four of the Ten Commandments) and introduces a further one dealing with man's duty to his neighbour: Thou shalt not defraud (unless this represents the last commandment, Thou shalt not covet). When the enquirer replies: "All these things have I done from my youth up," Jesus "looked upon him and loved him" [14]—in other words, the outlook of Jesus conformed with that of the most observant of his fellow Jews and was based on the Law.

Yet again, one of the *Scribes* asked Jesus: "What is the first of all the commandments?" and Jesus replies: "Hear, O Israel, the Lord our God, the Lord, is one: and thou shalt love the Lord thy God with all thy heart and with all thy soul . . . this is the first commandment, and the second is like unto it: Thou shalt love thy neighbour as thyself. There is no commandment greater than these."

Thus Jesus gives virtually the same answer as Hillel and Rabbi Akiba to a similar question. The Scribe replies to Jesus: "Of a truth, master, thou sayest well, for God is one and there is none else save he; and to love him with all the heart and with all the soul . . . and to love thy neighbour as thyself is greater than all the burnt offerings and sacrifices." Whereupon Jesus said to him—to the Scribe whom the Gospels treat, together with the Pharisee, as the very symbol of hypocrisy and cant—"Thou art not far from the kingdom of heaven." [15]

The Scribes and Pharisees were not, therefore, so very far removed from Jesus' standards, although he attacked them *generally* (though not nearly to the same extent as we find recorded in the Gospels); and even the great attack on the Pharisees (which Matthew, chapter xxiii, compiled out of isolated sayings, uttered at various times and on various occasions, which, however justifiable in so far as they apply to the worst of the Pharisees, referred to in the *Talmud* as the "Pharisaic plague," are unjustifiable as applied to the Pharisees in general)—even that attack Jesus prefaces by the fine words: "The Scribes and Pharisees sit in Moses' seat (*i.e.*, continue

[14] Mark x. 17-21.
[15] Mark xii. 18-34.

the teaching of Moses and adapt it to present needs) ; [16] all things therefore whatsoever they bid you, these do and observe: but do not ye after their works ; for they say, and do not." [17]

The last words can be applied to the best of religious bodies and to the best of people. The *Talmud* also severely condemns those "who require what is good but do not practise it ;" [18] "Seemly are the words when they come from the mouth of them which practise them ; some there be which require what is good and also practise it : Ben Azzai requires what is good but does not practise it." [19] It was even complained against Tolstoy, the moral giant of our generation, that he "required good" in the way of abolition of property, but did not "practise the good," in that he lived on his own country estate. Yet this did not render his teaching valueless. Is there any system of teaching in the world (that of Christianity first and foremost) which in course of time is not corrupted by its adherents and does not, to a large extent, deteriorate into a condition of "requiring good but not practising it ?"

But the *positive* attitude of Jesus towards Judaism, both Prophetic and Pharisaic, is made clear in the famous passage from the so-called "Sermon on the Mount" (which, as has already been explained, is really a collection of isolated sayings which are, in Mark and Luke, distributed throughout the entire Gospel, but in Matthew artificially collected into a single discourse) : "Think not that I came to destroy the Law or the Prophets: I came not to destroy but to fulfil ; [20] for verily I say unto you, Till heaven and earth pass away, one jot or one tittle [21] shall in no wise pass away from the law till all things be accomplished.[22] Whosoever therefore shall break one of these least commandments and shall teach men so, shall be called least in the kingdom of heaven: but whosoever shall do and teach them, he shall be called great in the kingdom of heaven." [23]

Then follow the words which are an *addition* to the Law of Moses and the Prophets: "Except your righteousness shall exceed the righteousness of the scribes and Pharisees, ye shall in no wise enter

[16] S. Krauss (*The Emperor Hadrian: the first explorer of Palestine, Ha-Shiloach*, XXXIX p. 430) supposes that in the synagogues there actually was a "Seat of Moses" upon which the Scribes and Pharisees used to sit; and this theory receives apparent confirmation from the seat which Dr. N. Slouschz discovered in his excavation of the synagogue at Tiberias. See *Qobetz ha-Hebhra l'haqirat Eretz-Yisrael*, Vol. I, Tel Aviv, 1921, p. 30.
[17] Matt. xxiii. 2-3.
[18] *Hagiga* 14a (R. Yochanan ben Zakkai) ; *Yebamoth* 63b.
[19] T. *Yebamoth* VIII 4 (near end).
[20] Almost the same phrase occurs in Aramaic in the *Talmud* (see above, p. 45 ff.) : "I came not to lessen the Law of Moses nor [but] to add to the Law of Moses" (*Shabb.* 116b).
[21] *Menahoth* 29a, 34a; cf. *Ex. R.* §6; *Lev. R.* §19; *Cant. R.* on *Rosho kethem paz.*
[22] Cf. Luke xvi. 17.
[23] Matt. v. 17-19.

into the kingdom of heaven." [24]   Jesus' displeasure is directed only against those who regard the ceremonial laws as of greater importance than the moral laws: he is far from annulling the former: "Woe unto you Pharisees! for ye tithe mint and rue and every herb and pass over judgment and the love of God: but these ought ye to have done, and not to leave the other undone." [25]   This verse (also occurring in Matthew with slight differences) [26] proves in the strongest possible fashion that never did Jesus think of annulling the Law (or even the ceremonial laws which it contained) and setting up a new law of his own.

But not only from the Gospels is it manifest that Jesus remained a Jew in his positive attitude to the Law generally: there is other tangible and irrefutable evidence.   It is only necessary to read carefully the "Acts of the Apostles" to be convinced that all the Apostles observed the ceremonial laws, visited the Temple, there paid their vows, and generally conducted themselves as true Jews.   Simon Peter, the "rock" of the society which Jesus created (see above, p. 300ff), long resisted the permitting of forbidden foods and the reception of non-Jews into the first body of Christians; Paul opposed his opinion, calling the stricter "Judæo-Christians" "false brethren;" [27] while James, the "brother of the Lord," who did not join the Apostles until after the crucifixion, and who remained a Jew and an orthodox believer in the Jewish religion, changing but one element in it (in place of a *future* Messiah he believed that the Messiah had already come in the person of Jesus)—this same James writes in the Epistle attributed to him (which Joseph Halevy has said might have been written by a *Tanna*): "For whosoever shall keep the whole law, and yet stumble in one point, he is become guilty of all" [28]—thus advocating a severer standard than did the Pharisees.

It is likewise apparent that the earliest Christians, generally, considered that the Gospel of the kingdom of heaven was to be preached for the benefit of the Jews alone: during the first seventeen years after the Crucifixion they made no attempt to spread the teaching of Jesus among the Gentiles. [29]   If, in truth, Jesus had said: "Many shall come from the east and from the west and shall sit with the children of Abraham, Isaac and Jacob in the kingdom of heaven, but the children of the kingdom (the Jews) shall be cast out in outer darkness: there shall be weeping and gnashing of teeth" [30] —it is inconceivable that for seventeen years nothing should have been done to evangelize the Gentiles, or that Paul should have been compelled to contend with Simon Peter and James, the brother of the Lord, on

[24] Matt. v. 20-28.
[25] Luke xi. 42.
[26] Matt. xxiii. 23.
[27] Acts x. 11 and 16; Galatians, ch. ii and elsewhere.
[28] Epistle of James ii. 10.
[29] Galatians i. 13; ii. 10.
[30] Matt. viii. 11-12.

the question of abolishing the ceremonial law and of baptising the uncircumcised.

Jesus was a Jew and a Jew he remained till his last breath. His one idea was to implant within his nation the idea of the coming of the Messiah and, by repentance and good works, hasten the "end." [31]

[31] See B. Jacob, *Jesu Stellung zum Mosaischen Gesetz*, Göttingen, 1893.

III. POINTS OF OPPOSITION BETWEEN JUDAISM AND THE TEACHING OF JESUS

Ex nihilo nihil fit: had not Jesus' teaching contained a kernel of opposition to Judaism, Paul could never *in the name of Jesus* have set aside the ceremonial laws, and broken through the barriers of national Judaism. There can be no doubt that in Jesus Paul found justifying support. In detailing the life of Jesus we have already come across various opposing points of view between the teaching of Jesus and that of the Pharisees (the latter representing traditional and also Scriptural Judaism).

Jesus eats and drinks with publicans and sinners, thereby disregarding ritual separatism and the principles of clean and unclean even to the extent to which they were accepted by the "sages" at the close of the Second Temple period. Jesus, on the Sabbath, heals diseases which are not dangerous. Jesus justifies his disciples when they pluck ears of corn on the Sabbath, thereby lightly esteeming the laws of Sabbath observance.

Jesus attaches little importance to the "washing of hands," and, in the subsequent argument, permits the eating of forbidden foods. Jesus, unlike the Pharisees and the disciples of John, does not fast often, and in answer to protests points out the impossibility of combining the old and the new: "No man seweth a piece of new cloth on an old garment, else that which should fill it up taketh from it, the new from the old, and a worse rent is made; and no man putteth new wine into old wine-skins, else the wine will burst the skins, and the wine perisheth and the skins: but they put new wine into fresh wine-skins." [1]

In other words, whatever change there is must be fundamental and not gradual or partial—not as with the Pharisees, who used to read forced new interpretations into the old Scriptures, changes never intended, in order that such new explanations demanded by daily life might not seem to set aside any principle in the Law. In the opinion of Jesus, such cautious changes, such combining of the old and the new, are nothing more than sewing patch upon patch, patching up an old, out-worn garment which can no longer adhere to the new patches and will, in the end, tear away completely: New matter must take on a completely new form.

As opposed to the *Tannaim* who taught, "Look not at the vessel but at what is contained therein: a new vessel may be full of old

[1] Mark ii. 21-22.

369

wine," [2] Jesus taught that new wine must be contained in a new bottle. Matthew [3] preserves a noteworthy passage to the same effect. After likening the kingdom of heaven to treasure hidden in a field, and telling how, when a man knew of it, he sells all that he has and buys that field; or to a merchant in search of fine pearls who, when he has found a pearl of great price, sells all that he has and buys that pearl; and, finally, to a fishing-net which, spread in the sea, brings up fish of many kinds of which the bad are thrown aside and the good gathered into vessels—after these simple metaphors Jesus asks his hearers: "Do ye understand these things?" and they answer, "Yea, Lord;" whereupon he utters these weighty words: "Therefore every scribe who hath been made a disciple to the kingdom of heaven (μαθητευθεὶς εἰς τὴν βασιλεία τῶν οὐρανῶν) is like unto a man that is a householder, which bringeth forth out of his treasure things new and old." [4]

The point is clear. The Scribes and Pharisees also believe in the kingdom of heaven. But in it they are no more than householders: they are not strong enough to clear away the old for the sake of the new, but overlay the one with the other, the useless and the useful together—just like a householder with his store of possessions. But Jesus, the *king* in the kingdom of heaven, the King-Messiah, is minded to separate the new from the old: the new he would gather into his vessels and the rest he would cast aside.

We saw above how, when one asked Jesus how to attain eternal life, Jesus enumerates six only of the Ten Commandments, precisely those which embody plain, human, ethical principles, but makes no mention of the four which comprise the known ceremonial religious duties (the first four of the Ten Commandments). [5] Not without reason was there attributed to Jesus the apocryphal saying according to which, on seeing a man working on the Sabbath, he said: "If thou knowest what thou doest thou art blessed, but if thou knowest not thou art accursed and a transgressor of the Law." [6]

Such is the subconscious attitude of Jesus towards traditional Judaism. It is instinctive rather than conscious: by his parables and by certain acts of his disciples which he leaves unrebuked, sometimes also by his own doings (such as healing on the Sabbath when the disease was not dangerous), by that juxtaposition of "It was said to you of old time (in the written or oral Law)" and "But I say unto you," and, above all, by his indiscriminate attack on the Pharisees—by these means he so decries the value of the ceremonial

[2] *Aboth* IV 20.
[3] Matt. xiii. 44-52.
[4] Matt. xiii. 52.
[5] See above, p. 365 ff.
[6] Added in Codex Bezae to Luke vi. 4; see A. Resch, *Agrapha*, 2 Aufl., Leipzig, 1906, pp. 45-48; B. Pick, *Paralibomena*, Chicago, 1908, pp. 61-62; and see above, p. 69.

laws as to make them of secondary importance compared to the moral laws, and *almost* to nullify them.

But only "almost:" Jesus never carried his teaching to its final conclusion. He himself observed the ceremonial laws (though not with the scrupulousness and pedantry of the Pharisees) till the last night of his life. Such a final conclusion—the abolition of the ceremonial laws and the consequent opening of the doors to the uncircumcised Gentiles—it was left for another, a Pharisee also, to reach—namely, Saul of Tarsus after he was become Paul the Apostle. But had not Jesus lent some support towards this negative attitude to the ceremonial law and to the body of traditional belief transmitted, generation by generation, from Moses to the Pharisees, Paul would never have supported himself on Jesus in his efforts to overcome the "Christian-Judaism" founded by Simon Peter and James the brother of the Lord.

But Judaism could not agree with such an attitude. For the Jews their religion was more than simple belief and more than simple moral guidance: it was a *way of life*—all life was embraced in their religion. A people does not endure on a foundation of general human faith and morality; it needs a "practical religiousness," a ceremonial form of religion which shall embody religious ideas and also crown every-day life with a halo of sanctity.

Jesus did not give any new ceremonial law to replace the old (except, perhaps, the brief form of prayer, "Our Father, which art in heaven . . ."), and so he taught no new national ways of life in spite of abolishing, or hinting at the abolition of the old ways. By this very fact he raised the nation out of its national confines: for is there not but one moral law for all nations alike? The Prophets, too, found cause for indignation in that the commandments had become a "law of men which could be taught," and that the external, ceremonial laws, such as sacrifices, were made the first principle, and righteousness, judgment and mercy matters of secondary importance.

Yet the Prophets could insist on the observance of the ceremonial laws when they served to fulfil a national-religious need (*e.g.*, the Sabbath in Jeremiah and "Second Isaiah," and circumcision in Ezekiel). Furthermore, even in their stern reprobation we feel a strong air of *nationalist, Jewish* history in its close connexion with the great events of universal human history. Hence the Prophets brought it to pass that other nations "were joined unto the house of Jacob" (as actually happened from the time of the Babylonian Exile till the time of Jesus and the conversion of the royal house of Adiabene). The Pharisees and the *Tannaim*—even the earliest of them—did, indeed, "pile up the measure" of the ceremonial laws, and they so overlaid the original nucleus with a multiplicity of detail and minutiæ as unwittingly to obscure the divine purpose of these laws.

This habit Jesus rightly opposes: but he fails to see the *national*

167

aspect of the ceremonial laws. He never actually sets them aside, but he adopts towards them an attitude as to outworn scraps in the new "messianic garment," and depreciates their religious and moral worth; he does not recognize the connexion which exists between national and human history, and he entirely lacks the wider political perspective shown by the Prophets, whose sweeping vision embraced kingdoms and nations the world over. Hence, all unwittingly, he brought it to pass that part of the "House of Jacob" was swallowed up by those other nations who, at the first, had joined themselves to that part. . . .

The problem is a very wide one and turns on fundamental principles.

All arts and sciences have their root in religion. From religion there developed the early stages of mathematics and indirectly astronomy, music as well as poetry, history in connexion with drama. In course of time the Greeks succeeded in separating art and science from religion and the Romans and European nations followed their example; but with the oriental nations—the Egyptians, the Assyrians and Babylonians, Tyre and Sidon—arts and sciences remained inseparable from religion.

In the East the learned were found only among the priests and higher officials (who also came from the priestly caste). The Jews, likewise, did not succeed in creating sciences and arts independent of religion. In one thing only did they differ from other orientals —they wrested religion from the monopoly of priests and placed its development and exegesis in the hands of laymen; thus they made religion more democratic and, in general, more nationalistic.

We have seen [7] that the "Scribe" (and his successor the *Tanna*) was not only a "Rab" and teacher, but also a lawyer, a judge, a notary (in matters of divorces and contracts), a law-maker, a physician (expert in questions touching the fitness of cattle for food, and menses), a botanist, an agriculturalist (in matters of tithes and mixed crops), and so forth. Similarly Jewish religious literature touches on such topics as algebra, surveying, medicine and astronomy (*e.g.*, in the *Book of Enoch*), zoology and botany, law and politics, history and geography, (*e.g.*, in the *Book of Jubilees*).

These did not approach the status of "science" in the Greek or in the modern sense, but they served as a substitute. They served to widen the horizon, increase the interests in life and enlarge material and spiritual culture. They preserved the national life from concentrating on a confined circle of ethico-religious ideas, and gave it a wider, more vital and more universal scope. As to the excessive meticulousness, reaching to such an extremity of far-fetched definition, hair-splitting, sophistry and casuistry, usually alleged against the *Tannaim*—this lay in the nature of the case: in the wish to embrace the whole of life in all its incidental forms

[7] See above p. 224.

(casûs), the Jewish "sages" were forced to concern themselves even with abnormal and unseemly cases.

For this Jesus, sometimes rightly, found fault with them; but they were right in their fundamental principle, namely, in their desire to bring religion and life together into a higher synthesis, to make religion life, and sanctify life with the sanctity of religion. This does not fit in with the needs of the present time, a time of narrow specialization in the sciences, when politics and culture are kept apart from religion. But in those early days, and in that Eastern world saturated with simple and all-embracing faith, this association of science and art with religion was a great boon to the nation: religion escaped the danger of exclusiveness and one-sidedness, and national life, the danger of stagnation and dryness. If it be a fact that Christianity has endured throughout nineteen hundred and twenty years and attracted thousands of millions of believers, it is equally a fact that *Talmudic* Judaism endures, alive and active, capable of rising superior to the most difficult conditions that human imagination can conceive, and that it possesses the ability of taking a lead in every new movement, both itself creating new things and also absorbing and digesting the best and newest things of others' creation—and this, too, throughout a period of some eighteen hundred and fifty years.

What did Jesus do?

Had he come and said: Instead of religion alone, I give you here science and art as national possessions independent of religion; instead of scripture commentaries—learning and poetry, likewise independent of religion; instead of ceremonial laws—grown so oppressive as to crush the warmer religious feelings—a practical and theoretical secular culture, national and humanistic. Had Jesus come with such a Gospel his name would have endured as a blessing among his nation.

But he did not come and enlarge his nation's knowledge, and art, and culture, but to abolish even such culture as it possessed, bound up with religion, a culture which the Scribes and Pharisees (unlike the Prophets who, though they ignored it in their wider political purview, did not annul it) seized upon and held tightly, as though it were the single anchor of safety left to the nation—a nation not minded to be only a religious community, but a real nation, possessed of a land, a state and authority in every sense.

Civil power!—that is naught: "Give unto Cæsar that which is Cæsar's, and unto God that which is God's;" it is not worth while to fight against the political oppression of Rome, for the political freedom of the nation. What does it matter if you *do* pay tribute to Cæsar, if only you are at peace with the Lord your God!

Civil justice, state efforts at reform of debased social conditions, would be impossible when one must "resist not evil" and when, if struck on the left cheek, the only response is to stretch out the right cheek also! How can the state endure if Jesus requires that a man "swear not at all (ὅλως)"?[8] What culture can there be in the world when Jesus ordains that man shall share all his goods with the poor and teaches that "it is easier for a camel to go through the eye of a needle than for a rich man to enter the kingdom of heaven?"[9] Even family life must break down for one who would be a true disciple of Jesus, since the Messiah accounts praiseworthy those "which make themselves eunuchs for the kingdom of heaven's sake."[10]

How can family affairs be righted if Jesus forbids the divorce of the wife on any ground whatsoever[11] ["save only for fornication"[12] —conforming with the School of Shammai: "except he have found in her a matter of lewdness"[13] —being only a later interpolation]? What interest has he in labour, in culture, in economic or political achievements, who recommends us to be as "the lilies of the field which toil not neither do they spin" but whose apparel is more glorious than that of king Solomon, or like the ravens whose mother birds are careless of their young, but the Holy One, blessed be He, supplies them with food without their labour or care (a thought drawn from, "Who giveth food to the cattle and to the ravens that call upon him,"[14] and paralleled by the *Talmudic* passage,[15] "I have never seen a gazelle a fruit gatherer, a lion a porter, or a fox a shop-keeper [nor a wolf a jar-seller] but they get their food without care)"?

In all this Jesus is the most Jewish of Jews, more Jewish than Simeon ben Shetah, more Jewish even than Hillel. Yet nothing is more dangerous to national Judaism than this *exaggerated* Judaism; it is the ruin of national culture, the national state, and national life. Where there is no call for the enactment of laws, for justice, for national statecraft, where belief in God and the practice of an extreme and one-sided ethic is in itself enough—there we have the negation of national life and of the national state.

To take one example: Jesus said, "Judge not that ye be not judged."[16] This recurs with greater emphasis in Luke and becomes a lofty ethical rule.[17] In the same Gospel occurs this brief incident: "And one of the people said to Jesus, Master, speak, I pray thee,

[8] Matt. v. 34.
[9] The many far fetched explanations of "the eye of a needle" and "the camel" ("small door of courtyard" or "rope") are uncalled for in view of the *Talmudic* expression "the elephant that enters the eye of a needle," *Berachoth* 55b; *Bab. Metz.* 38b.
[10] Matt. xix. 12.
[11] Mark x. 9, 12.
[12] Matt. v. 32.
[13] *Gitt.* IX 19 (end).
[14] Ps. cxlvii. 9.
[15] *Qidd.* 2b; *T. Qidd.* V 15, ed. Zuckermandel, p. 343, note on line 13.
[16] Matt. vii. 1.
[17] Luke vi. 37.

unto my brother that he divide the inheritance with me. And Jesus
said unto him: Man, who made me a judge or a divider over you?" [18]
Jesus thus disregards justice generally, even when it is a case of
natural civil interest, free of any ill motive; he thus ignores anything
concerned with material civilisation: in this sense he does not belong
to civilisation.

Many scholars have concluded that the Gospel of Luke is akin
in spirit to the Ebionites, the earliest Christian heresy, and that consequently whatever Luke contains that is not contained in Matthew
has been revised in a "Communist-Ebionite" spirit. [19] But had not
the teaching of Jesus contained a clear communist tendency, community of goods would never have been the first step taken by the
first Christian brotherhood, [20] nor would James, the brother of the
Lord, the first head of this brotherhood, have been so pronounced an
Ebionite and ascetic.

Again, Clement of Alexandria [21] also tells us that this tendency
towards the abolition of private property and abstention from material pleasures was closely connected with the beginnings of Christianity, and that those who held such views regarded Jesus as their
teacher and exemplar.

Yet again, the beatitude in Luke, "Blessed are ye poor, for yours
is the kingdom of heaven," is the natural form, and corresponds with
the later, "Blessed are ye that hunger," and the corresponding
"Woes:" "Woe unto you that are rich, for ye have received your
consolation; and woe unto you that are filled, for ye shall hunger;" [22]
whereas, on the contrary, the forms, "Blessed are the poor in spirit
(עניי הרוח or עניים ברוח in the sense 'thirst after the Spirit,'
πτωχοὶ τῷ πνεύματι)" and "Blessed are they that hunger and thirst
after righteousness" [23] are by no means natural. They are artificial
expressions which Matthew fashioned after Christianity had absorbed many adherents from the non-Jewish world and some from
the richer classes.

The parable of the rich man and Lazarus, occurring only in
Luke [23a] is not, therefore, an addition by Luke, but it has been omitted
by Matthew (such parables and sayings are on the whole rare in
Mark) for his own purpose. In this parable the rich man commits
no wrong: he inherits Gehenna simply and solely because he was
rich and derived pleasure from this world; and the poor man,
Lazarus, sits "in the bosom" of our "father Abraham" (a common
Hebrew figure of speech) [23b] not because he is righteous nor because

[18] Luke xii. 13-14.
[19] On the Gospel of Luke and its character, see Ed. Meyer, *op. cit.* I 1-51.
[20] Acts iv. 32, 36.
[21] *Stromata* III 6.
[22] Luke vi. 20-25.
[23] Matt. v. 4 and 7.
[23a] Luke xvi. 19-31.
[23b] 49 *Qidd. 72b; Pesiqta Rabbati* §43 (ed. Friedmann 180b); see

he had done good, but simply and solely because he was poor and had
had no joy in this world.

There is certainly no systematic teaching of communism, for
Jesus, in the selfsame Gospel, promises his disciples [24] that "there is
no man that hath left house, or wife, or brethren, or parents, or
children, for the kingdom of God's sake, who shall not receive
manifold more *in this time,* and in the world to come eternal life."
There is no conviction here that private property will disappear,
together with poverty, from this earth: at Bethany Jesus plainly says,
"The poor ye have always with you." [25]   This negative attitude to
property arises, rather, from the non-political and non-cultural stand-
point which was apparent in the beginnings of Christianity in the
Ebionite-Communistic movement.

This negative attitude led the Jacobins, during the French Revolution, to hail Jesus as "le bon sansculotte," and the Bolshevists to
style him "the great communist;" though it is very doubtful whether
Jesus, who opposed the struggle against evil, would have consented
to the terrible murders during the great French, and the still greater
Russian Revolution.   But it is unquestionable that throughout his
entire teaching there is nothing that can serve to the upkeep of the
state or serve towards the maintenance of order in the existing
world.

The Judaism of that time, however, had no other aim than to save
the tiny nation, the guardian of great ideals, from sinking into the
broad sea of heathen culture and enable it, slowly and gradually, to
realize the moral teaching of the Prophets in *civil life* and in the
present world of the Jewish state and nation.

Hence the nation as a whole could only see in such public ideals
as those of Jesus, an abnormal and even dangerous phantasy; the
majority, who followed the Pharisees and Scribes (*Tannaim*), the
leaders of the popular party in the nation, could *on no account*
accept Jesus' teaching.   This teaching Jesus had imbibed from the
breast of Prophetic and, to a certain extent, Pharisaic Judaism; yet it
became, on one hand, the negation of everything that had vitalized
Judaism; and, on the other hand, it brought Judaism to such
an extreme that it became, in a sense, *non-Judaism.*   Hence the
strange sight:—Judaism brought forth Christianity in its first form
(the teaching of Jesus), but it thrust aside its daughter when it saw
that she would slay the mother with a deadly kiss.

also A. Geiger, *Elieser u. Lazarus bei Lucas u. Johannes (Jüdische
Zeitschrift,* 1868, VI 196-201); H. P. Chajes, *Adda bar Ahaba e Rabbi
(Rivista Israelitica,* 1907, IV 137-139); and see also W. Bacher's notes and
the reply of Chajes, *op. cit.* 1907, IV 175-182; *R.E.J.* 1907, LIV 138 n. 1);
cf. *Abel Rabbati (Semahoth)* §8: "When R. Ishmael wept when he was
going out to be killed, R. Shimeon said to him, Thou art but two steps from
the bosom of the righteous ones, and dost thou weep!"

[24] Luke xviii. 29-30.
[25] Mark xiv. 7; Matt. xxvi. 11.

IV. JESUS' IDEA OF GOD

That Jesus never regarded himself as God is most obvious from his reply when hailed as "Good master:" "Why callest thou me good? There is none good but one, God." [1] When the disciples would know the exact time of the coming of the kingdom of heaven, he tells them: That day and that hour no man knoweth, not even the angels of heaven, nor the Son, but the Father only. [2] Jesus is thus not omniscient: he and the Father are not equal in knowledge. When we remember that, in the Garden of Gethsemane, he begs the Father to let the cup pass from him; and that, during the crucifixion, he cries out: My God, my God, why hast thou forsaken me!—it is perfectly manifest that in no sense did he look upon himself as God. Like every Pharisaic Jew he believed in the absolute unity of God, and he turned to God in time of trouble.

Nor did he regard himself as Son of God in the later Trinitarian sense; for a Jew to believe such a thing during the period of the Second Temple is quite inconceivable: it is wholly contradictory to the belief in the absolute unity.

Jesus may have made great use of the terms "Father," "My Father," "My heavenly Father," and perhaps also "Son;" but the last is no more than the Biblical "Israel is my first-born" [3]—other nations are sons of God, but Israel is God's first-born. We likewise find: "Ye are sons of the Lord your God." [4] "I have said, Ye are gods, and ye are all sons of the Highest," [5] "And God shall call thee, Son;" [6] "I will exalt the Lord, (saying) Thou art my Father," [7] "Beloved are Israel, for they are called 'Sons of the Highest;'" [8] and, most noteworthy, the striking passage: "Even if they are foolish, even if they transgress, even if they are full of blemishes, they are still called 'Sons.'" [9]

The phrase "Our Father, who art in heaven" is so common in the *Talmudic* literature as to render quotation superfluous for those

[1] Mark x. 18; Luke xviii. 19; on Matthew's version, see above, p. 364.
[2] Matt. xxiv. 36.
[3] Ex. iv. 22.
[4] Deut. xiv. 1.
[5] Ps. 82, 6.
[6] *Ben Sira* 4, 10.
[7] *Ben Sira* 51, 10. In *Fourth Esdras*, a wholly Pharisaic production, the Messiah is called "My Son" (7, 28-29; 13, vv. 25, 34, 37, 52; 14, 9). See Klausner, *Ha-Ra'yon ha-Meshihi* II 64.
[8] *Aboth* III 3.
[9] *Sifre* on Deut. §308 (ed. Friedmann, 133a and b).

377

with some knowledge of Hebrew.[10] Less common, however, is the use of the singular pronoun, "*My* heavenly Father," though it is somewhat frequent in such expressions as: "What shall I do, when my heavenly Father hath so commanded me?"[11] or "These buffettings have made me to love my heavenly Father;"[12] and we also find the "diminutive of affection:" "Abba who is in heaven," "Since I have done the will of Abba who is in heaven."[13] Jesus undoubtedly used the term "Abba who is in heaven" mainly in the same sense in which it is used in the *Talmudic* literature: God is a merciful father, father of all created things, and like a father he is indulgent and forgiving, good and beneficent to all, from the flowers of the field and fowls of the air, to the sinful wrongdoer, in whose death God finds no pleasure, but only in his repentance.

In this also Jesus is a genuine Jew.

Jesus, however, makes far more use of such expressions as "Father," "My Father," "My Father in heaven," than do the Pharisees and *Tannaim;* and often when he employs it, it receives an *excessive* emphasis. The reason is plain. From the day when he was baptised by John, Jesus looked upon himself as the Messiah, and as the Messiah he was closer to God than was any other human being. On the one hand, as Messiah he is "the Son of man coming with the clouds of heaven" and "drawing near to the Ancient of days;"[14] thus, literally, he is near to the Godhead.

On the other hand, it is he, the Messiah, who is spoken of in the Psalms: "Thou art my son, this day have I begotten thee."[15] In Jesus' time it was never doubted that these words referred to the Messiah, for earlier the Psalm says definitely: "And the rulers take counsel together against the Lord and against his *anointed.*"[16] The Messiah is, therefore, the nearest to God: God is his father in a closer sense than to the rest of mankind.

It was this excessive emphasis which made Kaiaphas, the High Priest, rend his clothes at the trial of Jesus, though Jesus did not then call himself "Son of God;" it was enough that he did not deny that he was the Messiah who was to come "with the clouds of heaven" and "be brought near to the ancient of days" and sit at his right hand ("at the right hand of Power"). Such words were more terrible in the ears of this Sadducæan High Priest, for whom the Messiah was only a great earthly king, than they were to a Pharisee, whose idea of the Messiah was more spiritual.

Arising out of this *exaggerated* sense of nearness to God is Jesus'

---

[10] See, *e.g.*, *Yoma* VIII 9; *Sota* IX 15 (*Baraita*); *Aboth* V 20, etc.
[11] *Sifra* on Levit. "*Qedoshim*" (end), 20, 26 (ed. Weiss 93b).
[12] *Mechilta*, "*Behodesh*," *Yithro*, §6 (end), ed. Friedmann 68b); *Midrash Tehillim* ("*Shoher Tob*") XII 5 (end) (ed. Buber 55a).
[13] *Lev. R.* §32 (a little before "My Father who is in heaven").
[14] Dan. vii. 13.
[15] Ps. ii. 7.
[16] Ps. ii. 2.

constant emphasis and insistence in "But I say unto you," as opposed to "them of old time," *i.e.*, the Law of Moses, the Prophets, and also the Pharisees.[17] A danger lurked in this exaggeration: it unwittingly confused Jesus' pure monotheism; it gave the impression that there was one man in the world with whom God was exceptionally intimate and for whom God bore especial love. Judaism knows this "God-nearness" in connexion with the *Tzaddiq* (the leader among the eighteenth and nineteenth century *Hasidim*); but such nearness was shared by many *Tzaddiqim*, and not claimed by one alone.

This preference of *one* man over the rest of mankind showed a species of favouritism on the part of God, which might induce (and after the time of Paul did, in fact, induce) a more or less idolatrous belief in Jesus as the "Paraclete," the advocate for man before God. Such a conception of the messianic title "son of God," signifying that he is nearest to God of all men (a fundamentally Jewish conception), Judaism was unable to accept. Jesus' own teaching is poles apart from the Trinitarian dogma; but it contained the germ which, fostered by gentilic Christians, developed into the doctrine of the Trinity.

There was yet another element in Jesus' idea of God which Judaism could not accept.

Jesus tells his disciples that they must love their enemies as well as their friends, since their "Father in heaven makes his sun to rise on the evil and on the good, and sends his rain upon the righteous and upon the ungodly." [18] Here it is no case of Jesus' justifying himself against the Pharisees who blamed him for eating with publicans and sinners—"they that are whole need not the physician but they that are sick;" the "sick" are no longer under consideration: both publicans and sinners are "whole" in the sight of God: sinners and non-sinners, evil and good, ungodly and righteous, all alike are of the same worth in God's sight. It follows, therefore, that God is not *absolute righteousness*, but *the good* before whom is no evil ("There is none *good* save one, and he—is God"). He is not the God of justice, in spite of his Day of Judgment: in other words, *he is not the God of History*.

With this, Jesus introduces something new into the idea of God. The *Talmud* also tells how "the rain falls equally for the righteous and for the sinful;[19] as to the sun's rising upon both good and evil (a thought also occurring in Seneca)[20] the *Talmud* relates a remarkable story concerning Alexander the Great and the King of Katsia:[21] when Alexander said to the king of Katsia that in his

[17] See Ahad ha-Am, Collected Works, IV 42-44.
[18] Matt. v. 45.
[19] *Taanith 7a.*
[20] *De beneficiis*, IV 26, 1.
[21] *Gen. R.* §33; *Lev. R.* §27; *J. Baba Metzia* II 6; *Tanhuma, "Emor,"* §9 (ed. Buber p. 88 f.); *Pesiqta d'R. Kahana*, §9 ("*Shor o keseb*"), ed. Buber,

country they would have put to death those two scrupulous men (who had both refused the ownership of certain hidden treasure since they did not, at the time of buying the land where the treasure was found, know of its existence) and confiscated the treasure, the African king asked Alexander: Does the sun rise in your country? and are there lean cattle in it? When Alexander answered in the affirmative, the other remarked: Then the sun rises in your country through the merit of the lean cattle; you wicked rulers are not worthy of it.

Such is the Jewish conception of God: the wicked are not worthy that God's sun should rise upon them.[22] Not that Judaism does not also rate highly the repentant sinners; none say more about the value of repentance than do the authorities of the *Talmud;* it is they who said, "Where the repentant stand, the wholly righteous do not (*i.e.* are not worthy to) stand."[23] But the unrepentant *destroy the world,* they break down the *moral* order, and therefore destroy the *natural* order too. If there is no righteousness in the world, it is not worth while that this world, with its sun and moon and stars and fixed laws of nature, should continue (hence the "Flood").

God is good; but he also requires justice. He is "merciful and compassionate, long-suffering and of great kindness;" but, none the less, "he will by no means acquit the guilty." It is for this reason that the Jews acclaim their God, in the same breath, "Our Father; our King:" he is not only "Father of mercies" but "King of Judgment," the God of the social order, the God of the nation, the God of history. Jesus' idea of God is the very reverse. However lofty a conception it may represent for the *individual* moral conscience, it stands for ruin and catastrophe for the *general* conscience, for the public, social, national and universal conscience, that conscience for which "Weltgeschichte ist Weltgericht;" and such an idea of God Judaism could by no means accept.

pp. 4-5. It is noteworthy that this story of a Greek character is repeated throughout the Jewish *Midrashic* literature but is not found at all in Greek literature; it was not in accordance with the Greek spirit.

[22] See Joseph Klausner, *Torath ha-Middoth ha-Q'dumah b'Yisrael,* Vol. I Odessa, 1918, p. 57.

[23] *Berachoth* 34b; Sanh. 99a.

V. THE ETHICAL TEACHING OF JESUS

The main strength of Jesus lay in his ethical teaching. If we omitted the miracles and a few mystical sayings which tend to deify the Son of man, and preserved only the moral precepts and parables, the Gospels would count as one of the most wonderful collections of ethical teaching in the world. These sayings and parables are to be found chiefly in Matthew and are mainly grouped together in what is called "The Sermon on the Mount." [1] Such sayings are comparatively few in Mark, and those which occur in Luke and are lacking in Mark and Matthew, are open to suspicion as emanating from a period later than Jesus. An attempt will here be made to give the moral principles as we find them in Matthew, using in addition what is common to Mark and Luke,[2] but drawing, in the main, from the Sermon on the Mount.

The "blessed," they whose "reward is great in heaven," are the poor, they that hunger and thirst, the meek, the mourners, the merciful, the pure in heart, the peace-makers, the persecuted, and those who are reviled and blasphemed. A man may not be angry with his brother; [3] he may not call his fellow "rascal" or "fool." Before making a religious offering a man should be reconciled with any whom he may have offended. He who looks on a woman and lusts after her, commits adultery in his heart. He who divorces his wife (and marries another) commits adultery, and a divorced woman who is married to another also commits adultery; for "whom God hath joined together let not man put asunder." Better is it not to marry at all.[4]

"If thy right eye" or "thy right hand offend thee," "pull out thine eye" and "cut off thine hand: it is better that one of thy members perish than that thy whole body go down to Gehenna." [5] It is forbidden to swear any oath, even on the truth. It is forbidden to fight

---

[1] Matt. chh. v-vii.

[2] No treatment of the ethics of Jesus along the lines of objective scholarship yet exists in any language. The best is Ehrhardt, *Der Grundcharacter der Ethik Jesu*, Freiburg, 1895. Christian apologetic works containing unbiassed treatment are: E. Grimm, *Die Ethik Jesu*, 2 Aufl. Leipzig, 1917; F. Peabody, *Jésus-Christ et la question morale* (trad. H. Anet), Paris, 1909; H. Monnier, *La Mission historique de Jésus*, Paris, 1906.

[3] The words "without a cause" are added in the Syriac text translated by A. Merx, *Die 4 kanon. Evv. nach ihrem ältesten bekannten Texte*, Berlin, 1897, p. 9.

[4] Matt. viii. 21-22; also xix. 3-10.

[5] Matt. v. 29-30, and more explicitly Matt. xviii. 8-9.

381

against evil, and "whosoever smiteth thee on thy right cheek, turn to him the other also. And if any . . . would take away thy coat let him have thy cloke also. . . . Give to him that asketh thee, and from him that would borrow of thee turn not thou away." "Love your enemies and pray for them that persecute you . . . for if ye love them that love you, what reward have ye? Do not even the publicans the same? . . . Ye therefore shall be perfect as your heavenly Father is perfect."

Almsgiving should be in secret so that the left hand may not know what the right hand is doing: "When thou doest alms sound not a trumpet before thee . . . in the synagogues and in the streets." Display in prayer is likewise forbidden, or "much speaking as do the Gentiles;" but prayer should be brief, in secret, behind closed doors.

When men pray they must forgive the sins which others have committed against them, that God may forgive them that pray, the sins which they have committed against God. Not once only, nor seven times only, must a man forgive his neighbour who has sinned against him—but seventy times seven.[6] When a man fasts he must not make display of the fact nor change his appearance that men may know that he is fasting; it is enough that his heavenly Father alone knows it. Therefore Jesus, contrary to the accepted Pharisaic usage,[7] allows washing and anointing during a period of fasting.[8]

One should lay up treasure in heaven, by means of almsgiving and good works, and not on earth where "moth and rust doth corrupt and thieves break through and steal." "The lamp of the body is the eye: if therefore thine eye be single, thy whole body is full of light; . . . if the light that is in thee be darkness, how great is the darkness!"

No man can serve two masters, God and Mammon (the world). So let him take no thought for the morrow: "sufficient unto the day is the evil thereof." "Consider the lilies of the field, how they grow; they toil not, neither do they spin, . . . yet Solomon in all his glory was not arrayed like one of these; but if God doth so clothe the grass of the field which to-day is, and to-morrow is cast into the oven, shall he not much more clothe you, O ye of little faith?"

"Judge not, that ye be not judged. For with what measure ye mete it shall be measured unto you." Let not a man look on the mote that is in his brother's eye and ignore the beam that is in his own eye. "All things whatsoever ye would that men should do unto you, even so do ye also unto them: for this is the law and the prophets." To enter into the kingdom of heaven it is not enough to call Jesus, "Lord, lord!" Rather let a man do the will of his heavenly Father.

[6] Cf. Matt. vi. 14-15 with xviii. 21-35.
[7] During an ordinary fast the *Mishnah*, too, permits washing and anointing (*Taanith* I 4 and 5); but both are forbidden during exceptional fasts (*Taanith* I 6) and on the Day of Atonement (*Yoma* VIII 1).
[8] Matt. vi. 16-18

Such are the ethical principles contained in the "Sermon of the Mount." The other ethical injunctions, which may with scarcely any doubt be accepted as genuine, can be summarized as follows:

He that would follow after Jesus may not even go to bury his father: "Let the dead bury their dead."[9] He that loves father, mother or son or daughter more than Jesus, is not worthy of him,[10] "for he that findeth his soul shall lose it, and he that loseth his soul for Jesus's sake shall find it."[11] "Everyone that doeth the will of my heavenly Father, he is my brother and sister and mother."[12] "Be ye hated of all men for my name's sake."[13] "Fear not them that can kill the body but are not able to kill the soul; but rather fear him which is able to destroy both soul and body in hell,"[14] for "what shall it profit a man if he gain the whole world and lose his soul?"[15] "Man is lord of the Sabbath" and "It is lawful to do good on the Sabbath," and therefore it is permitted to pluck ears of corn on the Sabbath and, on the Sabbath, to heal even in cases where life is not endangered.

"Every idle word that men shall speak, they shall give account thereof in the day of judgment."[16] Foolish vows do not bind a man, and unwashen hands do not defile him; what defile a man are evil thoughts and evil deeds—murder, theft, violence, adultery, false-witness and blasphemy.[17] Let none despise or offend children or the innocent or the ignorant, or even sinners; for if a man have a hundred sheep and lose one of them, when he have found the one "he rejoiceth over it more than over the ninety and nine which have not gone astray."[18]

"The first shall be last and the last shall be first."

It is like a king who made a marriage feast for his son and invited the chief people of the city and they did not come; then said he to his servant; Since these came not, summon from the market place and from the way side the wicked and the maimed, that they may fill the places of the guests.[19] "If thy brother sin against thee" reprove him, and if he hearken unto thee, well; if he hearken not, warn him in the presence of two or three witnesses, "and if he refuse to hear them, tell it unto the church (*ekklesia*), and if he refuse to hear the church also, let him be unto thee as the Gentile and the publican."[20]

[9] Matt. viii. 21-22.
[10] Matt. x. 37. A stronger form is given in Luke xiv. 26.
[11] Matt. x. 39.
[12] Matt. xii. 50.
[13] Matt. x. 22.
[14] Matt. x. 28.
[15] Matt. xvi. 26.
[16] Matt. xii. 36.
[17] Matt. xv. 1-20.
[18] Matt. xviii. 1-14.
[19] Matt. xx. 16; xxii. 1-14.
[20] Matt. xviii. 15-17.

The greatest commandment is, "Thou shalt love the Lord thy God with all thy heart and with all thy soul," and the second is like unto it, "Thou shalt love thy neighbour as thyself: on these two hang all the Law and the Prophets." [21] He that would win everlasting life and follow after Jesus, must not only keep the commandments— Thou shalt not kill, Thou shalt not commit adultery, Thou shalt not steal, Thou shalt not bear false witness, Thou shalt honour thy father and thy mother, and Thou shalt love thy neighbour as thyself —but he must also sell all that he has and give to the poor, for "it is easier for a camel to go through the eye of a needle than for a rich man to enter the kingdom of heaven." [22]

In the kingdom of heaven the great ones will not be like the great ones in this world whom *others* serve; but *they* shall serve others as does the Son of man.[23] The sin of the Scribes and Pharisees is twofold: What is of primary importance they make secondary, and what is secondary they make of primary importance; and they pay more regard to the letter of Scripture than to the spirit.[24] He who performs a good work for the humblest of creatures is as though he performed a good work for Jesus' sake.[25] They who take up the sword shall perish by the sword.[26]

The two mites that the widow gives to the Temple treasury are of more worth than the rich offering of the wealthy man: the latter gives of his superfluity, but she of her lack.[27] Let him who feels himself free from sin throw the first stone at the harlot.[28] "It is better to give than to receive." [29]

These are the underlying principles of Jesus' ethical teaching.[30] Not all of these sayings may have been uttered by Jesus, but they are all in accordance with his spirit and they are all of distinct originality. Yet, with Geiger and Graetz, we can aver, without laying ourselves open to the charge of subjectivity and without any desire to argue in defence of Judaism, that *throughout the Gospels there is not one item of ethical teaching which can not be paralleled either in the Old Testament, the Apocrypha, or in the Talmudic and Midrashic literature of the period near to the time of Jesus.*[31]

[21] Matt. xxii. 35-40.
[22] Matt. xix. 16-26.
[23] Matt. xx. 45-48.
[24] Matt. xxiii (the entire chapter).
[25] Matt. xxv. 34-45; cf. x. 42 (end).
[26] Matt. xxvi. 52.
[27] Mark xii. 41-44; Luke xxi. 1-4.
[28] An apocryphal saying, included in the Fourth Gospel, viii. 7, and, in certain versions, in Luke xxi. 38; but actually belonging to Mark xii. 18 or xii. 35.
[29] Acts xx. 35 (Paul in the name of Jesus).
[30] They are collected in a Hebrew translation in *Dibhrē Yeshua*, Leipzig, 1898, a supplement to the two works of A. Resch, *Aussercanonische Parallel-texte zu den Evangelien*, Theile 1-5, 1893-1897, and *Agrapha* 2. Aufl., 1906; and also separately in *Dibhrē Yeshua: Τά λόγια Ἰησοῦ* 1898.
[31] See above, pp. 110 and 114.

Furthermore, sayings similar to those in the Gospels, though found in literature later than the time of Jesus, must have been current orally among the Jews many scores of years before they were fixed in writing in the *Mishna, Talmud* or *Midrash,* because there are no grounds whatever for assuming that the Gospels influenced the authorities of the *Talmud* and *Midrash.* There are ethical sayings attributed to Jesus which recur word for word in *Talmud* or *Midrash.* For example, the saying, "With what measure ye mete it shall be measured unto you," in the Sermon on the Mount [32] occurs in exactly the same form in the *Mishna* (לו מודדים בה מורד שאדם במדה). [33] The parable of the mote and the beam, in the same chapter,[34] is uttered by the early *Tanna* and enemy of the *Gillayonim* and *Books of the Minim,* R. Tarphon: "If he (the reprover) say to him, Take the mote from thine eyes (or, according to another reading, Thy teeth), the other replies, Take the beam from thine eyes." [35] Sufficient for the day is the evil thereof,[36] is a typical *Talmudic* expression.[37]

The bulk of the rest of the sayings are to be found in the *Talmud* in a slightly different shape. For example, the saying, "He who looks on a woman to lust after her hath already committed adultery with her in his heart," [38] is found in the *Talmud* in the form, "He who deliberately looks on a woman is as though he had connexion with her;" [39] or, stated by the early *Amora,* R. Shimeon ben Lakish, "For thou mayest not say that everyone that committeth adultery with his body is called an adulterer; he that committeth adultery with his eyes is also to be called an adulterer." [40]

Jesus' saying, "It is better that one of thy members perish than that thy whole body go down to hell," [41] is also uttered by R. Tarphon, "Better that his belly burst that he go not down to the pit of destruction." [42] As to the forbidding of oaths, the *Talmud* requires "a righteous yea and a righteous nay," [43] and R. Eliezer says, "Yea is an oath and nay is an oath." [44] As a parallel to the requirement that almsgiving should be in secret, and that the left hand shall not know what the right hand does,[45] we have the saying of the early *Tanna,* R. Eliezer: "He who giveth alms in secret is greater than Moses our master;" [46] and that that is the most excellent form of almsgiving when "he gives and knows not to whom he gives, or takes and knows not from whom he takes," [47] while "he who ostentatiously gives alms to the poor—for this, God will bring him to judgment." [48] The Greek translators have probably made a mistake in the passage

[32] Matt. vii. 2.
[33] *Sota* I 7.
[34] Matt. vii. 3-5.
[35] *Baba Bathra* 15b; *Arakhin* 17b.
[36] Matt. vi. 38.
[37] *Berakhoth* 9b.
[38] Matt. v. 28.
[39] *Massekheth Kallah.*
[40] *Lev. R.* §23.

[41] Matt. v. 29-30; xviii. 8, 9.
[42] *Nidda* 13b.
[43] *Baba Bathra* 49b; *J. Shebi'ith* X 9.
[44] *Shebuoth* 36a.
[45] Matt. vi. 3.
[46] *Baba Bathra* 9b.
[47] *Ibid.* 10b (beginning).
[48] *Hagiga* 5a.

where Jesus is made to forbid "the blowing of a trumpet" (when giving alms) in the streets and synagogues;[49] the original reference may have been to the שופר של צדקה, the horn-shaped receptacle for alms, which stood in the Temple and synagogues, and, possibly, in the streets also.[50]

As a parallel to the "treasure in heaven" where "neither moth nor rust doth corrupt nor thieves break through and steal," we may quote the *Talmudic Baraita*: "It happened with Monobaz that he squandered his wealth and the wealth of his fathers (in alms) during a time of famine. His brethren and his father's house gathered around him and said: Thy fathers laid up treasure and added to their fathers' store, and dost thou waste it all! He answered: My fathers laid up treasure below; I have laid it up above. My fathers laid up treasure where the hand (of man) controlleth it; but I have laid it up where no hand controlleth it. . . . My fathers laid up treasure of Mammon; I have laid up treasure of souls. . . . My fathers laid up treasure for this world; I have laid up treasure for the world to come."[51] Here we have Jesus' ideas repeated almost word for word. Again, those "who are anxious for the morrow" Jesus calls "of little faith,"[52] exactly as does the early *Tanna*, R. Eliezer ben Hyrcanus: "R. Eliezer the Great said, He who has a morsel of bread in his vessel and yet says, What shall I eat to-morrow? is of those of little faith (מקטני אמנה);"[53] and in the same way R. Eliezer Modai says: "He who created the day, created also food for the day. Thus R. Eliezer Modai used to say, He who hath ought to eat to-day and says, What shall I eat to-morrow, such a one is lacking in faith" (מחוסרי אמנה).[54]

Within the Sermon on the Mount is to be found the "Lord's Prayer," perhaps the single religious ceremony or institution (except for the appointment of the "Twelve" Apostles, or disciples) which Jesus authorized during his lifetime. He requires of his disciples and followers that "they use not vain repetitions as to the Gentiles, who say in their heart, that they shall be heard by their much speaking."[55] The same thing was said by the author of Ecclesiastes: "For God is in heaven, and thou upon earth: therefore let thy words be few."[57]

Like a real Jew, Jesus regards the prayers of the heathen as "vain repetition," "babbling." He therefore composed this brief prayer: "Our Father which art in heaven, Hallowed be thy name. Thy kingdom come. Thy will be done, as in heaven, so on earth.

[49] Matt. vi. 2.
[50] *Shek.* VI 1; *Erubin* 32a; *Gittin* 60b; *Pes.* 90b.
[51] *Baba Bathra* 11a.
[52] Matt. vi. 30–34.
[53] *Sota* 48b.
[54] *Mechilta*, Exodus, "*Way'hi b'shallach*," §2 (ed. Friedmann 47b).
[55] Matt. vi. 7.
[56] Eccles. v. 1–2.

Give us this day our daily bread (the *Gospel to the Hebrews* reads, "our bread for to-morrow"). And forgive us our debts as we also have forgiven our debtors. And bring us not into temptation, but deliver us from the evil one." [57]

It is a remarkable prayer, universal in its appeal, earnest, brief and full of devotion. Every single clause in it is, however, to be found in Jewish prayers and sayings in the *Talmud*. "Our Father which art in heaven" is a Jewish expression found in many prayers; one ancient prayer, said on Mondays and Thursdays before returning the Scroll of the Law to the Ark, begins four times with the introductory clause: "May it be thy will, O our Father which art in heaven." [58] "May thy name be hallowed and may thy kingdom come" occurs in the *"Kaddish,"* so widespread among the Jews, and containing many very ancient elements: "Exalted and sanctified be his great name in the world which he created according to his will, and may he bring about his kingdom (or 'rule in his kingdom')" [59]

"Thy will be done, as in heaven, so on earth" occurs in the "Short Prayer" (precisely as with Jesus) of the early *Tanna* already referred to, R. Eliezer: "What is the short prayer? R. Eliezer said: Do thy will in heaven, and on earth give comfort to them that fear thee, and do what is right in thy sight." [60] The phrase "Give us this day our daily bread" is found not only in the Old Testament ("Give me the bread that is needful for me") [61] but also in a variant of R. Eliezer's "Short Prayer": "May it be thy will, O our God, to give to every one his needs and to every being sufficient for his lack." [62] "Forgive us our debts" is the Sixth Blessing in the "Shemoneh-Esreh" prayer; and in Ben Sira we also find, "Forgive thy neighbour's sin and then, when thou prayest, thy sins will be forgiven; man cherisheth anger against man, and doth he seek healing (or, forgiveness) from the Lord?" [63] Finally, the clause "bring us not into temptation" comes in a *Talmudic* prayer: "Lead us not into sin or iniquity or temptation," [64] a prayer that has been included among the "First Blessings" of the Book of Prayer used throughout Jewry to the present day.

We see, therefore, that the "Lord's Prayer" can be divided up

---

[57] Matt. vi. 9-12; Luke xi. 1-4. We disagree with some modern scholars who would regard this prayer, also, as late; in such a case virtually nothing at all would be left to Jesus: and from nothing we cannot get anything but nothing.

[58] *Siddur Rab Amram Gaon*, ed. Frumkin, Jerusalem, 1912, p. 158.

[59] See Zvi Karl, *Ha-Kaddish, Ha-Shiloach,* XXXV 45.

[60] *T. Berachoth* III 11; *Berachoth* 29b; cf. "Peace among men," Luke ii. 14.

[61] Prov. xxx. 8.

[62] *T. Berachoth* III 11; *Berachoth* 29b.

[63] *Ben Sira* 28, 2-5; cf. in *Talmud, Rosh ha-Shana* 17a and b; *Yoma* 23a, 87b; *Meg.* 28a; J. *Baba Qama* VIII 10.

[64] *Berachoth* 60b; cf. "He will never lead men into temptation," *Sanh.* 107a.

into separate elements every one of which is Hebraic in form and occurs in either the Old Testament or the *Talmud.* The same applies to virtually everything which Jesus uttered. If we remember that Hillel also said that the commandment, "Thou shalt love thy neighbour as thyself," or the ethical law, "What is hateful to thyself do not unto thy neighbour," was the whole Law and the rest but commentary; [65] and that the *Talmud* says: "They who are insulted yet insult not again, who hear themselves reproached yet answer not again, who act out of love and rejoice in afflictions . . . of them Scripture says, They that love him are as the going forth of the sun in his might;" [66] and that Scripture enjoins that a man restore his enemy's ox or his ass and "help the ass of his enemy when it croucheth under its burden—" [67]: then how much more should he aid his enemy himself; and that God compels Jonah the Prophet to save Nineveh, the city of his enemies who have destroyed (or were about to destroy) his native country; and that it is said in a *Midrash,* "How doth it affect the Holy One, blessed be he, whether a man slay a beast according to *Halakha* or not, and eat it? doth it profit Him or harm Him? or how doth it affect Him whether a man eat food unclean or clean? . . . the commandments were not given save as a means to purify mankind;" [68] and the wonderful saying, "Almsgiving and good works outweigh all the commandments in the Law;" [69]—if we call to mind all these high ethical ideals (and there are very many more like them) we are inevitably led to the conclusion that Jesus scarcely introduced any ethical teaching which was fundamentally foreign to Judaism.[70] So extraordinary is the similarity that it might

[65] *Shab.* 31a.
[66] Judges vi. 31; *Yoma* 23a; *Shab.* 88b; *Gitt.* 36b.
[67] Ex. 23. 4-5.
[68] *Tanhuma, Shemini,* 12 (ed. Buber p. 30); *Gen. R.* §44 (beginning); *Lev. R.* §13.
[69] T. *Peah* IV 19.
[70] The book giving *all* the Hebrew passages illustrating the Synoptic Gospels is Shack-Billerbeck, *Kommentar zum Neuen Testament aus Talmud und Midrasch,* Vol. I-II, München, 1922-4. The following give important material: J. Eshelbacher, *Ha-Yahaduth u-mahuth ha-Natzriyuth* (Hebrew translation, ed. Ha-Zeman, Wilna, 1911); B. Balzac, *Torath ha-Adam,* vol. 2, Warsaw, 1910; F. N. Nork (S. Korn), *Rabbinische Quellen und Parallelen zu Neutestamentlischen Schriften,* Leipzig, 1839; A. Wünsche, *Neue Beiträge zur Erläuterung der Evangelien aus Talmud und Midrasch,* Göttingen, 1878; G. Friedlander, *The Jewish Sources of the Sermon on the Mount,* London, 1911; H. P. Chajes, *Rivista Israelitica,* 1904 (I) 41-57; 105-6; 214-225; 1906 (III) 83-96; 1907 (IV) 52-58; 132-136, 209-213 and elsewhere; H. P. Chajes, *Ben Stada (Ha-Goren,* IV 33-37). See also "Ahad ha-Am," *Al sh'te ha-S'ippim* (Collected works, IV 38-58); G. Dalman, *Christentum und Judentum,* Leipzig, 1898; H. G. Enelow, *A Jewish View of Jesus,* New York, 1920; Z'eb Markon, *Ha-Talmud w'ha-Natzruth (Ha-Shiloach* XXXIII 20-32, 170-176, 469-481). See also L. Bäck, *Das Wesen des Judentums,* 3. Aufl. Frankfort a. M., 1923; M. Güdemann, *Jüdische Apologetik,* Glogau, 1906; *Die Grundlagen der Jüdischen Ethik (Die Lehren des Judentums nach den Quellen,* herausgegeben vom Verband der Deutschen Juden) bearbeitet von S. Bernfeld, Th. I-II,

almost seem as though the Gospels were composed simply and solely out of matter contained in the *Talmud* and *Midrash.*

But there is a new thing in the Gospels. Jesus, who concerned himself with neither *Halakha* nor the secular knowledge requisite for *Halakha,* nor (except to a limited extent) with scriptural exposition—Jesus gathered together and, so to speak, condensed and concentrated ethical teachings in such a fashion as to make them more prominent than in the *Talmudic Haggada* and the *Midrashim,* where they are interspersed among more commonplace discussions and worthless matter. Even in the Old Testament, and particularly in the Pentateuch, where moral teaching is so prominent, and so purged and so lofty, this teaching is yet mingled with ceremonial laws or matters of civil and communal interest which also include ideas of vengeance and harshest reproval.

Although there is, in the *Mishna,* an entire tractate devoted exclusively to ethical teaching, viz., *Pirke Aboth,* it is but a compilation drawing on the sayings of many scores of *Tannaim* and even (in the supplementary sixth chapter, "*Kinyan Torah*") of *Amoraim;* but the ethical teachings of the Gospel, on the contrary, came from one man only, and are, every one, stamped with the same peculiar hall-mark. A man like Jesus, for whom the ethical ideal was everything, was something hitherto unheard of in the Judaism of the day. "Jesus ben Sira" lived at least two hundred years earlier. Hillel the Elder reached an ethical standard no lower than that of Jesus; but while Jesus left behind him (taking no count of the recorded miracles) almost nothing but ethical sayings and hortatory parables, Hillel was equally, if not more, interested in *Halakha.*

Everything, from leprosy signs, *Nidda* and *Halla,* to lending on usury, comes within the scope of Hillel's teaching. He introduces amendments in civil law and marriage disputes (the *Prozbol, Batē Homah* [Lev. xxv. 31], the drafting of the marriage-settlement, and the like). He sits in the Sanhedrin. Not only is he teacher and Rabbi, but he likewise serves his nation as judge, lawgiver and administrator.

In Jesus there is nothing of this. In its place there is a far greater preoccupation in questions of ethics, and the laying down of virtually nothing but ethical rules (not, as with Hillel, religious and legal injunctions too). Hillel was all for peace and quietness and the avoiding of quarrels, and was prepared to compromise with his opponents to this end (as in the matter of Ordination on a Feast Day).[70a] Jesus, on the contrary, was, as the preacher of a moral standard, a man of contention, saying harsh things of the Pharisees and Sadducæan priests, opposing by force the traffickers in the Temple, and even suffering martyrdom for his opinions.

Berlin, 1920-1921; Irsael Abrahams, *Studies in Pharisaism and the Gospels,* First Series, Cambridge, 1917; Second Series, Cambridge, 1924.
    [70a] *Betza 20a.*

In this he is more like Jeremiah than Hillel, but while Jeremiah intervenes in the *political life* of his nation, contending not only with priests and the popular teachers, but also with *kings* and *princes*, prophesying not only against Judah and Jerusalem, but also against the Gentiles and foreign powers, and the whole of the then known world, enfolding them all in his all-embracing grip, and scrutinizing them with the acute vision of the eagle—Jesus, on the contrary, confines his exhortations within the limits of Palestine and against the Pharisees and priests of Jerusalem; as for the rest. . . . "Give unto Cæsar the things that are Cæsar's, and to God the things that are God.'s."

Thus, his ethical teaching, apparently goes beyond that of *Pirkē Aboth* and of other *Talmudic* and *Midrashic* literature. It is not lost in a sea of legal prescriptions and items of secular information. From among the overwhelming mass accumulated by the Scribes and Pharisees Jesus sought out for himself the "one pearl." But we have already pointed out that, in the interest of Judaism (and, therefore, of humanity as a whole through the medium of Judaism) this is not an advantage but a drawback.

Judaism is not only religion and it is not only ethics: it is the sum-total of all the needs of the nation, placed on a religious basis. It is a national world-outlook with an ethico-religious basis.

Thus like life itself, Judaism has its heights and its depths, and this is its glory. Judaism is a national life, a life which the national religion and human ethical principles (the ultimate object of every religion) embrace without engulfing. Jesus came and thrust aside all the requirements of the national life; it was not that he set them apart and relegated them to their separate sphere in the life of the nation: he ignored them completely; in their stead he set up nothing but an ethico-religious system bound up with his conception of the Godhead.

In the self-same moment he both annulled *Judaism* as the *life-force* of the Jewish nation, and also the nation itself as a nation. For a religion which possesses only a certain conception of God and a morality acceptable to *all* mankind, does not belong to any special nation, and, consciously or unconsciously, breaks down the barriers of nationality. This inevitably brought it to pass that his people, Israel, rejected him. In its deeper consciousness the nation felt that then, more than at any other time, they must not be swallowed up in the great cauldron of nations in the Roman Empire, which were decaying for lack of God and of social morality.

Israel's Prophets had taught that man was created in the image of God; they had proclaimed their message to all nations and kingdoms and looked forward to a time when they would all call on the name of the Lord and worship him with one accord.

Israel's spiritual leaders, the Scribes and Pharisees, also looked for the time when "all creatures should fall down before one God" and all be made "one society (a League of Nations) to do his will with a perfect heart." [70b] And the people knew, if once they compromised their nationality, that that ideal would be left with none to uphold it, and that the vision would never be fulfilled. Religion would be turned to mere visionariness, and morality would be torn and severed from life; while the manner of life of the Gentiles who were not yet capable of realizing such an ethical standard nor of being raised to the heights of the great ideal, would remain more barbarous and unholy than before.

Two thousand years of non-Jewish Christianity have proved that the Jewish people did not err. Both the instinct for national self-preservation and the cleaving to the great humanitarian ideal, emphatically demanded that Judaism reject this ethical teaching, severed, as it became, from the national life: the breach which, all unintentionally, Jesus would have made in the defences of Judaism, must needs have brought this Judaism to an end.

Yet another cause brought about this rejection: the "self-abnegation" taught by Jesus.

It is difficult to suppose that Jesus was, like John the Baptist, an ascetic. We have seen [71] how the Pharisees and the disciples of John reproved Jesus for not fasting like them, and for sitting at meat with publicans and sinners; and we have seen how he used to defend himself on the grounds that he is "the bridegroom" (and "the bridegroom is like unto a king," [72] and he, Jesus, is the "King-Messiah"), while his disciples are the "children of the bride-chamber," and neither "bridegroom" nor "children of the bridechamber" fast during the seven days of the wedding-feast. Jesus is not, therefore, the complete ascetic; he was, frequently, not averse to the pleasures of life (e.g. when the woman at Bethany poured the cruse of spikenard over his head).[73]

Yet after he had failed to arouse a great, popular movement, and after he had realized the severe opposition to his life-work, and also, perhaps, after he had begun to be persecuted by the Herodians and Pharisees, he began to adopt a "negative" attitude towards the life of this present world.

Like all who have become immersed in ethics and nothing else, he became a "pessimist;" life, the life as it is lived in this world, is valueless; nothing is to be gained by resisting evil or fighting against Roman oppression ("Give unto Cæsar the things that are Cæsar's"). Let possessions be divided amongst the poor; no rich man can be worthy of the "days of the Messiah" ("It is easier for a camel to go through the eye of a needle than for a rich man to enter

[70b] The *Shemoneh-Esreh* Prayer for New Year and the Day of Atonement.
[71] See above, p. 274.
[72] *Pirke d'R. Eliezer*, §16 (end).
[73] Mark xiv. 2-9; Matt. xxvi. 6-13.

the kingdom of heaven"). Let swearing be forbidden altogether, even swearing by the truth. It is preferable not to marry at all. It is forbidden to divorce a wife even though it be impossible to live with her owing to her unfaithfulness. For the sake of the kingdom of heaven, let a man forsake father and mother, brother and sister, wife and children. Let him desist from all litigation, even when it is a legal matter affecting inheritance.

Let him stretch out the left cheek to one who strikes him on the right cheek, and let him give his cloak to the one who would take away his coat. Let him take no thought for the morrow, nor amass wealth or material for the furthering of culture. He need not labour for the sake of food or raiment, but let him be like the "lilies of the field" or the "fowls of the air" which labour not, but receive everything from God.

As ethical rules for the individual, these may stand for the highest form of morality. We find similar sentiments in isolated sayings from the *Tannaim* and mediæval Jewish thinkers. On the theoretical side Judaism possesses everything that is to be found in Christianity. Judaism has also its ascetic tendencies—the Essenes, systems of thought such as are to be found in works like "The Duties of the Heart," the "Testament of R. Yehudah the Pious;" and a lofty individualistic morality has been a feature in Judaism from the time of Ezekiel ("The soul that sinneth it shall die") till the time of Hillel ("If I am not for myself, who will be for me?" and "If I am here, all is here").

But as a sole and self-sufficient national code of teaching, Judaism could by no means agree to it. The most ascetic remark to be found in the *Mishna* is that of R. Jacob (the teacher of R. Yehudah ha-Nasi): "This world is as it were an ante-chamber to the world to come;" [74] yet the same R. Jacob also says: "Better is a single hour of repentance and good works in this world than all the life of the world to come." [75] Thus *this* world is the main thing, and the moral life is to be realised *here*. The same thing happened with Jesus' ethical teaching as happened with his teaching concerning God. Jesus made himself neither God nor the Son of God, and, in his view of the Godhead, he remained a true Jew; yet by over-emphasis of the divine Fatherhood in relation to himself, he caused Paul and his contemporaries to attribute to him a conception which was both foreign to his own mind and little removed from idolatry.

So too with regard to his ethical teaching.

Judaism also knows the ideal of love for the enemy, and exemplifies it in the law dealing with an enemy's ox or ass and in the ethical teaching of the *Book of Jonah;* but Judaism never emphasized it to such a degree that it ultimately became too high an ideal for ordinary mankind, and even too high for the man of more than average moral

[74] *Aboth* IV 16. [75] *Aboth* IV 17.

calibre.[76] The same applies to the ideal of "stretching the other cheek." Judaism also praised them "who when affronted affront not again," but it never emphasized the idea unduly, for it would be difficult for human society to exist with such a basic principle. Judaism did not forbid swearing and litigation, but enjoined "a righteous yea or nay"[77] and, in the person of Hillel, laid down the principle, "Judge not thy neighbour till thou art come into his place."[78]

Everything which Jesus ever uttered of this nature is Jewish ethical teaching, too; but his *overemphasis* was *not* Judaism, and, in fact, brought about *non-*Judaism. When these extreme ethical standards are severed from the facts of daily life and taught as religious rules, while, at the same time, everyday life is conducted along completely different lines, defined in the prevailing legal codes (which are not concerned with religion) or in accordance with improved scientific knowledge (which again is not concerned with religion)—it is inevitable that such ethical standards can make their appeal only to priests and recluses and the more spiritually minded among *individuals,* whose only interest is religion; while the rest of mankind all pursue a manner of life that is wholly secular or even pagan.

Such has been the case with Christianity from the time of Constantine till the present day: the religion has stood for what is highest ethically and ideally, while the political and social life has remained at the other extreme of barbarity and paganism. The Spanish Inquisition was not thought to be incompatible with Christianity. The Inquisition was concerned with everyday life, it was political religiousness, whereas Christianity was pure religion and ethics lifted above the calls of everyday life. This, however, can never be the case when, as with Judaism, the national religion embraces every aspect of the national life, when nation and belief are inseparable; then it is impossible to use an extreme ethical standard as a foundation.

The nation desires freedom: therefore it must fight for it. As "possessor of the state" it must ensure the security of life and property and, therefore, it must resist evil. A national community of to-day cannot endure without civil legislation—therefore the community must legislate. Swearing on oath cannot always be dispensed with. The national community of today cannot exist without private property—therefore there must be private property; the point is, rather, in what manner the rich man makes use of his property. The social system is based on the family, therefore there is no

[76] It is worth noticing to what extremes apologists for the ethical teaching of Jesus are reduced, *e.g.*, E. Grimm, *Die Ethik Jesu*, 2 Aufl., Leipzig, 1917, pp. 122-134, 104, in order to be convinced how contrary to nature this teaching is.
[77] *Baba Metzia* 49a; *J. Shebi'ith* X 9.
[78] *Aboth* II 4.

place for teaching "celibacy for the kingdom of heaven's sake" as the most exalted virtue in those who would fit themselves for the kingdom of heaven. As to freedom of divorce, now, nineteen hundred years after Jesus, "enlightened" Christianity the world over is fighting for it.

What room is there in the world for justice if we must extend both cheeks to our assailants and give the thief both coat and cloak? Human civilisation is wholly based on the difference between man and nature, between human society and the brute beast and vegetable world; it is, therefore, neither possible nor seemly for man to become as "the lilies of the field" or "the fowls of the air."

But when, in reality, did Christianity ever conduct itself in accordance with these ethical standards of Jesus? In the small fellowship of his disciples community of goods was practised; but even so, the system was adopted only in part and temporarily. The earliest of Jesus' disciples married; they indulged in litigation, they hated and reviled not only their enemies but all who opposed them. Did Jesus himself abide by his own teaching? Did he love the Pharisees —who were not his enemies but simply his theoretical opponents? Did he not call them "Hypocrites," "Serpents," "Offspring of vipers?" and did he not threaten that "upon them would come all the innocent blood that was shed in the land?" [79]   Did he not condemn the ungodly to hell where there would be "weeping and gnashing of teeth?"

Did he not resist evil with acts of violence—by expelling the money-changers and them that sold doves in the Temple?

Did he not promise houses and fields and even judgment thrones in the future to those who followed him? When he sent out the Twelve as his messengers to the cities of Israel did he not warn them to be "subtil as serpents and simple as doves," [80] and at the same time say that, for the city which would not receive them, it "would be more tolerable for Sodom and Gomorrah in the day of judgment than for that city." [81]   And did he not say to his disciples that "whosoever denied him (Jesus) before men, Jesus would deny him also before his Father in heaven?" [82] and in this is there not vengeance, bearing of malice, unforgiveness and hatred of enemies? And what of those words: 'Think not that I came to bring peace upon earth: I came not to bring peace but a sword," [83] "not peace, but dissension?" [84]

And what of those harsh, definite words: "I came to cast fire on the earth, and what will I if it is already kindled!" [85]   And what of his injunction "to sell the cloak and buy a sword?" [86]   And what of

[79] Matt. xxiii. 35.
[80] Matt. x. 16.
[81] Matt. x. 15.
[82] Matt. x. 33.

[83] Matt. x. 34.
[84] Luke xii. 51.
[85] Luke xii. 49.
[86] Luke xxii. 36.

those cruelest of words, "Give not what is holy to the dogs and cast not your pearls before swine?" [87]

Where in all this do we find tenderness, pardon "till seventy times seven," love of the enemy and putting forth the other cheek? This is not an arraignment against Jesus: he maintained a high moral standard in all his doings, and his stern words and the expulsion of the traffickers and money-changers were in themselves a lofty moral protest; but such contradiction between precept and practice cannot but prove that this extreme ethical teaching cannot possibly be carried out in practice in everyday life, even by so exceptional a man for whom society was naught and the individual soul everything. Then how much more impossible must it be in the sphere of political and national life?

This it was left for Judaism to perceive. We have before us two facts. In the first place, "Christian morality" was embodied in daily life by—Judaism: it is Judaism, and Judaism only, which has never produced murderers and pogrom-mongers, whereas indulgence and forgiveness have become the prime feature in its being, with the result that the Jews have been made moral (not in theory but in living fact) to the verge of abject flaccidity. In the second place, monasticism is typical not of Judaism but of Christianity, in the same way as it is typical of Buddhism. Had there been no ascetic and monastic element in Jesus' teaching, monasticism would not have become a peculiarity of Roman and Orthodox Christianity.

The Protestant Reformation which abolished monasticism and the celibacy of the clergy was a reversion to Judaism. Christianity is the halfway station between Judaism and Buddhism. Pharisaic Judaism *as a whole* (as distinct from certain individual moralists, from the time of the Essenes till the time of the writer of the *Shebet Musar,* who educed from Pharisaic Judaism an extremist ethical code) was alive to the fact that the Law "was not given to the ministering angels," [88] and it endeavoured to take account of existing conditions, but to raise them and to sanctify them. It did not teach the abolition of marriage, of oaths or of property: it sought rather to bridle sexual desire, to limit the use of oaths and lessen the evils of wealth.

By embracing life as a whole Judaism rendered an extremist morality impossible; but it hallowed the secular side of life by the help of the idea of sanctity, while rendering the idea of sanctity real and strong and palpable by contact with actual reality. Judaism is an all-embracing, all-inclusive political-national social culture; therefore together with the noblest abstract ethic, it comprises both ceremonial rules of purely religious interest and entirely secular human points of view.

[87] Matt. vii. 6.
[88] *Berachoth* 25*b; Yoma* 30*a; Kiddushin* 54*a; Mc'ila* 14*b.*

Thus in the Levitical "Code of Holiness" [89] we find, side by side, "Thou shalt love thy neighbour as thyself," and rulings about "unclean foods" and the "sacrificial remnants;" "Thou shalt not take vengeance nor bear any grudge," side by side with rulings about "mixed materials" and "cross-breeding;" "The stranger that sojourneth with you shall be as the home-born among you, and thou shalt love him as thyself," side by side with rulings about "the acquired bondmaid" (Lev. xix. 20); alongside of the lofty thought, "Ye are the sons of the Lord your God," comes the ceremonial rule, "Ye shall not cut yourselves."

"Thou shalt not take vengeance nor bear any grudge" can occur in the same book in which it is written, "Remember what Amalek did unto thee," and "Harass the Midianites;" the command to help "the ass of thine enemy that is fallen under its load" does not exclude from the Law of Moses the command, "Thou shalt not leave a soul alive," and "of the foreigner shalt thou exact usury," and "of the stranger shalt thou exact it" (Deut. xv. 2—in whatever sense this is taken).

Within the same Old Testament is included the *Book of Jonah*, teaching in unrivalled fashion the duty of forgiveness to enemies and preserving the destroyer of the fatherland; and also the *Book of Esther* describing in most garish colours the vengeance wreaked on the enemy.

All such feelings and attitudes *exist* within a people and must find place in its literature: they are all human, deeply implanted in man's nature and they may not be changed in a moment at will. A proof of this is before us in the fact that even Christianity, in addition to the New Testament, *was forced to accept unchanged the whole of the Old Testament as Canonical Scripture*, a sign that the New Testament alone did not suffice.

It did not suffice because it did not embrace the whole of life, whether civil or national, communal or private, religious or ethical, theoretical or practical.

The *Talmud* also, like the Old Testament, is all-embracing and all-inclusive. The Old Testament ideal is the Prophet Jeremiah: he is a moralist, but he is also a political worker and a great fighter on his nation's behalf.

The *Talmud* ideal is Hillel the Elder: he, no less than Jesus, was a moralist of high degree, humble, a peace-maker, and a lover of his fellow men; but he was no fighter nor politician: instead his teaching embraced the whole of the social and national life. Hillel took up his position in the centre of affairs, laboured together with the community (his favourite saying was, "Do not keep yourself apart from the community"), took within his purview all the requirements of life from every possible point of view, embodied just such ethical standards as were possible in practice, and thus sanctified and raised the tone of ordinary, every-day life, and made his ethical

[89] Lev. xix.

teaching popular and widespread. He rendered it possible of practice to any man, and not merely to the chosen few who could withdraw from the affairs of everyday life.

Jesus surpassed Hillel in his ethical ideals: he changed Hillel's "Golden Rule" from the negative form ("What thou thyself hatest do not unto thy neighbour"—in which the *Book of Tobit* [90] anticipates Hillel) to the positive form ("What thou wouldest that men should do unto thee, do thou also unto them"—in which the "Letter of Aristeas" [91] anticipates Jesus), and concerned himself more with ethical teaching than did Hillel; but his teaching has not proved possible in practice.[92]

Therefore he left the course of ordinary life untouched—wicked, cruel, pagan; and his exalted ethical ideal was relegated to a book or, at most, became a possession of monastics and recluses who lived far apart from the paths of ordinary life.

Beyond this ethical teaching Jesus gave nothing to his nation. He cared not for reforming the world or civilisation: therefore to adopt the teaching of Jesus is to remove oneself from the whole sphere of ordered national and human existence—from law, learning and civics (all three of which were absorbed into the codes of the *Tannaim-Pharisees*), from life within the State, and from wealth in virtually all its forms. How could Judaism accede to *such* an ethical ideal?—that Judaism to which the monastic ideal had ever been foreign!

The ethic of Jesus is, however, founded on the special character of his belief in the Day of Judgment and the kingdom of heaven (the "Days of the Messiah"). Only after we have understood the nature of this belief can we comprehend how Jesus the *Jew* attained to such an extreme in his ethical teaching.

[90] *Tobit* iv. 15; the Rule is also found in Philo, as quoted by Eusebius, *Praeparatio Evangelica*, VIII 7, 6; and also in what is, in the main, a Jewish work, the *Didache*, I. 2.

[91] Ed. Wendland, p. 207; see Kautzsch, *Apocryphen und Pseudepigraphen des Alten Testaments* II 22, n. a. See the Slavonic *Enoch* LXI 1.

[92] See "Ahad ha-Am," Collected Works, IV 45-50; G. Friedlander, *The Jewish Sources of the Sermon on the Mount*, London, 1911, pp. 230-238. Maimonides, however, in his *Sefer ha-Mitzvoth, Mitzvoth 'Asēh* §206 (ed. H. Heller, Petrokoff 1914, p. 64), gives positive and negative forms together and regards them both as equally Judaism.

The Messiahship of Jesus

By Hans Joachim Schoeps

THE MESSIAHSHIP OF JESUS

So-called "scriptural proof," based on the Old Testament, has always had immense importance for both Christians and Jews. Such proofs are comprehensible to men of today only when they consider that the Bible has been a document not only of revelation, history, and law, but also of prophecy. In it, future events are already anticipated by way of suggestion or by type—typological exegesis. For example, in the fate of the Patriarchs is seen that of their descendants; Edom, according to the *Haggadah,* is of the type of Rome and so forth. Early Christian congregations had every incentive to interpret specific passages in such a way that they would refer to Jesus; for example, Isaiah 7:14, which describes the birth of a descendant of David by the name Immanuel, is thought to have been Jesus. The messenger of the Lord in Malachi 3:1 is seen as John the Baptist, representing Elijah, and thus predecessor of the Nazarene. Similarly, the 110th Psalm is seen as containing a prophecy of the heavenly tribunal, with Jesus sitting at the right hand of God. There are many other such passages. Jewish scholars replied to such exegesis by referring the passages in question to other historical events, often to King Hezekiah; but the Christological exegeses of the Church Fathers (in spite of the school of historical criticism), mediated by medieval literature, have been taken over by Christian theology of our own day.[13]

194

The form of demonstration peculiar to early Christianity was to build everything upon the word of the Bible, proving every statement with biblical quotations, ignoring in the process the context in which the quotation was located or giving any consideration to the historical conditions under which it was written. This process certainly witnesses to the absolute sovereignty and exclusive authority of Scripture; but, in this "naïve" form, it cannot be adopted by our present mode of thought. J. Ziegler (*ibid., pp.* 64 f.) correctly points out that the persuasive power of the Gospel can be rightly understood only when the skill with which the new doctrine assimilated this method of proof is properly recognized. The Christian reader of today, out of touch with this "Jewish" thought pattern, can only rarely give this fact its due. This is especially so when—Strack-Billerbeck notwithstanding—he does not give close enough attention to references to the corresponding passages of Scripture or parallels in the contemporary writings of the rabbis, and the *specific* recasting of common Jewish doctrines of the period. The following examples may serve here to illustrate the method of scriptural proof: Jesus was born in Bethlehem, and is accordingly the Messiah, *for* it is written in the prophet Micah (5:1) "But thou, Bethlehem . . . Out of thee shall one come forth unto Me that is to be ruler in Israel." (Matt. 2:5 f.) Jesus was in Egypt for a time, and is accordingly God's Son, *for* we read in Hosea 11:1: "Out of Egypt I called My son." (Matt. 2:15) Jesus rides into Jerusalem upon an ass, *for* it says in Zechariah 9:9: "Behold, thy king cometh unto thee . . . Lowly, and riding upon an ass." (Matt. 21:5) Jesus innocently suffered much, and accordingly he is the Messiah, *for* Isaiah teaches (53:4): "Surely our diseases he did bear, and our pains he carried." (Matt. 8:17) This recurrent appeal to prophecy was either a so-called *vaticinium post eventum* (prophecy after the event), with the event itself inserted into the life of Jesus in order subsequently to confirm the word of the prophet; or, conversely according to the principle *lekayyêm mâh shenê'-emâr;* that is, in order to fulfill what is written, Jesus conformed his acts to prophetic statement. Whichever it may be, recognition of this exegetic device confirms that the proponents of the new doctrine conducted their disputes quite in the Jewish manner. Much emphasis is placed upon these conclusions, because to a degree which cannot be overlooked, they contribute to the reading of the New Testament as *Haggadah.* Long passages of the New Testament are, indeed, actually nothing less than *new and different exegesis* of the Jewish Bible, the difference being determined by belief in the divine sonship of Jesus. It is thus already a "justification" of *the* Scriptures.[14]

Of decisive importance in this process of "biblical proof" (which the Church Fathers found highly developed among the Alexandrian Jews and ready to be put to their own use) was the vision of the Suffering Servant of God (*'ebhedh ha-shêm*) in Isaiah 52-53. The Church interpreted this as referring to Jesus, and declared the prophecy to have been fulfilled through his passion and death. For the most part, the rabbis replied by deeming the entire nation of Israel to be the Suffering Servant, an interpretation which the Church Father Origen records in *Contra Celsum* as the view of a Jewish scholar. The rabbis saw Israel's historical destiny of suffering predicted here, declaring that the Suffering Servant passages had nothing to do with Jesus or even with the Messiah. That Israel was intended by Isaiah to be a suffering missionary remained the pervading interpretation of the majority of Jewish biblical exegetes of the Middle Ages (Rashi, Ibn Ezra, David Kimhi, *et al.*).

Christological doctrine in itself—the belief that God has become man and has allowed his only-begotten son to suffer sacrificial death as a propitiation for the sins of mankind—has remained, as Paul rightly says, a "stumbling block" to the Jews. It is an impossible article of belief, which detracts from God's sovereignty and absolute otherness—an article which, in fact, destroys the world.[15] Indeed, the Sadducean High Priest (heeding the rabbinic directive on the conduct of a judge upon hearing blasphemy) rended his clothing in horror at the assertion of an incarnation of the eternal God. Similarly, according to Acts 7:54-60, when Stephen confessed his faith in the heavenly Son of God, he was stoned. It is the same passionate belief which can be heard in an admittedly late homiletical midrash: "It is not permitted a human mouth to say, 'The Holy One—blessed be he—has a son.' If God could not look on in anguish while Abraham sacrificed his son, would he then have suffered his own son to be killed, without destroying the entire world?" (Agadah Bereshit 31) And in another passage: When Nebuchadnezzar used the expression, " 'He is like a son of the gods' " (Dan. 3:25), an angel came down from heaven, smote him on the mouth, and said, "Blasphemer! Does God then have a son?' " (T. J. Shabbat 8; similarly, Midr. Samuel V, 7) Further, Midrash Rabbah explains, in reference to Exodus 20:2: " 'I am the Lord thy God': Compare therewith a king of flesh and blood. He reigns, and has a father or a brother or a son. The Holy One—blessed be his name—said, I am not so. 'I am the first,' for I have no father; 'and I am the last,' for I have no son; 'beside Me there is no God' (Isa. 44:6), for I have no brother." (R. Abbahu, an Amora of the second generation, prior to 300)[16]

In matters of Christology, we can attach more weight to the material preserved by the Tannaitic sources which can be referred in the narrower sense to the historical Jesus. Such material consists of a few scattered notices—incidental remarks which, as is often the case in the Talmud, are inexact and uncertain in regard to their historical significance. They admit only the conclusion that the early Tannaim did not think the events around the year of Jesus' death to be especially important; in that period, proponents of irregular doctrines and convictions based on messianic heresy were not unusual. The only item of importance is that Yeshu ha-Noṣri is called (using an idiom common at that time) a man who "burned his food in public," that is, caused a public scandal, became an apostate (Sanh. 103a, and elsewhere). His views are recorded because he ridiculed the words of the wise (according to Matt. 23), led the people of Israel astray, and induced them to apostasy (Sanh. 43a; 107b; Soṭah 47b).[17] Only at the close of the tannaitic era, about two centuries after the crucifixion, does R. Eliezer ha-Ḳappar, a contemporary of the rabbi who was redactor of the Mishnah—plainly influenced by discussions with Gentile Christians—accuse Jesus of elevating himself to the status of divinity (according to Yalḳuṭ Shim'oni 765 on Num. 23:7). As justification for this charge, a decisive objection (in the Jewish view of that period) was raised against any possible messiahship on the part of Jesus: the possibility of referring the crucifixion to the passage in the Torah, "he that is hanged is a reproach unto God." (Deut. 21:23) The fatal import of this statement also made great difficulty for Paul (Gal. 3:13). The much-cited "scandal of the cross" hinges on this passage!

Rabbinic passages of the above-mentioned kind can be found with others collected *in toto* by Joseph Klausner, as well as by the Christian theologians Heinrich Laible, Gustaf Dalman, and Hermann Strack. It must be emphasized once more that these are incidental remarks, which never assumed central importance. They are of value to the historian of religion who wishes to obtain information about the intellectual climate of the period and gain familiarity with the peculiarities of polemic of that time. The attitude of present-day Judaism—as remains to be shown—has altered decisively, and these statements possess *no* normative force. This whole process of free midrashic exegesis is found among the Amoraim and also, as a pattern of thought, among the Church Fathers; it is important solely for the light it casts on the historical doctrinal convictions of the time.

Only after the growing Church began to develop a Christological doctrine—that is, after the middle of the third century—do we find such statements of the Amoraim, thus motivated, concerning the doctrine of the incarnate God. These are intended to illustrate the impossibility of Christological doctrine for strict Jewish transcendental monotheism. As the passages referred to show, this doctrine ultimately had to be rejected as being quite impossible, given the basis of the Jewish experience of God. God, who is without form, cannot be incorporated in any shape, no matter how fashioned; without boundary and prior to all form, it is he who creates forms. No rabbinic exegete ever felt it necessary to enter into a discussion of the content of Pauline teaching. Christian soteriology restricted the distinctive mark of the Jewish nation, the *'ebhedh ha-shêm,* to a single individual who suffers vicariously as a propitiation for the sins of his fellow men, being therein and thereby the Messiah. To the rabbis, this must have seemed just so much "Greek" speculation. Had a Jew propounded such a doctrine as being *the* meaning of the Torah, according to the Jewish way of thinking he would thereby have surrendered the true meaning and content of revealed monotheistic religion. Furthermore, this un-Jewish shift of ideas contradicted all the realistic expectations of the "messianic age" shared by that period, from Judas Maccabeus to Simon bar Kokhba. This age was to bring a real end to Roman oppression, together with peace on earth under the victorious scepter of the royal Messiah, as well as the supernatural miracle of cessation of sin. Above all, the royal Messiah was expected to be a human being. The postexilic name for the Messiah, *ben' âdhâm* ("son of man"), which occurs especially in the book of Daniel, was obviously formed in contradistinction to ideas of a "Son of God" common among contemporary pagans. It was intended as an anti-mythological Jewish term. It is true, however, that these pagan conceptions penetrated into the messianic doctrine of the apocalyptic books of the first century after Christ, especially IV Ezra.

A final word on the idea that the devout believer—including and, in particular, the one sent by God—must suffer *as a man*. This opinion is and was well known to Judaism. This was the reason that the Jews of the fourth century could enter into political alliance with the Arian Christians, who acknowledged the human Jesus, but denied his divinity. The idea that God becomes man, suffers of his own free will, and is defeated by the evil of the world—this is an impossibility for Judaism! Of course, it is no secret that even the Talmud speaks of a suffering forerunner Messiah (e.g., in Sukkah 52a), the Messiah ben Joseph, of the tribe of Ephraim, who is even defeated in battle and killed. Only then after his death, does the Messiah ben David appear, who will bring final deliverance. This doctrine developed only very late (according to G. Kittel, certainly no earlier than the second century). It can be viewed as a reflected answer to the question of the Messiah as newly stated by the Christians—an attempt to connect the demonstration of the Messiah's power with the problem of suffering. It was not, however, the *figure* of the Messiah which became decisive for later Judaism, but rather the earthly *kingdom* expected for the messianic age, in which "the Lord shall be King over all the earth; In that day shall the Lord be One, and His name one." (Zech. 14:9)

Jesus: Jew or Christian?

By Ben Zion Bokser

*T*he Hebrew Bible was the source that fed the living tradition of Judaism. But there were two tributaries that also flowed from the same source, Christianity and Islam. There were influences other than the Bible that helped shape the Christian and Islamic traditions, but the Hebrew Bible was the cornerstone on which they were reared. And the process by which these traditions transformed the biblical element into their own image was also a process of interpretation analagous to the *midrash* by which the Rabbis created the Oral Torah. The Islamic tradition falls outside our present inquiry, but we shall study the Hebrew Bible as the formative elment in the rise of Christianity. The directing force behind the origin of Christianity was of course the ministry of Jesus.

A mist of legend hovers over the historical personality of Jesus and the teachings he imparted to his disciples and left as his legacy to posterity. There are no reports written from a detached and objective viewpoint on the basis of which to reconstruct those events in which he was the central figure. Our knowledge must be drawn from the New Testament writings, principally the synoptic Gospels—Mark, Matthew, and Luke. But none of the Gospels were written by an immediate disciple of Jesus, nor did they originate in the primitive Christian community where firsthand reports might have been preserved as oral tradition. They originated in the Greek Christian community and were composed by people who were more than one generation removed from the events chronicled.

The Gospel writers sought to defend the dogmas which the Church had woven about the role of Jesus in the scheme of salvation. The Gospels are both polemical and defensive. They are not directed at an objective portrayal of the master's life and of his work. In the words of the noted contemporary New Testament scholar Rudolf Bultmann: "We conclude that the whole framework of the history of Jesus must be viewed as an editorial construction, and that therewith a whole series of typical scenes which, because of their ecclesiastical use and their poetic and artistic associations, we had looked upon as scenes in the life of Jesus, must be viewed as creations of the evangelists." [1]

The commingling of a kernel of historical fact with homiletical embroidery in the Gospel narrative was recently touched on by Msg. Myles M. Bourke of St. Joseph's Seminary in an article in the *Catholic Biblical Quarterly*. Writing on "The Literary Genus of Matthew 1–2," he declared: "Admittedly, the gospel presents Jesus' ministry, death and resurrection as events which really happened. But that the author of such a work might have introduced it by a midrash of deep theological insight, in which Jesus appears as the new Israel and the new Moses (thus containing the theme of the entire gospel), and in which the historical element is very slight seems to be a thoroughly probable hypothesis." [2]

The Gospel portrayal of Jews is generally hostile, as many Christians as well as Jewish scholars have observed. The Gospels were written after the Christian community had broken with Judaism, after Jewish practices had been repudiated as ineffectual

[1] Rudolf Bultmann and Karl Kundsin: *Form Criticism*, Frederick C. Grant (trans.) (New York: Harper & Row; 1962), p. 28.

[2] Quoted by James M. Robinson in *Ecumenical Dialogue at Harvard*, Samuel H. Miller and G. Ernest Wright (ed.), (Cambridge, Mass.: The Belknap Press of Harvard University Press; 1964), p. 102.

at best, and new formulae for man's salvation, faith in Jesus, the rites of the Eucharist meal and baptism had been developed by Church authorities. They were written, too, after Christian leaders had resigned themselves to the realization that the Jewish community by and large would remain adamant in rejecting the claims of Christianity, and that the future of the Christian movement was therefore to be sought among the pagans of the Roman Empire. It therefore suited the purpose of the Gospel writers to present Jesus as a noble figure who struck out against the spiritual decadence of the Jewish faith, and who was consistently at war with the Jews and with their leaders. The events were so shaped as to suggest that the Jews were the prime movers in the tragedy of the crucifixion, while the involvement of the Romans was played down.

It is significant therefore that when subjected to searching inquiry, the Gospel accounts themselves disclose to us that Jesus lived and died as a Jew, within the framework of Jewish belief and Jewish practice. "The schematic representation according to which the Pharisees and scribes are from the outset the sworn enemies of Jesus is certainly unhistorical," declared Bultmann. He even doubts that Jesus himself thought of himself as the messiah: "Indeed, it must remain questionable whether Jesus regarded himself as the messiah, and did not rather first become messiah in the faith of the community." [3]

A detailed examination of the teachings of Jesus disclosed him to have been within the mainstream of the living tradition of Judaism. The pioneer of critical studies in the Old and New Testaments, Julius Wellhausen, declared categorically: "Jesus was not a Christian; he was a Jew. He did not preach a new faith, but taught men to do the will of God; and in his opinion, as also in that of the Jews, the will of God was to be found in the Law of Moses and in the other books of Scripture." [4] Some of the findings of Wellhausen, especially in his Old Testament studies, have been questioned by contemporary historians, but his judgment on the Jewishness of Jesus is fully supported by modern scholarship.

[3] Bultmann and Kundsin: *Form Criticism*, pp. 35, 71.
[4] Julius Wellhausen: *Einleitung in die drei ersten Evangelien* (n.p.: Berlin; 1905), p. 113.

The New Testament portrayal of Jesus, Joseph Klausner has noted, shows him to have been obedient to the traditional practices of Judaism.[5] He attended the Temple and respected the institution of sacrifices. He was a regular worshipper in the synagogue. He wore fringes on the corners of his garment, as prescribd by Jewish tradition. He celebrated the religious festivals and recited the prayers customary at such occasions.

When asked to define the way one might earn eternal life he replied (Mark 10:17–19): "You know the commandments: 'Do not kill, Do not commit adultery, Do not steal, Do not bear false witness, Do not defraud, Honor your father and mother'" (Exodus 20:12–16, Deuteronomy 5:16–20). When asked to single out the primary commandments he replied (Mark 12:29–31): "The first is [Deuteronomy 6:4–5] 'Hear, O Israel: The Lord our God, the Lord is one; and you shall love the Lord your God with all your heart, and with all your soul, and with all your mind, and with all your strength.' The second is this [Leviticus 19:18], 'You shall love your neighbor as yourself.' There is no other commandment greater than these." The commandments quoted by Jesus as the way to gain eternal life are selected from the Ten Commandments. But "Do not defraud," included in the Gospel of Mark, does not appear in either version of the Decalogue. The parallel discussion in Matthew 19:17–19 omits "Do not defraud" and substitutes for it "You shall love your neighbor as yourself" (Leviticus 19:18). This discussion is also paralleled in Luke 18:18–23, and here, too, "Do not defraud" is omitted, but Luke did not substitute any other commandment for it.

We also face difficulty in the formulation of the two primary commandments (the love of God and the love of neighbor). In the original Hebrew the verse commanding the love of God does not have "with all your mind." The parallel passage in Matthew 22:37 has "with all your mind," but it omits "with all your strength." In Luke 10:37 the passage reads: "With all your heart, and with all your soul, and with all your strength, and with all your mind."

[5] Joseph Klausner: *Jesus of Nazareth*, Herbert Danby (trans.) (New York: The Macmillan Company; 1953), pp. 363–8.

The disagreement of the Gospels in quoting the words of Jesus and the slight deviation of each version from the original Hebrew is readily understood when we recall that one of the Gospel writers personally witnessed the events they describe. Dependence on an oral tradition going back to events more than a generation earlier leads to inaccuracy—in which the Gospel abounds. While it is thus impossible to fix the precise words of Jesus, it remains clear that he walked firmly on the ground of Jewish piety and the authority that he invoked as a guide to life was the authority of Scripture, which was embodied for him in the Hebrew Bible.

The distinction that Jesus made in the relative importance of the commandments was also in the spirit of Judaism. The Rabbis discussed this subject often. Rabbi Akiba, for example, dealt with the same question, but his answer was more radical than that of Jesus. He was content with singling out one commandment—the one which Jesus quoted from Leviticus (19:18)—as the summation of the whole Torah: "You shall love your neighbor as yourself."

Some have seen a cleavage between Jesus and his Jewish heritage in the sharp invective that he is quoted as having spoken against the Pharisees, who were presumably the official representatives of Jewish piety in his time. We have already noted that historians tend to doubt whether the denunciations of the Pharisees that the Gospels put into Jesus' mouth are really genuine. They are rather inclined to think that these denunciations reflect the later hostility between the early Church and the Jews, after the Jews had confounded the hopes of Christian leaders by refusing to acknowledge the messiahship of Jesus. Indeed, Jesus appears to have lived his life in conformity to Pharisaic teachings. But apart from this, a critical attitude toward the Pharisees was not inconsistent with loyalty to Judaism. The name Pharisee was, indeed, an honorable name in Judaism, but there were instances when the name became a mask and a pretense, a byword for shallow and insincere faith, for a rigorous attention to the externals of religion and an unconcern for its inner essence.

The Talmud, too, was impatient with such Pharisees and

spoke out sharply against them. The Talmud (Yerushalmi Berakot 9:7 and Sotah 5:7) speaks derisively of the "shoulder Pharisee," who exhibits his good works on his shoulder for public view; the "wait-a-bit Pharisee," who announces to people with whom he is engaged in business that he must interrupt himself to do a good work; the "calculating Pharisee," who seeks to keep statistics on his transgressions and his good works; the "economizing Pharisee," who asks, What economy can I practice to save a little for the purpose of doing a good deed; the "show-me-my-fault Pharisee," who says, Show me my fault and I will correct it by a balancing good deed; the Pharisee who serves out of fear, like Job. Only one kind of Pharisee is dear to God, the Talmud adds, one who serves out of love, like father Abraham.

The Pharisees were the architects of popular Jewish piety. In the ideological battle they had once waged with the Sadducees, they won the people to their side. But the Pharisees remained a distinct party, with customs and disciplines of their own which set them apart from the rest of the people. While the people recognized them as the custodians of the tradition, this did not prevent the people, in some instances, from resenting the Pharisees as a group apart in the community. Jesus, as Yehezkel Kaufmann suggested, followed the Pharisaic tradition without formally being a member of the group.[6] This would explain his general adherence to Pharisaic principles, as well as the freedom of criticism which he voiced against them.

The Gospels, W. D. Davies reminds us, preserve "only the whisper of the voice of Jesus."[7] It is difficult to believe that Jesus could really have employed against the Pharisees the abusive language imputed to him in the Gospels. Did he not denounce anger as a vile emotion? Did he not advocate returning good for evil and turning "the other cheek"? But wide is the margin between what good men preach and what they are able to practice in their own life. The most dedicated and selfless idealists in religious and ethical pursuits have often made fierce adversaries of those with

[6] Yehezkel Kaufmann: *Goleh ve-Nekar* (Tel-Aviv; 1929), I, 353.
[7] W. D. Davies: *The Setting of the Sermon on the Mount* (New York: Cambridge University Press; 1964), p. 436.

whom they disagreed. A contemporary of Jesus, Rabbi Eliezer the son of Hyrcanus, had a favorite maxim: "Let your friend's honor be as precious to you as your own, and be not easily provoked to anger" (Avot 2:15). But when he became engaged in debate over some principle he proved a most recalcitrant opponent. In one instance he defied the consensus of his colleagues and sabotaged the proceedings of the academy with bitter and unyielding words. In the end he was voted in contempt of the academy and excommunicated from its deliberations.

Some have grounded the Jewish opposition to Jesus in his claims to being the messiah. The sources in the New Testament are by no means clear that Jesus himself laid claim to messianic status. Julius Wellhausen, Rudolf Bultmann, and Charles Guignebert, among others, tend to doubt this, attributing this claim to the Christian community after his death. Adolf Harnack and others believe that he did make such a claim.[8] Assuming that Jesus himself laid claim to being the messiah, this would not automatically have made him a heretic to bring the wrath of the Jewish authorities against him. Preceding Jesus and following him, there were various figures in Jewish history who were imbued with the redeemer's zeal and thought of themselves as messiahs. The best known of these was Bar Kokba, whose cause won a following among the highest circles of religious leadership in Judaism, including Rabbi Akiba, one of the most renowned teachers in the rabbinic academies of his time. Bar Kokba became the central figure in a movement for the liberation of Jewish Palestine from the Roman yoke which had its heyday in 135 C.E. Jesus conceived of messiahship in other terms than did Bar Kokba; his was otherwordly in emphasis and was less concerned with the injustices of Roman imperialism. But however he conceived his messiahship, this could not have created an impassable barrier between him and the Jewish authorities of his day.

Jesus has on occasions been presented as a universal spirit who was impatient with the introverted, narrow Jewish piety of his

[8] Adolf Harnack: *What Is Christianity?* (New York: G. P. Putnam's Sons; 1904), p. 133. (Now available in a Harper Torchbook soft-cover edition.)

time. The record, however, points clearly in the opposite direction. The Pharisees were concerned with bringing the message of their faith to the outside non-Jewish world. The New Testament itself states that the Pharisees would travel over land and sea to make a single convert for their faith (Matthew 23:15).

The Jewish missionary effort as guided by Pharisaic principles, we have noted earlier, did not concentrate primarily on seeking formal conversions to Judaism. It was content to make "God fearers," men who acknowledged the existence of a universal God and the claims of the moral law, even though they remained technically within their ancestral faith. Jesus, on the other hand, did not concern himself with the non-Jewish world. He centered his interests on his own people. He was reluctant to help a Canaanite woman because, as he explained to his disciples, he was sent "only to the lost sheep of the house of Israel" and that "it was not meet to take the children's bread and cast it to the dogs" (Matthew 15:21–27). He instructed his disciples when charging them to continue his ministry (Matthew 10:5–6): "Go nowhere among the Gentiles, and enter no town of the Samaritans, but go rather to the lost sheep of the house of Israel."

A contrary position is expressed in Jesus' parting message to his disciples, where he is quoted as charging them: "Go therefore and make disciples of all nations, baptizing them in the name of the Father and of the Son and of the Holy Spirit" (Matthew 28:19). But Jesus is here quoted as speaking after his resurrection, as an apparition seen by his disciples. It cannot therefore have the authenticity of the earlier encounters reported in his lifetime. The reference to the three persons of the trinity also stamps the final scene as a later formulation, after the trinitarian doctrine had been established. John C. Fenton, in his commentary on Matthew, cites the actual hesitation of the first disciples of Jesus to preach to gentiles, as reported in Acts 11:1–2, 19, and concludes that "it is improbable that Jesus said this." [9] He notes also that the first disciples of Jesus baptized in the name of Jesus, and not in the name of the trinity (Acts 2:38). D. E. Nineham, in his commentary on

[9] J. C. Fenton: *The Gospel of St. Matthew* (Baltimore: Penguin Books; 1963), p. 453.

Mark, regards the call to preach to all the nations "a saying current in a Gentile Church but not an actual saying of Jesus" [1] Indeed, the verses in Mark charging the disciples to preach to all the nations (16:14–16) are regarded by most scholars, Protestant as well as Catholic, as spurious. They relegate them as part of an appendix to the Gospel of Mark, written sometime in the second century.

Some have maintained that the God of Judaism is remote and austere, and that Jesus broke new ground in religion by proclaiming the nearness of God, and His accessibility to man, no matter what his condition. Thus it has been pointed out that Jesus called God *abba,* "father," a term of nearness and endearment. Joachim Jeremias, a prominent German Lutheran scholar of both Testaments, put it thus: "As a form of address to God the word abba is without parallel in the whole of late Jewish devotional literature. . . . There is no parallel to the authority with which he dares to address God as *abba.* . . ." [2] It is difficult to know where Professor Jeremias received his information, but he is of course very much mistaken. He is a noted authority on the history of Christianity, but his knowledge of post-biblical Judaism is limited. Jewish devotional literature abounds in the use of "father," as a term of address to God. It generally uses the Hebrew terms *avinu* or *av,* rather than the Aramaic *abba.* One prayer, recited on fast days and the Day of Atonement, consists of some forty verses, each of which begins with *avinu.* Sometimes the term appears in combinations as *av harahamim,* "Merciful Father"; *av shebashamayim,* "Heavenly Father"; *av lekol ha-olam,* "Father to the Whole World"; *avinu av harahamim* "Father, Merciful Father." In the words of Martin Buber: "The pious Jews of pre-Christian times called their God 'Father'. . . . It is not as though these men did not know that God is also utterly distant; it is rather that they know at the same time that however far away God is, he is never unrelated to them, and that even the man who is farthest away

---

[1] D. E. Nineham: *The Gospel of St. Mark* (Baltimore: Penguin Books; 1963), p. 449.

[2] Joachim Jeremias: *The Problem of Historical Jesus,* Norman Perrin (trans.) (Philadelphia: Fortress Press; 1964), pp. 18–21.

from God cannot cut himself off from the mutual relationship." [3]
The Rabbis' use of the term "Father" in various combinations,
when addressing God, is well documented by A. Marmorstein in
his *The Old Rabbinic Doctrine of God*.[4] Jesus was no innovator
when he used this term; he merely drew on one of the basic concepts of Jewish piety.

The Sermon on the Mount has sometimes been cited as a pronouncement by Jesus which appears to abrogate the old law in
favor of a new law propounded by him. Our principal source for
this body of teachings is Matthew 5–7. Commentators on the
Gospels tend to believe however that, as formulated, these teachings express the editorial hand of the evangelist himself and are
not to be seen as a direct utterance of Jesus. John C. Fenton, principal of Lichfield Theological College in England, and editor of
the Gospel of Matthew, put it thus: "Whatever the pattern of
this block of teachings is, it has almost certainly been contrived
by the Evangelist himself, because it is almost certain that Matthew has collected together here sayings of Jesus which were not
all spoken on the same occasion. The words and deeds of Jesus
seem to have been remembered and preserved in the period before they were written down as isolated small units of not more
than a paragraph each; and the arrangement of these paragraphs
and sayings was the work of the Evangelists." [5]

The Sermon on the Mount proceeds in the form of antithesis:
"You have heard. . . . But I say unto you." We cite a passage
from this sermon to illustrate its method as well as its substantive
direction: "You have heard that it was said to the men of old,
'You shall not kill [Exodus 20:13, Deuteronomy 5:17]; and whoever kills shall be liable to judgment.' But I say to you that everyone who is angry with his brother shall be liable to judgment;
whoever insults his brother shall be liable to the council, and
whoever says, 'You fool!' shall be liable to the hell of fire. . . .
You have heard that it was said [Exodus 21:21, Leviticus 24:20,
Deuteronomy 19:21], 'An eye for an eye and a tooth for a tooth.'

[3] *The Writings of Martin Buber*, Will Herberg (ed.) (New York:
Meridian Books; 1956), p. 268.
[4] (London: Oxford University Press; 1927), pp. 56–62.
[5] Fenton: *The Gospel of St. Matthew*, p. 78.

But I say to you, Do not resist one who is evil. But if anyone strike you on the right cheek, turn to him the other also; and if anyone would sue you and take your coat, let him have your cloak as well; and if anyone forces you to go one mile, go with him two miles. Give to him who begs from you, and do not refuse him who would borrow from you" (Matthew 5:21-22, 38-42).

An analysis of this passage and of the Sermon as a whole does not support the impression that we have here an abrogation of the old law taught by Judaism in favor of a new law propounded by Jesus. The Sermon on the Mount does not abrogate the original commandments of Judaism but seeks to remind us that law in itself does not fulfill the full demand of our moral responsibilities, that there is a zone of moral concern beyond the law which a good man must attend to.

Moshe Greenberg, Ellis Professor of Biblical Studies at the University of Pennsylvania, expressed it thus "The New Testament does not contain a corpus of criminal laws. While several sayings of Jesus touch upon points of biblical law, they do not themselves take the form of law, but of exhortation to saintly behavior (e.g., Matthew 5:21-32, note vs. 20). Jesus' pronouncement on talion is a case in point: what is rejected is far more than the literal application of 'an eye for an eye and a tooth for a tooth,' which, as suggested above, can hardly have been a juridical penalty even in ancient Israel. The Tannaitic understanding that monetary compensation alone is implied (Mekilta at Exodus 21:23; Misnah Baba Kamma 8:1) would be no less repugnant to Matthew 5:38-41. For the demand here is that the injured waive his rights to sue for reparations of any sort whatever. This saintly teaching is, of course, the very antithesis of a legal prescription." [6]

In protesting the moral insufficiency of law as such, Jesus expressed a familiar doctrine in rabbinic Judaism. The Rabbis often emphasized the importance of the law, but they were well aware that a morally sensitive person cannot content himself with merely conforming to the law, but must often go beyond it. In

[6] Moshe Greenberg [erroneously cited as J. Greenberg]: "Crimes and Punishments," *The Interpreter's Dictionary of the Bible* (Nashville, Tenn.: Abingdon Press; 1962), I, 742 ff.

one instance the Rabbis declared that Jerusalem was destroyed because the people therein were content to act in accordance with the strict demands of the law (Baba Metzia 88a). Good people must act *lifnim mishurat ha-din*, "beyond the letter of the law" (Mekilta on Exodus 18:20).

In the Sermon on the Mount Jesus expressed what the Rabbis called *midat hasidut*, "a standard of saintliness," by which rare spirits live. The Rabbis idealized the person who accepts offense without retaliation and submits to suffering cheerfully (Yoma 23a). Does not the Amidah include in the final liturgical meditation these words: *venafshi keafar lakol tihyeh*, "and may I be like dust to all." It is a strange idiom but it is obviously a prayer for a state of self-effacement that would make a person wholly non-responsive to injury. In the *Ethics of the Fathers* we have the following evaluation of human character (5:13): "He who says, What is mine is mine, and what is yours is yours, is a medium type, and some say that his type is like that of the wicked city of Sodom. . . . He who says, What is mine is yours and what is yours is yours, is a saintly man." The Mishnah (Sotah 3:4), in one instance, cautioned against excessive "saintliness" because it may prove quite unrealitic, but there have always been "unrealistic saints" in the history of Judaism.

The exhortation to the "standard of saintliness" presupposes an existing social order with a system of justice to protect the innocent and judge the guilty. But good men render a precious service to the world by reminding us of a higher standard where men are protected by a more potent safeguard, a mutuality of love, a degree of self-effacement and non-retaliation to hurt which establishes peace through love rather than the fear of force. In projecting such a standard Jesus did not necessarily negate the right of men—even their duty, in some circumstances—to resist aggression. He was within the tradition of his people in projecting another order of life in which saintliness would render the dependence on force a moral anachronism.

This interpretation of the two major elements by which the structure of this sermon is developed will account for an otherwise insoluble problem in its text. As David Daube noted: "Twice in the sermon on the mount, 'Ye have heard' leads up to a quotation not really found in the Old Testament: 'Ye have heard, Thou shalt not kill, and [only] he who kills shall be in danger of the judgment,' and 'Ye have heard, Thou shalt love thy neighbor and hate thine enemy' [Matthew 5:21]. The clauses, 'and only he who kills shall be in danger of the judgment' and 'thou shalt hate thine enemy,' do not occur in the Pentateuch at all. However, as soon as we proceed from the translation 'You have literally understood,' the additions cease to be troublesome." [7] It was not the Pentateuchal law as such which Jesus castigated, but its vulgarization by an interpretation of strict literalism. The clauses missing in the Pentateuchal text are simply an interpretation of that text which Jesus found offensive.

Those who have studied the Sermon on the Mount critically tend to see it not as a call to abrogate the law of Judaism but as an effort to redefine that law in terms of the higher demands of its inner spirit. "You have heard. . . . But I say unto you," according to Professor Daube, is not meant to oppose the old law with a new law, but rather to contrast two interpretations of the old law; the conventional interpretation, which is literal and narrow, and the interpretation advocated by Jesus, which seeks to fulfill not only the letter but also the spirit and the underlying ideal of that law. In the words of Professor Daube: "In Matthew, in the sermon on the mount, we find a series of injunctions intended to illustrate Jesus as upholder, not destroyer of the Law. They all, more or less, follow this pattern: 'Ye have heard what was said by them of old time, Thou shalt not kill. But I say unto you, That whosoever is angry with his brother shall be in danger of the judgment.' This form falls into two parts. The first gives a Scriptural rule narrowly interpreted, the second a wider demand made by Jesus. . . . The relationship between the two members of the form is not one of pure contrast; the demand that you must not be angry with your brother is not thought of as utterly irreconcilable with the prohibition of killing. On the contrary, wider and deeper though it may be, it is thought of as, in a sense, resulting from, and certainly including, the old rule." [8] W. D. Davies,

[7] David Daube: *The New Testament and Rabbinic Judaism* (London: University of London; 1956), p. 56.

[8] Ibid., p. 60.

after quoting the statement of Daube, adds the following: "To interpret on the side of stringency is not to annul the Law, but to change it in accordance with its own intention. From this point of view . . . we cannot speak of the Law being annulled in the antithesis, but only of its being intensified in its demand, or reinterpreted in a higher key." [9]

Elwyn E. Tilden, Jr., of Lafayette College, Easton, Pennsylvania, in his brief commentary on Matthew (5:21–48) in the *Oxford Annotated Bible*, regards the Sermon on the Mount similarly as an exposition of what the old law really demands and as a protest against its narrowing by conventional interpretations. He describes the provisions of this Sermon as "illustrations of the true understanding of the Law." The theme was a common one among the Rabbis as well, who were ever seeking to lift the spiritual vistas of their people by showing them the wider implications of the law, and the broader principles which lie beyond the zone of law. Principles or laws once adopted shrink or broaden in scope depending on the people who live by them.

The ground of authority on which Jesus took his stand was the Hebrew Bible, but for him too, just as for the Rabbis, the Bible was not a rigid document. Jesus supplemented the biblical word with a kind of *midrash*, an interpretive elaboration, which made the Bible an efficacious instrument for dealing with life as he understood it. The Oral Torah is of wide latitude and it permitted diverse interpretations. This diversity was balanced by the unity of a common adherence to the authority of the scriptural word itself and to the principles of hermeneutics by which the text was expounded to yield new inferences. The interpretations quoted in the name of Jesus are not incompatible with the structure of the Oral Torah or with the method by which its provisions were drawn from the written text.

Jesus is quoted in the Gospels as expounding the biblical text on a number of subjects. We quote his exposition concerning the Sabbath. The report in Mark 2:23–28 is as follows: "One sabbath he was going through the grain fields; and as they made their way his disciples began to pluck ears of grain. And the Pharisees said to him, 'Look, why are they doing what is not lawful on the Sab-

[9] Davies: *Setting of the Sermon on the Mount,* p. 102.

bath?' And he said to them, 'Have you not read what David did [I Samuel 21:1–6, II Samuel 8:17], when he was in need and hungry, he and those who were with him: how he entered the house of God, when Abiathar was high priest, and ate the bread of the Presence, which it is not lawful for any but the priests to eat, and also gave it to those who were with him?' And he said to them, 'The sabbath is made for man, not man for the sabbath; so the Son of man is, also lord even of the sabbath.' "

The same report is quoted in Luke 6:1–5. This report is also cited in Matthew 12:1–8, but with a slight change. After quoting the precedent of David, who ate the "bread of the Presence," he cites an additional consideration: "Or have you not read in the law [Numbers 28:9–10] how on the sabbath the priests profane the sabbath, and are guiltless? I tell you, something greater than the temple is here. And if you had known what this means [Hosea 6:6], 'I desire mercy and not sacrifice,' you would not have condemned the guiltless. For the Son of man is lord of the sabbath."

Another case involving the Sabbath law is reported in Mark 3:1–6, and it is also reported in substantially the same form in Luke 6:6–11. As reported in Mark the case was as follows: "Again he entered the synagogue, and a man was there who had a withered hand. And they watched him to see whether he would heal on the sabbath, so that they might accuse him. And he said to the man who had the withered hand, 'Come here.' And he said to them, 'Is it lawful on the sabbath to do good or to do harm, to save life or to kill?' But they were silent. And he looked around at them with anger, grieved at their hardness of heart, and said to the man, 'Stretch out your hand.' He stretched it out, and his hand was restored."

The issue under discussion is the application of the scriptural law which forbids work on the Sabbath. Jesus is quoted as propounding the view that the prohibition was not meant in an absolute sense, that it was not to be applicable where the work contemplated was to assuage hunger, to heal the sick, to save life. In the case of the disciples who plucked grain on the Sabbath, Jesus is quoted as citing scriptural support for condoning it. Had not David and his associates violated a law to assuage their hunger?

The priests in the Temple regularly ignored the Sabbath to perform the sacrificial rites. Since Scripture itself testifies that an act of mercy is preferable in the eyes of God to the rites of sacrifices, it should certainly be proper to set aside the usual Sabbath restrictions to meet human needs, such as assuaging hunger. In the second case cited, no specific scriptural text is quoted, but it is implied. Since there is nothing higher than saving life, healing cannot be forbidden on the Sabbath.

The principle propounded by Jesus acknowledges the authority of the biblical prohibition to labor on the Sabbath, but it surrounds it with qualifications. This is precisely how the Sabbath law is treated by the Rabbis. The rabbinic principle is *pikuah nefesh dohe shabbat*, "the saving of life supersedes the Sabbath." And this principle is given even broader scope in several well-known maxims: "The Sabbath has been given for you, you were not given for the Sabbath" (Mekilta on Exodus 31:13) and "the Sabbath has been placed under your authority, you have not been placed under its authority" (Yoma 85b).

The Rabbis specifically permitted various categories of communal business on the Sabbath, such as meeting for the purpose of making grants to charity, and when necessary, they allowed attending meetings with Roman officials on the Sabbath, even if this meant going to see them at "theaters, circuses, and basilicas." They likewise allowed making arrangements on the Sabbath for the betrothal of a young girl, or for a child's education, including training for a trade.

The Rabbis quoted Isaiah 58:13 as a source for their views: "If you honor it [the Sabbath], not going your own ways, or pursuing your own business. . . ." One's own "business" must not be attended to on the Sabbath, but acts of service to others—good deeds—are the Lord's "business" and are therefore permitted (Shabbat 150a).

The additional statement attributed to Jesus, "The Son of man is lord of the sabbath," is of uncertain meaning. Some have taken it as directed at Jesus himself, that he, in his role as "Son of man," is Lord of the Sabbath. This would imply that the authority to break the Sabbath derives from the special status of Jesus, but is not the point of the homily that it is the fact of human *need* which sanctions labor on the Sabbath, and if so, is not *any* man in such instance justified in ignoring the restriction against work on the Sabbath? The Rabbis made it a point to emphasize that the suspension of Sabbath restrictions in order to save life does not require specific sanction from religious authorities, but that each individual must act on his own and "the quicker one does so, the more praiseworthy he is" (Yoma 84b). Professor Morton Scott Enslin and others have suggested that "Son of man" in the present passage is to be understood simply as *man*, any man, in other words, and it does not refer to Jesus at all.[1] If *any man* be acknowledged as lord over the Sabbath, then the statement attributed to Jesus would be an exact parallel to the maxim of the Rabbis. The discourse of Jesus on the Sabbath law, as quoted in the Gospels, is thus within the general pattern of thought developed by the Rabbis in the Oral Torah.

The principle attributed to Jesus in qualifying the law of the Sabbath is clearly the principle well recognized in rabbinic Judaism, but the application given it in the Gospels is less certain. If the disciples were in a state of starvation to the point where their health was really imperiled, or if the man with the withered hand faced some special jeopardy through the persistence of his condition, then the principle enunciated would be clearly applicable. On the other hand, if this were not the case, then there was no real cogency for the action *on the Sabbath*. There would have been no serious loss in delay. D. E. Nineham has noted this point when he declared: "The difficulty with this is that the man with the withered hand was in no danger of death; there was no question of saving or destroying life; if there had been, the rabbis themselves would have been completely at one with Jesus, for they were quite clear that the sabbath law might and must be broken in cases of danger to life. But Jesus seems to extend this principle so as to make it justify healing work of all kinds—and, indeed, all other kinds of benevolent work—on the sabbath. If that was his meaning the effect would have been to supersede the sabbath law entirely, for the prohibition on sabbath work would

[1] Morton S. Enslin: "Son of Man," *An Encyclopedia of Religion* (New York: Philosophical Library; 1945), p. 726; cf. Nineham: *The Gospel of St. Mark*, p. 108.

become simply a prohibition of evil and life-destroying activity on the sabbath, and that is forbidden on any day." [2]

Students of the Gospel texts have indeed questioned whether these reports may be considered historical. One may, for example, question the rather strange coincidence that the Pharisees were present as Jesus and his disciples passed the cornfield. The coincidence suggests rather a deliberate stage setting, in other words, the work of the evangelist who wrote the Gospel.

Rudolf Bultmann is of the opinion that these reports reflect not the practice of Jesus himself but that of the later Christian community, which had broken with the practices of Judaism. To justify their action, they told stories to show that their master had sanctioned their conduct. As Bultmann puts it: "The 'disciples,' i.e. the primitive Christian church, have broken with the old customs in this matter, and they are defending themselves against criticism by means of the stories, through which they make their appeal to a saying of Jesus." [3]

Another incident in which Jesus is involved in what appears to be an attack on Jewish practice deals with the question of divorce. The report is quoted in Mark 10:2–12: "And Pharisees came up and in order to test him asked, 'Is it lawful for a man to divorce his wife?' He answered them, 'What did Moses command you?' They said, 'Moses allowed a man to write a certificate of divorce, and to put her away' [Deuteronomy 24:1–4]. But Jesus said to them, 'For your hardness of heart he wrote you this commandment. But from the beginning of creation, "God made them male and female." "For this reason a man shall leave his father and mother and be joined to his wife, and the two shall become one" [Genesis 1:27, 5:2, 2:24]. So they are no longer two but one. What, therefore, God has joined together let no man put asunder.' And in the house the disciples asked him again about this matter. And he said to them, 'Whoever divorces his wife and marries another, commits adultery against her; and if she divorces her husband and marries another, she commits adultery.'"

The same case is reported in Matthew 19:1–9, with the usual variation in details. But here a radical difference appears in the

[2] Nineham: *St. Mark*, p. 109.
[3] Bultmann and Kundsin: *Form Criticism*, p. 44.

concluding statement of Jesus. In the Matthew version, Jesus is quoted thus: "And I say to you: whoever divorces his wife, except for unchastity, and marries another, commits adultery." According to Matthew, the rejection of divorce is not absolute. Divorce is sanctioned on grounds of unchastity.

The differences between Matthew and Mark on so crucial an aspect of the views of Jesus are a dramatic reminder of the uncertainty we face in defining what is authentic in the views of Jesus. But both reports proceed clearly on the common ground of scriptural authority. The moral element in the position of Jesus derives from the biblical conception of marriage as founded in the design of creation, which intended male and female to separate themselves from their respective fathers and mothers and to join themselves to one another, as one flesh (Genesis 1:27, 2:24).

The apparent sanction of divorce which reflected current Jewish practice and which was rooted in Deuteronomy 24:1–4, where it is taken for granted that a man may give his wife a bill of divorcement and send her away and she may then marry another, is cited as a challenge to Jesus. He replies by redefining the provision in Deuteronomy in a manner typical of the Midrash, by an interpretive supplement. The sanction of divorce in Deuteronomy, he expounds, does not represent the true scriptural ideal. It is a concession granted to men, because of their weakness. Jesus, however, asks his followers to rise above the compromise and reach out for the scriptural ideal, which is less permissive. The entire exposition proceeds with all the presuppositions of the Oral Torah and with its basic methodology of defining a scriptural text in the light of other texts, and in the light of our general understanding of what the Torah really wants for human life.

Not only in method but in the substance of his thought, the position of Jesus remains in consonance with general rabbinic thinking on the subject. Even more explicit than the verses from Genesis quoted by Jesus is the declaration of the prophet Malachi (2:13–16): "And this again you do. You cover the Lord's altar with tears, with weeping and groaning because he no longer regards the offering or accepts it with favor at your hand. You ask, 'Why does he not?' Because the Lord was witness to the covenant between you and the wife of your youth, to whom you have been

faithless, though she is your companion and your wife by covenant. . . . So take heed to yourselves, let none be faithless to the
wife of his youth. For hateful is [literally, he hates] divorce says
the Lord, the God of Israel, and covering one's garment with violence, says the Lord of hosts. So take heed to yourselves and do
not be faithless." The Rabbis took the verse from Malachi as the
occasion for many touching statements in abhorrence of divorce.
Said Rabbi Elazar: "Whoever divorces the wife of his youth,
causes even the altar to shed tears for his treachery, as it is written, 'And this again you do. You cover the Lord's altar with tears
. . . because the Lord was witness to the covenant between you
and the wife of your youth, to whom you have been faithless.'"
Rabbi Johanan read his exhortation into the very words of the
prophet: "Hateful is divorce" (quoted in Yalkut Shimeoni *ad
locum*).

There was no division of opinion among the Rabbis on the
moral issues involved in divorce. The severance of the marriage
bond is a tragic event, which desecrates a covenant meant to be
holy and binding for all time. But the facts of life sometimes confront us with grievous situations, in which the ideal is defeated or compromised. The unity of marriage is founded ultimately on the love that should relate husband and wife to each
other. Sometimes, however, one partner may be unfaithful to the
other. Sometimes even without formal grounds, husband and wife
prove unsuited for each other, and love turns to hate. In the face
of certain tragic circumstances, is not the dissolution of a marriage a preferable alternative? Shall the law shut its eyes to these
realities and insist that husband and wife must continue to live
with each other in a marriage which has in truth ceased to exist?

Rabbinic jurists were realistic and under certain circumstances
sanctioned divorce. The School of Hillel, which was also joined
by Rabbi Akiba, was not concerned with objective considerations. Given the subjective fact of incompatibility, the law must
acknowledge what life has wrought, and must permit the dissolution of the marriage. The School of Shammai, on the other hand,
insisted on objective grounds, and it sanctioned divorce only for
reasons of unchastity. The formal basis of these divergent opinions was centered in the interpretation of Deuteronomy 24:1:

"When a man takes a wife and marries her, if then she finds no favor in his eyes because he has found some indecency in her, and he writes her a bill of divorce. . . ." The School of Shammai saw the term "indecency" as implying a case of unchastity; Rabbi Akiba quoted, "if then she finds no favor in his eyes" as the significant consideration, which is all subjective; the School of Hillel cited "some indecency," the qualification *some* implying to them *any* fault which the husband deems an indecency (Mishnah Gittin 9:10).

If Matthew's version be correct and Jesus allowed divorce on grounds of unchastity, then he would be in agreement with the views of the School of Shammai. If so, it may appear strange that Jesus did not follow the scriptural interpretation of the Shammaites, and base his view on the word "indecency." Jesus may well have agreed that the verse in Deuteronomy has the more permissive meaning, especially since the general practice followed the School of Hillel. Jesus found firmer ground for his views, whether as reported in Matthew or in Mark, by calling for the higher ideal which Scripture clearly affirmed, rather than the compromise sanctioned by the law. The theory that biblical law sometimes accommodates itself to human weakness and demands of man less than the highest was a familiar view in rabbinic circles. It was invoked, for example, to account for the permission granted by the Bible (Deuteronomy 21:10–14) to Israelite warriors to marry women taken captive in war (Kiddushin 21b).

Another exemplification of the method of the Oral Torah, precisely as taught by the Rabbis, is afforded us in Matthew 22:23–23, with a close parallel in Mark 12:18–27: "The same day Sadducees came to him, who say there is no resurrection; and they asked him a question, saying, 'Teacher, Moses said [Deuteronomy 25:5], If a man dies, having no children, his brother must marry the widow, and raise up children for his brother. Now there were seven brothers among us; the first married, and died, and having no children left his wife to his brother. So, too, the second and third, down to the seventh. After them all, the woman died. In the resurrection, therefore, to which of the seven will she be wife? For they all had her.' But Jesus answered them, 'You are wrong, because you know neither Scriptures nor the power of God. For in the resurrection they neither marry nor are given in marriage, but are like angels in heaven. And as for the resurrection of the dead, have you not read what was told to you by God [Exodus 3:6], I am the Lord God of Abraham, and the God of Isaac, and the God of Jacob. He is not God of the dead, but of the living.' And when the crowd heard it, they were astonished at his teaching."

The Sadducees as we know from Josephus and from rabbinic sources did not believe in the resurrection as the crowning event of "the end of days." They did not believe in the general extension of the teachings of the Torah through the method of *midrash*, which had been developed by the Pharisees. They were strict constructionists of the biblical text, and they accepted only what was explicitly in the text. In the passage quoted, Jesus stands as the champion of Pharisaic teachings, which in his time had become normative in general Jewish doctrine. He affirms the resurrection, and he affirms the method of *midrash* by which the doctrine of the resurrection found support in the biblical text.

The statement of Jesus is paralleled substantively in the teachings of the Rabbis. One teacher put it thus (Berakot 17a): "In the world to come there is no eating or drinking, no begetting of children, no commerce, no envy, no jealousy no hatred and no competition—there is only this, that the righteous sit with crowns on their heads and take delight in the splendor of God's presence."

The proofs cited by the Rabbis for the resurrection do not differ in substance from the proof given by Jesus. Here is one such proof quoted in the Talmud (Sanhedrin 90b) in the name of Rabbi Simlai: "Whence do we infer the belief in the resurrection from the Torah? From the verse [Exodus 6:4], 'And I also have established My covenant with them [the Patriarchs] to give them the land of Canaan.' It does not say 'to give you,' but 'to give them,' implying that they would be restored so that the land might really be given to them." These "proofs" are all of one character—they are attempts to find some scriptural allusion, to confirm a doctrine deemed vital, but which some circles continued to challenge.

The exponents of the Oral Torah did not confine themselves

to scriptural interpretations. They often expressed views directly, without reference to proof texts. The Torah was conceived in broad terms allowing for new insights which were in harmony with its basic teachings, though they might not flow directly from a text. Jesus, too, expounded many ideas directly, not relating them to Scripture, though they were always within the spirit of the Bible and the rabbinic tradition which had grown out of it. Jesus extolled poverty, he spoke for the simple life, he attacked involvement in mundane concerns and asked for a concentration on the life of the spirit, on faith in God, and the pursuits of mercy and love. The most important of his teachings was the messianic doctrine. Whether he himself believed that he was the promised messiah is still a subject of speculation among scholars. But he believed and taught as a basic article of his faith that the messianic promise, long spoken of by the prophets, was reaching fulfillment, that the present world was about to end, and the eschatological visions of a divine kingdom to supersede the present order, were about to become a reality. The change, he taught, was to be effected through God's intervention, and then would follow the Last Judgment, and the promised bliss for the righteous and retribution for the wicked. Jesus called on his adherents to prepare for the end by penitence (cf. Matthew 25:31–46). The ascetic trend in his teachings, and the apparent disdain for the world and its problems, stemmed in great part from this belief in the imminent destruction of the present order and the inauguration of the new order, the Kingdom of God.[4]

Jesus is quoted as having said that the Kingdom would be established in his own generation (Mark 13:30, Matthew 10:23), and to have assured his listeners that some among them would "not taste death before they see the Kingdom of God come with power" (Mark 9:1). Those who took his prophecy of the imminent end seriously could not but respond with a radical shift in their center of interest; the world paled in its appeal for them. The Thessalonian Christians concluded from this belief that it was foolish to work. This faith fostered an uprootedness from the existential world, its claims and its responsibilities.

[4] Nineham: *St. Mark*, p. 48; Fenton: *St. Matthew*, p. 21; Bultmann and Kundsin: *Form Criticism*, p. 101.

The sources from which the belief in imminent world destruction was drawn were varied. In part it represented the action of an innate mystical tendency that is especially pronounced in certain natures. In part it was an influence of apocalyptic visionaries who were then active in the Jewish world and who were preoccupied with pointing to the impending end of the present epoch and its replacement by a new heavenly order which would cancel all mundane existence with its effrontery to the life of the spirit. The call of Jesus for recognition of his own role as mediator of divine power in healing, in forgiveness of sin, and in the qualification of those who are to be admitted to God's kingdom, if historical, is a parallel to the conceptions found in apocalyptic writings.

This belief was also fed, no doubt, by the evils of the Roman occupation and the yoke which bore heavily on the land, which set Jews to dream of redemption and deliverance. There were some who were aware that the work of redemption depended at least in part on human initiative. But Jesus belonged to those who waited for a miraculous deliverance through an intervention by God and His angelic hosts. For Jesus, as Maurice Goguel put it, "the entry into the Messianic Kingdom depends on divine and not on human initiative." [5]

According to some scholars, the journey of Jesus and his followers to Jerusalem was to witness and share in the epochal event which was to inaugurate the new order, the Kingdom of God. According to Paul Winter, the entry to Jerusalem "has the appearance of an unmistakable messianic demonstration. As such it would have been an open defiance of imperial authority—a proclamation of the will to national independence from Roman rule." [6] The kingdom which Jesus proclaimed was not of this world, but spirit does not exist in total detachment from substance. Certainly for his followers, this "kingdom" could not but appear as the antithesis of the existing power structure, and a reinauguration of the ideal kingdom of ancient days, the kingdom of

[5] Maurice Goguel: *The Life of Jesus*, Olive Wyon (trans.) (New York: Barnes & Noble; 1958), p. 314.

[6] Paul Winter: *On the Trial of Jesus* (Berlin: Walter de Gruyter & Co.; 1961), p. 141.

David. No wonder his followers greeted Jesus with royal acclaim, shouting among other things (Mark 11:10): "Blessed be the name of the kingdom of our father David, that cometh in the name of the Lord; Hosanna in the highest."

It was his messianic proclamation which brought on the tragedy of Calvary. As Professor Solomon Zeitlin reminds us: "On the cross was inscribed in Hebrew, Greek and Latin: *Jesus Nazarenus, Rex Judaeorum,* 'Jesus of Nazareth, the King of the Jews.' It was the Roman custom to write the reason for the execution on a placard and attach it to the body of the victim. Pilate followed the established method. Jesus was crucified for claiming to be the king of the Judeans." [7]

As we shall have occasion to note later on, the offense of Jesus was clearly an offense against the existing order. Jewish officials no doubt played a part in the proceedings, but they were Roman appointees and served as collaborators of the Roman authorities. Charles Guignebert, professor of the History of Christianity at the University of Paris, tends to doubt that Jesus regarded himself as a messiah. But it was the messianic movement, the call to expect an immediate end to the existing order and the dawn of the heavenly kingdom, which made Jesus a menace to the Roman authorities. The account in the Gospels that places the blame for the crucifixion on the Jews, Professor Guignebert further maintains, is clearly inaccurate and represents an anti-Jewish bias, as well as a desire to curry favor at the hands of the Roman authorities: "According to all appearances, the efforts of our Evangelists to absolve the Roman of guilt, and lay upon the Jews the entire responsibility for the crime, are not inspired by a desire to be true to the facts, but by a desire to humor the Roman authorities, for they were writing at a time when these authorities were the sole support of the Christians against the animosity displayed toward them by the synagogues." [8]

Paul Winter, in his more recent study of the trial of Jesus, offers us the same conclusion: "The Gospel records, when criti-

[7] Solomon Zeitlin: "The Dates of the Birth and the Crucifixion of Jesus," *Jewish Quarterly Review,* LV:1 (July 1964), 56 ff.

[8] Charles Guignebert: *Christianity, Past and Present* (New York: The Macmillan Company; 1927), pp. 37, 38, 43.

cally examined, furnish clear evidence of the fact that Jesus was executed on a charge of sedition at the order of the Emperor's representative. . . . That he was executed as a rebel, together with others who were executed on the same charge, by no means proves that he did work for the overthrow of the existing political system. So far as the procurator [Pontius Pilate] was concerned, it would have been sufficient reason for ordering the crucifixion if he had come to the conclusion that Jesus' itinerant preaching tended to excite the masses to expect the end of the existing order." [9]

Our primary concern, however, is not the personal destiny of Jesus, but his exemplification of the Jewish interpretive tradition in the study of Scripture. We have noted that the teachings of Jesus, insofar as it is possible to reconstruct them from layers of later New Testament reinterpretations, are expressive of the method and the substance of the Oral Torah as developed by the great masters of rabbinic Judaism. If, in some details Jesus hewed an independent line, this was normal in rabbinic Judaism, which allowed a wide latitude for individual teachers to think independently. If, in some instances, his views might have aroused opposition from contemporary teachers, this, too, was a normal phenomenon in Judaism. The debates between the School of Shammai and the School of Hillel on the interpretation of tradition and its application to contemporary life were sometimes fiercely acrimonious, but there was never any doubt that both were legitimate lines for the exposition of Judaism. Jesus, declared Professor Guignebert, "did not come bearing a new religion, nor even a new rite, but only a conception personal rather than original of the piety embedded in the Jewish religion. Nor did he aim at changing either its creed or its Law or its worship. The central point of his teaching was the Messianic idea, which was common property of all his compatriots as much as to him, and only his conception of it was his own. . . . To attribute to him the desire to found a Church, his Church, to provide it with rites and sacraments, visible signs of his grace, and to prepare it for the conquest of the whole world—these are just anachronisms. I prefer to say

[9] Winter: *On the Trial of Jesus*, p. 148.

that they are distortions of his ideas which would have shocked him, had he known them." [1]

Jesus himself declared his loyalty to the institutions of Judaism when he said (Matthew 5:17-18): "Think not that I have come to abolish the law and the prophets; I have come not to abolish them but to fulfill them. For truly, I say to you, till heaven and earth pass, not an iota, not a dot shall pass from the law until all is accomplished." But the process of seeking to fulfill the law often involved going beyond it, to supplement the written word with new elaborations. This process of supplementation and elaboration was achieved primarily through an interpretive technique represented by the Midrash, and exemplified in the Oral Torah.

The Jesus of history was a son of his people, who shared their dreams, who was loyal to their way of life, who died a martyr's death because of a commitment to his vision of their highest destiny. The image of Jesus as depicted in Christian writings was not founded on historical reality. It is rather a work of idealization and myth-building, reflecting the faith, primarily, of those who were under the influence of the non-Jewish, Hellenistic world, and who conceived Jesus in accordance with their own understanding of the hero in the drama of salvation. Professor Frederick C. Grant, writing in the language of Christian piety, but also as a historian, puts it thus: "In a profoundly true sense it is not— and never has been—the Jesus of history who is the redeemer of men and the hope of the world, but the spiritual Christ, the risen and exalted Lord of the church's faith." [2] Rudolf Bultmann reached the same conclusion. Summarizing Bultmann's views, Joachim Jeremias put it bluntly: "For Bultmann, the history of Jesus is part of Judaism, not of Christianity. . . . The study of Jesus and his message may be very interesting and instructive for the historical understanding of the rise of Christianity, but it has no significance for faith." [3] Bultmann himself expressed it thus: "The message of Jesus belongs to the presuppositions of the the-

[1] Guignebert: *Christianity, Past and Present*, p. 44.
[2] *The Gospels: Their Origin and Their Growth* (New York: Harper & Brothers; 1957), p. 9.
[3] Jeremias: *Historical Jesus*, pp. 9-10.

ology of the New Testament and is not a part of that theology itself." [4] In other words, the teaching of Jesus is only a preface to Christianity, which does not really begin until after the death of Jesus.

Indeed, many Christian scholars have abandoned the quest for the historical Jesus because this leads to Judaism and not to Christianity. Christianity was a work of construction by Jesus' disciples, who made him the center of an original conceptual system, which included among its formative elements "the Easter experiences of the disciples, the Messianic expectations of Judaism and the mythology of the pagan world with which Jesus of Nazareth was to be clothed." [5]

The question may well be raised as to why the teachings of Jesus did not enter the classic literature of Torah supplementation. In the time of Jesus, as Professor Harry A. Wolfson has pointed out,[6] Jewish teachers were officially affiliated with schools, the School of Shammai or the School of Hillel. Those schools preserved the teachings of affiliated masters. In the official literature preserved from this period, the heads of the schools are quoted by name, while the individual masters are quoted collectively, in the consensus which eventually summed up their views. Independent teachers, like Jesus, were free to teach, but their words were often lost to posterity. The recent discovery of the Dead Sea Scrolls is a reminder that a literature of vast scope flourished in Judea, which was lost until our own day.

The teachings of Jesus were preserved by his followers—but in a context that obscured their original character. They were reinterpreted to conform to the new role that Jesus assumed after his death, as the central figure in a new religion that was essentially hostile to Judaism. But the historical Jesus, to the extent that we can envision him from the reinterpreted versions left by his followers, represents a point of development running unbroken from the Hebrew Bible and linked to it through an interpretive supplement that is characteristic of the great literary creation of the Rabbis, the Oral Torah. As Yehezkel Kaufmann put it: "The

[4] Cited by Jeremias: ibid., p. 9.
[5] Ibid., pp. 9 ff.
[6] *Menorah Journal*, XLIX (1962), 25–31.

attitude of Jesus to the Torah is the very same attitude one finds among the masters of *halakah* and *haggadah* who followed in the Pharisaic tradition. The Torah is the everlasting foundation on which they base their own views and doctrines, even when they appear to digress sharply from its literal meaning. . . . Jesus believed that his teachings were only a completion or a clarification of the teachings of the Torah, guideposts inviting man how to live and conduct himself in its spirit." [7]

[7] Kaufmann: *Goleh ve-Nekar*, p. 342.

Two Types of Faith

By Martin Buber

T HE Jewish position may be summarized in the sentence:
fulfilment of the divine commandment is valid when
it takes place in conformity with the full capacity of the
person and from the whole intention of faith. If we
want to give a parallel formulation to Jesus' demand that is
transcending it, the sentence may run like this: fulfilment
of the divine commandment is valid if it takes place
in conformity with the full intention of the revelation
and from the whole intention of faith—in which however
the conception of the intention of faith receives an
eschatological character. The first of these two positions
starts from the actuality of the acting individuals and
the conditionality of their ability, the second on the
one hand from the actuality of God at Sinai and the un-
conditionality of its claim, on the other hand from the
eschatological situation and the readiness incumbent on it
to enter into the kingdom of God which draws near. Both
conflict with Paul's critical attitude to the Torah.

I say 'Torah' and not 'law' because at this point it will
not do to retain the Greek mis-translation which had such

56

far-reaching influence upon Paul's thought. In the Hebrew Bible Torah does not mean law, but direction, instruction, information. *Moreh* means not law-giver but teacher. God is repeatedly called this in Old Testament texts. 'Who is a teacher like Him?' Job is asked (Job xxxvi. 22), and the prophet promises the future people of Zion: 'Thine eyes shall see thy Teacher' (Isa. xxx. 20); man is ever expectant that the God who forgives will teach Israel 'the good way' (see especially 1 Kings viii. 36) and the Psalmist asks as a matter of inward certainty (Ps. xxv. 4, xxvii. 11): 'Teach me Thy paths'. The Torah of God is understood as God's instruction in His way, and therefore not as a separate *objectivum*. It includes laws, and laws are indeed its most vigorous objectivizations, but the Torah itself is essentially not law. A vestige of the actual speaking always adheres to the commanding word, the directing voice is always present or at least its sound is heard fading away. To render *torah* by 'law' is to take away from its idea this inner dynamic and vital character. Without the change of meaning in the Greek, objective sense the Pauline dualism of law and faith, life from works and life from grace, would miss its most important conceptual presupposition.

It must not of course be overlooked that from the very beginning in Israel itself, with the existence of the Tables, all the more with that of a 'Book of the Covenant' and more than ever of a 'Holy Scripture', the tendency towards the objectivizing of the Torah increasingly gained ground. We become acquainted with its results best in Jeremiah's great accusation (viii. 8 f.), in whose eyes the current saying, 'We are wise, the Torah of JHVH is with us' means a scorning of the divine *word*. In the period of the beginning of Christianity the Hebrew Torah conception became yet more static, a process which brought it near the conception of law, and indeed caused it to be blended with it; the narrow

57

but deeply-felt idea that the Torah has actually been given to Israel and that Israel possesses it thereafter tends effectively to supplant the vital contact with the ever-living revelation and instruction, a contact which springs from the depths of the primitive faith. But the actuality of faith, the undying strength of hearing the Word, was strong enough to prevent torpidity and to liberate again and again the living idea. This inner dialectic of Having and Being is in fact the main moving force in the spiritual history of Israel.

For the actuality of the faith of Biblical and post-Biblical Judaism, and also for the Jesus of the Sermon on the Mount, fulfilment of the Torah means to extend the hearing of the Word to the whole dimension of human existence. This demand made it necessary to struggle against a withering or hardening, which knew of no other fulfilment than the carrying out of rules, and so made the Torah in fact into a 'law' which a person had merely to adhere to as such, rather than to comprehend its truth with every effort of the soul and then to realize it. Indeed the constant danger of the form of faith which tends to the realization of a revealed divine will, is that the keeping of it can persist apart from the intended surrender to the divine will, and can even begin as such, which surrender can alone invest the attitude with meaning and thereby with its right. The beginnings of this process of making the gesture independent go back to the early times of the Sinai-religion. The struggle against it runs through the whole history of Israelite-Jewish faith. It begins in the accusations of the prophets against a sacrificial service robbed of its decisive meaning by the omission of the intention to surrender one's self, gains a new impulse in a time of increased danger in the zeal of the Pharisees against the many kinds of 'tinged-ones', i.e. those whose inwardness is a pretence, and in their contending for the

58

'direction of the heart', and continues through the ages until at the threshold of our era it receives a peculiar modern form in Hasidism, in which every action gains validity only by a specific devotion of the whole man turning immediately to God. Within this great struggle of faith the teaching of Jesus, as it is expressed in particular in one section of the 'Sermon on the Mount', has a significance, to understand which one must see Jesus apart from his historical connexion with Christianity.

The teaching of Jesus is in this regard fundamentally related to that critical process within Judaism, especially to its Pharisaical phase, and yet at one decisive point stands out against it.

In the Sermon on the Mount it says (Matt. v. 48), 'Ye therefore shall be perfect,[1] as your Heavenly Father is perfect'. The Old Testament commandment, five times repeated (Lev. xi. 44 f., xix. 2, xx. 7, 26), which is likewise founded upon a divine attribute and so likewise summons to the imitation of God, runs similarly yet differently: 'Ye shall be holy, for I am holy'. In the former instance 'ye' refers to the disciples who have gone up the 'mount' to Jesus, in the latter to Israel assembled around Sinai. The address to Israel concerns the sacred principle of the lasting life of the nation, that to the disciples arises out of the eschatological situation and refers to it, as that which demands what is definitely extraordinary, but which also

[1] Torrey's opinion (*The Four Gospels*, 291, cf. *Our Translated Gospels*, 92 f., 96) that in the Aramaic original the adjective means' all inclusive' is quite mistaken; the references from the Talmud assembled by him lack all force of proof, and Matt. xix, 21, where the word has obviously the same meaning as here, but has to be translated by Torrey by 'perfect', most clearly contradicts it. Bultmann (*Jesus* 111) understands by the adjective: faithful and straight, but proceeds from an Old Testament meaning and not that which was current in the writings at the time of Jesus.

59

makes it possible. In accordance with this the command to the disciples says, transcending humanity: 'as'; the command to the people says only: 'for'; in the breaking-in of the Kingdom according to the teaching of Jesus man ought to and can touch the divine in his striving after perfection, while the people in the revelation-hour of its history is only required and expected to strive, for the sake of the divine holiness, after a human holiness which is essentially different from the divine. There is in the course of history a human holiness, which only corresponds to divine holiness; there is no perfection in the course of history, and in Israel—in distinction from Greek philosophy and the mysticism of Islam—it is an essentially eschatological conception. This becomes apparent also in the only other passage in the Gospels where (probably in a secondary text stratum) the adjective occurs (Matt. xix. 21): he who would be 'perfect' must give up everything and follow Jesus on his eschatological way. It is of course possible that the Matthew-text in the Sermon on the Mount does not give the original words, which may be found in the parallel reference in Luke's Gospel (vi. 36), it too following the commandment to love one's enemy. There we find 'compassionate' instead of 'perfect', and compassion can be imitated, while perfection cannot. In this form the saying coincides almost verbally with the well-known Pharisaic one dealing with the imitation of God (Bab. Tal. Shabbat 133b, Jer. Pea 15b): 'Be thou compassionate and merciful as He is compassionate and merciful'. Nevertheless the Matthean passage remains worthy of notice as the expression of a doctrine of perfection of the Church (cf. xix. 21) in which there still dwells a strong eschatological impulse.

Some Old Testament commandments speak of perfection in quite a different way. 'And let your heart be perfect (complete) with JHVH your God', it says in the concluding

60

sentence of Solomon's speech of consecration (1 Kings viii. 61), and certainly not unintentionally the one responsible for the redaction of the book recognizes soon afterwards in the same words (xi. 4) that Solomon's own heart did not remain perfect with JHVH his God. Obviously a general human attribute is not meant here, but a degree of devotedness to God which reaches completeness. The same is intended when, in connexion with the warning against Canaanite superstition, it says (Deut. xviii, 13): 'Thou shalt be entire (undivided) with JHVH thy God'.[1] This does not refer to a perfection which emulates the Divine perfection, but to completeness, undividedness, entirety, in the relation to God. The Torah addresses the constant nature of man and summons him to the elevation granted to him, to the highest realization of his relationship to God which is possible to him as a mortal being; Jesus on the other hand, as represented by Matthew, means to summon the elect in the catastrophe of humanity to come as near to God as is made possible to it only in the catastrophe.

The spiritual struggle within Judaism is determined by those primitive commandments, and it is concerned with their truth. In our connexion we have to deal neither with the prophets nor with the Hasidim, but with the Pharisees. The Jesus of the Synoptic tradition addresses them from the point of view of his eschatological radicalism (especially Matt. xxiii. 13 ff., Luke xi. 39 ff.) in a way which is scarcely different from that in which they themselves address those who only seem to be Pharisees;[2] it sounds like a declaration directed against unhappy confusions when the Talmud (Bab. Sota 22b) makes King Jannai, the Sadducee, tell his

[1] It should be noted that the Septuagint renders both adjectives, *shalem* and *tamim*, by τέλειος.

[2] Cf. Chwolson, *Das letzte Passamahl Christi* (1892), 116 ff., and *Beiträge zur Entwicklungsgeschichte des Judentums* (1910), 60 f.

61

wife that she shall not be afraid of the Pharisees, but 'of those tinged-ones who look like Pharisees'. Jesus misses the mark when he treats the Pharisees as people who close their eyes, and they miss their mark when they treat him as one subject to hallucinations; neither party knows the inner reality of the other. Much in the stories in which 'the Pharisees and scribes', half chorus and half spiritual police-patrols, 'test' Jesus, are snubbed by him and then begin their testings again, is certainly unhistorical, and originates from the polemical tension of early Christianity, in which the generalizing point against 'the Pharisees' may have been added in the Hellenistic diaspora[1]; yet there remains enough of real difference over against the true outlook of the Pharisees, even if never quite so great as to exceed the bounds of the dialectics within Judaism. Nevertheless, whether the sentence from the Sermon on the Mount (Matt. v. 20)—which sounds somewhat 'Pauline' and yet is not really Pauline—'For I say unto you, if your proving true is not greater than that of the scribes and Pharisees, you will not enter into the Kingdom of God' originally contained the reference to the Pharisees or not, yet undoubtedly the criticism which is expressed in it applied not to a lax observance of moral or religious commandments by some circle of the people, but to the dominant *view* about the relationship to them, a view which was essentially determined by that of the Pharisees. And in the preceding declaration of Jesus[2] (v. 17) that he has not come to dissolve the

[1] The *ad quosdam, non ad omnes* in the Jewish-Christian pseudo-Clementine 'Recognitions' 6, 11 is worthy of notice; cf. now Schoeps, *Theologie und Geschichte des Judenchristentums* (1949), 145 n. 2.

[2] I cannot accept Bultmann's view ('Die Bedeutung des geschichtlichen Jesus fuer die Theologie des Paulus', *Theologische Blaetter* VIII, (1921), 139, cf. *Die Geschichte der synoptischen Tradition*, 2. ed. 146 f., 157 f., *Theologie des Neuen Testaments*, 15) that Matt. v. 17–19 is not genuine and is a 'product' of the polemics of the Church'. When the 'fulfilling'

62

Torah but to 'fulfil' it, and this means indeed to make it manifest in its full original meaning and to bring it into life, it becomes altogether clear that here doctrine has to stand against doctrine, the true disclosure of the Torah against its current, erroneous and misleading usage. (The doing belongs of course to this, as is expressly stated in the next verse but one: as in the report of Sinai hearing succeeds doing, so here teaching succeeds doing—only on the basis of doing can a person truly teach.) The attitude of the Sermon on the Mount to the Torah accordingly appears to be the opposite of that of the Pharisees; in reality it is only the sublimation of a Pharisaic doctrine from a definite and fundamental point of view, the character of which can again be made clear by comparison. Of course there can be no question of influence, since the Pharisaic doctrine to which I refer is not attested until after the time of Jesus; here also we have only to show the homogeneous elements as such. It is to be emphasized that among the rabbis of the period other views of the subject are to be found, for the inner dialectics continues within Pharisaism itself; but the great and vital lineage of this doctrine is unmistakable.

The doctrine can best be described as that of granting direction to the human heart. The heart of man—this unformulated insight is at the basis of the doctrine—is by nature without direction, its impulses whirl it around in all directions, and no direction which the individual gathers from his world stands firm, each one finally is only able to intensify the whirl of his heart; only in Emunah is persistence: there is no true direction except to God. But the heart

is correctly understood it does not seem to me that the contrasting of the verses with 'other words of Jesus' and with the 'actual attitude of Jesus' yields any contradiction other than that which is biographically acceptable.

63

cannot receive this direction from the human spirit, but only from a life lived in the will of God. Hence the Torah has assigned to man actions agreeable to God, in the doing of which he learns to direct his heart to Him. According to this purpose of the Torah the decisive significance and value does not lie in the bulk of these actions in themselves but in the direction of the heart in them and through them. 'One does much, the other little', was the device of the college of Jabne (Bab. Berachot 17a) 'if one only directs the heart to heaven!' (Heaven is to be understood here, as in all related contexts, as God.) The Scripture-verse (Deut. vi. 6), 'This, which I this day command thee, shall be on thy heart' is explained (Bab. Megilla 20a) to mean that everything depends on the direction of the heart. Therefore the Temple was called after David and not Solomon because 'the Merciful One desires the heart' (Bab. Sanhedrin 106b): it is a matter, not of the one who completed it, but of him who directed his heart to God for this work and who dedicated it to Him. The doctrine applies not only to actions which are commanded, but to all: 'All thy works shall be for the sake of Heaven' it says in the Sayings of the Fathers (ii. 13). Sin is recognized by the fact that in it a man cannot direct his heart to God; he who commits it denies to God the directing of his heart to Him. Therefore the project of sin and the reflecting upon it and not its execution is the real guilt. The play of the imagination upon the sin is explained (Bab. Joma 29) as being even more serious than the sin itself, because it is this which alienates the soul from God. The most virtuous conduct in the matter of the performance of precepts can exist together with a heart which has remained or become without direction, a heart waste or devastated. On the other hand it may even happen that a person in his enthusiasm for God transgresses a commandment without being aware of it, and then not the sinful

64

matter in his action but his intention is the decisive thing: 'The sin for God's sake is greater than the fulfilling of a commandment not for God's sake' (Bab. Nazir 23). Accordingly, he who has a waste heart cannot truly teach another the Torah; he cannot teach how to obtain the direction, and without it the individual is not able for that for which all learning by the mouth of man is but the preparation: to open his heart to the living Voice of the Divine Teacher. Therefore the Patriarch Gamaliel II ordered that it should be proclaimed (Bab. Berachot 28a) that no scholar whose inwardness did not equal his outwardness ought to enter the schoolroom. From this there was coined two hundred years later the principle (Bab. Yoma 72b): 'A scholar whose inwardness does not equal his outwardness is no scholar'.

There is much to be said for the critical view of the Sermon on the Mount which suggests that we have in it a later composition from different words of Jesus, spoken at different times, with the addition of some from the community, which probably were contained already in the source used by Matthew and Luke. It seems to me however that the blessings belong essentially together from the start, whereas the sayings which concern us here, in spite of formal elements common to them—which obviously caused them to be joined together—'Ye have heard . . . and I say unto you', are different in meaning and purpose, and are therefore probably to be assigned to different groups. Three of them (murder, adultery, oaths) derive essentially from three of the Ten Commandments and transcend them, but what they demand is to be found also in Pharisaic teachings, yet without these approaching the forcefulness of their address. The other three (divorce, formula of the talion, love to one's neighbour), which have obviously been further arranged and adapted to the form of the first three[1], refer to commandments and precepts outside the decalogue, and either contradict them (the first two) or contradict at least an accepted, apparently popular interpretation (the third); rabbinical writings present either no analogy to them or none sufficient. Only that group—in which 'the thesis' stands 'in the form of a prohibition' which 'is not rejected but surpassed'[2]—can in essence be regarded as 'fulfilment' of the Torah, and not those also which are concerned 'not with a prohibition, but with an instruction or concession', which 'is not surpassed but abolished'. That nevertheless even these sayings aim at a 'fulfilling' is shown when we place together the one in which 'Jesus directly annuls a Mosaic ordinance'[3] with the related Synoptic texts which at all events are nearer to the original version. In one of these (Luke xvi. 17 f.) a saying against divorce (which incidentally agrees with the strict view of the school of Shammai) is conjoined with one which repeats, almost verbally yet rather more sharply, a sentence from that section of the Sermon on the Mount: 'It is easier for heaven and earth to pass than for one tittle of the law to fall'. How this is to be understood becomes clear when we refer to the narrative (Mark x, Matt. xix, Luke xvi) in which Jesus actually says this against divorce, according to which the remarriage of a divorced person shall reckon as adultery. In both instances, the 'Pharisees' appeal to Moses, who

[1] In distinction from those they obviously do not belong originally together; vv. 39 and 44 derive, I presume, from the same unity (cf. Luke vi. 27 ff.); the joining of the first with the talion formula is secondary, probably also v. 43 and vv. 31 f. constitute an independent saying (see further below). In both of the first the Old Testament quotation has been, I imagine, pre-fixed subsequently: probably also in the first (cf. Luke xvi. 18); whereas in the other group the quotations are an organic part of the text.

[2] Bultmann, *Die Geschichte der synoptischen Tradition*, 144.

[3] Wellhausen, *Das Evangelium Matthaei*, 21.

66

(Deut. xxiv. 1) instituted the form of divorce. Thereupon Jesus makes a significant double reply. In the first place, Moses wrote down this commandment 'because of the hardness of your hearts'; about which a modern commentator[1] truly remarks that 'lying at the basis of this hard word is the deep Jewish idea that the Torah is never a fixed law, considered apart from the persons to whom it was given, but rather "instruction" given in a dialogue between God and a partner whose heart and ear are not always open to this teaching of God'. In the second place, Jesus refers to God's word in Paradise (Gen. ii. 24) that a man shall leave his father and mother and cleave to his wife, and they shall become one flesh. Jesus understands this as a commandment: he appeals from the Mosaic revelation to that of creation. Therefore in the end it is the same with the second group as with the first: starting from the inwardness of the divine claim Jesus demands that the inwardness of men shall surrender to it. The divine claim in its outwardness has been made known in the historical situation and has reached the externality of man, the outward conduct of man; the inwardness from above presents itself in the eschatological situation and the inwardness from below can now appear before it. Fulfilment of the Torah accordingly means here disclosure of the Torah. Seen in regard to man the Pharisaic doctrine of the direction of the heart comes here to an heightened expression, and indeed to one so radical that in contrast to Pharisaism, it affects the word of the Torah itself—for the sake of the Torah. Jesus speaks throughout as the authentic interpretor: as long as he remains standing on Sinai he teaches what the Pharisees teach, but then Sinai cannot satisfy him and he must advance into the

[1] Lohmeyer, *Das Evangelium des Markus*, 200 (apparently under the influence of my hints, both verbally and in writing, to this circumstance).

67

cloud-area of the intention of the revelation, for only now his words (familiar in form also to rabbinic discussion) 'but I say unto you' or 'and I say unto you' are opposed to the tradition of the generations. Now too we hear a specifically eschatological-present command like 'Resist not the evil', which must have been unacceptable and even intolerable to the Pharisees, who supposed that they had to live and teach, not in the breaking-in of God's rule, but in continued historical preparation for it under Roman rule. They also indeed enjoined that one should not oppose with force the wrong done to one in personal life, and promised to the one who submits that all his sins would be forgiven him; but a principle which forbade action against the wrong-doer in general or which might at least be so understood, increased in their eyes the area of injustice in the world. They rejected in general the position of the Zealots; but in their heart, as is to be noticed in particular in the recorded conversations with the Romans, they obviously felt themselves to be the opponents of the evil power, which they opposed by their own spiritual methods.

From this point of view the last and highest of these pronouncements, that of love for the enemy, is also to be considered. It proceeds (v. 43) from the Old Testament commandment to 'love one's neighbour' (Lev. xix. 18) which Jesus in another place, in the reply to the scribe's question about the greatest commandment (Matt. xxii. 39; Mark xii. 31), declares to be the greatest alongside that of love to God, and appends to it the interpretation which was indeed popular but was presumably derived in part from the strong words of the Pharisees against the enemies of God, that a man is allowed to or even shall hate his enemy. He opposes this with his commandment 'love your enemies'. In its fundamental meaning it is so deeply bound up with

68

Jewish faith and at the same time transcends it in so particular a way that it must be especially discussed at this point.

In the quotation from the Sermon on the Mount about the command to love it is first of all noteworthy that the word usually translated by 'as yourself' is missing, whereas in the reply to the scribe the sentence is quoted in its entirety (only outwardly shortened by Luke); the reason may be that a 'love your enemies as yourself' ought not to follow it. But the 'as yourself' is only one of the three falsely rendered words which follow one another in this sentence in the Septuagint and the other current translations. The word so translated refers neither to the degree nor the kind of love, as if a man should love others as much as himself or in such a way as himself (the idea of self-love does not appear in the Old Testament at all); it means, equal to thyself, and this means: conduct thyself in such a way as if it concerned thyself. An attitude is meant and not a feeling. It does not say, one should love someone, but 'to someone'. This strange construction of the dative is found in the Old Testament only in this chapter of Leviticus. Its meaning is easy to ascertain when once the question is put in this way: the feeling of love between men does not in general allow its object—designated by the accusative—to be prescribed; whereas an attitude of loving-kindness towards a fellow creature—designated by the dative—can indeed be commanded to a man. And finally the noun *re'ah* translated in the Septuagint by 'the one near by, the near' means in the Old Testament first of all one to whom I stand in an immediate and reciprocal relationship, and this through any kind of situation in life, through community of place, through common nationality, through community of work, through community of effort, especially also through friendship; it transfers itself to fellow-men in general and

69

so to others as a whole.[1] '*Love thy re'ah*' therefore means in
our language: be lovingly disposed towards men with
whom thou hast to do at any time in the course of thy life;
for this of course there was also required a soul not given
to feelings of hatred, and so the commandment was pre-
mised (*v.* 17): 'Do not hate thy brother (synonym for
re'ah) *in thy heart*'. However in order that no limitation of
the idea might result in the people's consciousness to whom
the first half of the sentence ('Do not take vengeance on
and do not bear ill-will to the sons of thy people') could
easily be misleading, later in the same chapter (*v.* 33)
another commandment is added, to meet with love
also the *ger*, the non-Jewish 'sojourner' who lives in
Israel; 'for ye were once sojourners in the land of

[1] It is customary to base the generally accepted interpretation
'fellow-countryman' incorrectly on the fact that in the first parallel
phrase of the sentence the reference is to the 'sons of thy people'.
That in texts of this kind, as in general, the parallelist form of
expression may not be pressed, is made clear, for example, by *v.*
15, in which 'the humble man' and 'the great man' are made
parallel. Moreover, man on the threshold of history (and from
such a one, I am convinced, originates the sentence transplanted
into a late text) often uses 'fellow-countryman' and 'man' inter-
changeably, as he does the designations 'land' (own land) and earth,
because he knows by living contact only that which belongs to him,
and includes that which is other according to the degree in which it
becomes vitally familiar to him. In Israel he says 'fellow-countryman'
and means accordingly the man with whom he *lives;* when he wishes
to denote him as such, he says 'companion' (*re'ah*); and because he also
lives with other people as well as fellow-countrymen, that is with
'foreign-settlers' (*gerim*) [real 'foreigners', *nochrim*, he learns to know
only from his or their journeyings or in war, he does not 'live' with
them], he refers in particular to them. Our *idea* of 'fellow-creature' is a
late one, derived from the reflection (stoicism) which strove to *overcome* the fact of foreignness, and from the great religious missionary
movements in which this first became possible on a large scale (Hellenistic mystery religions, Jewish and Christian missions to the heathen).

70

Egypt', which means, ye have yourselves known what it means to be treated as sojourners, unloved. The first commandment ends with the declaration 'I am JHVH', the second with 'I am JHVH thy God'. Translated into our language: this is not a moral commandment but a commandment of faith; the declaration means accordingly: I command this to you not as human beings as such, but as *My* people. The connexion between the actuality of faith and the commandment to love is disclosed more deeply still to us if we turn to the passage where, in apparent contradiction to our conclusions, the commandment is construed with the accusative (Deut. x. 19): 'Ye shall love the sojourner, for ye were sojourners in the land of Egypt'. The full understanding of this sentence is first disclosed in its connexion with the three references to love in the previous verses. Israel is summoned to love God (*v.* 12); it is said of God (*v.* 15) that He loved Israel's fathers when they were foreign-settlers; and then it is said of Him (*v.* 18) that He loves the sojourner—not this or that one, but the man dependent upon a foreign nation in general, 'to give him bread and raiment', (cf. the words of Jacob on his way to become a *ger*, Gen. xxviii. 20), as He does right to the person within the nation who is dependent upon others, 'the orphan and the widow'. With God there is no difference between love and the action of love. And to love *Him* with the complete feeling of love[1] can be commanded, for it means nothing more than to actualize the existing relationship of faith to Him, as in trust so in love, for both

[1] Bultmann (*Jesus*, 105 ff.) attacks the view that a feeling is involved in the commandment to love God and one's neighbour. Certainly a 'sentimental' feeling (110) is not involved, but a great feeling is never sentimental, and the love of God is the greatest; 'to submit one's own will in obedience to God's' (105) does not describe love to God; when and so far as the loving man loves he does not need to bend his will, for he lives in the Divine Will.

71

are one. But if a person really loves Him, he is led on by his own feeling to love the one whom He loves; naturally not the sojourner only—it merely becomes quite clear in his case what is meant—but every man whom God loves, according as a person becomes aware that He does love him. To the loving attitude towards one's fellow love itself is added here, awakened by the love to God.

The maxim from the Sermon on the Mount stands over against this Old Testament view of the connexion between the love of God and the love of man, or, if one prefers the derived categories to original realities, between 'religion' and 'ethics'. Its kinship with the maxims of Deuteronomy and its distance from them is shown at once in the argument about the love of God for all men (v. 45). By His grace in the realm of Nature He sheds His love upon all without distinction, and we are to imitate His Love (both of these are the doctrine of the Talmud also). But 'all' does not mean in this case what it did there: not only Israel but also foreigners, but: evil and good, just and unjust. God does not select the good and the just in order to love them; so also we ought not to select them.

We have seen that the Old Testament commandment of love in its primitive meaning of re'ah does not admit of the interpretation that one ought to hate the enemy. Obviously Jesus starts from a changed meaning which had taken place in the noun. The question here is not the much-discussed problem as to whether at the time of Jesus only fellow-countrymen were included in it, because he nowhere indicates here that he has non-Jews in mind: rather it is about the fact that in his time the word referred mostly to the personal friend: over against love of a friend, love to a person who loves me, he set love towards a person who hates me. But the interpretation quoted in the text which was apparently a popular saying, that one was free to hate

72

the enemy, misunderstood not merely the wording of the commandment to love; it stood also in contradiction to the express commandments of the Torah (Exod. xxiii. 4 f.), to bring help to one's 'enemy', 'the person who hates one'. Nevertheless amongst the people appeal may have been made, as already indicated, to certain expressions on the part of the Pharisees.

In the sayings of the Pharisees exceedingly strong expression is given to the universality of the command to love, so when (Jer. Nedarim 41c, Sifra on Leviticus xix. 18) one of two great rabbis declares, like Jesus, that the Leviticus statement about love for one's neighbour was the greatest precept in the Torah, his companion, obviously because of the possibility of the text being misinterpreted, places another verse of Scripture still higher, namely (Gen. v. 1): 'This is the deed of the generations of Adam. . . . In the image of God He created him': since everyone originates from God's image, discriminating between men or the races of men is in the end inadmissible, the question as to the worthiness of this or that person to be loved is therefore directed against God Himself. It actually says in a Midrash (Genesis rabba XXIV): 'Know whom thou despisest. He created him in the image of God', and another (Pesikta zut. on Numbers viii), emphasizing his absolute value: 'Whoever hates a man is as if he hated Him Who spake and the world was'. In sayings like these the strong basing of the morality upon the actuality of faith is not inferior to that in the saying of Jesus. What according to this doctrine God thinks in particular of national hatred becomes evident when an early school of interpretation, which attributes a share in eternal life to all men, even to evil-doers, makes God reply (Bab. Sanhedrin 105a) to the angels' question as to what He would do if David complained before His throne about the presence of Goliath, that it is incumbent

73

upon Him to make the two friends with each other. Nevertheless a limit is often described, owing to the Biblical idea of the 'enemies of God' or 'haters of God', of whom the Psalmist (Ps. cxxxix. 21 f.) avows that he hates them fundamentally as his own enemies. How shall a man, may precisely one who is convinced of the truth of his faith easily ask himself, not hate them, and particularly those too whose 'hostility' to God manifests itself in the denial of His presence? To the question of a philosopher as to who among men is absolutely deserving of hatred, a rabbi replies (Tos. Shebuot III, 6): 'He who denies his Creator'. Especially with the increase of a formalized 'believing that', this opinion is hardened: unbelievers and heretics do not merely cause confusion in the world of man, but they disturb God's saving activity, and one must fight them and destroy them —and very rarely can hatred be absent from such a conflict. So by appealing to this Psalm, a saying comes about like that (Abot de R. Natan XVI. 32) which begins by contradicting a limitation of the commandment of love, in order then to continue: 'Love all—and hate the heretics, the apostates and the informers'. In this case it is shown crudely how dangerously unstable the boundary-line is. To one assured of his possession of the God of Israel it was but a short step to hold (Sifre 22) that one who hates Israel is 'as one who hates God'. Such opinions are easily transferred to the personal sphere, so that many among the people understand their own enemies as God's, instead of reckoning with the Psalmist God's enemies as their own. But we do not come to know the real danger on such lowlands as these, but rather upon the heights of faith. Not merely fanatics but precisely genuine prophets often cannot but attribute opposition to the message—God's message!—to malice and hardness of heart and in their zeal for it they lose the simple love. The Gospel in which the Sermon on the

74

Mount appears knows the same thing in Jesus' angry outbursts against the 'generation of vipers' of the Pharisees (Matt. xii. 34, xxiii, 33), the authenticity of which, it is true, has been justifiably contested.

All in·all, the saying of Jesus about love for the enemy derives its light from the world of Judaism in which he stands and which he seems to contest; and he outshines it. It is indeed always so when a person in the sign of the *kairos* demands the impossible in such a way that he compels men to will the possible more strongly than before. But one should not fail to appreciate the bearers of the plain light below from amongst whom he arose: those who enjoined much that was possible so as not to cause men to despair of being able to serve God in their poor everyday affairs.

However, by our view of the difference between 'Jewish' and 'Christian' faith and of the connexion between Jesus and the former, we have not yet done full justice to the saying.

'Love your enemies', it runs in the concise version of Matthew, 'and pray for your persecutors, that you may become the sons of your Father in heaven'. To illustrate by paradox and with the help of a Greek conception, yet with the greatest possible faithfulness: men become what they are, sons of God, by becoming what they are, brothers of their brothers.

Moses says to the people (Deut. xiv. 1): 'Ye are sons of JHVH your God . . . for ye are a people holy unto JHVH your God'. In the people holy unto God, because they are that and in so far as they are that, all men are sons of God. The prophets deny that the desecrated people belong to God, they are no longer JHVH's people (Hos. i. 9); but they promise (ii. 1): 'Instead of it being said to them: "ye are not My people", it will be said to them: " sons of the living

75

God!"'' Through the new consecration of Israel its people will be newly admitted into sonship. In a late yet pre-Christian book, the Book of Jubilees, the promise is expressed in this way (i. 23 ff.): 'Your soul will follow Me, they will do My commandment. I will be Father to them and they will be sons to Me. They will all be called sons of the living God. All angels and all spirits shall know and perceive that they are My sons and I am their Father in faith and truth, and that I love them'. There has come down from the first half of the second century after Christ a conversation (Bab. Baba Batra 10) between Rabbi Akibah, imprisoned by the Romans, and a high Roman official; on the basis of a verse from Scripture the Roman asserts that the God of the Jews treats them as insubordinate slaves; Akibah refers against this to the 'Ye are sons', but the Roman sees in the difference between the two statements the difference between two stages in the relationship to God: 'If you do God's will you are called sons, if you do it not you are called slaves'. Still more precisely a Midrash text (Pesikta rabbati XXVII) holds: 'If thou doest His will, He is thy Father and thou art His son; if thou doest it not He is thine owner and thou art His slave'. The statement of Jesus about love to an enemy is to be seen in connexion with this process of a progressive dynamization of the sonship. But nowhere else is love to man precisely made the presupposition of the realized sonship to God as here, and that in the unheard-of simple form of this 'so that', in the form, that is, of open entrance for everyone who really loves. Originating from the enthusiasm of eschatological actuality, this statement, viewed from the point of view of Israel's faith, implies at the same time a supplement to it. Somewhere, apparently quite on its own accord, the most daring arc has been described, and yet a circle has thereby been completed. Seen in relation to the history of faith in Christianity,

76

the arc must of course appear as the beginning of another figure, perhaps of an hyperbole. How this figure is continued is shown to us in the sentence in the prologue of John's Gospel (i. 12), where the Logos which appeared gives power to 'those who believe on his name' to become children of God, and in the sentence related to this (1 John v. 1), declaring everyone who believes that Jesus is the Messiah to be 'born of God', or already by Paul's direct speech to the converted Gentiles (Gal. iii. 26): 'For ye are all sons of God through faith in Christ Jesus'.

Entirely within Judaism and outside all Christian influence the question, which has concerned us here, found in its three essential points at the threshold of our age a parallel answer in Hasidism. As the clearest examples three reports from the life of the Zaddikim, from leaders of the Hasidic body, may be cited. The first concerns the 'enemy' in general. A Zaddik commands his sons: 'Pray for enemies that things go well with them. And if you think, that is no service of God: know that more than any other prayer, this is service of God'. The second story concerns the extent· of the idea of the 'neighbour'. A Zaddik speaks to God: 'Lord of the world, I beseech Thee that Thou mayest redeem Israel. And if Thou willest it not, redeem the Gentiles!' The third concerns the 'enemy of God'. A Zaddik is asked by a pupil whether one can love a person who rises up against God. He replies: 'Dost thou not know that the primeval soul came from God and that every human soul is a part of it? And when thou seest how one of the holy particles has become entangled and is near to be suffocated wilt thou not show mercy to it?'

That the principle of love to the enemy in this instance has in such a way expanded in the pure form of faith, and not in a form essentially ethical, merely enjoined by God, is to be understood from the fact that even in Hasidism the

77

messianic inspiration of Judaism made one of its high flights, and that without employing in general the form of eschatological actuality: paradoxically expressed, it is a messianism of continuity. Even the Hasidim, at all events those of the first generations, experience a nearness of God's rule, yet one which demanded not the readiness to change everything, but the continuity of a life of faith which was both enthusiastic and yet strove after the cohesion of the generations.

Come now, you rich. . . . You have
condemned and put to death the just,
and he did not resist you.
JAS. 5:1, 6 [CCD]

The Crime of Deicide

By Jules Isaac

PROPOSITION

FOR EIGHTEEN HUNDRED YEARS IT HAS BEEN GENERALLY
TAUGHT THROUGHOUT THE CHRISTIAN WORLD THAT
THE JEWISH PEOPLE, IN FULL RESPONSIBILITY FOR THE
CRUCIFIXION, COMMITTED THE INEXPIABLE CRIME OF
DEICIDE. NO ACCUSATION COULD BE MORE PERNICIOUS
—AND IN FACT NONE HAS CAUSED MORE INNOCENT
BLOOD TO BE SHED.

Having come to the threshold of the last phase,
    prepared to enter it with such meditation, such a trembling of heart,
    but without withdrawing before the texts,
    let us listen first to the barbaric clamor rising from the depths of the
centuries, the choir of the Christian accusations, the Christian imprecations—that is, emanating from those who call themselves Christians,
for they harmonize ill with the words of charity, mercy, and love
which are the major teachings and the glory of Christ.

All these cries of death—can there be "Christian" cries of death?

And even the previous, even the odious Jewish accusations, Jewish
imprecations do not justify them.

Murderers of Jesus, of the Christ-Messiah, murderers of the God-
Man,

DEICIDES!

Such is the accusation hurled at the whole Jewish people, without exception, without any kind of distinction, the blind violence of ignorant
masses being closely linked to the cold reasoning of theologians.

A capital accusation, to which is tied the theme of capital punishment, the terrifying curse weighing down Israel's shoulders, explain-

233

ing (and justifying in advance) its wretched destiny, its cruel trials, the worst violences committed against it, the rivers of blood flowing from its constantly reopened and inflamed wounds.

In such wise that by an ingenious technique of alternating learned judgments and popular passions, God is made responsible for acts which, seen in human terms, are surely the doing of man's incurable vileness, of that perversity, variously but skillfully exploited from century to century, from generation to generation, which culminated in Auschwitz, in the gas chambers and crematory ovens of Nazi Germany.

One of those Germans, those servile killers, one of those chief murderers (baptized a Christian) said: "I could not have any scruples because they were all Jews."

Hitler's voice? Streicher's voice?

No. *Vox saeculorum.*

o   o   o

Stricken with horror, I could not move one step forward before I felt myself taken by the arm, by both arms. At my right, at my left: two theologians, sympathetic, inexorable.

The first said:

We would like to address a reminder to the Jews.

When they make the Church responsible for their immense misfortunes because of having accused them . . . of deicide, they forget that God, Yahweh himself, by choosing them as the unique messianic and God-bearing people, was bound to make them odious and mark them for the hostility of the world and pagan peoples long before the Incarnation, long before the deicide. Let them recall the time of the Pharaohs, Exodus 1:9, or the time of Esther 3:8–9: "There is a certain people scattered abroad and dispersed among the peoples in all the provinces of your kingdom; their laws are different from those of every other people, and they do not keep the king's laws, so that it is not for the king's profit to tolerate them. If it please the king, let it be decreed that they be destroyed. . . ." In Egypt in the thirteenth century before Christ, in Persia in the fifth, there were already pogroms.[1]

What shall I reply? In my own name, in my name as victim?

First of all, let us leave the Church to itself. Let us leave to it the task of seeking for itself what share of responsibility it has had in

[1] Father Charles Journet, *Destinées d'Israël*, Paris, Egloff, 1945, pp. 199–200.

such a tragedy, whether it has truly had none, whether it has truly had no hand in the atrocious deviations in which so many of its members, so many of its faithful have found themselves involved,[2] whether it has truly done everything that its duty as the Church of Christ required it to do in order to prevent such deviations, correct them, brand them, punish them. Yes, let us leave the Church to face itself, to face God.

The case of ancient Egypt is historically complex; it goes well beyond the framework of Israel. Victim of great Semitic invasions, Egypt regained its independence at the price of long and bloody battles which necessarily engendered feelings of mistrust and hatred regarding all Semite peoples.

This said, it is quite true that there was a strain of anti-Semitism in the pagan world preceding Christian anti-Semitism, though it is perceptible in history only beginning in the third century B.C.;

it is quite true that this anti-Semitism sometimes unleashed bloody conflicts and pogroms;

it is quite true that a determining cause of this anti-Semitism was Israel's exclusivism, the separatism of Israel dispersed in the pagan world, a separatism essentially religious, dictated by Yahweh, commanded by Scripture,[3] without which Christianity could obviously not have been born; for it is owing to this, to Jewish separatism, that the Yahwist faith, the worship of the one God could be transmitted intact, preserved from all taint from generation to generation until the coming of Christ.

But in what way does the reminder of these historic facts justify you?

Because a pagan anti-Semitism existed whose source is in effect the divine commandment, in what way does Christianity find itself justified for having followed suit (after having itself been a victim of it for a time), and more, for having pushed the virulence, the evil-mindedness, the murderous calumnies and hatred to paroxysm?

Let us complete this "reminder" with another reminder:

while it is true that the pagan world experienced a current of anti-Semitism—though also the countercurrent of proselytism, of Judaizing paganism—it is nonetheless true that the Jews generally

---

[2] Father Journet straightforwardly recognizes "the faults of Christians," though not of the Church, in *ibid.*, p. 201. His generous thought is expressed forcefully on p. 188.

[3] See p. 5, above.

enjoyed a privileged status in that world, particularly in the Roman Empire, which lasted several centuries,

until the day when the Empire became Christian.[4]

The second theologian, who was waiting his turn, came forward. And from the outset I shivered. For he was armed from head to foot with sacred texts, but I soon doubted that there was a man, a soul with God living in it, inside that armor. He looked like a brother of the scribe in the Gospels (and not of the one who was "not far from the kingdom of God"), and entrenched himself in Scripture as in a blockhouse.

Opening his Bible, he turned to Acts, chapter 2, where Peter is addressing the Jews, and he read:

Men of Israel, hear these words: Jesus of Nazareth, a man attested to you by God with mighty works and wonders and signs which God did through him in your midst . . .—this Jesus, delivered up according to the definite plan and foreknowledge of God, you crucified and killed by the hands of lawless men.

                                                                Acts 2:22–23

Then, turning the pages quickly with a dry, cold hand, see here, he said, Acts 2:36; 3:15; 4:10, 27; 5:30; 7:52; 10:39; 13:27–28, not forgetting 1 Thessalonians 2:14–16:

. . . for you suffered the same things from your own countrymen as they [the churches of God] did from the Jews, who killed both the Lord Jesus and the prophets, and drove us out, and displease God and oppose all men by hindering us from speaking to the Gentiles. . . . But God's wrath has come upon them at last!

What more do you want? he asked. Are you challenging these texts? Isn't the crime of the Jewish people—the inexpiable crime— explicitly denounced the very morrow of the Crucifixion by the mouth of the Apostles, of Peter, Paul, by Holy Scripture? We, accusers of Christian posterity, are only plumbing a sacred source. And we say: "God is not mocked with impunity." [5] You denied, you crucified His Son; believe in His "wrath," and bow before it.

Such icy conviction emanated from this prosecutor (for God) that I had difficulty collecting myself. Finally, I replied:

Historian I am, and no theologian, but I am inclined to believe

[4] The questions raised here on pp. 234–236 and commented on briefly are studied more closely in Jules Isaac, *Genèse de l'antisémitisme*, Paris, Calmann-Lévy, 1956.
[5] Jean Bosc, "Le Mystère d'Israël" [The Mystery of Israel], *Réforme*, November 23, 1946.

that history precedes theology in all respects and that the theological validity of a text remains subordinate to its historic validity. These venerable and sacred texts with which you bombard us are historical evidence first, and as such must be passed through the sieve of critical analysis beforehand—which will be done in due time and place. For the moment, I will observe simply that even if one accepts as literally exact speeches which were reproduced approximately half a century after they were delivered,

one cannot state that any one of them was directed at the Jewish people taken all together. Some were addressed expressly to the ruling caste, to the Sanhedrin (Acts 4:10; 5:30; 7:52), others to the Jews of Jerusalem or residing in Jerusalem (2:22–23, 36; 3:15). This is said plainly and unequivocally in Paul's discourse in the synagogue at Antioch of Pisidia:

For those who live in Jerusalem and their rulers, because they did not recognize him [Jesus]. . . . yet they asked Pilate to have him killed.

Acts 13:27–28

While "the peoples of Israel" are mentioned in Acts 4:27, it is in conjunction with "the Gentiles," and one cannot endow this pious effusion—the prayer of the faithful after the release of the Apostles— with the slightest validity as historic information. Moreover, the section of Peter's discourse in Acts 10:39 must be understood in the same light as similar portions of others of Peter's speeches.

In the second place, none of these texts formulates the capital accusation, of deicide, against the Jewish people. What is spoken of is homicide ("a man . . . you crucified and killed by the hands of lawless men"); not only that, but homicide out of ignorance, and in words which are terms of remission, singularly worthy of meditation; for the Apostle Peter, addressing the Jews of Jerusalem, still called them "brethren," thus setting a high example (which would not be followed):

And now, brethren, I know that you acted in ignorance, as did also your rulers.

Acts 3:17

As for the canonic Epistles, even the Epistles of Paul, they say nothing more. The Epistle of James (why ignore it? why this persistent neglect?) takes umbrage exclusively at the rich: "Come now, you rich. . . . You have condemned and put to death the just . . ." (5:1, 6 [CCD]). According to Paul in 1 Corinthians 2:8, it was "the rulers of

257

this age," temporal or satanic powers,[6] who "crucified the Lord of glory." The Jews denounced in 1 Thessalonians 2:14–16 are manifestly not all the Jewish people but the Pharisee and Jerusalemite clique—of which Saul of Tarsus was previously a zealous member— expressly named in Acts 13:27; "Paul was not thinking of the Jewish people as such, that is quite clear," writes Jacques Maritain.[7] When the "Apostle to the Gentiles" examines all aspects of the problem posed by the unbelief of a "part of Israel" (Rom. 11:25) in his masterful Epistle to the Romans, where does anyone see the faintest allusion to Israel's guilt, to its crime?

Saint Paul speaks of "trespass," of "disobedience," of "blindness," but he goes no farther; and taking care to put the Gentile brothers on guard against any judgment out of pride, he concludes:

For God has consigned all men to disobedience, that he may have mercy upon all.

Rom. 11:32

You exhort me to believe in God's wrath. I believe in it, as in His mercy. But I believe in it for all men.

And I believe too that it is rash, if not impious, to inscribe it automatically in the history of human turpitude.

o   o   o

The way cleared, let us follow the course of the centuries now.

From one generation to the next, the tone grows more heated. We know how far religious passion can go, whether it is Jewish or Christian, Catholic or Protestant: in all ages, the relentlessness of hangmen has made the saintliness of martyrs, Christian martyrs, Jewish martyrs. A vehement dialogue developed between adherents to the Ancient Covenant, persecutors at first, and adepts of the New Covenant, persecuted at first. This nascent Christianity, of Jewish stock, preached by Jewish Apostles who went from synagogue to synagogue and initially recruited only among Jews or Judaizers, not without re-

---

[6] Both interpretations have had currency, the first seeming more plausible. The "rulers of this age" would thus be the secular powers, Roman and Jewish authorities. Alfred Loisy holds the contrary opinion in *La Naissance du christianisme*, Paris, Nourry, 1933, p. 18, n. 4.

[7] Jacques Maritain, *La Pensée de saint Paul* [The Thought of Saint Paul], New York, Maison Française, 1941, p. 141, n. 1. [See, in English, as *idem*, ed., *The Living Thoughts of St. Paul*, tr. Harry Lorin Binsse, New York, McKay, 1941, p. 87.—Tr.]

sistance but also not without success—as the Acts of the Apostles witness [8]—broke away from the Mosaic Law in a bold sweep, and passing from a hardly relaxed exclusivism to absolute universalism, turned toward the masses of the Gentile world. In less than a century, it would sever the ties which attached it to Judaism and simultaneously take wing in a flight that nothing would ever stop again, contempt or ridicule, insults or polemics, persecutions or killings—pagan after Jewish; not even its own internal dissensions, the seething of its heresies. It conquered souls, it conquered the Empire: a redoubtable triumph, it was elevated to the rank of the official religion. But the victory, miraculous though it was, did not pacify the wrath that arose against the most detested of the vanquished.

When the Jewish people as a whole proved irreducible, it became necessary, imperatively necessary for the edification of the faithful, that the Jewish people as a whole prove evil, fundamentally evil, unworthy, laden with crimes, opprobrium, and maledictions. And when this became necessary, this became true, with a theological truth which infinitely outdistanced historic truth, and where need be obliterated it. Nothing easier, nothing more human, albeit not more equitable, more Christian (in the Gospel sense of the word). Where Jesus had said, "the chief priests, the scribes, and the Pharisees"—which was already a substitution of the whole for the part—people exaggerated, people said: "the Jews," "the Jewish people." Where Saint Paul had said, "those who live in Jerusalem and their rulers"—which was once more a substitution of the whole for the part—people said, people said again: "the Jews," "the Jewish people." Where only Temple flunkeys, inflamed followers of the powerful, brutish pagan soldiery figured, people repeated obligingly: "the Jews," "the Jewish people," "all the people," "all Israel." Where only a withered fig tree appeared, people declared calmly: "symbol of Israel." And to discredit contending adversaries more positively, people pointed fingers at them to ignorant populaces and said: "God-killers! Deicides!"

[8] The crescendo of conversions can be followed in the Acts of the Apostles: "a hundred and twenty" in 1:15; "about three thousand" in 2:41, "And the Lord added to their number day by day those who were being saved," 2:47; "about five thousand" in 4:4; "And more than ever believers were added to the Lord . . . ," 5:14; ". . . and the number of the disciples multiplied greatly in Jerusalem . . . ," 6:7; "So the church throughout all Judea and Galilee and Samaria had peace and was built up; and walking in the fear of the Lord and in the comfort of the Holy Spirit it was multiplied," 9:31; further increases at 13:43, 14:1, and 18:4; "You see, brother, how many thousands there are among the Jews of those who have believed; they are all zealous for the law. . . ," 21:20.

Thus began the elaboration in (if I dare call it so) Christian consciousness of the theme of the Crime, the Infamy, the Curse, the Punishment of Israel, collective punishment like the Crime itself, without appeal, encompassing "carnal Israel" in perpetuity, fallen, outcast Israel, Judas-Israel, Cain-Israel. A theme which interlaced but did not blend with another theme, turned into a doctrinal thesis, that of the Witness People. Reserved by God, the Jew Saint Paul had said, for the fullness of final conversion. Wretched witness "of their own iniquity and of our truth," [9] said Saint Augustine three hundred years later; marked by God with a sign, as was Cain, which preserved them and singled them out at the same time, singled them out for the loathing of the Christian world.

•   o   •

"Deicide." At what moment did the defamatory epithet appear, the brilliant find—itself murderous—which would be made into an indelible brand, generating frenzies and crimes (homicide, genocide)? It is impossible to say exactly. But we can discern in the roiled stream of Judeo-Christian polemics the current whence it issued.[10]

The contents of the Gospels, begun in the mid-first century, carry visible marks of these polemics; this is particularly true of the first Gospel, Matthew's, and the fourth, John's. We have pointed these marks out, and we will have occasion to return to them, for the account of the Passion is relevant in this regard, owing to the obvious eagerness it exhibits to slide the whole weight of responsibility for the Crucifixion from Roman onto Jewish shoulders. In the apocryphal gospels, written in the following era, this eagerness would become a

[9] Augustine, *Enarratio in Ps. LVIII* [Discourse on Psalm 58], 1:22, in Father Jacques-Paul Migne, ed., *Patrologia latina*, 221 vols., Paris, Garnier, 1844–1864, XXXVI, 705.

[10] We will use data here furnished by the learned work of Jean Juster, *Les Juifs dans l'Empire romain*, 2 vols., Paris, Guethner, 1914, vol. I. In addition, before the present book went to press, we were able to consult two other writings in which we found valuable information: Rev. James Parkes, *The Conflict of the Church and the Synagogue: A Study in the Origins of Antisemitism*, London, Soncino, 1934 [repub. New York, Meridian, 1961]; and especially Marcel Simon's *Verus Israël*, Paris, Boccard, 1948 [rev. ed. 1964], an indispensable work for anyone who wants to study the origins of Christian anti-Semitism. [Dr. Parkes's distinguished contribution to the study of various aspects of Jewish-Christian relations extends over the last thirty years; see also, for example, his *History of the Jews*, 6 vols., Philadelphia, Jewish Publication Society of America, 1945. Marcel Simon is honorary Dean of the Faculté des Lettres, University of Strasbourg.—Ed.]

veritable obsession with their authors, who would stick at no improbability to attain their aim of making the Jews more criminal, more odious. A man of deeper learning, the great third-century theologian Origen, battling with the pagan Celsus, was still taking the trouble to mention Pilate while declaring that Jesus' condemnation was above all the act of the Jewish authorities; but let him speak theology and he did not hesitate to simplify, writing: "The Jewish nation . . . has been condemned by God . . . ," for "they crucified him [Jesus]." [11] And such language became common usage.

From this to pronouncing the supreme outrage, "deicide," is not far. The first step was taken in the fourth century. Eusebius, the Church historian, reporting the Emperor Constantine's letter on the Council of Nicaea, had him express himself thus:

For their [the Jews'] boast is absurd indeed, that it is not in [Christians'] power without instruction from them to observe these things [Easter]. [12] For how should they be capable of forming a sound judgment, who, since their parricidal guilt in slaying their Lord, . . . are swayed by every impulse of the mad spirit that is in them? [13]

"Such was the reward," wrote Eusebius in his *Church History*, "which the Jews received for their wickedness and impiety against the Christ of God." [14]

The Church Fathers go much farther. We have already heard Saint Ephraim call the Jews "circumcised dogs." [15] Saint Jerome—all the while asking them for Hebrew lessons—denounced the "Judaic serpents" of whom Judas was the model and consigned them to the hatred of Christians. [16] But the honors go to Saint Gregory of Nyssa and Saint John Chrysostom, rivals for truculence in sacred invective.

---

[11] Origen, *Against Celsus*, 2:34; *On the Principles*, 4:1:8. [Quotations taken from *idem, Against Celsus* and *De principiis*, tr. Rev. Frederick Crombie, in *The Ante-Nicene Fathers*, ed. Rev. Alexander Roberts and James Donaldson, rev. ed. Rev. A. Cleveland Cox, 10 vols., New York, Scribner, 1917–1925, IV, 445, 356.—Tr.]

[12] In that period, many Christians celebrated Easter at the same time as the Jews celebrated Passover.

[13] Eusebius of Caesarea, *The Life of Constantine*, 3:18. [Quotation taken from *ibid.*, tr. Ernest Cushing Richardson, in *A Select Library of the Nicene and Post-Nicene Fathers of the Christian Church*, second series, ed. Revs. Philip Schaff and Henry Wace, 14 vols., Grand Rapids, Mich., Eerdmans, 1952–1961, I, 524.—Tr.]

[14] *Idem, Church History*, 3:6:32. [Quotation taken from *ibid.*, tr. Rev. Arthur Cushman McGiffert, in *A Select Library* . . . , I, 141.—Tr.]

[15] See p. 21, n. 4.

[16] Simon, *op. cit.*, p. 271; see Jerome, *Psalmus CVIII* [Psalm 108], in Migne, *op. cit.*, XXVI, 1155 ff.

In a *Homily on the Resurrection* that spilled a potful of abusive attributes on the head of the Jews—"adversaries of grace," "enemies of God," "devil's advocates," "brood of vipers," "sanhedrin of demons"; and I am skipping—Gregory did not fail to fulminate first the principal grievance: "murderers of the Lord," "slayers of the prophets." [17] And what should we say about the sermons delivered at Antioch by Saint John Chrysostom in the years 386–387! Israel "since the deicide" has been given over to "commerce with demons"; the Jews have all the vices of beasts, and "are good for nothing but slaughter"; gluttons, drunkards, sensualists, "living for their belly . . . , they behave no better than pigs and goats in their lewd vulgarities"; how could the faithful not be ashamed to associate "with those who spilled the blood of Jesus Christ"? Their crime leaves them no hope of mending their ways or being pardoned. The synagogue is now "a brothel, a den of thieves, a lair of wild beasts"—and the translation palliates the crudeness of the terms used.[18]

Even Saint Augustine, teaching the catechumens, put all the resources of his orator's genius to work to carve a gripping image of the deicide, calculated to inflame those novice hearts:

The Jews held Him, the Jews insulted Him, the Jews bound Him, they crowned Him with thorns, they dishonored Him by spitting upon Him, they scourged Him, they heaped abuses upon Him, they hung Him upon a tree, they pierced Him with a lance. . . .[19]

Simple vehemence of language? Alas, no. It was translated into law and deeds. Anti-Semitism would be able to bloom and diversify in the eras to come: it found its finished model there in the fourth century. Under the influence of the Fathers of the Church, and notably Saint John Chrysostom, imperial legislation tended to alter to the detriment of the Jews, to take on even the tone of the anti-Jewish polemic. Material violence followed: synagogues were confiscated and burned, sometimes at the instigation of ecclesiastic authorities; and when the

[17] Gregory of Nyssa, *Homily on the Resurrection*, in Father Jacques-Paul Migne, ed., *Patrologia graeca* [Greek Fathers], 165 vols., Paris, Garnier, 1857–1866, XLVI, 685.
[18] John Chrysostom, *Adversus Judaeos* [Against the Jews], 1, 2, in Migne, *Patrologia graeca*, XLVIII, 847, 861; quoted in Simon, *op. cit.*, p. 257.
[19] Augustine, *Sermo ad catechumenos* [Sermon to the Catechumens], in Migne, *Patrologia latina*, XL, 634. See also Bernhard Blumenkranz, *Die Judenpredigt Augustins* [Augustine's Sermons on the Jews], Basel, Helbing & Lichtenhahn, 1946. [Quotation taken from Augustine, *The Creed*, tr. Sister Marie Liguori Ewald, I.H.M., in *Saint Augustine: Treatises on Marriage and Other Subjects*, ed. Roy J. Deferrari, "The Fathers of the Church" series, 60 + vols., New York, Fathers of the Church, 1955, XXVII, 301.—Tr.]

emperor wanted to deal severely with these acts in protection of public order and of a noble tradition of equity, Saint Ambrose threatened him with excommunication.[20]

Among the Christian masses—the more malleable as they tended to grow more ignorant, more crude, more mixed with barbarians—everything combined to mold this anti-Jewish mentality, permeated with a sacred horror of "the deicide people." As the admirable Christian liturgy, so persuasively efficacious, took form, the hymns and prayers, the readings and sermons insistently recalled "the odious crime perpetrated by the Jews." The majesty of the setting, the solemnity of the ceremony, the beauty of the words and voices helped incise in the hearts of the faithful sentiments which would nevermore be blotted out, which would be transmitted from century to century and would ultimately aggregate to form what could be called "the Christian subconscious." Listen to the *Improperia*,[21] the very moving hymn from the liturgy for Good Friday, which has risen and soared over an unfathomable depth of meditation at the hour of adoration since about the ninth century:

O my people, what have I done to thee? or wherein have I aggrieved thee? answer me. Because I led thee out of the land of Egypt, thou has prepared a Cross for thy Saviour. . . .

I gave thee a royal sceptre: and thou didst put a crown of thorns upon my head.

O my people, what have I done to thee? . . . I raised thee up with mighty power: and thou didst hang me upon the gibbet of the Cross.[22]

---

[20] See Simon, *op. cit.*, p. 266.

[21] In the *Improperia*, or Reproaches, Christ addresses tender plaints to his "people," for whom he has done so much good and who in return have done him such ill. Christ's voice merges with Moses'. [The beginning of the *Improperia* is drawn from Micah 6:3–4.—Ed.]

[22] [*The Missal in Latin and English*, ed. Father J. O'Connell and H. P. R. Finberg, New York, Sheed & Ward, 1953, "Masses of the Season," pp. 383–385. Let us listen also to the Oriental liturgy:

Awake, singer David. . . .
"The people who do not know mercy,
pitilessly pierced the hands of the Son. . . .
Like dogs, they have surrounded him who keeps silence.". . .
Awake, noble Malachy.
Make the wicked people ashamed who crucified Christ. . . .
Awake, prophet Daniel.
Look at Emmanuel whom Gabriel reveals to you, tortured by the children of
    Israel.
Woe to the prevaricating people. . . .

(Chaldean rite, quoted in Sister Marie Despina, "Jews in Oriental Christian Liturgy," *Sidic* [Rome], October–November, 1967, p. 16.)—Ed.]

The Church does indeed know its duty; it has never failed to join mercy to reprobation. "We must have pity on them [the Jews], fast and pray for them," we read in the Didascalia, a liturgical breviary dating from the third century.[23] One must "pray for them," Saint Justin said, Saint Augustine repeated. But there is prayer and prayer. The prayers for the Jews would soon be reduced to the single contemptuous Good Friday prayer, already known to Gregory of Tours in the sixth century, the only one which remained in the liturgy into our own time. "*Oremus et pro perfidis Judaeis . . .*"—"Let us also pray for the perfidious Jews. . . ." And soon, too, it would be specified that for this single *Oremus*, the ritual genuflexion should be omitted.[24]

Let us say quite plainly: better no prayer than a prayer like that. What can human hearts retain of this too skillfully blended mixture of mercy and reprobation? No mercy; and far worse than reprobation —disgust and hatred and horror toward the deicide people. Come an opportunity, whether a crusade, a plague, or a famine, and the anger sustained and accumulated over centuries, strengthened in the credulous minds of the people by absurd calumnies like the accusation of ritual crimes inherited from paganism, exploded—some monk was always there to trigger it—to be followed by the thousand and one medieval pogroms which pious eloquence and theological learning would then be able to raise to the rank of "providential punishment" and "divine vengeance." [25] "By the twentieth century," writes Jean-Jacques Bovet, "the Jews were no longer being accused of slaughtering children. . . ." [26] Wrong, alas. As the first edition of the present work was being published, there were still churchmen in Poland to

<hr/>

[23] See Juster, *op. cit.*, I, 311–312.

[24] [In 1949, following Pope Pius XII's authorization to translate *perfidis* as "unbelieving" or "without faith," Jules Isaac had an audience with the Pope. He pointed out that the change was insufficient; he pressed for total suppression of the word and also for the reinstatement of the ritual genuflexion. The latter was restored in 1955; and in 1959, Pope John XXIII eliminated the word *perfidis* from the prayer forever. Finally, Pope Paul VI removed any mention of conversion and the assertion that Jews needed deliverance "from their darkness," and he introduced the reference to the Jews as "the people of Abraham beloved by God" (see "Prayers on Jews Revised by Pontiff," *New York Times*, April 1, 1965, pp. 1, 9).—Ed.]

[25] Louis-Claude Fillion, *Vie de Notre Seigneur Jésus-Christ*, 22nd ed., Paris, Letouzey, 1929, III, 197, 248.

[26] Jean-Jacques Bovet, "L'Étoile" [The Star], *Le Christianisme social*, October–December, 1946, p. 416.

hawk foul calumnies against the Jews and incite credulous populaces to pogrom.[27]

o   o   o

I will not stop to follow the high roads and bypaths of history traced by the sanguinary course of the teaching, whose major theme remained the accusation of deicide: this would need a book, and

[27] See *La Quinzaine*, January, 1947, p. 30. [Rare is the twentieth-century nation, in fact, which has not turned on its Jewish citizens or neighbors with precisely the accusations which Bovet claims to be bygone. In Eastern Europe, the Russian city of Kishinev launched a pogrom at Easter in 1903; so did Bialystok in 1906. Twenty thousand people were killed in 200 Ukrainian pogroms between 1919 and 1921, and Poland itself foreshadowed the Holocaust with a pogrom at Przytyk in 1936. Again in the Ukraine, its capital city of Kiev was the setting for the trial in 1911–1914 of Mendel Beiliss on a charge of ritual murder; Beiliss was found innocent, and emigrated to the United States. (These and other instances are discussed in detail in Lucy S. Dawidowicz, *The Golden Tradition*, New York, Holt, Rinehart and Winston, 1967, pp. 46–81.) More recently, Jews have been accused of using human blood for rituals in the Uzbek Republic of the U.S.S.R.: at Margelan two days after Rosh Hashanah in 1961, and at Tashkent shortly after Passover, 1962 (reported by Label Katz, president of B'nai B'rith, at a press conference, Washington, D. C., January 23, 1963).

[The same libel has been circulating in the Arab world along with the infamous and proven forgery, *The Protocols of the Elders of Zion*. In its issue of June 21, 1967, the popular illustrated weekly *Akher Saa* (Cairo) carried an article by Ibrahim Saada entitled "The Secret of the Blood Practices Israel Is Enjoined To Observe." Under the heading "Some of the Ritual Rabbis Perform with Christian Blood," the author writes, "What is the secret of the Jewish dough mixed with blood? . . . The kidnapping of children in Syria and Lebanon for the purpose of sucking their blood on the Jewish Passover."

[While political motivations presumably underlie Near Eastern anti-Semitism in part, not even this excuse can be summoned for physical and moral attacks on Jews in Western countries. A lives of the saints for children, issued at Valencia with an imprimatur in 1963, teaches that "They [the Jews] remember the passion on Good Friday by stealing a child and crucifying it" (quoted in Fathers René Laurentin and Joseph Neuner, S.J., *The Declaration on the Relation of the Church to Non-Christian Religions of Vatican II*, "Vatican II Documents" series, Glen Rock, N. J., Paulist Press, 1966, p. 55). Numerous scurrilities, laying heavy stress on the deicide charge, were printed and distributed broadside to the representatives at the Vatican Council in Rome, 1962–1965, and one of the lengthier —a pseudonymous book—has since appeared in English in the United States, in 1967. (The editor has examined or possesses four such pieces of hate literature, and others are discussed by Rabbi Arthur Gilbert in *The Vatican Council and the Jews*, New York, World Publishing, 1968.) These materials were neither sponsored nor sanctioned by any official Church voice, but this may not be said of the opinion expressed by Bishop Luigi Carli that ". . . Judaism must be held responsible for deicide, reprobated and accursed by God . . ." (see p. 392, n. 10, below). And one cannot help sensing an undertone of the same injurious tradition in the words spoken by Pope Paul VI himself on Passion Sunday, 1965 (see p. 263, n. 76, below).

[Finally, though the United States may claim never to have mounted a po-

surely that book must be written,[28] but the undertaking surpasses the framework I have set for myself.[29] Having marked the point of origin clearly, I will limit myself to showing where it has led: its contemporary existence and virulence. At the most, I think it useful to erect some landmarks so as to make the continuity of the current visible.

I can therefore only mention the anti-Jewish legislation of the Middle Ages, arising from that system of interdicts, exclusions, degradations applied to the Jews which spread across not several years, like its Nazi imitation, but some fifteen centuries: this constitutes a gauge of its dreadful effectiveness. Actually this system, which began to evolve as soon as the Church united with the State, was not developed fully until the eleventh, twelfth, and thirteenth centuries,[30] the era when there was really a Christendom, in that "great light of the Middle Ages" (Gustave Cohen *dixit*),[31] which to be sure also bore some shadows; it is not an accident that the institution of the *rouelle* or disc, of the various ignominious badges imposed on the Jews, coincided with the apogee of pontifical theocracy: before Hitler, Innocent III; before the Nuremberg Laws, the decrees of the Fourth Lateran Council.

But at the root of this anti-Jewish legislation was deicide, as dei-

grom, the Jews of this country too have suffered the degradation of "foul calumnies" and death at the hands of "credulous populaces." In August of 1915, Leo Frank was lynched in Atlanta for a murder of which he was later found innocent. Two days before Yom Kippur, 1928, Rabbi Berel Brennglass was accused by the mayor of Massena, New York, of committing the ritual murder of a four-year-old child (see Morton Rosenstock, *Louis Marshall, Defender of Jewish Rights*, Detroit, Wayne State University Press, 1965, pp. 264–267). And a pamphlet published in Birmingham, Alabama, in 1962 lists hundreds of "well-authenticated" cases of "ritual murder" throughout the world in the present century; the copy in the editor's possession carries the date of October, 1964, and the claim, "Republished by Popular Demand."
[So it is that we, like Jules Isaac, must still answer Jean-Jacques Bovet's allegation of more than twenty years ago: "Wrong, alas."—Ed.]

[28] [Since the initial appearance of *Jésus et Israël* in 1948, and frequently under its inspiration, numerous books have been written on this subject. Notable in the United States is Father Edward H. Flannery's *The Anguish of the Jews: Twenty-Three Centuries of Anti-Semitism*, New York, Macmillan, 1965. Father Flannery is the first Roman Catholic priest who has had the courage to write at length about the history of Christian anti-Semitism.—Ed.]

[29] [Jules Isaac undertook such a work, but time was not left him to complete it. He was able to cover only the period up to the year 1000, in *Genèse de l'antisémitisme* (see n. 4, above).—Ed.]

[30] Prior to the Middle Ages, notably in the Carolingian age, the Jews experienced long periods of tranquillity and prosperity. When one speaks of "providential punishment," then, it is well to distinguish between eras.

[31] Gustave Cohen, *La grande Clarté du moyen-âge* [The Great Light of the Middle Ages], New York, Maison Française, 1943.

cide was the origin of the massacres. "The mob of massacrers shouted,
'They killed our Savior—let them convert or let them die!' " [32] These
people were only translating into their own unrefined terms a thesis
of the medieval Church to which how many Christians—or would-be
Christians—might be disposed to subscribe even in our day. Even
those who tried out of Christian charity and theological reasoning to
curb popular frenzies recognized the merits of the thesis and of the
capital accusation on which it rested. Saint Bernard of Clairvaux, a
most noble and powerful figure of twelfth-century French Christendom, wrote in a letter addressed both to "the English people" and
to "all the clergy and people of Eastern France [the Rhineland] and
Bavaria" in 1146:

The Jews are not to be persecuted, killed or even put to flight. . . . The
Jews are for us the living words of Scripture, for they remind us always
of what our Lord suffered. They are dispersed all over the world so that
by expiating their crime they may be everywhere the living witnesses of
our redemption. [33]

And the illustrious thirteenth-century doctor, Saint Thomas Aquinas,
said in a consultation given the Duchess of Brabant: "It would be
licit, according to the law, to hold the Jews in perpetual servitude because of their crime." Saint Thomas was only restating the formula of
the great Pope Innocent III: "The Jews," guilty of having "crucified
the Lord," have been "subjected to perpetual servitude." [34]

After the relative tolerance of the Renaissance popes, the popes of
the Counterreformation reverted to Innocent III's principles, applying
them strictly. By his Bull of July 12, 1555, Pope Paul IV re-estab-
lished the most rigorous anti-Jewish legislation in the Papal States:
confinement in the ghetto, obligatory wearing of a distinctive mark
(the yellow hat), prohibition from practicing most professions. [35]

[32] Father Joseph Bonsirven, S.J., in Father Henri de Lubac, S.J., et al., Israël
et la foi chrétienne, "Manifeste contre le Nazisme" series, Fribourg, Switz., Éd.
de la Librairie de l'Université, 1942, p. 133.

[33] Bernard of Clairvaux, Lettres, ed. Father P., Lyons, 1838, III, 105. [Quota-
tion taken from Letters of St. Bernard, ed. Bruno Scott James, Chicago, Regnery,
1953, p. 462, para. 6.—Tr.]

[34] Thomas Aquinas, letter to the Duchess of Brabant, in De regimine princi-
pium [On the Primary Rule], Turin, Marietti, 1924, p. 117; Innocent III, CXXI
[(letter) 121], in Migne, Patrologia latina, CCXV, 694. Quoted in Father Hippo-
lyte Gayraud, L'Antisémitisme de saint Thomas d'Aquin [Anti-Semitism in Saint
Thomas Aquinas], Paris, Dentu, 1896, p. 71; Journet, op. cit., p. 260; Father Joseph Bonsirven, S.J., Les Juifs et Jésus, Paris, Beauchesne, 1937, p. 186.

[35] David Lasserre, "L'Antisémitisme de l'Église chrétienne," Cahiers protestants, no. 1, January–February, 1939, p. 9.

A medieval thesis, then, with Counterreformation postscripts? No;
just as much a modern thesis, a classic thesis that Jansenism adopted
for its own account in the person of Blaise Pascal:

It is an amazing thing . . . to find the Jewish people surviving after so
many years, and to see them in a state of wretchedness; but in order to
prove the claims of Jesus Christ it was essential that they should both survive and be wretched because they crucified him. . . .[36]

". . . in order to prove the claims of Jesus Christ . . ."? Isn't it most
astonishing of all that Jesus Christ should need this proof?

o   o   o

But the Reformation?

Wouldn't the Reformation, whose primary inspiration was to go
back to the purest sources—the Word of Christ—have been led by
this very fact to move away from the traditional viewpoint? Not in
the least.

Indeed, Luther—as Muhammad before him—began by lavishing
fine words and welcomes on the Jews, with the undisguised hope of
rallying them to his cause. He published *Christ Was Born a Jew* in
1523; "Please God that the time [of Israel's conversion] be close, as
we hope." [37] But ten years had not passed before the reformer, disap-
pointed in his hope, opened fire against them with all the violence of
an impulsive, quick-tempered Germanic temperament. The Jews were
then but abominable deicides for him, fit for drowning in the Elba if
they asked for baptism: about 1531 or 1532, he declared that if he
found some pious Jew to baptize, he would lead him out on the
bridge over the Elba, attach a stone to his neck, and throw him in the
river, saying: "I baptize you in the name of Abraham!" [38] We read in
Luther's *Table Talk:* "The destruction of Jerusalem was cruel,
lamentable. . . . It was really too much [for God] to see his own people lead his own Son before the gates of the city to crucify him." [39]

[36] Blaise Pascal, *Opuscules et pensées*, ed. Léon Brunschvicg, Paris, Hachette,
1897, para. 640. [Quotation taken from *idem, Pensées*, ed. and tr. Martin Turnell,
New York, Harper, 1962.—Tr.]
[37] [Martin Luther, *Das Jhesus Christus eyn geborner Jude sey* (Christ Was
Born a Jew), Wittenberg, 1523.—Tr.]
[38] Quoted in Reinhold Lewin, *Luthers Stellung zu den Juden* [Luther's Attitude Toward the Jews], Berlin, Trowitzsch, 1911, p. 37.
[39] [Martin Luther, *Tischreden* . . . (Table Talk . . .), Eisleben, Gaubisch,
1566.—Tr.]

And in one of his last writings, entitled *On the Jews and Their Lies*, the filthiest insults—in the style of Saint John Chrysostom—alternate with frenzied summonses to the worst violence:

Venomous beasts, vipers, disgusting scum, cancers, devils incarnate. . . . Rather than touch the pearl and balm of the word of God, you should handle pig excrement. . . . Their [the Jews'] private houses must be destroyed and devastated; they could be lodged in stables. . . . I beseech our magistrates to exercise severe pity toward these wretches in case it might contribute to their salvation. . . . Let them take care to burn their synagogues . . . and whatever escapes the fire must be covered with sand and mud. . . . Let them force them to work. And if all this avails nothing, we will be compelled to expel them like mad dogs in order not to expose ourselves to incurring divine wrath and eternal damnation! [40]

Patience, Luther, Hitler will come. Your wishes will be granted, and more! Let us recognize here the family ties, the blood ties, uniting two great Germans, and let us place Luther in the place he deserves, in the first row of Christian precursors—of Auschwitz.

John Calvin, more in control of himself, did not deviate from doctrinal considerations. But such was the intransigence of the theologian that it took him to the point of denying Christ's merciful pardon:

When Christ, moved with an affection of mercy, asked God for pardon of those who pursued him, this did not at all prevent him from acquiescing in God's righteous judgment, the which he knew to be ordained for the reprobate and obstinate.[41]

And Calvinist rigidity, as we know, did not hesitate to steal a march on God's judgment against "the reprobate and the obstinate"; in 1632, a pastor, Nicolas Antoine, would be strangled in Geneva for apostasy and conversion to Judaism.

o   o   o

Wrath of God, vengeance of God, Crime and Punishment—choice theme for great preachers. The oratory of a Bossuet gave it an unequaled magnificence, first in the sermon preached at Metz around 1653, *On the Goodness and Stringency of God*, and then, some twenty

---

[40] [*Idem, Von den Jüden und jren Lügen*, Wittenberg, Lufft, 1543. See, in English, as *idem, The Jews and Their Lies*, St. Louis, Christian Nationalist Crusade, n.d.—Tr.]

[41] Jehan Calvin, *Sur la Concordance ou Harmonie composée de trois évangélistes, asçavoir S. Matthieu, S. Marc et S. Luc*, vol. 1 of *Commentaires de M. Jehan Calvin sur le Nouveau Testament*, Paris, Meyrueis, 1854.

years later, in the second part of his *Discourse on Universal History*, Chapters XX and XXI.[42] Everything is there.

The definition of the crime:

It was the greatest of all crimes: an unprecedented crime, that is, deicide, which also occasioned a vengeance the like of which the world had never seen.

A striking, graphic description of the "vengeance" of God:

At the moment the Emperor Titus laid siege to the city, the Jews were there in crowds to celebrate Passover. . . . Surely you were remembering, O great God, that it was in the Passover season that their fathers had dared to imprison the Savior; you paid them back, O Lord! and in the same Passover season you imprisoned their children, imitators of their obstinacy, in the capital of their country. . . .

Divine justice demanded an infinite number of victims; it wanted to see 1,100,000 struck down . . . : and even after that, pursuing the remains of this disloyal race, he dispersed them over all the earth. For what reason? As magistrates, having had a number of malefactors broken on the wheel, ordered that their torn and sundered limbs be displayed at several places on the major roads, to strike terror in other villains. This comparison horrifies you: the fact remains that God behaved about the same way. . . .

Finally, the serene affirmation of the traditional doctrine:

By this profound plan of God, the Jews still exist in the midst of the nations, where they are dispersed and captive: but they exist stamped by their reprobation, visibly blighted by their unfaithfulness to the promises made to their fathers, banished from the Promised Land, having no land to cultivate even, slaves everywhere they are, without honor, without freedom, without form as a people. They fell into this state thirty-eight years after they crucified Jesus Christ.

Unfortunately, beauty of style dominates solidity of content. I do not know how the *lex talionis* can be reconciled with the Sermon on the Mount, but as Bossuet speaks of tearing and sundering, I owe it to truth to observe that it is history which finds itself torn and sundered in the hands of the vigorous Bishop of Meaux. Not only is the Dispersion anterior to the events of A.D. 70 by a number of centuries, but there was not even a dispersion of the Palestinian Jews at that date: the proof lies in the second Judean war, fought in 132–135 under

---

[42] Jacques-Bénigne Bossuet, *Discours sur l'Histoire universelle*, vol. V of *Oeuvres de Bossuet*, Paris, Méquignon Junior et Leroux, 1846, pt. II, Chap. XXI, pp. 408–409; idem, *Sur la Bonté et la rigueur de Dieu* [On the Goodness and Stringency of God], in *Sermons choisis de Bossuet* [Selected Sermons of Bossuet], ed. Ferdinand Brunetière, Paris, Firman-Didot, 1882, pp. 40 ff.

the Emperor Hadrian.[43] The "visibly blighted" condition of the Jews was the result of the system of debasement which we have discussed. Finally, if the Jews after a certain period had "no land to cultivate" any more, it was because Christian princes, at the instigation of the Church, progressively withdrew from them the right to own land and the means of practicing agriculture (in the eighth century, there were still Jews in southern Gaul who were great landowners).

o   o   o

Prefacing the contemporary era came the torrential revolutions which seemed—in France, at least—to carry away all the barriers, break all the chains, and which, freeing the Jews from all servitude, restored their human dignity and rights as citizens. In this new climate of freedom, to which public subservience adapted not without difficulty—no more easily than secular privileges, prejudices, and debasements; in this world convulsed as if by an earthquake, there is nothing surprising in the fact that the traditional current nonetheless continued to flow (below ground or in the open), that the traditional teaching continued to shape souls. The incriminating thesis lost nothing of its strength and rigor—far from it. All the varieties of anti-Judaism could wax and flourish in the layer of humus deposited by the silt of centuries: the ground was well prepared. And modern techniques of distribution and publicizing would assure it a monstrous growth.

Works by clerics and laymen, by doctors, professors, men of letters and journalists, Catholic or Protestant, the reading material offers us too much to choose from. And our choice will go by preference to the most qualified, the most reputable.

Among nineteenth-century Protestant theologians, John Nelson Darby stands as an innovator; in what terms did he speak of the Jews? "We can see in Cain a type of the Jews, murderers of the Lord: they carry the mark of it on their forehead." [44] We have already pointed out the merciless severity—inherited from Calvin—of a

---

[43] [Moreover—were further proof needed—the establishment of the State of Israel in 1948 (after the initial publication of the present book) adds to the implausibility of Bossuet's theses.—Ed.]

[44] John Nelson Darby, *Introduction à la Sainte Bible* [Introduction to the Holy Bible].

Frédéric Godet [45] and an Henri Bois.[46] More recent commentators on
the Gospels, Gunther Dehn and Hébert Roux are no less implacable
prosecutors in their indictment of Israel. "An internal necessity," the
first assures us, "impelled the Jewish people to nail Jesus to the cross,
because he destroyed their pretensions." "Israel," the second decrees,
"is maintained as a people, as a race, for the day of judgment to
come. . . . Just as the descendants of Israel were the object of God's
special grace and as it was first to them that Jesus came, so they
would be the object of a special judgment, they who took 'innocent
blood' upon themselves and who would have to make an
accounting." [47] I admire these superior spirits who have penetrated
God's designs to the point of being initiated into the secret of His
judgments.[48]

More recent yet is an article in the foremost French Protestant periodical, *Réforme*, which, after disdainfully brushing aside "the controversies concerning exegesis and history," reminds us in a hard tone
that

. . . willingly or unwillingly: this is the key word in the [Jewish] enigma.
The Jewish people have fulfilled and are still fulfilling their mission, but it
is *unwillingly*. After centuries of abusing the patience of their God without exhausting it, the decisive moment in [their] history arrived. Jesus
Christ came on earth. He came to establish the Kingdom of God. . . . Thus
he declared himself king of the Jews. The Jews refused to recognize him as
their king: they scoffed at him, condemned him, crucified him. In so doing,
they trampled underfoot the mission they had received, they said "no" to
God. . . . [Dispersed over all the earth and persecuted by reason of the
curse brought down on them,] they [nonetheless] continue to fulfill their
function as witnesses. They effectively remind all men and the nations
where they dwell that God is not mocked with impunity.[49]

[45] See p. 126, above; and in Godet's work (*Commentaire sur l'Évangile de Jean*,
Paris, Fischbacher, 1876), see also III, 518.
[46] See pp. 101 and 205; n. 67, above; and in Bois's book (*La Personne et
l'oeuvre de Jésus*, Neuilly, La Cause, 1926), see also pp. 110, 120–122.
[47] Gunther Dehn, *Le Fils de Dieu, commentaire à l'Évangile de Marc*, Paris,
Je Sers, 1936, p. 148; Hébert Roux, *L'Évangile du Royaume*, Geneva, Labor et
Fides, 1934, p. 289.
[48] [More telepathy, this time American: "In the Judgment Day, the scriptures
in which they [The Jews] trusted will therefore judge and condemn them" (*Gospel of John* [Assembly of God], 1965, p. 24; quoted in Gerald Strober, ms. in
preparation, New York [Xerox], p. 53).—Ed.]
[49] Bosc, *op. cit.*; and see the editorial "Le Point de vue de Réforme" [The
Viewpoint of Reform] in the same issue of *Réforme*, November 23, 1946. [This
"hard tone" can be heard in some American Protestant voices which are recorded
by way of example in Bernhard E. Olson's book *Faith and Prejudice* (New Haven,
Yale University Press, 1963, pp. 35, 242). One says: "When the Jews quote God's
promise to Abraham, 'I will curse them that curse Thee,'. . . ask them how that

In other words, God uses the Jews as Sparta did its drunken Helots.[50]

Thus is a theological tradition maintained in all its rigidity which in fact has only a very remote relation to exegesis and history and, one could even add, to the Gospel of Christ.

So faith, hope, love abide, these three; but the greatest of these is love.

1 Cor. 13:13

o   o   o

Alternating choruses: Catholic voices reply to Protestant.

Lamennais, who at that moment was still Father Lamennais, pre-echoed John Nelson Darby, and his eloquence and orthodoxy seemed to announce a new Bossuet, more hotblooded—and more absolutist:

Universal, perpetual miracle, which will demonstrate to the end of days the inexorable justness and the holiness of God, whom this [Jewish] people dared to deny. . . . Even to our own time all peoples have seen them pass, all have been gripped with horror at their sight; they were marked with a sign more terrible than Cain's; on their forehead an iron hand had written: Deicide! [51]

It is Cain, again Cain (oh, the convenience—and arbitrariness—of that device, the figure of speech!) whom Father Lagrange himself evokes in his interpretation of Matthew 23:35:

So the chosen people, whose election was prefigured by Abel, adopted Cain's attitude against the Messiah, brother born of their blood who had been sent to them. . . . No man is punished except for his faults, but this time the nation would take responsibility for a crime which summed up all the crimes accumulated since the origin of the world, and its punishment, long deferred, would be definitive.[52]

promise could apply to the Jews whom Jesus Himself condemned. Jesus in very strong terms denounced the Jews, and pronounced judgement upon them. . . . This explains why these judgements are falling upon the Jews, from Jesus' time until today; they are receiving just what they measured out to Christians" (*Women's Voice*, vol. XI, no. 8, March 26, 1953, p. 1). And another: "Because they rejected their Messiah at His first coming, demanding that His blood be on them and their children, the Jews have had an unhappy lot for centuries" (*Adult Teacher* [Scripture Press], October–December, 1953, p. 116).—Ed.]

[50] [The reference is to Plutarch's report that Helots were forced to appear in public drunk on certain occasions as a lesson to Spartan youth.—Tr.]

[51] Félicité de Lamennais, *Essai sur l'indifférence en matière de religion* [Essay on Indifference in Religious Matters], 4 vols., Paris, 1817–1823, vol. III.

[52] Father Marie-Joseph Lagrange, O.P., *L'Évangile de Jésus-Christ*, Paris, Gabalda, 1928, p. 456.

Less well known, but no less effective for the fact, are the manuals for seminary use which have molded generations of priests. Father Jean-Joseph Rivaux's *Church History Course* was widely distributed at the end of the nineteenth century; I extract a few typical sentences:

Divine wrath already pursued this deicide race everywhere. . . . Everything combined finally to hasten that catastrophe which would consummate the destruction of the deicide nation. . . . Thus this deicide nation is experiencing a punishment comparable to the crime which was the original cause of its misfortunes; and the idolatrous soldiery, by crucifying these wretches, repaid them all the outrages they themselves had heaped on the Son of God at Golgotha.[53]

The place of favor of Father Rivaux's work in Catholic teaching passed to Father Léon Marion's *History of the Church*, "the standard manual in most French seminaries," which contains almost identical formulas on the manifestations of God's "justice toward the deicide people." [54] Sooner or later, the traditional epithet flows from the pen (and certainly from the lips) of the Catholic professor; commenting on Luke 23:27–31, where Jesus, carrying the cross, speaks to the "Daughters of Jerusalem," A. Brassac inserts these parentheses: "If it goes so hard with the tree that is still green (that is, with our Lord), what will become of the tree that is already dried up (that is, of the Jewish nation which is committing an infamous deicide)?" [55]

Better yet—or worse—is one of the more recent history texts for use in Catholic primary schools. It states:

The punishment of the deicide (God-murdering) Jews was not long in coming. Thirty-six years after the Savior's death, the Roman Emperor Titus seized Jerusalem and completely destroyed the Temple. The Jews, dispersed throughout the world, have never again been able to form a nation. They have wandered everywhere, considered a cursed race, an object of contempt to other peoples.[56]

[53] Father Jean-Joseph Rivaux, *Cours d'histoire ecclésiastique à l'usage des séminaires* [Church History Course for Use in Seminaries], 3 vols., 10th ed., Grenoble, Baratier, 1895.

[54] Father Léon Marion, *Histoire de l'Église* [History of the Church], 3 vols., 4th ed., Paris, Roger et Chernoviz, 1905–1922, I, 127–128.

[55] Father A. Brassac, *Nouveau Testament*, vol. III of Fathers Fulcran G. Vigouroux and A. Brassac, *Manuel biblique, ou Cours d'Écriture sainte à l'usage des séminaires*, ed. Fathers A. Brassac and Louis Baceuz, 4 vols., 12th ed., Paris, Roger et Chernoviz, 1906–1909, p. 698. [Father Brassac's insertions aside, the wording of Lk. 23:31 here is from RK, which also carries this note: "This verse is generally understood to mean, If crucifixion is the lot of the innocent, what punishment is to be expected by the guilty (that is, the Jews)?"—Tr.]

[56] Henri Guillemain and Canon François Le Ster, *Histoire de France: Manuel du certificat d'études*, rev. ed., Paris, Éd. de l'École, 1947. This text was oblig-

Let us move up a few degrees. Let us come to that great Catholic work by the Reverend Father Dom Prosper Guéranger, *The Liturgical Year*, the volume devoted to *The Passion and Holy Week*. Dom Guéranger gives us brimful measure:

The most general characteristic of the prayers and ritual of this fortnight is profound grief at seeing the Righteous One oppressed by his enemies to the death [ah, what heart would not endorse this! but Dom Guéranger adds:] and strenuous indignation against the deicide people. . . . Sometimes Christ himself reveals the agonies of his soul; sometimes there are frightful imprecations against his tormentors. The punishment of the Jewish nation is displayed in all its horror.

Here, Dom Guéranger does say, "The Church does not seek to stir up fruitless feeling; it wishes primarily to strike salutary dread in the hearts of its children. If they are terrorized by the crime committed in Jerusalem, if they feel that they are guilty of it, their tears will always flow amply. . . ." But the hearer will persuade himself of the Jew's guilt more readily than of his own. Dom Guéranger continues: "These considerations on the justice of the punishment of the impenitent Jews will succeed in destroying the attachment we have to sin. . . ."

ingly communicated to me by Miss M.-M. Davy, of the faculty at the École de Hautes Études. Canon Le Ster very adequately expressed to me his regret at having allowed such locutions to pass into print, and he corrected the text in a new edition, of 1948. [The revised edition was reprinted in 1957 and was still in use in France in 1967.—Ed.] To see how active this tradition continues to be in Catholic teaching, the reader may refer to the inquiry conducted by Paul Démann, *La Catéchèse chrétienne et le peuple de la Bible* [Christian Catechesis and the People of the Bible], Paris, Éd. des *Cahiers sioniens*, 1952.

[See also Canon François Houtart and Jean Giblet, eds., *Les Juifs dans la catéchèse: Étude des manuels 'de catéchèse de langue française*, Louvain, Centre de Recherches socio-religieuses and Centre de Recherches catéchétiques, 1969. This broad-based study of catechetical materials documents all too painfully "how active" the anti-Jewish "tradition continues to be in Catholic teaching" still today —more than two decades after *Jésus et Israël's* writing. The quotations which the study incorporates, and on which the editor has drawn freely, parrot the misguided commentaries cited by Professor Isaac. Listen to the familiar ruthlessness underlying these words from an instruction text: "But Jews, his [Jesus'] fellow countrymen, refused to let themselves be loved by Jesus. This is why they will be burned like dried-out vine branches. And the temples [sic] of these Pharisees will be nothing but ruins" (J. de Lorimier, *Histoire de notre salut*, teacher's manual, Ottawa, Fides, 1962, p. 157). To this the author joins a corresponding sentence in the pupil's text: "But the Jews, his fellow countrymen, men like the one you see [in the picture of an "Old Jew"], refused to let themselves be loved by Jesus" (*ibid.*, student's text, p. 157). And consider again the brutalizing effect on young ears of such words as these: "The Jews remain those who refuse Christ and the people whose ancestors solemnly called for his blood to fall on them" (A. Ravier, *L'Église du Dieu Vivant* [The Church of the Living God], 2nd ed., "Fils de lumière" series, Paris, Gigord, 1962, p. 152; all quoted in Houtart and Giblet, *op. cit.*, pp. 132, 166, 137).—Ed.]

Alas! They will also succeed in destroying any feeling of humanity that defenseless hearts have toward the "deicide" Jews, whose reprobation is sounded page after page, in words of unparalleled vehemence:

The blood that was spilled by the Jewish people on Calvary . . . is the blood of a God. The whole world must know and understand this from the mere sight of the punishment of the murderers. . . . The spectacle of a whole people drenched with malediction in all its generations, for having crucified the Son of God, gives Christians matter for reflection. They learn from it that divine justice is terrible, and that the Father demands an accounting for the blood of His Son down to the last drop from those who have spilled it. Let us hasten to wash in this precious blood the stain of complicity which we have with the Jews. . . .[57]

But how many faithful will be tempted to cry out here, "First let us wash it in Jewish blood!"

The one and the other, the exegete and the theologian, both accusers, each throwing his stone (in the name of Christ), each decreeing himself final judge by proxy for God: "God's vengeance would sweep down pitilessly on this deicide race and would demand an accounting for all the blood spilled wrongfully," writes Father Prat.[58] "Behind the Roman appears the great bearer of guilt, and it is not Judas alone, it is the leaders of that crowd, and it is 'all the people' who cried out, 'His blood be on us and on our children!' " intones Father de Grandmaison.[59] "The deicide of the Jews"—the stock phrase recurs under Louis-Claude Fillion's pen: the crucifying of the Jews in the year 70 "was a horrible spectacle in which it is hard not to see the punishment that the deicide nation had thus called down upon itself." [60] Father Lebreton, like Calvin, takes the occasion of Jesus' very pardon to crush the Jews: "Those for whom he [Jesus] interceded were neither only nor primarily the soldiers. . . . They were the chief offenders, those against whom Jesus' death armed divine justice, those who called down on themselves the curse of the spilled blood: the Jews." [61] "A murderous people," says Father Fessard, who

[57] Dom Prosper Guéranger, O.S.B., *La Passion et la Semaine sainte*, vol. III of *L'Année liturgique* (6 vols.), 24th ed., Tours, Mame, 1921.
[58] Father Ferdinand Prat, *Jésus-Christ, sa vie, son oeuvre, sa doctrine*, 2 vols., Paris, Beauchesne, 1938, II, 235.
[59] Father Léonce de Grandmaison, S.J., *Jésus-Christ, sa personne, son message, ses preuves*, 2 vols., Paris, Beauchesne, 1928.
[60] Fillion, *op. cit.*, vol. III.
[61] Father Jules Lebreton, S.J., *La Vie et l'enseignement de Jésus-Christ*, 2 vols., Paris, Beauchesne, 1931, II, 422.

assigns Israel a "negating mission," defines the Jews as "enemies of everything that is specifically Christian and everything that is human," denounces the transmutation of the divine favor "into infernal falseness and hatred" through the fault of the Jewish people, and like Bossuet, like so many others who have been less concerned with historic truth than with theological rationalization, finds this eloquent —if not charitable—image to describe Israel's wretchedness:

When they accompanied Jesus to Calvary, at the gates of the City, where he would be crucified by the Romans, who among the Jews foresaw that the destiny of the whole people would be to be crucified by the pagans outside the Holy City, and hence to remain, Witness of God, eternally nailed to the crossroad where Humanity's destinies would converge and traverse, in order to show passersby that we are the meaning of History . . . ? [62]

Imprimatur, imprimatur.[63]

If priests—excellent priests; if pastors, professors, learned men express themselves thus, what can we expect from laymen, men of letters, whose works have (perhaps) less authority, certainly greater distribution and readership, and whose imagination, stimulated by faith, knows no bounds? The uneven but visionary and powerful writer Léon Bloy has won an enthusiastic following, especially since his death, through the appeal of a fierce independence, a holy (but grumbling) poverty, an inspired heart. In the strange book Salvation Is from the Jews (written in 1892), "the only one that I would dare present to God without any fear," he said, and one in which the sublime and the ignoble admix in equal measure, he sees fit to call up "the unrivaled ignominy" of that Jewish people who have "butchered the Word made flesh" and "the prodigious spectacle of their endless punishment." He writes:

Demoniac people . . . , anathema of a race . . . [who] were always for Christians an object of horror and at the same time the occasion of a myste-

---

[62] Father Gaston Fessard, S.J., Pax nostra, 8th ed., Paris, Grasset, 1936.

[63] The quotations can be multiplied. I open the May 15, 1930, issue of the Bulletin catholique de la question d'Israël, where it is said that Israel's rejection of Jesus "is like a sort of second original sin that the deicide people drag through the world. From that time on, the deicide people would be ostracized by society" (Robert John, "Israël: La grande Tragédie de l'histoire du monde et la question juive" [Israel: The Great Tragedy of the History of the World and the Jewish Question], p. 13). Note that this bulletin was published by the missionary priests of Notre-Dame de Sion. But it should also be noted in fairness that after 1948, when Paul Démann took over its direction, this journal was totally transformed. Retitled Cahiers sioniens, not only did its appearance change; its soul changed.

rious fear. . . . they had waited more than two thousand years for an occasion to crucify the Word of God.[64]

This is only a prelude, I know; the deep meaning of the book goes far beyond it; but how many readers penetrate the deep meaning, and how many savor this infamous prelude?

In a Giovanni Papini, one may not recognize any kind of true talent, but one cannot contest that his works in translation have a large Catholic audience. Glancing through his *Life of Christ*, I discover as soon as the subject is broached that "The progeny of those god-killers has become the most infamous but the most sacred of all the peoples"; I learn (not without some surprise) that after the destruction of Jerusalem, "The end of the god-killing people, the partial and local ending, had taken place"; and I perceive in Giovanni Papini, as he comments on the destruction of the Holy City, an emulator of Bossuet or Father Rivaux: "The hills made of stone like the heart of the deicides would only send back the echo of their howling, and the mothers' children would fall in pools of warm blood which would compensate in some feeble way for the blood of Christ." [65] One would like to disregard these oratorical platitudes, but they have currency and they insinuate themselves into innocent hearts. And I say that they lead—yes—they lead to Auschwitz.[66]

[64] Léon Bloy, *Le Salut par les Juifs* [Salvation Is from the Jews] (1892), Paris, Mercure de France, 1933, pp. 47, 51, 56; 95, 126, 189.

[65] Giovanni Papini, *Histoire du Christ*, tr., Paris, Payot, 1922; a wholly new translation appeared in 1946. [Quotations taken from *idem*, *Life of Christ*, tr. Dorothy Canfield Fisher, New York, Harcourt, 1923, pp. 46, 273. The last passage is not included in the English edition.—Tr.]

[66] [Other such "oratorical platitudes" which turn into complete distortions of the Gospels still have currency, to wit in the Oberammergau Passion Play, which was staged again in 1950, 1960, and 1970. The presentation of the drama dates from the seventeenth century; the Oberammergau villagers vowed in 1633 that if they escaped the plague which beset Europe during the Thirty Years' War (1618–1648), they would enact a Passion play every ten years. The first performance took place in 1634, and the script was rewritten in 1860. The Nazis endorsed the play as "a racially important cultural document." The official German text of the play was not significantly modified in 1970. Translated into English from the "revised and newly published" 1970 version by the Community of Oberammergau, *The Passion Play of Oberammergau* includes such lines as these:

> [*Narrated Prologue:*] Even Pilate is moved to sympathy for him
> [Jesus]. . . .
> But around the Saviour of all, in wrath is raging
> A furious, blinded people which ceaseth not its clamour
> Till the unwilling judge
> Cries: So take him and crucify him! [p. 97].
> *All:* Pilate must consent—all Jerusalem demands it of him!
> *Pilate:* Can not even this pitiful sight win some compassion from your hearts?

And of how many others will I say as much? Of my old colleagues
in academicians' robes Jérôme and Jean Tharaud, entitling the most
biased of accounts *When Israel Is King;* [67] of the raving Louis-Ferdi-
nand Céline, dug into a corner of Hitlery during the Second World
War; passing by the hanged Julius Streicher and the obstinate
Charles Maurras, sentenced to life imprisonment, mentor and ora-
cle for numerous French youth, frenetic virtuoso of incitement to
murder.

As for me, because so much stench gives me a desperate desire to
breathe a little clean air, I cannot restrain myself from recalling here
the memory of hours of anguish, the memory of a poor woman, a Jew,
threatened with deportation and consoling a frightened son, a small
Emmanuel seven years old, with words that I do not hesitate to characterize as sublime: "Stop, now, Emmanuel. You mustn't cry. God is
with us. He was with us when we came here. He will be with us if we
have to leave. He will be in the train that will carry us away. He will
be with us everywhere, always." A Jew, a simple Jewish woman, as
Jesus was "a simple Jew." But the ashes of millions of Jewish martyrs
had not yet cooled before the pious tradition of gratuitous insults and
accusations was resumed.

How could the friendship that I had until so recently with Daniel-
Rops have stood up under the reading of such sentences as I will
quote, gathered in 1946 from his *Sacred History: Jesus in His Time*—
a work carrying a nihil obstat signed with the respected name of Joseph Huby and an imprimatur, and assured of the largest distribution
by the most skillful promotion?

All: Let him die! to the cross with him!
Pilate: So take ye him and crucify him at your peril.
   I will have nothing to do with it [p. 101].
Pilate: I am compelled by your violence to yield to your desire.
   Take him and crucify him [p. 104].
Caiphas: Triumph! The victory is ours! The enemy of the Synagogue is
   destroyed! . . .
People: Up and away! Away to Golgotha! Come and see him upon the cross! O
   joyful day! The enemy of Moses is thrown down. . . . He deserves cruci-
   fixion! Happiest Passover! Now is peace returned to Israel! [p. 106].
People: Drive him with violence that we may get on to Calvary. . . .
Priests and People: Do not let him rest. On, drive him with blows! [p. 109].

[And these words were revived in 1950, less than ten years, Dr. Robert Gor-
ham Davis reminds us, after "bulldozers were literally covering with hills of earth
the mass graves of Jewish women and children" ("Passion at Oberammergau,"
Commentary, March, 1960, p. 199).—Ed.]

[67] Jérôme and Jean Tharaud, *Quand Israël est roi* [When Israel Is King],
Paris, Plon-Nourrit, 1921.

This last wish of the people he had elected ("His blood be on us and on our children!") was granted by God in his justice. Through the span of the centuries, in all the lands where the Jewish race has been dispersed, the blood falls; and eternally, the cry of murder hurled at Pilate's praetorium covers a cry of pain repeated a thousand times. The face of persecuted Israel fills History, but it cannot make one forget that other face sullied with blood and spit, which the Jewish crowd did not pity. It doubtless did not rest with Israel not to kill its God after having failed to recognize him, and, as blood calls mysteriously to blood, it perhaps no more rests with Christian charity to prevent the horror of the pogrom from compensating for the unbearable horror of the Crucifixion in the secret balance sheet of the divine intentions.

Dreadful sentences, impious sentences, themselves of an "unbearable horror," aggravated by a note which says:

Among modern-day Jews . . . , a certain number . . . try to throw off the weight of this heavy responsibility. . . . Understandable feelings, but History will not be contravened . . . and the terrible burden of [Jesus' death] which weighs on Israel's forehead is not among those which it rests with man to throw off.[68]

I will add: sentences taken out of context and thereby sidetracked from their original (and infinitely less cruel) meaning, for the majority of them are translated from German and taken from an essay by an anonymous German Catholic, "The Blood Falls," [69] written some eight years earlier. Daniel-Rops made them his own. Let him bear the "heavy responsibility" for them, or rather (as I hope) let him have the heart to disavow them.[70]

[68] Henry Daniel-Rops, *Histoire sainte: Jésus en son temps*, Paris, Fayard, 1945, pp. 526–527.

[69] Anon., "Le Sang retombe" [The Blood Falls], in Paul Claudel *et al.*, *Les Juifs*, "Présences" series, Paris, Plon, 1937, p. 19. The note which I wrote to Daniel-Rops severing our friendship, after I had read his *Jésus en son temps*, was published under the title "Comment on écrit l'Histoire (sainte)" [How (Sacred) History Is Written] in *Europe*, July 1, 1946.

[70] I have let this paragraph stand as originally published in 1948. It must be added, and this is thoroughly to Daniel-Rops's honor, that after the note I addressed to him breaking our friendship, the sentences incriminated were modified in subsequent editions. The 1951 printing of *Jésus en son temps* carries this notice: "New Edition, Revised and Corrected in July, 1951." [And in the 1962 edition, Daniel-Rops says, on the subject of Jewish responsibility: ". . . the present text (1961) differs from that written in 1945–1946; this change translates the evolution of the author's thought during these fifteen years" (p. 683, n. 1). Concerning this evolution, Jules Isaac wrote: ". . . I have received the new edition of *Jésus en son temps*, radically revised, far better inspired toward Judaism . . ." (*L'Enseignement du mépris*, Paris, Fasquelle, 1962, p. 144; see, in an abridged English edition [i.e., appendixes dropped], as *idem*, *The Teaching of Contempt: Christian Roots of Anti-Semitism*, tr. Helen Weaver, New York, Holt, Rinehart and Winston, 1964). In a later book, Daniel-Rops remarked: "We must cite in a

o   o   o

These innumerable voices (there are a thousand others), this concert of outrages, this unparalleled accusation, insistent, persistent, repeated from century to century, perpetually reinforced by that stirring liturgy, that magisterial teaching—we cannot underestimate their effectiveness, their penetration into souls, their ineradicable influence and marks, beginning in childhood and for life.

This is perfectly seen and described by Sören Kierkegaard in his *Training in Christianity:*

Then tell the child what befell Him [Jesus] in life, how one of the few that were close to Him betrayed Him, that the other few denied Him, and all the rest scoffed at and derided Him, until at last they nailed Him to the cross—as the picture shows—requiring that His blood might be upon them and their children, whereas He prayed for them that this might not come to pass, that the heavenly Father would forgive them their fault. . . . Tell the child that contemporary with this loving One there lived a notorious robber who was condemned to death—for him the people demanded release, they cried, "Viva! Long live Barabbas!" But as for the loving One, they cried, "Crucify, crucify!" . . . What effect do you think this narrative will make upon the child? . . . The child would have decided that when he grew up he would slay all those ungodly men who had dealt thus with the loving One.[71]

Kierkegaard adds: "When the child became a' youth, he would not have forgotten the impression of childhood, but he would now understand it differently. . . ." Perhaps, but the first impression will govern his thoughts, often without his being conscious of it.

Desirous of teaching children after adults, Daniel-Rops takes care to tell them: "Rather than hate the people who crucified Jesus, it is better to be grateful to them for all the true and admirable things that they have given humanity." [72] Here are good intentions. A shame that they are obliterated by the massive affirmation, the poisonous ac-

class by itself the moving plea by Jules Isaac, *Jésus et Israel* . . . , to which our final stage [of thinking] owes many elements" (*La Vie quotidienne au temps de Jésus*, Paris, Hachette, 1961, p. 533; see, in English, as idem, *Daily Life in the Time of Jesus*, tr. Patrick O'Brian, New York, Hawthorn, 1962).—Ed.]

Yet it remains very painful that Daniel-Rops could have written such words even a single time—and that time being immediately after Auschwitz.

[71] Sören Kierkegaard *École du Christianisme* tr. P.-H. Tisseau, Paris, Berger-Levrault, 1937. [Quotation taken from idem, *Training in Christianity*, tr. Walter Lowrie, London, Oxford University Press, 1941, pp. 176–177.—Tr.]

[72] Henry Daniel-Rops, *Histoire sainte de mes filleuls* [Sacred History for My Godchildren], Paris, La Colombe, 1946, p. 215. [See, in English, as idem, *The Book of Books: The Story of the Old Testament*, rev. ed., tr. Donal O'Kelly, New York, Kenedy, 1956, pp. 163–164.—Tr.]

cusation they innocently introduce: "the people who crucified Jesus"; nothing more is needed to arouse hatred.

I say to all Christian educators: it is a serious thing, a thing of the greatest seriousness, to infuse hatred—in the name of Christ—in the heart of a child. That these sentiments, inculcated and almost innate (through heredity), thrust their roots deep into the Christian masses I find further proof on a page of Romain Rolland's *Jean-Christophe:*

His grandfather did not like Jews; but as an irony of fate would have it, his two best music students—one become a composer, the other an illustrious virtuoso—were Israelites, and the good man was very unhappy; for there were moments when he would have wanted to embrace those two good musicians; and then, he recalled with sadness that they had put God on the cross; and he did not know how to reconcile those irreconcilable feelings. . . . As for his mother, she was not sure that she was not committing a sin when she went to work [for Jews] as a cook. . . . she bore them no ill will; she was full of pity for those unfortunates, whom God had damned. . . .[73]

Indubitably, there are exceptions to the rule. There is Péguy, for example, who wrote in those last moving pages of his *Appended Note on M. Descartes and Cartesian Philosophy*, in the last hours of his life as a writer (the eve of the 1914 mobilization):

And I will tell my whole thought, for I will say: if God were fully served in his Church (he is served in it with exactitude, but with such miserly exactitude), he would perhaps not need to recall, when he wants to grant a great grace of thought, that there still exist and he still has in his hand the people of his first servants.[74]

The marvelous resonance of that voice, the purifying clarity of that glance, which Death was besetting.

Yet the accusation lives on, even in the most generous declarations made during the last several years to protest against racist theories and practices: "Christ . . . who took His human nature from that people which was to nail Him to the Cross . . . ," wrote Pius XI; [75] "The Jews . . . stoned the prophets and crucified the Son. [But] their guilt . . .

---

[73] Romain Rolland, *La Révolte*, vol. IV of *Jean-Christophe*, 10 vols., Paris, Ollendorff, 1904–1910, pp. 79–80. [See, among many English editions, as *idem, Revolt*, pt. IV of *Jean-Christophe*, tr. Gilbert Cannan (1910), New York, Modern Library, 1941, Bk. I, p. 401.—Tr.]

[74] Charles Péguy, *Note conjointe sur M. Descartes et la philosophie cartésienne* [Appended Note on M. Descartes and Cartesian Philosophy], in *Oeuvres complètes de Charles Péguy*, Paris, NRF, 1924, IX, 135.

[75] Pius XI, *Mit brennender Sorge* [With Burning Sorrow], encyclical, 1937. [Quotation taken from *The Church in Germany*, Vatican Press tr., Washington, D. C., National Catholic Welfare Conference, 1937.—Tr.]

is in the fact that not Jew nor pagan nor Christian is justified before God." [76]

I know too, I know very well everything that can be presented to counterbalance the somber picture I have painted.[77] But no counterbalancing will unmake the veracity of this picture. The question which arises now is thus not one of rehabilitating Christian charity— God forbid my ever doubting it; the question is one of discovering whether the accusation of deicide, thrown in the face of the Jewish people for more than fifteen centuries, is justified or not.

[76] Declaration of the Reformed Church of Basel, 1938, in *Foi et Vie*, the first of eight issues devoted to Jewish studies (see p. 328, n. 30, below), April, 1947, pp. 213–222. [And Pope Paul VI stated on Passion Sunday in 1965: "[The Gospel for Passion Sunday is] a grave and sad page because it narrates the conflict, the clash between Jesus and the Hebrew people, a people predestined to await the Messiah but who, just at the right moment, not only did not recognize Him but fought Him, abused Him and finally killed Him" (quoted in "Pope Cites Cross as Timely Lesson," *New York Times*, April 5, 1965, p. 33). The Pope said later that he did not mean to imply collective Jewish guilt. This is an unfortunate example of Christian insensitivity resulting from centuries of a religious teaching of contempt.—Ed.]

[77] [Since this was written, even some Catholic theologians have seen the light. It is all to Father Gregory Baum's credit that he relates, in his Introduction to his own book, how he himself had "repeated the long litany of theological legends" about the Jews and "thought [the Jews] a people condemned for murder" until, he says, "I came upon a book which shattered me: *Jésus et Israël*" (*Is the New Testament Anti-Semitic?*, Glen Rock, N. J., Paulist Press, 1965, p. 12). Among other Christian leaders who have issued statements opposing anti-Jewish "theological legends," Bishop L. A. Elchinger, of Strasbourg, hopes for "doctrinal orientations" such that "the Jews of today feel they are recognized" as members of "a religion which has a place in God's plan" (symposium address, Strasbourg, July 20, 1967; in *Amitié judéo-chrétienne de France*, no. 2, April–June, 1968, p. 15). See also pp. 319, n. 16, and 364, n. 107, below.—Ed.]

PROPOSITION 17

NOW, IN THE GOSPELS, JESUS WAS CAREFUL TO NAME IN AD-
VANCE THE PARTIES RESPONSIBLE FOR THE PASSION:
ELDERS, CHIEF PRIESTS, SCRIBES—A COMMON SPECIES
NO MORE LIMITED TO THE JEWS THAN TO ANY OTHER
PEOPLE.

Enough heard from the scribes. Let us listen to Jesus now:

[Mark:] And he began to teach them that the Son of man must suffer many things, and be rejected by the elders and the chief priests and the scribes, and be killed, and after three days rise again [8:31].

. . . he was teaching his disciples, saying to them, "The Son of man will be delivered into the hands of men, and they will kill him; and when he is killed, after three days he will rise" [9:31].

Once more taking the Twelve aside he began to tell them what was going to happen to him: "Now we are going up to Jerusalem, and the Son of Man is about to be handed over to the chief priests and the scribes. They will condemn him to death and will hand him over to the pagans, who will mock him and spit at him and scourge him and put him to death; and after three days he will rise again" [10:32–34 (JB)].

[Matthew:] From that time Jesus began to show his disciples that he must go to Jerusalem and suffer many things from the elders and chief priests and scribes, and be killed, and on the third day be raised [16:21].

As they were gathering in Galilee, Jesus said to them, "The Son of man is to be delivered into the hands of men, and they will kill him, and he will be raised on the third day" [17:22–23].

And as Jesus was going up to Jerusalem, he took the twelve disciples aside, and on the way he said to them, "Behold, we

264

are going up to Jerusalem; and the Son of man will be delivered to the chief priests and scribes, and they will condemn him to death, and deliver him to the Gentiles to be mocked and scourged and crucified, and he will be raised on the third day" [20:17–19].

[Luke:]   [Jesus added:] "The Son of man must suffer many things, and be rejected by the elders and chief priests and scribes, and be killed, and on the third day be raised" [9:22].

. . . he said to his disciples, "Let these words sink into your ears; for the Son of man is to be delivered into the hands of men" [9:43–44].

And taking the twelve, he said to them, "Behold, we are going up to Jerusalem, and everything that is written of the Son of man by the prophets will be accomplished. For he will be delivered to the Gentiles, and will be mocked and shamefully treated and spit upon, they will scourge him and kill him, and on the third day he will rise" [18:31–33].

No ambiguity in these texts, which are essential in the eyes of the Christian faith. Three prophetic utterances enunciated by Jesus: one accuses elders, chief priests,[1] and scribes, initially responsible for the Passion Jesus was to suffer; another "men"; and still another "the Gentiles"—the Romans—from whom he would undergo insult, scourging, and death. In all three cases, not one word about Israel, about the Jewish nation, not one which could be interpreted as signifying its participation in the tragedy, its collective responsibility.

Will John 5:18, 7:16–25, 8:28–40, 10:31–32, and other passages be entered in rebuttal?

This is why the Jews sought all the more to kill him, because he not only broke the sabbath but also called God his Father, making himself equal with God [5:18].

So Jesus answered them [the "Jews"], ". . . Why do you seek to kill me?" The people answered, "You have a demon! Who is seeking to kill you?" . . .

Some of the people of Jerusalem therefore said, "Is not this the man whom they seek to kill? . . ." [7:16, 19–20, 25].

---

[1] The term "chief priests" applies here not only to those invested with that supreme office but to all the high dignitaries of the priesthood and those close to them. [In ancient Judaism, there was one high priest appointed for a certain length of time. However, a high priest "who had held the office only for a day retained the title and also sat in the Sanhedrin" (Joseph Klausner, *Jesus of Nazareth: His Life, Time, and Teaching*, tr. Herbert Danby, New York, Macmillan, 1953, p. 340). On the other hand, the hierarchy of the priesthood contained several grades of chief priests besides the high priests.—Ed.]

So Jesus said [to the "Jews"], "When you have lifted up the Son of man, then you will know that I am he . . . ."

". . . I know that you are descendants of Abraham; yet you seek to kill me. . . ."

[44] ". . . you seek to kill me, a man who has told you the truth which I heard from God . . ." [8:28, 37, 40].

The Jews took up stones again to stone him. Jesus answered them, "I have shown you many good works from the Father; for which of these do you stone me?" [10:31–32].

An invalid rebuttal. In keeping with good orthodoxy, can it be otherwise? Will the evangelist's words overshadow Christ's words? They will not, for the major reason—and we know it already—that the fourth Gospel frequently gives the word *Jews* a special, limiting (and abusive) meaning. In an earlier chapter,[2] we fully demonstrated that editorial procedure, bearing the mark of the time the Gospel was written—around the year 100. To designate Jesus' adversaries— elders, scribes, and chief priests—the evangelist (in whom tradition recognizes a Jew, moreover: the Apostle John, son of Zebedee) adjudged it good to say quite indiscriminately "the Jews," and in such a contemptuous tone! Forthwith, opprobrium rained down on the entire Jewish nation, now hardened in unbelief. And we know how the whole army of Christian writers since then, from Saint Augustine to François Mauriac inclusively, has passed through that open breach into the thick of the theological fight.

What of it, it's a fair fight. What of it, nobody thought anything much about it. (And you, Jews, pick up your dead.)

o   o   o

But why follow Saint John blindly, beyond the boundaries sovereignly established by Jesus?

Here we are led to examine a new problem—or a new aspect of the problem—of responsibility. Is Christian theology justified in making Israel as a whole jointly liable for the fault, the sin, the crime of some? Is it justified in pronouncing a collective condemnation? And in pronouncing thus, does it not commit a legal error, is it not mistaking one collectivity for another?

Its thesis is as follows: a people is committed by its qualified leaders and representatives, in the present case Pharisees and chief

[2] See pp. 112–116, [and n. 20], above.

priests, "the two great parties which contrived Jesus' death." Father Lagrange's opinion is categoric on this point: ". . . the leaders of the nation, by which he [Saint John] means above all the chief priests and the Pharisees. . . . the religious and political leaders, responsible for the practice of the cult and zealous about the Law, were perfectly qualified to represent the people and could be vested with their name ["the Jews"]." [3] With the burden on the people, reciprocally, of bearing the whole weight of the decisions and acts of its chiefs—of their crimes.

A like thesis leads far and deserves examination.[4] From having traversed centuries and rendered some services, it does not follow that it is correct. It is not enough to say at present: Pharisees and chief priests were the qualified representatives of Israel; this must be proved, and it must be proved as well that they are the guilty ones. To elucidate such a problem, we must leave none of its givens in shadow: from the hostility toward Jesus to his influence in Israel, the power exercised, the role he played, and the acceptance by the people.

o   o   o

In the first ranks of Jesus' adversaries, commentators generally place the Pharisees and the scribes, as do the Gospels—and on the same level.

We have seen previously what these two groups were.[5]

The scribes, or doctors of the Law, were not all Pharisees; their authority, their prestige profited from the immense respect that all Is-

---

[3] Father Marie-Joseph Lagrange, O.P., ed. and tr., *Évangile selon saint Jean*, Paris, Gabalda, 1924, p. cxxxii. [A recent American commentary, equally categoric: "The Lord Jesus was officially rejected by the Jewish nation at his trial before Pilate" (*Young Teen Teacher* [United Methodist Church], April–June, 1968, p. 7; quoted in Gerald Strober ms. in preparation New York [Xerox]. p. 57). —Ed.]

[4] The question of "German guilt" for the genocide of the Jews has been penetratingly studied by the German philosopher Karl Jaspers, as also by Eugen Kogon in his book *Organized Hell*. But Kogon does not accept the notion of collective responsibility as formulated by the Allied victors (*L'Enfer organisé*, tr., "Pour servir à l'histoire de ce temps" series, Paris, La Jeune Parque, 1947). [See, in English, as idem, *The Theory and Practice of Hell*, tr. Heinz Norden, New York, Farrar, Straus & Young, 1950.—Tr.] One will agree, however, that the responsibility of the Jewish people in the killing of Jesus and that of the German people in the extermination of six million Jews (1,800,000 of them children) are radically different cases.

[5] See p. 39, above.

rael professed for the Law. Those of them who sat in the Sanhedrin alongside the chief priests and elders held a part of the political and judiciary powers, which must also be defined.

The Pharisees, devotees of the written Law and oral tradition—the Torah and the Mishnah—exercised an influence in Israel's religious life which can be called unequaled. But of what order? Bearing less on persons than on customs, legislation, beliefs. Would we call them "religious leaders"? The terms "guides," "teachers," "inspirers" would seem preferable. Again I would attach some reservations, for their very piety, their devout formalism, their extreme concern with purity made them "separate"; avoiding all contact with the ignorant and impure mass of the *ammei ha-aretz*,[6] they formed a sort of caste of "saints," apart from the people.

Scribes and Pharisees had the loftiest image of themselves, certainly; they considered themselves the elite of Israel. Did this alone suffice to fetter the whole of Israel to them forever? After all, the scribes were only an association, the Pharisees only a party, a sect, a group—most influential, true, and most esteemed; but there were others, and of all sorts, and sometimes antagonists. John the Baptist issued from Israel too, before Jesus.

What do we know of their hostility to Jesus? How can we explain it, measure it? We know it only through the Gospels; thus we must take ourselves to the Gospel texts, never forgetting that the Gospels are prosecution evidence, written in a time when Christianity, in the process of de-Judaization, had no enemies more determined than the Pharisee doctors, the vanguard of official Judaism.[7]

The major texts occur mainly in the Synoptics; the controversies reported in the fourth Gospel carry less weight because, as we have seen, doctrinal inspiration prevails in Saint John's writing. The principal grievances of the scribes and Pharisees against Jesus are these:

Usurping God's sovereign power to forgive sins: Mk. 2:5–7 (Mt. 9:2–3; Lk. 5:20–21)

[6] "But this crowd, who do not know the law [and who admire Jesus], are accursed" (Jn. 7:49).

[7] According to Father Joseph Bonsirven, S.J., such observations are a sign of a bias common to most Jewish authors (*Les Juifs et Jésus*, Paris, Beauchesne, 1937, p. 173). But exactly the contrary is true: to omit such an observation is to neglect a fundamental principle of historical criticism, to refuse to acknowledge facts, and consequently to display a blind apriorism. It is of course easier to adopt as an axiom that the Gospels are "clear and irrefutable testimony" (*ibid.*, p. 172). R. Travers Herford speaks more objectively (*Les Pharisiens*, tr. Gabrielle Moyse, Paris, Payot, 1928, p. 246).

Eating and drinking with tax collectors and sinners (or, in Loisy's
  phrase, fraternizing with "the dregs of Judaism"): Mk. 2:16 (Mt.
  9:2; Lk. 5:30, and see 15:2)
Failing to have his disciples fast: Mk. 2:18 (Lk. 5:33)
Breaking the Sabbath: Mk. 2:23–24 (Mt. 12:1–2; Lk. 6:1–2);
  3:1–6 (Mt. 12:10–14; Lk. 6:6–11); Jn. 9:16
Working miracles through powers from Satan: Mk. 3:22 (Mt. 9:34,
  and see 12:24; Lk. 11:15)
Failing to observe the ritual cleansing of hands: Mk. 7:1–5 (Mt.
  15:1–2, 12)
Displaying excessive indulgence toward an adulterous woman: Jn.
  8:3–9
Attacking wealth: Lk. 16:13–14
Exhibiting messianic pretensions in Jerusalem: Lk. 19:39

The most relentless said of him, "He is a blasphemer! He is not a man
of God but of the devil!" In league with the chief priests, they sought
to seize him and have him killed (Mk. 11:18; 14:1; Mt. 21:46; Lk.
19:47), whether by stoning him themselves, Jewish fashion (Jn. 8:59;
10:31), or by delivering him to the Romans (Lk. 20:20).

Rages sustained, driven to paroxysm by vehement retorts from
Jesus, who hardly dealt tactfully with them, accusing them publicly
of pride, hypocrisy, sham, greed, iniquity, blindness, of themselves
having "neglected the weightier matters of the law, justice and mercy
and faith" (Mt. 23:1–39, quotation at 23:23; Mk. 12:38–40; Lk.
11:39–52; 20:45–47); assuring them that "Truly, . . . the tax collectors
and the harlots go into the kingdom of God before you" (Mt. 21:31).

At first sight or first reading of the Gospels, the opposition thus
seems absolute and irreducible.

At closer view, it is less simple.

We can in fact observe

that in his explicit prophecies of his Passion and death, Jesus mentions the scribes, never the Pharisees (Mk. 8:31 and 10:32–34, and
parallels);

that quite obviously, the scribes and Pharisees who hounded Jesus
are "some" among the Pharisees and scribes (it is easy, but arbitrary,
to generalize);

and that conversely, if Jesus' indictment seems to condemn the
scribes and Pharisees en bloc, it is only polemical violence, the vehemence of the angered prophet, scornful of nuances. It would be ab-

surd to take these sublime imprecations literally. Father Lebreton says of the apocalyptic discourse, "Nothing proves apriori that the words [of Jesus] must be interpreted more literally than similar expressions of Isaiah, Jeremiah, Ezekiel, or Joel." [8] Just as much may be said of the reprimand of the "scribes and Pharisees, hypocrites!" Who would dispute this? The scribes and Pharisees were not all vain and blind, not all hypocritical and greedy, not all iniquitous, without mercy and faith;

that in addition, as is apparent in certain texts (for example, Jn. 9:16), a number of the Pharisees who approached Jesus found favor with him;

and that, as other Gospel texts allow us to see, relations between the Pharisees and Jesus were not uniformly hostile:

Pharisees consult Jesus, asking his opinion: Mk. 10:2 (Mt. 19:3);
    12:13–17 (Mt. 22:15–22; Lk. 20:20–26), 28–34 (Mt. 22:34–40;
    Lk. 10:25–37); Lk. 17:20–21; Jn. 3:1–2 (in some instances the
    evangelists say that Jesus was approached to be tested, but such a
    proceeding does not imply unremitting antagonism)
Jesus recommends observance of the Pharisees' teachings: Mt. 23:1–3
Jesus is invited to eat with Pharisees: Lk. 7:36; 11:37; 14:1
Pharisees warn Jesus against Herod: Lk. 13:31
A Pharisee opposes Jesus' arrest: Jn. 7:50–51

If these passages are placed side by side with those discussed a moment ago, we see clearly that they express a different reality. What can we properly deduce from this?

First, that the Pharisees were not all committed enemies of Jesus. Some maintained a wait-and-see attitude, hesitant and questioning, not intentionally hostile; some, more or less openly but quite genuinely, approved of him, admired him, believed in him. "Nicodemus and Joseph of Arimathea were only the most prominent of a fairly numerous group"; [9]

again, that the distance between the two teachings—the Pharisee and the Gospel—was not so great or the opposition so sharp, since when he attacked the hypocrisy of the Pharisees Jesus himself took pains to begin with this public declaration: ". . . so practice and observe whatever they tell you . . ." (Mt. 23:3). Father Lagrange, citing

    [8] Father Jules Lebreton, S.J., *La Vie et l'enseignement de Jésus-Christ*, 2 vols., Paris, Beauchesne, 1931, II, 206.
    [9] Lagrange, *op. cit.*, p. 343.

Saint Augustine, comments that "What is involved is only the authority of the Pharisees when they proclaim the Law." [10] When they proclaim it or interpret it. Even if we accept this restricted meaning, it is
difficult to present Jesus' teaching as the negation of Pharisee
teaching.

The bonds between the Gospel and Phariseeism, which we have already discussed,[11] are undeniable, no less than the Gospel's bonds
with Essenism. Let us restrain ourselves from going too far along this
path out of an instinctive reaction against the summariness and inex-
actitude found in tradition; let us leave to others the sophomoric view
of Jesus as only a kind of dissident Pharisee teacher. It remains that
the Gospel texts, examined impartially, oblige us to reject the traditional interpretation and to conclude:

it is not at all certain that the Pharisee party took a united position
against Jesus and conspired to bring about his downfall; Father de
Grandmaison acknowledges that among the Pharisees, "An imposing
minority had not sinned against the light"; [12] actually, what grounds
are there for speaking about "majority" or "minority"?

The only firm fact, going by the Gospels, is that Jesus set against
himself and relentlessly fought against that common species of Pharisees and scribes, the undistinguished species (but look around you,
don't you recognize it?) of deadly mortarboards, fortified with their
theological virtuosity and their pompous authority, puffed up with
scholarship and self-satisfaction; certified righteous men, sanctimo-
nious hypocrites, who lent to God at weekly interest but genuflected
profusely, who had "their works" and "their poor" as one has an all-
inclusive (of hell too) insurance policy; pietistic and puritanical Tar-
tuffes, a baleful standing army pilloried in the Talmud [13] as in the
Gospels—all these, and they are surely numerous (in all times, in all
places);

but not the others, not the respected and respectable masters of
the Pharisee school, successors to Hillel, the Gamaliels, of whom perhaps Jesus and certainly Saint Paul were disciples, that Gamaliel who
would say in the midst of the Sanhedrin, according to the Acts of the
Apostles:

[10] *Idem,* ed. and tr., *Évangile selon saint Matthieu,* Paris, Gabalda, 1922, p.
437.
[11] See p. 84, above.
[12] Father Léonce de Grandmaison, S.J., *Jésus-Christ, sa personne, son message,
ses preuves,* 2 vols., Paris, Beauchesne, 1928, I, 263.
[13] See p. 39, above.

Men of Israel, take care . . . . for if this plan or this undertaking is of men, it will fail; but if it is of God, you will not be able to overthrow them. You might even be found opposing God!

Acts 5:35, 38–39

In the last analysis, nothing allows us to believe and assert that the Pharisee masters, Judaism's true religious guides, the nation's spiritual elite, who alone may rightly be said to have been Israel's qualified representatives in certain respects, fought against Jesus, and even less that they wanted, demanded, and plotted his death.

Moreover, do we not have testimony from a historian of a nature to put us on guard against tendentious accusations, foolhardy generalizations? The only Jewish evidence—valid evidence—that we can erect in the face of Christian evidence—for the prosecution. It relates to a later event, but that event was the trial and execution of James, "the Lord's brother" (Gal. 1:19), head of the Christian church in Jerusalem. Now, what does Josephus say about this? "Those . . . inhabitants of the city [Jerusalem] who were considered the most fair-minded and who were strict in observance of the law were offended at this [judgment]." [14] Weren't these "fair-minded" men, "strict" observers of the Law, Pharisees for the most part, pious Israelites of a kind with Hillel and Gamaliel? We have every reason to believe that these were no more set against Jesus than against James.

o   o   o

When Father Lagrange speaks of "the religious and political leaders, responsible for the practice of the cult," he is thinking principally of the chief priests, of that higher clergy, the priestly aristocracy, who in effect formed the leading class in Judea and who through the Temple, through the Sanhedrin, held the majority of religious, political, and judiciary powers, at least those that the imperial master of the hour, the Roman procurator, agreed to allow them.[15]

About these, as about the scribes and Pharisees, we must therefore ask:

[14] Flavius Josephus, *The Jewish Antiquities*, 20:201 (=20:9:1). [Quotation taken from *ibid.*, tr. Louis H. Feldman, in *Josephus*, 9 vols., "Loeb Classical Library" series, Cambridge, Mass., Harvard University Press, 1965, IX, 497.—Tr.]

[15] "After the death of these kings [Herod and Archelaus], the constitution [of Judea] became an aristocracy, and the high priests were entrusted with the leadership of the nation," wrote Josephus in *The Jewish Antiquities*, 20:251 (=20:10:5). [Quotation taken from *ibid.*, tr. Feldman, IX, 523.—Tr.]

first, to what degree and why they took a position against Jesus; second (if their hostility be proven), to what degree they can be said, in Father Lagrange's phrase, to have been "perfectly qualified to represent the [Jewish] people," it being clear that "official representatives"—another phrase of Father Lagrange's applied to the chief priests [16]—does not necessarily signify "qualified representatives."

The chief priests are introduced rather late in the Gospels, particularly in the Synoptics. The texts mentioning their predisposition to hostility, their murderous designs are fewer than those where the Pharisees and scribes appear. The reason is simple: the chief priests were men of the Temple, of Jerusalem; according to the Synoptics, then, it would have been only at the end of his ministry that Jesus, arriving in Jerusalem, found himself contending with them directly. There is nothing improbable in the notion that the outcome of the conflict came promptly, almost immediately, on the part of an iron-fisted governing body, brutal guardians of the established order. Yet, as we have seen,[17] it is possible to believe that Jesus was not a newcomer to Jerusalem, that he had already visited there, that the leading oligarchy of chief priests thus had gathered information and taken a stand on him. The texts concerning them, and they are clear and in agreement, show no split, no trace of the divergences observed among the Pharisees.[18]

The text references are brief, with the exception of the Johannine passages at 7:31–32, 45–49 and 11:47–53. Even so, they show clearly that in the eyes of that political and authoritative higher clergy, Jesus was a dangerous dreamer, a miracle-worker, a crowd-charmer, a Galilean agitator of a strange breed ("Can anything good come out of Nazareth?"—Jn. 1:46) who seemed to be playing messiah, without his game being very clear to anyone, who dared to attack the authority of the priests even in the Temple itself, and who, disturbing the peace on the eve of the Passover celebrations, risked drawing Roman thunderbolts down on Jerusalem. Did they need any other reasons for eliminating this nuisance?

[16] Lagrange, . . . *Jean*, p. cxxxii.
[17] See p. 95, above.
[18] Mk. 11:18, 27–28 (Mt. 21:23; Lk. 20:2); 12:12, "they" being "the chief priests and the scribes and the elders" named in 11:27 (Mt. 21:45–46; Lk. 20:19); 14:1 (Mt. 26:3; Lk. 22:2); Mt. 21:15–16; Jn. 7:31–32, 45–49; 11:47–53. While the fourth Gospel does not mention the chief priests explicitly prior to 7:31–32, we know that when it says "the Jews," this can be understood to mean the chief priests, the scribes, and the Pharisees.

Let us admire in passing, let us admire for its credibility the dialogue reported in John 11:47–53, the unforgettable words of Caiaphas:
"You know nothing at all; you do not understand that it is expedient
for you that one man should die . . . and that the whole nation
should not perish" (vv. 49–50). Immortal Caiaphas! The echo of your
words has reverberated from century to century: didn't we ourselves
still hear it with miraculous clarity just before the turn of our own
century, in the course of that other famous debate in which French
Catholicism, almost unanimous behind its clergy, crushed an innocent
Jew? [19] Does the comparison shock you? It involves principles, not
persons. One trial throws light on the other, helps to fix responsibilities, bursts the national framework in which people try to enclose
them; for nothing resembles yesterday's conformists (Jewish) more
than today's conformists (Christian). The same species. The same
race.

Caiaphas. I concede to Father Lagrange that Caiaphas is a representative personage, eminently so; it remains to be seen in what
sense.

That year, then—which was the year of Jesus' Passion—Caiaphas
was high priest, that is, the highest dignitary in Israel, the supreme
head of the clergy, leader of the cult, head of the unique sanctuary—
the Temple, president of the Great Council, or Sanhedrin, in Jerusalem. What honors and powers gathered around one head, and what
responsibilities! Whoever became high priest in Israel retained the
post for life. Theoretically, at least. In fact, the high functionary sent
from Rome to govern Judea, the procurator, disposed of the high
priesthood as he saw fit, as Herod the Great, king of Palestine and a
tyrant detested by the Jews, had done before him. The hard and
greedy Roman found this profitable, monetarily and politically, for he
was paid dear for his favors, and as these could be revoked at any
time, the Jewish high priest was in a totally dependent position—so
much so that the Roman commandant of Antonia Fortress, which
dominated the Temple, kept under lock and key the sumptuous vestments which the high priest could use only three or four times a year,
for the high festivals, including Yom Kippur. Was ever a more humili-
ating servitude devised? [20] Hence the duration of the high priesthood
varied arbitrarily according to the will or the caprice of the Roman

---

[19] [Alfred Dreyfus.—Ed.]
[20] It was abolished by the Emperor Tiberius in the year 36 on application
from the Jews.

procurator and the obsequiousness, adroitness, subservience of the Jewish high priest: one would see himself dismissed like a valet hardly a year after his installation; another—a Caiaphas—would succeed in holding his place as long as eighteen years (A.D. 18–36), at what a price we can imagine; still, each retained from his turn at the high priesthood—whether brief or long—the title and dignity of high priest, which entailed certain privileges, such as sitting on the Sanhedrin.

But there is another aspect, and a typical one, which needs to be emphasized: the selection by the procurator, the true master of Israel, was made only within narrow limits, among a small number of families, three or four, and always the same. Thus, Caiaphas was the son-in-law of Annas (or Hanan or Anan or Ananos), who had himself been high priest from the year 6 to the year 15 and whose five sons attained to the supreme office in turn. The chief priests, or as some translators write, "the princes among the priests," thus formed a restricted and closed oligarchy, an exclusive caste, jealous of its privileges, both rich and rapacious—to the point of robbing the lower clergy of its share in the tithes;[21] harsh but compliant, despotic but servile, servile toward the all-powerful Roman but despotic toward the Jewish people, at least those of the lower classes, over whom police at its command, well-schooled police, exercised their fists and clubs according to the rules of the art. The ballad of the "wounds," a popular song included in the Talmud, has preserved the memory for us:

> Woe is me because of the house of Boethus; woe is me
>   because of their staves!
> Woe is me because of the house of Hanin [Annas], woe is
>   me because of their whisperings!
> Woe is me because of the house of Kathros [Kantheras],
>   woe is me because of their pens!
> Woe is me because of the house of Ishmael the son of
>   Phabi, woe is me because of their fists!
> For they are High Priests and their sons are [Temple]
>   treasurers and their sons-in-law are trustees and their
>   servants beat the people with staves.
>   Pesahim 57a [BT; line breaks added] [22]

[21] Josephus, op. cit., 28:8.
[22] Quoted in Joseph Klausner, Jésus de Nazareth, tr. Isaac Friedmann, Paris, Payot, 1933, p. 489 [and in idem, Jesus of Nazareth . . . , p. 337.—Tr.]. The terms "whisperings" and "pens" in the second and third lines would be allusions to secret denunciations, oral and written. [Klausner points out that the two closing lines may not belong to the song.—Ed.]

It is possible to believe, as we shall see, that this oligarchic caste
—four powerful families in all, brutal, cynical, and ill-famed [23]—bore
the heaviest part of the responsibility for Jesus' arrest and delivery to
the Romans. And it is this caste which our authoritative theologians
and exegetes, for lack of better, baptize as "perfectly qualified" representatives of the Jewish nation. "Perfectly disqualified" would be
more accurate. Vichy in Jerusalem. And worse yet, if we recall that
Vichy could at least claim some democratic basis and exhibited only
a secular (or military) dishonor.

o   o   o

There remain the "elders," expressly designated in Jesus' prophecies
(Mk. 8:31; Mt. 16:21; Lk. 9:22), members of the Sanhedrin along with
the chief priests and scribes, but about whom the Gospel texts say almost nothing elsewhere. Mark 11:27 and the parallel passages in Matthew 21:23 and Luke 20:1 mention them in the company of chief
priests and scribes when these came to ask Jesus, "By what authority
are you doing these things . . . ?" Matthew 26:3–4 and Luke 19:47
mention them likewise with chief priests as resolved to seize Jesus in
order to have him killed. John does not name them explicitly anywhere.

How is this silence to be filled? Because Matthew 26:3 says "the
elders of the people" and Luke 19:47 "the principal men of the people," must we see "qualified" representatives in the persons of these
elders? Not in the least. The elders were the notables of Jerusalem,
leaders and representatives not of the people but of the great families,
who, powerful through their wealth, constituted a secular aristocracy
alongside the priestly aristocracy. Both groups were Sadducees, conservative, rigidly protective of the established order, disposed to deal
severely with every innovation, every innovator arising from the
people and stirring them up dangerously. Perhaps too, in the case of
Jesus, these rich personages felt themselves to be the direct butt of
the scathing contempt he expressed with regard to money and the
wealthy: "But woe to you that are rich . . ." (Lk. 6:24); "You cannot
serve God and mammon" (Mt. 6:24).

[23] Another broadside in the same tractate reproaches these priestly families for
"defil[ing] the Temple of the Lord," for "desecrating the sacred sacrifices of
Heaven," for displaying a disgusting gluttony, and so forth (Pesahim 57a [BT]).

The attempts to veil these texts are useless; they explode in the midst of the Gospel. Péguy said, "Jesus' horror of the wealthy is terrifying. He loves only poverty and the poor." And again:

The terrifying anger that runs below the surface of the Gospels is not at all anger against nature or against man before grace [I would add: is not at all anger against the nation, against Israel]; it is uniquely anger against *money*, and truly, it must be that no one wanted to see it for this reprobation not to have blazed before everyone's eyes.[24]

But who says that no one wanted to see it, that no one saw it, with Jesus present and speaking, and that this "reprobation" blazing "before everyone's eyes" was not repaid in turn, mercilessly, by a coalition of the rich, "principal men of the people" or "princes among the priests"? Do we not have James's testimony (5:1, 6 [CCD]) on this?

Come now, you rich. . . . You have condemned and put to death the just. . . .

Embarrassing testimony, not to be cited.[25]

However, other testimony from Scripture puts us on guard against hasty generalizations. It gives us the name of one of these wealthy notables, "a respected member of the council": and it is Joseph of Arimathea, "who was also himself looking for the kingdom of God" (Mk. 15:43).

•   •   •

A specific number of chief priests, elders, and scribes made up the Sanhedrin.

When Jesus announced to the Twelve that he would be "rejected by the elders and the chief priests and the scribes," he was alluding to the Sanhedrin, and it is the Sanhedrin to which the Gospels—the Synoptics, at least—assign the primary role in Jesus' arrest, judgment, and sentencing to death.

What was the Sanhedrin, then? And what were its powers, particu-

---

[24] Charles Péguy, *Lettres et entretiens* [Letters and Conversations], ed. Marcel Péguy, Paris, Artisans du Livre, 1927 [repub. Paris, Éd. de Paris, 1954], pp. 160, 187.

[25] Father Joseph Chaine dates the Epistle of James in the neighborhood of the year 60 (*L'Épître de saint Jacques* [The Epistle of Saint James], Paris, Gabalda, 1927). Luther, who found it an impediment to his doctrine of salvation by faith alone, called it an "epistle of straw."

larly its legal powers? In our investigations of responsibilities, this is
a point which it is essential to determine.

But here history intervenes, and is compelled to make some painful
admissions It confesses honestly that it can provide only probabili-
ties, feeble and scanty, and almost no certainties. There does indeed
exist a tractate called Sanhedrin in the Mishnah, which contains a
minute description of the composition of the assembly, its functions,
its rules of procedure as a criminal court. But then, how rigorously
can we go applying to Jesus' time, to Caiaphas' Sanhedrin, a description drawn some 170 years later by writers who doubtless intended to
define the tradition but who were hardly concerned with historic considerations?

What we know, what we can reasonably conjecture, boils down to
very little.

All the testimony, the most valid of which is that of the Jewish historian Flavius Josephus, indicates that the Sanhedrin was an aristo-
cratic council, dominated by the priestly oligarchy and presided over
by the incumbent high priest. The doctors of the Law—the scribes—
had been members for about a century. Through them, or at least
through some of them, Pharisee trends were represented. Through the
chief priests and elders, the preponderant influence remained with
the Sadducees.

There is no sure indication of the size or the method of recruiting
the membership of the Sanhedrin. It is generally said, following the
indications in the Mishnah, to have numbered seventy or seventy-one;
this is possible, but nothing proves that it was so at the beginning of
the first century. It is supposed that the Sanhedrists recruited by co-
option and that their membership was for life; this is only a hypothesis, and another is not ruled out, is not less likely—that the Roman
authorities intervened in their selection as in the appointment of the
high priest. Father Lebreton, citing George Foot Moore, recognizes
"that they were perhaps named by the political authorities, Herod or
the Romans . . . ," and that "The most influential members were the
leaders of the priests." [26]

Because it was the supreme council of Jerusalem—the Holy City
—the Sanhedrin possessed a certain moral authority over all the Jews
of Palestine and of the Diaspora. Its actual authority extended only

[26] Lebreton, *op. cit.*, II, 361.

over the narrow confines of the procuratorial territory—essentially
Judea—and was under the procurator's control.

The Sanhedrin was both a government council and a court of justice. How far did its competence reach in criminal matters, and did it
or did it not have the right to pass a sentence of capital punishment
or to have the sentence carried out—by stoning, according to Jewish
custom [27]—in the case of a religious crime? This is the knot of the
problem.[28] Interminable debates, too often dominated by prejudice,
have not succeeded in unknotting it. In the opinion of some historians
—who reject the Gospel accounts in toto—the Sanhedrin had the
most extensive jurisdiction in religious matters, the right of con-
demning to death and also the right of carrying out the execution;
a number of capital executions in the period from the Crucifixion
to the destruction of the Temple would prove this (the execution of Stephen, Acts 6:12 ff.; 7:58–60; of James, Josephus' *Jewish Antiquities*, 20:200 [20:9:1]; of the daughter of a priest, Sanhedrin 52b).
From this it is deduced that Jesus, having been crucified and not
stoned, was judged and condemned by the Romans, not by the Jews.
In the opinion of other historians, who accept some of the Gospel accounts and compare them with certain talmudic texts, the Sanhedrin
lost the right to pass capital sentences, either (as in the Talmud) forty
years or so before the destruction of the Temple, which occurred in
the year 70, or (by a reasoning process, for lack of documentary evidence) on the establishment of the Roman regime in Judea, which
was in the year 6. Accordingly, Jesus would have been delivered by
the Sanhedrin to Pontius Pilate, the procurator, who alone possessed
the *jus gladii*, the "right of the sword" or power over life and death. A
third group of historians assume that the Gospel accounts correspond
with historic reality; and their thesis is that the Sanhedrin retained
the right to pronounce capital sentences, but under the control and on
condition of the procurator's confirmation, he alone being empowered
to carry out the sentence. This would explain the dual trial, Jewish
and Roman, the double sentencing, its execution by the Romans, the
nailing to the cross.

To tell the truth, if one holds strictly to the demands of sound his-

---

[27] The condemned could also be burned, decapitated, or suffocated, but not
crucified. Crucifixion was a specifically Roman punishment.
[28] [Paul Winter's *On the Trial of Jesus* (in English), Berlin, De Gruyter, 1961,
discusses this point extensively.—Ed.]

toric method, none of the arguments put forth—in any direction—
appears decisive, capable of producing complete certainty. The fact
that the procurator had the *jus gladii*, which is not debatable, does
not necessarily rule out that the Sanhedrin had power over life and
death, particularly where a religious crime was concerned. The capital sentences invoked in support of the first theory are troubling facts,
but it can be maintained, with the help of the texts, that they were irregular. The talmudic texts, however categoric they may seem, are
unreliable and contradict each other. And one is indeed forced to observe that the Gospel texts themselves, however worthy of respect
they may be, display serious divergences. Finally, if the condemnation brought down by the Jewish authorities was valid only after it
was approved by the procurator, it does not follow that a Roman
punishment like crucifixion had to be substituted for the usual Jewish
punishment in such a case, stoning. This is the opinion of Maurice
Goguel:

It seems indeed that what was taken away [from the Sanhedrin] was not
the right to pronounce capital sentences but only the right to carry them
out before they had received the approval of the Roman authorities. If Pilate had only ratified a condemnation passed by the Sanhedrin, as the Gospel accounts seem to suppose, Jesus would have suffered a Jewish punishment; he would have been stoned or strangled, he would not have been
crucified.[29]

For lack of certainties, we are thus reduced to conjectures. The
best-grounded, by analogy, seems to be the following. Thanks to legal
documents found in Egypt, we know today that in certain important
cases, the prefect of Egypt—the Roman governor of that imperial
territory—gave over to local authorities the task of investigating the
matter; we can say that the same should have been true in Judea, and
that consequently the Sanhedrin functioned in certain cases as a court
of judicial inquiry, a grand jury. Such would have been its role in the
matter of Jesus of Nazareth. And that in no measure diminishes its responsibility.

But that in no measure entails responsibility on the part of the Jewish nation. Whom did the Sanhedrin represent? Basically, an oligarchy of priests and the wealthy, itself completely dominated in Jesus'
time by the powerful Annas family, which circled within the Roman
orbit. Now, we know how vital, fierce, indomitable was the patriotism

---

[29] Maurice Goguel, "Christianisme primitif," in Raoul Gorce and Maxime Mor-
tier, eds., *Histoire générale des religions*, Paris, Quillet, 1945, II, 196.

of the Palestinian Jews, a patriotism solidly grafted onto their faith. And it is this patriot people that commentators want to make jointly liable for the crimes committed by its leaders, supposedly its qualified representatives [30] but in fact creatures of pagan Rome and representatives of a detested caste, whose single concern was to safeguard its powers, its privileges, and its goods!

o   o   o

Yet if there is one point on which the Gospel texts are agreed and positive, it is precisely the distinction which must be made between the people—the popular masses—and the oligarchic clan accountable for initiating the proceedings against Jesus. All the evangelists made a point of emphasizing that this clan acted unbeknownst to and despite the people. And it is evident that the leaders of the clan, its most active element, were the chief priests; associated with them were sometimes the scribes—or the Pharisees—and sometimes the elders. But Judas was not confused: when he had made his fatal decision, it was directly to the chief priests—doubtless to Caiaphas or Annas—that he went. Let us reread the texts:

[Mark:]   The chief priests and scribes heard of this, and looked for some means of making away with him; they were afraid of him, because all the multitude was so full of admiration at his teaching [11:18 (RK)].

And they tried to arrest him, but feared the multitude . . . [12:12].

It was now two days before the Passover and the feast of Unleavened Bread. And the chief priests and the scribes were

[30] Or its "spiritual leaders," according to Jacques Maritain's theory, leaders with whom all Israel would be jointly responsible "For the people of Israel is a *corpus mysticum*, a holy nation," and for whose error it must pay over centuries—indeed, "forever" (*Raison et raisons* [Reason and Reasons], Paris, Egloff, 1947, p. 232). [Maritain expounds the same argument in his *Ransoming the Time*, tr. Harry Lorin Binsse, New York, Scribner, 1946, pp. 151–155, and his *A Christian Looks at the Jewish Question*, New York, Longmans, Green, 1939, pp. 26–27.—Ed.] The thesis is fundamentally wrong. It does not follow from Israel's identity as a "mystical body" that it was implicated in the crime of a Caiaphas, who had no right whatever to the title of "spiritual leader." Jacques Maritain is careful to particularize that his "concept is only valid from the highest metaphysical and transcendent viewpoint" (*loc. cit.*). But in such a case it is hard to make an absolute distinction between the metaphysical plane and the other, the historical plane. Would the metaphysical thesis itself be conceivable without a historic basis? [Quotations taken from Jacques Maritain, *The Range of Reason*, New York, Scribner, 1952, p. 131.—Tr.]

seeking how to arrest him by stealth, and kill him; for they said, "Not during the feast, lest there be a tumult of the people" [14:1–2].

Then Judas Iscariot, who was one of twelve, went to the chief priests in order to betray him to them [14:10].

[Matthew:] When the chief priests and the Pharisees. . . . tried to arrest him, they feared the multitudes, because they held him to be a prophet [Mt. 21:45–46].

Then the chief priests and the elders of the people gathered in the palace of the high priest, who was called Caiaphas, and took counsel together in order to arrest Jesus by stealth and kill him. But they said, "Not during the feast, lest there be a tumult among the people" [26:3–5].

Then one of the twelve, who was called Judas Iscariot, went to the chief priests and said, "What will you give me if I deliver him to you?" [26:14–15].

[Luke:] And he was teaching daily in the temple. The chief priests and the scribes and the principal men of the people sought to destroy him; but they did not find anything they could do, for all the people hung upon his words [19:47–48].

Now the feast of Unleavened Bread drew near, which is called the Passover. And the chief priests and the scribes were seeking how to put him to death; for they feared the people.
 . . . [Judas] went away and conferred with the chief priests and captains [of the Temple] how he might betray him to them. . . . [Then he] sought an opportunity to betray him to them in the absence of the multitude [22:1–6].

While less clearly than in the Synoptics, the opposition between the leading clan and the people comes to light also in the fourth Gospel:

[John:] Yet many of the people believed him. . . . the chief priests and Pharisees sent officers to arrest him.
 . . . but no one laid hands on him.
The officers then went back to the chief priests and Pharisees, who said to them, . . . "Are you led astray, you also? Have any of the authorities or of the Pharisees believed in him? But this crowd, who do not know the law, are accursed" [7:31–32, 44–49].

Many of the Jews therefore, who . . . had seen what he did, believed in him. . . . So the chief priests and the Pharisees gathered the council, and said, ". . . If we let him go on thus, every one will believe in him. . . ." So from that day on they took counsel how to put him to death [11:45–48, 53].

Perfect agreement: not only of the four evangelists with each other, but of the event as they describe it with the prediction which Jesus had made to the Twelve. These texts are truly too emphatic to be challengeable.

o   o   o

Thus, the first stage of our inquiry into the crime and its responsible authors has already led us to some notable results.

According to the Synoptic Gospels, Jesus expressly predicted that he would be the victim of "the elders and the chief priests and the scribes"; he did not say "the Pharisees"; he never implicated the Jewish people.

According to the four Gospels, the Pharisees and the scribes were not solidly hostile to Jesus. Nothing proves that the elite of Judaism was involved in the murder plot; on the contrary, there are good reasons to doubt it.

According to historical evidence, the dominant influence in Jerusalem and in the Sanhedrin lay with a priestly and secular oligarchy composed of a few great families, the most powerful of which was that of Annas, father-in-law of the high priest Caiaphas. This oligarchy, Sadducee in outlook, cruel and tyrannical in conduct, was itself subjugated to Rome and detested by the people. It was this oligarchy, in all likelihood, which played the determining role. This is likewise the clearly expressed opinion of Father Lebreton: "It was the Sadducees who had played the decisive role in the trial of Christ." [31]

The Jewish nation could not have been identified with this caste in any way. Not only did the people have no part in the intrigue woven against Jesus, but the four evangelists testify that the leaders acted unbeknownst to the people, despite them, and in fear of them.

It is true that we are only on the threshold of the Passion. In the short moment which confines it,[32] it remains to discover whether there was a shift of opinion, whether the attitude of the people changed radically between one day and the next, whether—as it continues to be taught in print, by word, and through pictures—the Jew-

[31] In Father Jules Lebreton, S.J., and Jacques Zeiller, *L'Église primitive*, vol. I of Augustin Fliche and Victor Martin, eds., *Histoire de l'Église depuis les origines jusqu'à nos jours*, Paris, Bloud et Gay, 1934, p. 138.
[32] See p. 288, n. 2, below.

ish people joined Jesus' enemies in order to obtain his death, disparage him and grind him down, even on the cross.

But first, some preliminary observations are required on the
knowledge we have of the trial, the condemnation, and the execution
of the judgment.

The Crucifixion

By Haim Cohn

Jesus was brought to a place called Golgotha, meaning "the place of the skull" (Matt. 27:33; Mark 15:22; John 19:17), in the Lucan tradition rendered as Calvary (23:33), where, it seems, Roman executions were usually carried out. He was not the only prisoner to be led there that day—with him were two others (John 19:28), who are described in Mark and Matthew as *lestai*, wrongly translated in the King James Version as "thieves," for it signifies bandits or brigands[1] (Mark 15:27; Matt. 27:38), and described in Luke as *kakourgoi*, criminals[2] or "malefactors" (23:33). It has been suggested that both were probably rebellious zealots, sentenced to death for their part in a recent insurrection in Jerusalem.[3] Whatever their antecedents, the fact that they were put to death by crucifixion proves that, like Jesus, they were convicted by the Roman governor of a capital offense under Roman law.

It was widely believed, and has latterly been reasserted,[4] that the Romans had no monopoly of crucifixions, and that the Jews, even before the Roman occupation of Judaea, had adopted the mode from Persian patterns. The belief may rest on the Johannine tradition that it was the Jews, and not the Romans, who crucified Jesus; and we have shown that this tradition is contro-

208

verted in the Gospel of John itself (19:23). But it is currently reinforced by arguments and evidence from Jewish sources, giving it the appearance of a scientific discovery rather than a traditional belief, and though some of the arguments have by now been conclusively refuted,[5] the penological and lego-historical problems involved are yet to receive the attention which they deserve. And the question is not just of penological or legal interest; that a tradition which originated in a tendentious misrepresentation can be, and is today being, resurrected and vindicated under a show of impartial scholarship renders critical vigilance indispensable.

Much of the confusion is due to faulty terminology. It so happens that the modern Hebrew usage for "to crucify," *tselov,* is the old Aramaic word for "to hang": wherever the Bible speaks of hanging (Hebrew: *taloh*), the authoritative Aramaic translation is *tselov,*[6] from which it has quite unwarrantably been concluded that all biblical hangings were crucifixions. In fact, the Hebrew *tselov* is derived not from the Aramaic at all, but from another Hebrew root, *shelov,* which has the sense of fixing or bracing wooden planks or beams to each other,[7] while the Aramaic *tselov* in all likelihood comes from the Assyrian *dalabu,* "causing pain or distress."[8] It is true that in Assyrian there are at least two other words for hanging,[9] of which derivatives also occur in Aramaic,[10] and it has been said that, wherever these other words are used, the intention is to convey the notion of extrajudicial hangings, whereas judicial hangings are rendered as *tselivot.*[11] But one can infer nothing from the fact that the Hebrew "hanging" is rendered *tselov* in Aramaic, and that *tselov* in Hebrew means "to crucify": the identity of the Hebrew word for "to crucify" and the Aramaic word for "to hang" is more apparent than real. The distinction in Hebrew between "to hang" (*taloh*) and "to crucify" (*tselov*) is postbiblical and occurs for the first time in talmudic sources; biblical Hebrew, in contrast to Aramaic, does not know the word *tselov,* either for "crucifying" or at all; and even assuming—though not admitting—that the Aramaic *tselov* could have borne the meaning of crucifying, too, that would purport only that the Aramaic translators of the Bible held that in biblical language no distinction could or need be made between hanging on the cross and hanging on the gallows. It may, indeed, be that neither the Hebrew *taloh* nor the Aramaic *tselov* connotes any particular mode of hanging, and that the mode employed in a given case had to be discovered otherwise than from the word used for "hanging." There is no such difficulty with the talmudic sources, in which hangings as such are expressly differentiated from hangings carried out "in the way (or: mode) practiced by the government,"[12] a plain allusion to the special form of hanging practiced by the Roman governor's forces, namely, crucifixion. The phrase "in the way practiced by the government" in itself already conveys an undertone of strangeness, as if one wished to dissociate oneself from an alien and exotic method and had no room for it either in one's laws or in one's language.

The Hebrew *tselov*, "to crucify," is found once in the Dead Sea Scrolls. The verse, "The lion did tear in pieces enough for his whelps and strangled for his lionesses" (Nah. 2:12), is in the Commentary on the Book of Nahum interpreted as follows: "This is the young lion who wrought vengeance on them that sought smooth things, and crucified all of them on the same day; such a thing had never happened before in Israel, for it is written, he that is hanged is accursed of God" (Deut. 21:23). I have rendered the word *tsalav* in the text as "crucified"; most translators render it as "hanged alive."[13] On the assumption, then, that we must conclude from the use of the term *tsalav* that the sense to be conveyed is hanging by crucifixion, we find the commentator reporting not only that there was a Jewish "lion" who revenged himself on his enemies by crucifying them, but also that such a thing as hanging by crucifixion had never before happened in Israel. And it could not ever have happened before, because, from the Jewish point of view and by the most ancient Jewish tradition, hanging alive, by crucifixion or otherwise, was an "affront to God" and a defilement of the holy land.[14] A majority of scholars believe that the "young lion" was Alexander Jannaeus, king of the Jews, whom Josephus reports as ordering the death of eight hundred Pharisees and their wives and children, while he and his concubines caroused and reveled in the spectacle: the eight hundred were "crucified," and their wives and children "slaughtered" before their eyes.[15] Another suggestion is that the reference is to a killing of sixty of the elders of Israel, said to have been the act of a priest named Elyakim, who was a collaborator with the enemy,[16] but the expression to describe the killing is "slaughtered," not "crucified," and the text affords no evidence of hanging or crucifixion. Alexander Jannaeus, however, if Josephus is to be believed, had to hang his victims alive, because he wanted them, before expiring on their crosses, to behold the atrocities done to their beloved ones. Conjecture as we may what took place and who the "young lion" was that crucified his adversaries, all that can be learned from this Essene comment on Nahum is that the crucifying had left so indelible an impression in the minds of the common people, when once it had occurred, as not to be forgotten or forgiven, for it was unheard of in the annals of Israel and was in conflict with all custom and tradition.[17]

The modes of execution which we find prescribed or described in the Bible are stoning (Deut. 17:5, *et al.*), burning (Lev. 20:14, *et al.*), hanging (Josh. 8:29, *et al.*), and slaying (Deut. 20:13). For reasons into which we shall presently inquire, the mishnaic codifiers dropped the hanging and added "strangling."[18] As far as biblical hangings are concerned, a distinction is necessary between hanging alive and hanging after execution: there is no biblical law which prescribes hanging, as such, as a proper way to inflict death; all recorded instances of hanging are factual reports, not legal prescriptions. There is, however, an explicit law providing for hanging after execution: "If a man has committed a capital offense, and is put to death,[19] thou shalt hang him on a tree: his body shall not remain all night upon the tree, but thou shalt in any wise bury him that day, for he that is hanged, is accursed of God; that thy land be not defiled, which the Lord thy God giveth thee for an inheritance" (Deut. 21:22–23). Executions had to take place in the late afternoon,[20] so that the corpse was taken down from the "tree" straight after the hanging, before sunset.[21] So far from being a demonstration of triumph over the wrongdoer and of rejoicing at his death,[22] it was rather a formal, and hurried, compliance with the scriptural injunction to let all the people see "and fear, and do no more presumptuously" (Deut. 17:13) and to pillory the offender against the sun (Num. 25:4); public deterrence was, understandably, a main purpose of all punishment. "He that is hanged is accursed of God" has been authoritatively interpreted to mean that "it is a curse before God

308

to hang a man":[23] while, to deter potential offenders, it may be a dire necessity that convicts be hanged and publicly displayed, there can be no worse calamity in the eyes of God than to have to hang a fellow man. Reluctance to hang offenders, even after statutory execution, eventually led to a reform of the law: while biblical law did not distinguish between capital offenses with respect to the post-mortem hanging, it was later laid down that this hanging was to be confined to idolaters and men who had cursed God, pronouncing His ineffable Name: of such it could properly be said that they are hanged for cursing God, and when hanged are accursed of Him.[24] As a matter of law, therefore, hanging was never more than hanging after death, and hanging after death was ultimately reserved for idolaters and blasphemers.

As to the reported instances of hanging alive, it is submitted that they are all either non-Jewish or nonjudicial or both, and that there is no case in the Bible of a Jewish judicial execution by hanging alive. Examples of non-Jewish hangings are those ordered by Pharaoh, king of Egypt (Gen. 40:22), Ahasuerus, king of Persia and Media (Esther 7:10; 9:14), and the Philistines (II Sam. 21:9), all of whom may be presumed to have acted in conformity with their own laws and customs. Wherever we find Jews hanging men alive, it is in the course of wars or in warlike operations: Joshua hanged the king of Ai on a tree (Josh. 8:29), but even then he "commanded that they should take his carcass down from the tree as soon as the sun was down" (ibid.). We also find Joshua hanging five men after a previous execution by slaying (10:26). When David ordered the execution of the murderers of Ishboshet, his enemy, they were first slain, then their hands and feet were cut off, and finally their bodies were suspended over the pool in Hebron (II Sam. 4:12). The injunction to "hang up before the Lord against the sun" (Num. 25:4) any who had bowed down to alien gods has been correctly understood not as directed to judicial organs, but as a call to a warlike, wholly nonjudicial, operation;[25] it is, anyhow, open to grave doubts whether the term here used, hoqa, actually stands for "hanging"; the better opinion would favor a sense of pilloring.[26]

Biblical law thus knew hanging only as a means of deterrence after execution had taken place and death had supervened in some other mode: hanging was not then used to put a convict to death. It is only in subsequent periods that we find hanging alive as a form of execution imported into Jewish law from foreign sources. The most important evidence of this is in the Book of Ezra: in a decree ascribed to the Persian king, Cyrus, we read that "whosoever shall alter this word, let timber be pulled down from his house, and, being set up, let him be hanged thereon; and let his house be made a dunghill for this" (Ezra 6:11). The timber to "be pulled down from his house" could, of course, be made as well into a gallows as into a cross; but it is said that the decree had the effect of introducing the Persian mode of execution into Israel, and that that mode was exclusively crucifixion.[27] First, however, while records exist of crucifixion in Persia, it does not follow that it was the one and only kind of execution in vogue there: hanging and crucifixion alike may have been known and practiced. And, second, not a solitary instance is chronicled of a judicial execution carried out in ancient Israel in the manner authorized by Cyrus or in exercise of the specific power conferred by him. We know from biblical sources (viz., the Book of Esther) that the Persian king would hang his convicts "upon the gallows" (Esther 8:7, *et al.*), and from other sources that Persian kings would crucify their victims.[28] Even assuming, then, that crucifixion could be regarded as a—or the—Persian way of execution, the mere fact that the Jewish authorities then subject to Persian suzerainty were empowered to apply it, particularly for offenses under Persian law, such as disobedience to the royal "word," would not in itself mark any change in Jewish law or in the competence or practice of the Jewish courts as such. Nevertheless, it is said that we have here a "reception" of Persian law, attested by the Bible itself, and it is this "reception" which is called in proof of the contention that crucifying had become a Jewish mode of execution.

Another instance is provided by the Aramaic translation of the Book of Ruth. The translation is posttalmudic,[29] and hence several centuries later than the events with which we are concerned. Ruth's words, "When thou diest, will I die" (Ruth 1:17), were hermeneutically taken to mean that, among the other prescripts of Jewish law, Ruth also took upon herself those relating to capital punishment: as if she had said: In all the ways that you may be put to death under your laws, I, too, shall be ready to be put to death.[30] This interpretation is rendered in the authoritative Aramaic version as follows: "Naomi told Ruth, we have four legal modes of execution, namely, stoning, burning, slaying, and hanging; whereupon Ruth said, in whatever way you will die, I will die." Is it that in posttalmudic times the mishnaic tradition of strangling[31] had fallen into oblivion, and one of strangulation by hanging substituted for it? Or had there been another reform in the meantime, with the archaic mode of strangling replaced by the more merciful hanging? Or ought the text to be dismissed out of hand as an obviously erroneous statement of law by an ignorant layman? One conclusion at any rate, I think, may fairly be drawn from the substitution, namely, that, as in strangling, so also in the hanging here mentioned, death is caused by strangulation, and, as regards the physiological cause of death, there would then be no difference between hanging and strangling.[32] But in that case it would follow that the hanging here referred to cannot have been crucifixion, because in crucifixion, as we shall see, death is not due to strangulation at all.

Admittedly, hangings were carried out by Jewish authorities, or on their initiative, at one time or another during talmudic and posttalmudic eras; but it is submitted, and will be shown, that all of them were executions by strangulation, in which the condemned man died of suffocation and which might properly be classified, therefore, as "strangling." Crucifixion, on the other hand, is the one and only mode of hanging in which death is due not to suffocation but to exhaustion or exposure or other causes of which we shall speak. Thus in normal hangings death is instantaneous, whereas in crucifixion it may be delayed for hours and even days. If normal hanging may be regarded as a reasonably humane mode of execution, because of its instantaneity, crucifixion must be deemed utterly inhumane, if only because of its protractedness. What the two modes have in common is really nothing but the name: execution on the gallows and execution on the cross are equally referred to as "hangings." Even the crucifixion of Jesus is described in the New Testament as hanging, and his cross as the tree whereon he was hanged (Luke 23:39; Acts 5:30; 10:39).

The most notorious of Jewish hangings is that reported to have been decreed by Simon ben Shetah (2d century B.C.): eighty witches were hanged on a single day in Askalon.[33] The story, which is from a later period, goes that a scholar had a dream in which his dead master told him that the great Simon ben Shetah would have to suffer the pangs of hell because of women witches rampant in Askalon, against whom the law was not being enforced.[34] When Simon heard that, he promptly enforced the law, whether with the help of eighty young men whom, according to the story, he enlisted for the purpose or through other executioners. The historicity of this wholesale hanging has been challenged,[35] but if it did, in fact, take place, the question arises whether it was a result of judicial proceedings or an emergency measure undertaken on the personal responsibility of Simon, acting not as a court of justice but as an executive authority. The second possibility is bespoken by the fact, commented upon in the Talmud,[36] that rules of procedure and evidence were disregarded, yet Simon was known to insist, in his judicial capacity, on strictest compliance with all formalities and in particular the rules of evidence,[37] as well as by the fact that according to law these women .should have been stoned, not hanged.[38] Thus it became well established Jewish tradition that Simon's action was of emergent character, and it has been held that "no law may be inferred from emergency measures."[39]

While we have no information of the particular "emergency" which prompted Simon to do what he is reported as doing, we certainly know the law, which is that to incur the death penalty, the witch, or the sorcerer, must have committed a real and overt act of witchcraft or sorcery, and the act been proved by at least two eyewitnesses; merely claiming the talent to practice witchcraft, even performing feats of sleight of hand or juggling to make people believe in one's possession of magic capacity, is not enough.[40] At the same time, to claim the talent to practice witchcraft is also forbidden,[41] though not, strictly speaking, a criminal offense. If the witches of Askalon had not yet committed any real and overt acts of witchcraft proper which could be proved against them, but had purported to own supernatural powers and made people believe it, the authorities responsible for upholding public order and religion may well have felt called upon summarily to put a stop to this perilous trickery, the more so as it apparently threatened to become endemic, if as many as eighty women held themselves out as practicing witchcraft in a small town like Askalon.[42] Had the women been stoned, the false image might have been created of a regular execution following a regular trial; they were advisedly hanged, so as to demonstrate that they had forfeited their lives, although they could not be brought up to Jerusalem for trial and execution in due course of legal process. Such an extrajudicial forfeiture of life might, in the eyes of men like Simon ben Shetah, be justified by the divine command "Thou shalt not suffer a witch to live" (Exod. 22:17) or "There shall not be found among you a witch" (Deut. 18:10), commands directed not to the witch as prohibiting her craft, but to the citizen and, a fortiori, to the leaders of the community, enjoining them not to suffer the presence or activity of a witch in their midst, whether she has been or can be prosecuted judicially or not. This wide, but still literal, interpretation of the divine behest was invoked until late in the Middle Ages throughout Christendom to justify the persecution of witches.[43] The action of Simon against the witches of Askalon had to be swift to be successful: if word got around of the steps planned against them, they were likely to disappear. Therefore, he ordered the action completed on one day, even if it meant employing eighty executioners. And because execution had to be quick, hanging was the method, the speediest way of causing death. The witches would never have been crucified, because that would have entailed slow, protracted, and painful death.

Witches were not the only offenders that might be done away with even without due process of law: a similar license appears to have been allowed by law in respect of certain idolaters and temple desecrators caught in flagrante delicto,[44] and, some scholars say, in respect also of inciters to idolatry so apprehended.[45] But nowhere is there indication that death had, in any of these cases, to be inflicted by hanging; on the contrary, we find that in one case the mode prescribed or authorized was slaying by the sword, copying the "zealous" act of Phineas, who took "a javelin in his hand" and killed the offender in flagrante (Num. 25:7–8, 11).[46] To modern minds this kind of dispensation with due process of law may be odious, but for the ancients the example of Phineas had kept its full splendor. In the words of Philo Judaeus, a contemporary of Jesus: "Rightly are all those who are

313

imbued with virtuous zeal, entitled to inflict the punishment [on idolaters caught *in flagrante*] without dragging them before a court or a council or other authority; they are qualified by their hatred of evil and by their love for God . . . and they may be convinced that in that moment they are councillors, judges, commanders, assemblymen, prosecutors, witnesses, laws, even the people as a whole—all in one and at the same time."[47]

It follows that the hangings of Simon ben Shetah lend no support to the theory that hanging was an approved and common mode of Jewish execution. It was resorted to only when legitimate judicial modes were not legally available, or, possibly, also for the purpose of showing that the execution was nonjudicial. It was selected as an emergency mode for the reason that it led to a quick and relatively painless death; hence it could not have been hanging by crucifixion, on a cross, for that was as lingering as it was painful, but only hanging on a stake or gallows, where death was due to strangulation.[48]

How lingering and painful was death by crucifixion is revealed in the Gospels themselves.[49] The Gospel tradition fixes the hour of Jesus' crucifixion as the third (Mark 15:25), and when we take into account all that is said to have happened that morning, first in the palace of the high priest, then the escorting of Jesus to the *praetorium*, then the trial before Pilate, and finally the taking of Jesus to the place of execution, this was the earliest possible hour to fix. In the sixth hour, we are told, that is, when Jesus had already been on the cross for three hours, "a darkness was over all the earth" (Luke 23:44; Mark 15:33; Matt. 27:45), and three hours later, in the ninth hour, Jesus cried out in anguish, "My God, my God, why hast thou forsaken me?" (Matt. 27:46; Mark 15:34), or, "Father, into thy hands I commend my spirit" (Luke 23:46). Jesus survived on the cross for six hours.

Matthew tells that vinegar mingled with gall was given to Jesus to drink, but when he had tasted it he would not drink (27:34); according to Mark, it was wine mingled with myrrh, "and he received it not" (15:23). From Luke we know that "there followed him a great company of people, and of women, which also bewailed and lamented him" (23:27), and they would of a surety have followed him all the way to Golgotha. Combining both traditions, it may, I think, be permissible to infer that it was the women accompanying Jesus on his way to execution, and attending him in his last hours on the cross, who brought the wine and begged him to drink: it was an ancient Jewish custom that a condemned man, when led to the place of execution, had to be given a draft of wine with incense in it, "in order that he may lose his mind," that is, become unconscious; and it was "the dear women of Jerusalem who volunteered and brought the wine" and offered it to him.[50] This custom is told in the Talmud in connection with convicts about to be stoned, and stoning, too, as practiced in talmudic times, ends in a very swift death, not as the slow extremity of crucifixion. But, manifestly, if "the dear women of Jerusalem" saw to it that even a man about to die by stoning should be anesthetized against excess of pain, a fortiori would they be solicitous of one facing crucifixion; and if they did their act of grace to a man about to die by judgment of the Jewish court, with even greater compassion would they minister to one sentenced to death by the enemy governor. Jesus did not drink the wine, and his consciousness was awake throughout the six hours that he hung upon the cross.

According to Mark and Matthew, Jesus was silent all the time and did not speak until the sixth hour, when he gave up his spirit, but Luke and John report that he uttered. At the moment of crucifixion, he said, according to Luke, "Father, forgive them; for they know not what they do" (23:34), and when the "malefactors" who were crucified with him addressed him, he said to one of them, "Verily I say unto thee, To day shalt thou be with me in paradise" (23:43). According to John, when Jesus saw his mother and his disciple standing by, he said to his mother, "Woman, behold thy son!" and to the disciple, "Behold thy mother!" (19:26–27), and went on, "I thirst" (19:28). We are not concerned here with the theological implications of this or that utterance attributed to Jesus; suffice it to note the tradition, common at least to Luke and John, that while he was upon the cross he did speak, and his words could be heard.

We find in Roman sources, too, that men lived on for long hours on the cross, and spoke as they hung there. It is reported, for instance, of the Punic king Bomilcar, crucified by an exultant proletariat, that as he hung on the cross he addressed the crowd in chiding: his words are said to have been so moving that the

315

remorse and pity of the people were stirred, but when he fell silent, he breathed his last.[51] And the emperor Claudius once expressed a desire to witness a crucifixion, of which he had heard as being the most ancient form of execution: *more maiorum*,[52] whereupon several convicts were one day crucified before his eyes, and when he had gazed on them for many an hour, he became impatient or weary and ordered that they be killed.[53]

On one important question, penologically, the Gospels are mute: whether Jesus was nailed to the cross or bound to it. It appears that it was normal Roman practice to bind the convict to the cross by ropes,[54] not nail him to it. But it is ancient Christian tradition that Jesus was nailed to the cross: the earliest text to mention nails piercing the hands of Jesus is the story of the Doubting Thomas (John 20:25); Paul speaks metaphorically of "the handwriting of ordinances that was against us" as nailed by Jesus to the cross (Col. 2:14); and Justin Martyr seems to be the first to speak of nails through the feet.[55] The fact that Jesus expired on the cross after some six hours had passed forcefully sustains the tradition that he was nailed, not bound: the nailing opened wounds in his flesh, and he must have lost much blood, greatly hastening death. If only bound, he might have endured yet a while, even several days.[56] The theory that he was taken down from the cross still living,[57] and its recent elaboration that this stratagem had been contrived by him beforehand,[58] also presuppose binding in the first instance; it must have been known that nailing, with its inevitable aftermath of hemorrhage, would bring death speedily. A victim nailed to the cross may die of weakness induced or aggravated by loss of blood and complications of open wounds. A victim bound may die of hunger or thirst, or of inclemency of weather, or, especially at nights, by attack of vulture or jackal, none of them causes normally predictable. How the end of crucifixion could differ from one case to another is illustrated by the story of Josephus, who, finding three of his friends crucified, asked the emperor to pardon them: when they were taken down, two died, and only the third survived.[59]

The tradition that Jesus was nailed to the cross, not bound to it, has further corroboration in Jewish legal sources. Certain provisions of the purification laws in the Talmud are based on the premise that persons crucified not only stayed alive for a length

316

of time but lost blood throughout.[60] What is more, the "nail from the cross" (or the "nail from the crucified") is mentioned in the sabbatical laws as a medical appliance, and, as such, some authorities allow it to be carried on the Sabbath.[61] Medical opinion of the day seems to have been divided as to the use for which this nail ought to be recommended: there were those who thought it infallible in reducing swellings and inflammations;[62] others preferred it as a cure of nettle stings;[63] a later medical pundit insists on prescribing it for treatment of thrice-recurring fever.[64] But an assertion that all this superstitious nonsense imported from the heathen (the "Emorites") should not be clothed with statutory sanction was eventually voted down, on the view that the sabbatical laws must take cognizance of everything that the physicians may, at one time or another, accept as therapeutically useful.[65] That belief in the remedial efficacy of such nails was indeed an importation from Rome, presumably together with the cross itself, is highly probable: they seem to have been applied in Rome to treat epileptics,[66] and even to check the spread of infectious and epidemic diseases.[67]

The legal significance which Jewish canons assigned to nails of the cross, and to blood lost on it, suggests not only that the Romans in Judaea crucified by nailing, not binding, the victim to the cross, but also that such crucifixions were not uncommon. Crucifixion was, indeed, the only mode of execution "practiced by the government" of Rome in Judaea,[68] and it was practiced extensively enough. In the year 4 B.C., the Roman governor, Varus, ordered some two thousand Jewish underground fighters to be crucified in the mountains of Jerusalem;[69] after the crucifixion of Jesus, we find the governor Tiberius Alexander sentencing Jacob and Simon, sons of Judah the Galilean, to death by crucifixion;[70] within a few years, a second wholesale crucifixion of zealots was ordered by the governor Quadratus.[71] Then came Felix, who outdid his predecessors by crucifying not only rebels and zealots, but also any citizen suspected of collaborating with them,[72] and who succeeded him, on one single day had 3,600 Jews crucified, or killed on the way to the cross.[73] The emperor Titus bade that the prisoners taken during the siege of Jerusalem be crucified on the walls of the city, and day after day five hundred perished thus; the soldiers, Josephus reports, had to twist the wretched victims into the most gruesome postures, "as their number was very large, and there was no room for the many crosses, and not crosses enough for the many bodies."[74] It may be deduced, then, that crucifixion was not only the judicial mode of execution practiced by the Romans in Judaea, but also their non-judicial and quasi-military manner of dealing punitive death; and in view of the multitudinous crucifixions recorded by Josephus, it is hardly to be wondered at if the fate of crucified persons gave rise to legal problems of all kinds and those problems, again, to intricate discussion.

Apart from the context of purification and sabbatical ordinances, we find such discussion mainly in the laws of marriage and divorce. When a woman who has been married desires to remarry, she has first to adduce evidence that her husband has died; and the fact that he has been seen hanging on a cross is not in itself evidence of death.[75] The reason given for this rule is that "a rich matron might still come along and redeem him"[76]—another indication of how long the victim may linger on the cross before death comes. But there is a positive side to this: the longer life lasts, the brighter the prospect of ultimate redemption. We are entitled to infer that the wealthier matrons among the "dear women of Jerusalem," who, as we read, attended crucifixions, time and again succeeded in bribing Roman soldiers or officers to have a still-breathing victim taken down from the cross. If witnesses had beheld wild animals or vultures attacking the men on the cross, their testimony would be accepted as proof of death provided that the parts of the body seen to be so attacked were vital ("the parts where the soul goes out") ;[77] this points to the fact, seemingly established by experience, that death upon the cross not seldom was the result of rending by birds or beasts of prey. There is, as well, some evidence that not a few Roman emperors regarded crucifixion as only the prelude to throwing the corpse to the beasts.[78]

In the ensuing talmudic exegesis, it is said that people, places, and times differ from one another: one man dies more quickly because of his obesity, the other more slowly, being strong and athletic; in one place, where it is cooler, men will hold out longer than in another, where it is hot and dry; and physical suffering is easier to bear in winter than in summer.[79] No general rule can, therefore, be laid down for the length of time, or even minimal and maximal lengths of time, that a man can stay alive on the cross. But it is provided that where three days have elapsed after crucifixion, evidence is no longer admissible, not because it could reasonably be assumed that the victim was still alive, but because his features would no longer be recognizable, so that the witnesses cannot be relied upon to identify the man whom they saw hanging unless there are other means of identification.[80]

Another rule provides that if a man crucified speaks from the cross and orders a bill of divorcement to be written to his wife in his name, his injunction is to be complied with: his body may have become weak, but his mind is presumed still to be sound.[81] The same rule applies where he did not speak but nodded his head in agreement to the question whether he wished the bill written.[82] The object in writing such a bill is to avoid the trouble of proving death: the wife would be allowed to remarry not as a widow but as a divorcee.

The "dear women of Jerusalem" were wont, as we saw, to try to render unconscious the men about to be crucified, and so spare them pain and torment. Jesus would have none of their ministrations, and did not sip the drink which they held out, nor, it appears, did the two convicts crucified together with him. Both, like Jesus himself, were fully conscious throughout: according to Luke, one said to him, "If thou be Christ, save thyself and us" (23:39), and the other rebuked him, "saying, Dost not thou fear God, seeing thou art in the same condemnation? And we indeed justly; for we receive the due reward of our deeds; but this man hath done nothing amiss" (23:40–41). According to Mark and Matthew, the two who were crucified with Jesus joined the others present in reviling and railing at him (Mark 15:32; Matt. 27:44). Though Jesus said nothing, there is no doubt that he heard the abuse: his ignoring of it was not a sign of weakness or of indifference, but deliberate. When he sees fit to retort, his voice rings out: one of the two says, "Lord, remember me when thou comest into thy kingdom" (Luke 23:42), and Jesus bows down to him: "Verily I say unto thee, To day shalt thou be with me in paradise" (23:43).

We are concerned with the phenomenological rather than the theological implications of this story. From the theological point

319

of view, differing explanations have been offered to give the triple
crucifixion some deeper meaning: the commonest is that already
propounded by Mark, that Scripture had to be fulfilled, he that
"hath poured out his soul unto death" was to be "numbered with
the transgressors" (Isa. 53:12; see Mark 15:28), a prophecy which,
in a Lucan tradition, had been made by Jesus himself the evening
before (Luke 22:37). This tendency to make events occur so
as to demonstrate that Scripture fulfilled itself in Jesus we shall
find in other happenings reported as taking place at or instantly
after the crucifixion; but just as it is, of course, possible that the
events were framed to fit Scripture, so it is equally likely that they
did take place and that scriptural verses were afterward invoked
to point the desired theological moral. Fulfillment of a scriptural
prophecy by a particular event would not in itself render that
event improbable, even in the eyes of rational nontheologians; but
where a reported occurrence is in itself, on objective grounds,
improbable, its reporting may well be due to the theological
proclivity to see Scripture realized. It was, for example, pointed
out a century ago that the report of the "chief priests" (Mark
15:31) with "the scribes and elders" (Matt. 27:41) and the
"rulers" (Luke 23:35), not to speak of the common folk around,
mocking and reviling Jesus while he hung on the cross, could
have been inserted into the Gospel story for only one purpose,
namely, to affirm that Jesus verily underwent all that the Psalmist
had foretold: "All they that see me laugh me to scorn: they shoot
out the lip, they shake the head, saying, He trusted on the Lord
that he would deliver him: let him deliver him, seeing he delighted in him" (Ps. 22:7–8). Jesus was being ridiculed identi-
cally: "He trusted in God: let him deliver him now, if he will
have him" (Matt. 27:43). It simply will not bear belief that
priests or scribes or elders or rulers or any commoner should mock
and curse a fellow Jew hanging on a Roman cross, whatever his
crime was. Hence the theory that Scripture had to be fulfilled;[83]
and that, by the same stroke, the Jews could be presented as the
cruel and inhuman creatures, lacking the least decency, and true
to the vileness of character portrayed throughout the Passion
story, was only a further and more welcome ground for arranging
that Scripture fulfill itself.

The crucifixion was bad enough without all this execration, and the evangelists need not have tried to make it worse to aggravate the ordeal of Jesus. They may, in their days in Rome, have witnessed crucifixions where the mob was licensed to vilify the victim and people gave free rein to their baser instincts; or the normally concomitant scourgings may have impressed them as the kind of consequential vulgarity that had to be provided in the story of the crucifixion of Jesus no less. But irrespective of all attendant excesses, crucifixion was known in Rome as the gravest and cruelest death (*summum supplicium*),[84] originally practiced in the more barbarous and less gentle ages of bygone ancestors (*more maiorum*),[85] and kept on only as a mode of putting slaves and aliens to death, or for the most heinous crimes.[86] Tacitus reports a debate in the Roman senate, where a member protested against its infliction, arguing that "it is not what a depraved criminal may deserve, that we ought to inflict on him: in the days of an enlightened ruler and of a senate unfettered by precedent, hangman and cross and ropes should be abolished, and punishments provided for in the laws that can be inflicted without cruelty by the judges and that will not disgrace this generation."[87] There was no echo of this lonely voice, but it shows how much, even then, more liberal and progressive Romans recoiled from the use of crucifixion. The general horror that it existed can be felt in the names given to appurtenances of it: the victim was made to stand on an "unhappy" plank (*infelix lignum*) and was hanged on an infamous beam (*infamis stipes*).[88] Though other manners of execution practiced in Rome were not distinguished for any humaneness, this was, as Cicero put it, the most cruel and terrible penalty (*crudelissimum et teterimum supplicium*):[89] it was, as has recently been remarked, "the acme of the torturer's art."[90]

It is significant that in the Gospel According to John we find no report or mention of any insult or mockery hurled at Jesus by Jews in general or by the chief priests present (19:21) in particular. It is the Jews who are represented by the fourth evangelist as leading him away for crucifixion (19:16), and, at least by insinuation, as crucifying him (19:18). There could be no plainer, no more unmistakable, indication that the fourth evangelist was determined to outvie his predecessors in blaming and branding the Jews. All the same, he gave up the Marcan tradition of their tirades against Jesus on the cross, though Matthew and, to a less extent, Luke had adopted it. To be faithful to his tendentious purpose, he should have been quick to take it up and exploit it to the hilt. Be it noted that, as far as concerns the mockery of the Roman soldiers, John follows the tradition of the Synoptic Gospels, though he places it at a somewhat earlier stage (18:2–3) : the more remarkable, surely, that he knows nothing of any mockery by the Jews. To suggest that he did not mention this or that reviling because he "ignored the details which he regarded as merely accessory"[91] fails to do justice either to the dramatic quality or to the anti-Jewish bias of the Johannine accounts. And the hypothesis that John felt that for his account he had no need to speak of it, because his account had been "stripped of any element of proof from prophecy,"[92] is disproved by at least two instances of Scripture fulfilled recorded in John (19:28, 36). Either, then, John had a tradition of his own, which taught him surely that the Jews had not mocked Jesus, or he chose to pay no heed to the report of the Synoptic Gospels because of its inherent incongruity. Some scholars maintain that John must have been present in person at the crucifixion of Jesus and reported what had actually happened there, and in particular the exchange of words between Jesus and his mother and the disciple (19:25–27), as an eyewitness who heard them spoken and beheld the speakers;[93] that would be all the more reason to prefer his account of the events to that of the other evangelists and to discard, as he did, their tale of Jewish mockery and abuse. It seems that Luke had similar scruples: while his "rulers" sneered at Jesus, "the people stood beholding" (23:35), refraining, strangely enough, from participation in what, according to Mark (15:29) and Matthew (27:39), must have been a public pastime.

Evident though the incongruity of the Marcan account is, it is argued that there will always be people to derive "some sickening pleasure in the sight of the tortures of others, a feeling which is increased and not diminished by the sight of pain," and that "the cross represented miserable humanity reduced to the last degree of impotence, suffering and degradation,"[94] and hence a welcome target of popular contumely. This kind of ready-made psychology ignores, once again, the peculiar position of the Judaean Jews under Roman dominion: it is totally out of the question that the average, that is, the not particularly depraved, common man, see-

322

ing a compatriot crucified at the hands of the detestable Romans, would or could so have demeaned himself as to stop and pour vituperation on the hapless head of the victim, his own neighbor and fellow citizen and tribesman. If he could do nothing to hearten or comfort him, he might stand there mute, seeking at least to convey sympathy by his mere presence, but would never open his lips to hurt him. I do not think that any idiosyncratic Jewish trait need be invoked to establish this: the same might be said of any nation under foreign rule that has preserved a remnant of national pride and solidarity, and is not utterly devoid of elementary kindliness. However pleasurable the sight may be to perverts of a body writhing in agony, or motionless and impotent, no perversion will withstand the pressure of public opinion and the threat of clandestine vengeance by zealots; and the first and slightest attempt at "amusement" at Jesus' expense would have been energetically and efficaciously suppressed on the spot. Even on the unwarranted assumption that among the Jews were some who had had a hand, or an interest, in the execution of Jesus or in doing away with him otherwise, the imagination boggles at the thought that, having won their presumably secret purpose, they would now parade their triumph or satisfaction in public: on the one hand, they would have to fear the scorn of the masses, who would not lightly pardon so fatal a case of collaboration with the enemy; on the other, not only possible pangs of conscience, but simple common and sober prudence, would prompt them to hold back and stay home. Nor can they be supposed to have come to the scene of the crucifixion in an endeavor to quiet their guilty consciences in a bedlam of noisy jeers and rude insults: for if they really did regret what they had done to Jesus, they could still try to save him, and if Pilate had in truth been as reluctant as the evangelists make him out to be to see Jesus crucified, there must have been some chance still of obtaining a pardon from him before Jesus died. In short, everything speaks for the accuracy of the Johannine tradition that no chief priests and no elders, no scribes or rulers, and no Jews, whoever they may have been, cursed Jesus or mocked him after his crucifixion: all who were present were stricken dumb, in grief and bitter disappointment.

Another Johannine tradition has it that when Jesus knew "that all things were now accomplished," he said from the cross, "I thirst" (19:28). "Now there was set a vessel full of vinegar: and they filled a sponge with vinegar, and put it upon hyssop, and put it to his mouth. When Jesus therefore had received the vinegar, he said, It is finished: and he bowed his head, and gave up the ghost" (19:29–30). We do not hear who "they" were that put the drink to Jesus' lips. Luke reports that the soldiers who had mocked him came to him and offered him vinegar (23:36); but there is no mention of Jesus accepting it. According to Mark and Matthew, when Jesus had cried out, "My God, my God, why hast thou forsaken me?," of some of them that stood there, "one ran and filled a sponge full of vinegar, and put it on a reed, and gave him to drink" (Mark 15:35–36; Matt. 27:46–48); and when Jesus had taken from the drink, he "yielded up the ghost" (Matt. 27:50; similarly Mark 15:37). Here we have a tradition that in some form is common to all Gospels; and it is not without interest for our inquiry.

We can dismiss the Lucan version that the drink was offered to Jesus by the Roman soldiers, if only because Luke here is a sole dissenter. The other evangelists are unanimous in reporting that one or more from among the bystanders fetched the drink and gave it to Jesus; John says so not expressly but by reasonable implication. Whether it was on hearing the cry or sigh of Jesus, or on their own impulse, they brought him vinegar: not water, which would have quenched his thirst, or wine, which might have robbed him of his senses, but vinegar, which neither relieves thirst nor anesthetizes. They had brought it for Jesus to drink, knew that it worked to hasten death, and that, indeed, was what they proposed to do and shorten his agony. A medieval writer assures us that "according to certain people, the fact of drinking vinegar under conditions such as these, is apt to hasten death, or so it is said."[95] This cautious assurance is reminiscent of a talmudic debate whether vinegar has or has not a quality of refreshment: those who gainsay this allow its drinking on fast days, even on the Day of Atonement; those who hold that it refreshes forbid its drinking then.[96] Still, it may have the quality of speeding death where dissolution has set in, even though it may also be "refreshing"; and we do find it said that any drink, whatever its nature, would be apt to speed death in those circumstances.[97] Most scholars, however, are agreed that the evangelists chose vinegar as the draft offered to Jesus not because of any inherent virtue but, again, to make scriptural prophecies come true, as, for instance, "in my thirst they gave me vinegar to drink" (Ps. 69:21).[98] The Psalmist decries the giving of vinegar as wholly inept to quench thirst, but on that day people evidently thought that the drink which they offered Jesus would relieve him of his torment and bring him peace.

The episode lends further weight to the view that the people present, so far from wishing to harass Jesus and vilify him, were single-minded in purpose—to lighten his sufferings as best they could. Of course, the evangelists would not, or could not, admit that in so many words, and, clinging to their policy, put into the mouths of the people such phrases as would be bound, in the reader's eyes, to empty their deeds of all merit. That they had no valid tradition of what was actually said by the people may be inferred from the inconsistencies of the Gospel stories. According to Mark, the man who had run and brought the vinegar to Jesus said to him, proffering it: "Let alone; let us see whether Elias will come to take him down" (15:36). This, it would seem, was a little too much even for Matthew: that man was not the mocker, for he at least would be consistent; but "the rest said, Let be, let us see whether Elias will come to save him" (27:49). The fourth evangelist dismisses the Marcan version, even as moderated by Matthew, as either unreasonable or unnecessary: his story is straightforward, that when Jesus had said, "I thirst," they gave him of the vinegar, of which there was there already "a vessel full"; and when Jesus "therefore had received the vinegar, he said, It is finished" (John 19:28–30). The words "There was set a vessel full of vinegar" (19:29) imply that the vinegar was always kept available and handy at the place of crucifixion, and that what "they" did to Jesus "they" would do to any person dying on the cross, from compassion, to be sure, and not in ill will. Luke, we recall, lets the Roman soldiers administer the vinegar to Jesus, and they, confessedly, "mocked him" before offering it to him, and at once said to him: "If thou be the king of the Jews, save thyself" (23:36–37): we have already expressed our doubts as to the acceptability of the Lucan version that the vinegar was offered to Jesus by the Roman soldiers; but, having before him the Marcan story that those who did so mocked him at the same time, it is not at all surprising that Luke scouted the notion that they could have been Jews, and replaced them by the Roman soldiers.

The Gospel According to John goes on to tell that "The Jews therefore, because it was the preparation, that the bodies should not remain upon the cross on the sabbath day, (for that sabbath day was an high day,) besought Pilate that their legs might be broken, and that they might be taken away. Then came the soldiers, and brake the legs of the first, and of the other which was crucified with him. But when they came to Jesus, and saw that he was dead already, they brake not his legs: But one of the soldiers with a spear pierced his side, and forthwith came there out blood and water" (19:31–34). It was only after this episode that Joseph of Arimathaea "besought Pilate that he might take away the body of Jesus" (19:38). In contradistinction, Mark reports that "when the even was come, because it was the preparation, that is, the day before the sabbath, Joseph of Arimathaea . . . came, and went in boldly unto Pilate, and craved the body of Jesus. And Pilate marvelled if he were already dead; and calling unto him the centurion, he asked him whether he had been any while dead. And when he knew it of the centurion, he gave the body to Joseph" (15:42–45). If the Johannine version is to be accepted, the Jews came to Pilate and told him that Jesus had not yet died, and for those tidings Pilate would not have required confirmation from the officer commanding his troops, because the time elapsed since the crucifixion would not ordinarily have been long enough for death to supervene. The petition which the Jews desired to make of the governor was that he order the legs of the crucified to be broken: it was the eve of Sabbath and Passover, and the bodies should not be allowed to hang on the crosses after sunset; and the breaking of their legs would hasten death. The Jewish delegation which presented itself to the governor and submitted this plea must have left Golgotha while Jesus was still alive; otherwise it was pointless. In other words, when the delegation was absent pleading with Pilate, the people who had stayed behind heard Jesus say, "I thirst," and gave him of the vinegar. And Jesus must have died before the delegation came back with Pilate's commands. If the Marcan version is to be accepted, the whole incident of the breaking of legs is imaginary, because if it had really happened Pilate would not have expressed wonderment that Jesus had already died and have verified the information by questioning his centurion. This particular difficulty would not arise according to the Gospels of Matthew and Luke, for there Pilate is not reported as voicing surprise at Jesus' death (Matt. 27:58; Luke 23:52).

While, according to Mark, the governor was amazed that Jesus should already be dead, according to John he agreed to have the death hastened. The breaking of legs is not, nor is it meant to be, an extra torment: it is the *coup de grâce*, intended to bring the sufferings to a swifter end. The Jews who besought Pilate to have Jesus' legs broken are, however, reported to have acted not out of pure compassion but so that they might perform their religious duty and bury him before sunset. As far as Pilate was concerned, there was no objection whatever to letting the bodies hang on the crosses throughout the night and for days and nights to come; on the contrary, it was, as we have seen, the well-established Roman custom to expose the victims on the crosses, even after death, to jackal or vulture: to be devoured and dismembered by "the fowls of the heaven and the beasts of the earth"[99] was regarded as a supplementary and particularly degrading punishment, which was the condemned man's deserts, and of which he could be relieved only by an act of grace. By ordering the legs of the crucified men to be broken, Pilate in effect conceded waiver of some of the punitive incidents of crucifixion, and as the waiver was represented to him as a matter not of grace or mitigation but rather of religious observance, he saw no reason to refuse it.

It is true enough that Jews were strictly forbidden to let a corpse hang overnight "upon the tree" (Deut. 21:23), a prohibition which, although by the tenor of the law applying only to persons executed for capital offenses under Jewish law and by sentence of a Jewish court, was certainly enforced—perhaps by analogy—in respect of persons executed by sentence of a non-Jewish court as well. The approach of the Sabbath and feast day only lent a special urgency to what was a binding duty in any circumstances. If burial had to be finished before sunset on any working day, then it must be exceptionally hurried on the eve of a festival day, when people had to purify themselves in time to attend temple services, if they were to have sufficient leisure

after the interment to prepare for the feast. Now, if it had really
been the Jews who brought pressure upon Pilate, on this of all
days, that Jesus be crucified, how could it be that in all probability they did not know that his death might be delayed until
after sunset? From practical experience, to which the aforemen-
tioned rules of Jewish law bear ample witness, they must have
been aware that days would often pass until a man died on the
cross: if, nevertheless, they cried out for the crucifixion of Jesus
on that very morning, it must have been in the knowledge that
the night and the feast would be likely to supervene before he
died, and that they would have to let him hang on the cross
overnight and during the feast. It would seem that they did not
care. One might say, of course, that "the Jews" who clamored for
Jesus' crucifixion were not identical with "the Jews" who asked
Pilate to have his legs broken; but then there is no differentiation
between this and that kind of "Jews" in the Gospel of John. If,
for instance, the Jews who besought Pilate to hasten Jesus' death
were friends or disciples of Jesus, the evangelist would surely have
said so, just as he made no secret of the particular personal relationship of Joseph of Arimathaea to Jesus (19:38; similarly Luke
23:50–51; Matt. 27:57; Mark 15:43). If any differentiation were
permissible between the categories of "Jews," it would be consequential to distinguish between Jews learned in the law, and
conscious of their religious duty, who would see to due compliance with the rules in respect of the prescribed daylight burial
of the executed man and the proper keeping of Sabbath and feast
days, and other Jews who, on the eve of Passover, allegedly had
nothing better in their minds than to give vent to hysterical
clamor for the crucifixion of Jesus.

Moreover, if "the Jews" who desired to bury Jesus before nightfall were the same as "the Jews" who had cried out for his crucifixion, another query would arise. We read in John that the Jews
"went not into the judgment hall, lest they should be defiled; but
that they might eat the passover" (18:28). If, then, they desired
to keep themselves pure for the evening's ritual repast, how is it
that they were prepared, in the afternoon, to defile and sully
themselves by burying the dead? Whether it would have defiled
or sullied them to enter the judgment hall is open to the gravest
doubts, but that it would to take part in a burial is incontestable

(Num. 19:11–14). Either they had no compunction about un-cleanness in the morning, in which case they would have entered the judgment hall, or they had the strongest compunction about it in the afternoon, so shortly before the commencement of the feast, in which case they would have taken no steps enabling them to bury Jesus before the feast began. The truth is that in the morning, as we have shown, they did not enter the judgment hall, not for fear of being defiled, but for entirely different reasons beyond their control; and in the afternoon they were gladly pre-pared to become unclean, if only they could bestow on Jesus and his fellow convicts the last favor and honor of a proper Jewish burial.

It has been suggested that the episode of the breaking of the legs owes its *raison d'être* to the conclusion which the evangelist wished to reach: "For these things were done, that the scripture should be fulfilled, A bone of him shall not be broken" (19:36). It is only a "lamb without blemish" (Exod. 12:5) that is fit for Passover, as a sacrifice to God, and it is "without blemish" that, on the sanctification of Passover, Jesus would make his ultimate sacrifice to God. "Neither shall ye break a bone thereof" (Exod. 12:46) is an enlargement of the basic injunction to choose a lamb without blemish; but that the breaking of bones was singled out for special mention as spoiling the immaculacy of the paschal lamb plainly suggests that unbroken bones are the cardinal attribute of a flawless lamb. However usual the breaking of bones may have been with lambs prepared for a meal or a sacrifice, you would not normally break the bones of a man; and the fact that the legs of Jesus were unbroken would have been without sig-nificance, and would not have lent itself to any possible compari-son with the unblemished sacrificial lamb, were it not for the report of the breaking of the legs of the two convicts crucified together with Jesus, or for the general knowledge of a custom of breaking the legs of convicts hanging on the cross. It is after the legs of those two others had been broken that the miracle occurred of Jesus left intact: God took his spirit when he was still without blemish, his sacrifice was thus made perfect, as of the paschal lamb, and his "precious blood," spilled on the cross as was the blood of "a lamb without blemish and without spot" upon the temple altar, would redeem the sins of men (I Pet. 1:19).

"When they came to Jesus, and saw that he was dead already, they brake not his legs; But one of the soldiers with a spear pierced his side, and forthwith came there out blood and water" (John 19:33–34). This thrust, entailing, as it evidently did, the opening of a wound, would at first sight appear to nullify all the endeavors to leave Jesus intact and "without blemish"; but it may be that anything done to his body after death could no longer diminish his faultlessness, for it was at the moment of death that the sacrifice without blemish ascended to heaven. Or it may have been considered no less important than fulfilling the Scripture's "A bone of him shall not be broken" (19:36) to realize another prophecy of Holy Writ, namely, "They shall look on him whom they pierced" (19:37). The sentence is taken from a prophecy of Zechariah (12:10) in which God promises to "pour upon the house of David, and upon the inhabitants of Jerusalem, the spirit of grace and of supplications: and they shall look upon me whom they have pierced, and they shall mourn for him, as one mourneth for his only son, and shall be in bitterness for him, as one that is in bitterness for his firstborn. . . . In that day there shall be a great mourning in Jerusalem. . . . And the land shall mourn, every family apart" (12:10–12). The words "and they shall look upon me whom they pierced" are taken out of context in their quotation in John (19:37), and it may not be amiss to restore them to their place: the sight of the pierced—whoever he may be[100]—will cause general mourning and lamentation in Jerusalem; there will be no family and no household left unafflicted; that this prophecy was truly fulfilled in the death of Jesus is to be shown by the fact that his side was "pierced." As we established, a sense of general affliction there undoubtedly was, and there can be little question that the lamentation and mourning over Jesus were common and widespread throughout Jerusalem. But the authors of the Gospel According to John does not seem to have been sufficiently aware that the prophecy of a deep and universal affliction at the death of Jesus had anyhow come true, regardless of any "piercing."

It has been argued that, physiologically, the story of the piercing cannot be sustained, as blood and water would not come out together from a pierced corpse, certainly not so as to be discernible by the naked eye.[101] The whole story was seemingly in-

330

serted for the sake of fulfillment of the scriptural prophecy, not on the strength of any valid tradition of an actual happening. And what is true of the piercing would in all probability be true of the breaking of legs: that unsubstantiated tale, too, might have been written into the Gospel According to John for the very same reason. The blood and water issuing were interpreted as symbols of the Eucharist and of baptism,[102] as Jesus is said to have come "by water and blood" (I John 5:6); and this, for the evangelist, must have borne a special meaningfulness, since he insists on the veracity of the eyewitness on whose "record" he relies (John 19:35). But even that insistence has been found to fall short of counterbalancing the fact that these incidents, and the presence of mother, disciple, and eyewitness at the crucifixion, are not mentioned by the earlier evangelists: if this had been based on any sound tradition, the Synoptic Gospels could never have passed over them in silence.[103]

Nonetheless, it is submitted that the fourth evangelist may well have possessed information, or a sound tradition, of the breaking of the legs or bones of the two particular convicts, or of crucified convicts in general. We find that the emperor Augustus had the legs of one of his secretaries broken, for divulging official secrets;[104] and Tiberius did likewise with men who would not be indecently used by him.[105] These were instances of separate punishment, but we also find the breaking of legs as incidental to crucifixion,[106] not necessarily only as a means of speeding death, but also as a prelude to the actual crucifixion.[107] In contrast to the drawing of water and blood by the piercing of Jesus' side, for which there is no precedent or parallel, the breaking of legs appears to be in line with regular usage, and, if for this reason only, the Johannine tradition that the Jews asked Pilate to order the breaking of the legs of the convicts on the crosses cannot be dismissed offhand. It is not without interest that, while Pilate was asked to order his soldiers to break their legs and seems to have done so, no such plea had been made to him as to the piercing of the side of Jesus: it was "one of the soldiers" who, on his own prompting, as it appears, drove in the sword (19:34), and it is not clear from the record whether he wanted to make sure that Jesus had breathed his last or whether it was just another act of insult and reviling. Even, therefore, if it had happened at all and was not invented merely to have Scripture fulfilled, it would have no bearing on the role in which "the Jews" were cast.

It is "the Jews" (19:31) who are expressly credited with beseeching Pilate to hasten death by the breaking of legs. It is, needless to say, quite out of tune and out of context to find "the Jews" given the merit of humanity or kindliness: it might have dovetailed much more neatly into the general picture if Pilate himself had been fathered with the original will to cut short the sufferings of Jesus on the cross, whereupon we would, as a matter of course, expect the Jews to protest loudly and insist that his sufferings be intensified and protracted; the more distressful and the lengthier, the better. If, relentless persecutors and crucifiers of Jesus as they were depicted to be, the Jews asked Pilate that Jesus' legs be broken, surely they must have been urged by evil motives: maybe it was not at all to speed his death and abridge his pain, but to add to his torment and suffering, and the breaking of legs would certainly inflict anguish enough. It has, accordingly, been suggested that the Jews used the "preparation" for the approaching Sabbath as a pretext only, making it appear to Pilate as if they were concerned with hastening Jesus' death, whereas in truth they were out to aggravate his misery, to cause him greater hurt and ache; and the gullible Pilate, in his ingenuousness, yielded to their suasion and benignly condescended to confer on Jesus this last grace.[108]

If our thesis is correct that the Jews loved Jesus and identified themselves with him, and that, at the sight of what he had to endure, their love could not but gain depth on this—his last—day, and that neither they nor any of their leaders had a say in his prosecution or condemnation, then it becomes plausible that when they saw him in agony on the cross, fluttering between life and death, they ran to the governor, entreating of him a word to his officers that would bring death without further heart-rending pause. The rapid nearing of the holy feast was, as we have said, a welcome argument to put to Pilate; but that fact must have weighed on the mind of Jesus as heavily as on the minds of the onlookers: Jesus was the last person to wish or agree that the Sabbath be desecrated for his sake or the festal night profaned by letting a crucified man—the "curse of God"—hang overnight without burial. It was because they all knew of Jesus' own susceptibilities in the matter that the Jews were all the more anxious that the ultimate honors of the dead be paid to a beloved brother before the Sabbath entered.

If, on the other hand, it were true that the Jews had demanded the crucifixion of Jesus that very morning, and that Pilate had given in to them reluctantly and against his better judgment, not only would those same Jews not have dared now to come to him with this plea, but he would never have acceded to it had it been made: he would still harbor a grudge against them, and their further, and now altogether inconsistent, importunity could only arouse his fury and extinguish his last flicker of patience. Moreover, they would themselves have foreseen that, as likely as not, they would not be allowed to quit his palace unharmed. If the Jews did in fact beseech Pilate to hasten Jesus' death by ordering his legs to be broken, then this was the one and only time that they confronted the governor in the matter of Jesus: the one and only errand respecting Jesus that any Jews essayed to Pilate was an errand of mercy and compassion.

The story, common to all the Gospels, that the Roman soldiers who had crucified Jesus "parted his garments, casting lots upon them, what every man should take" (Mark 15:24; similarly Matt. 27:35; Luke 23:34; John 19:23), also preached fulfillment of a scriptural prophecy, namely, "They part my garments among them, and cast lots upon my vesture" (Ps. 22:18). There is authority for the contention that it was the right of the executioners in Rome to appropriate the convicts' garments,[109] but no such custom is reported in Judaea. As only Jesus' garments, and not those of the two convicts crucified with him, were divided among the soldiers, it would seem that the story had no purpose save fulfillment of Scripture, the more so as his garments were not outstandingly valuable, made of one piece of unseamed cloth (John 19:23) and apparently humble enough.

We find such special treatment again accorded to Jesus, in preference to his fellow convicts, in the matter of burial. We are told that Joseph of Arimathaea "craved the body of Jesus" (Mark 15:43; Matt. 27:58; Luke 23:52; John 19:38), but said nothing about the bodies of the others. By Jewish law and custom, it was to be expected that he would do the two the act of grace that he did Jesus. It may, of course, be that he did not, in fact, dis-

333

criminate, but buried all three, but that the evangelists did not mention it, simply because the fate of the two was no longer relevant to their story. We may assume that Joseph, described as a disciple of Jesus (Matt. 27:57; John 19:38), followed Jesus' teaching: "If ye love them which love you, what reward have ye? do not even the publicans the same? And if ye salute your brethren only, what do ye more than others? do not even the publicans so?" (Matt. 5:46–47) ; and that what he did for the man whom he loved he did, no less, for strangers whom he knew not.

While the Jews who went to Pilate to ask him to hasten Jesus' death are shrouded in anonymity, the name of the Jew who begged Pilate's permission to bury him has been preserved for eternal fame. Joseph of Arimathaea (in Hebrew: *Haramati*, or of the highlands) is said to have been a member of the Sanhedrin (Mark 15:43; Luke 25:50), and some scholars theorize that he was personally known to the evangelists and served them as source of primary information[110]—which can be neither proved nor disproved; but if the evangelists, or any of them, had firsthand intelligence from him of what took place at the meeting of the Sanhedrin the night before, they would certainly not have withheld their source, any more than they withheld his name in the burial episode. But it would also have to be anticipated that had this Joseph, this disciple of Jesus, taken part in a meeting of the Sanhedrin such as the Gospels describe, he would have spoken up and tried to exert some influence on the course of events; or if he reported the proceedings to the evangelists, that he would at least have asserted that he had done everything in his power to avert the tragedy. As far as we are concerned, we may safely accept the tradition that this disciple of Jesus, like other disciples and followers of his, was a member of the Sanhedrin and attended the session in the high priest's home the night before; but if he did report to any evangelist what had transpired, he did not— alas!—succeed in persuading them to transcribe his report in the Gospels. What—as we believe—had really taken place at the session is, assuredly, in total consonance with the membership in the Sanhedrin, and with the presence, of Joseph of Arimathaea as well as of any other disciple and follower or sympathizer of Jesus, at the meeting.

A recent writer has suggested that Jesus and Joseph were parties to a conspiracy: Joseph agreed to administer a drug which would keep Jesus alive but give him the appearance of death; then he would ask permission to take him off the cross, and pretend to bury him; and after a few days Jesus would rise again as if resurrected.[111] So far from subscribing to a theory which would, in effect, incriminate both Jesus and Joseph, if not legally, then at least morally and theologically, we prefer to content ourselves with the simple and very human story told in the Gospels, that Joseph was a friend and follower of Jesus who volunteered to bury him, and did bury him in his own land, before nightfall, in the finest of Jewish custom and tradition.

The Roman law was that a convict, after execution, might not be buried:[112] we have seen that the crucified, in particular, were left on the cross until beasts and birds of prey devoured them.[113] Guards were mounted on duty at the cross to prevent kinsfolk or friends from taking down a corpse and burying it; unauthorized burial of a crucified convict was a criminal offense.[114] The emperor or his officers might, exceptionally, grant kinsfolk or friends authorization to bury the convict,[115] and what in Rome was the imperial prerogative was in a province the right of the governor. What Joseph of Arimathaea asked of Pilate was, therefore, nothing unusual, nor is Pilate reported to have made any difficulty in granting his wish. We know from Josephus that the Jews were always very solicitous and particular about burying their dead, and those especially whom Roman crucifixions had killed,[116] and it would appear that they sought and got special burial permits in each individual instance. It is unarguable, however, that had it really been the Jews who petitioned Pilate to crucify Jesus or anybody else, and even had Joseph of Arimathaea not been one of them, the governor would have entertained their later petition for permission to have him taken off the cross and buried: if the governor had, indeed, "delivered" Jesus to the Jews for crucifixion, he would not now "deliver" him to them for burial. And it is highly improbable that he would have recognized Joseph of Arimathaea as having abstained from the persecution of Jesus that morning: these Judaeans were all much of a muchness in his eyes.

Jesus was buried in the grave which Joseph had dug on his own land (Matt. 27:60; Luke 23:53; John 19:41), proof that he was

not regarded as a convict executed by a judgment of a Jewish
court, which, indeed, he was not—we know that convicts executed
by order of the Jewish court must be interred in a cemetery set
aside for that special purpose and known as the court's grave-
yard.[117] The law was that private persons were not allowed to
bury such convicts, and that no one might mourn them, whereas
convicts executed by order of the Roman governor had to be
buried and mourned like any person who had died a natural
death.[118] It would not matter of what offense a convict had been
found guilty by the Romans: that it was a Roman court which
had sentenced him was enough to entitle him to the benefits of
Jewish burial and traditional Jewish mourning. So his mother and
Mary Magdalene sat down at the side of Jesus' grave and mourned
(Matt. 27:61; Mark 15:47), until the Sabbath came, after timely
readying of the spices and ointments for his body (Luke 23:56);
everything was done in "the manner of the Jews" in burying their
own dead (John 27:40). It was Jewish custom to clothe the dead
in white linen,[119] and so Jesus was "wound in linen clothes"
(John 19:40), "fine linen" bought by Joseph (Mark 15:46). He
was buried and mourned and honored as every Jew would have
been who, like him, had been the victim of persecution by the
Roman oppressors. It was in a garden that he was laid to rest,
near the place where he had been crucified; and in the garden was
a new sepulcher "wherein was never man yet laid" (John 19:41):
that was the last resting place that Joseph had chosen for his
master and teacher, and he would make sure that the homage
befitting the great dead of Israel would be accorded in full. Joseph
did his simple duty, as one Jew to another, and that he was not
alone in doing it is attested by John (19:39), who here again
brings in Nicodemus, the Pharisee (3:1), and who, for that
matter, could properly have brought in all the "Pharisees" of
Jerusalem to join hands in paying Jesus their farewell respects.

NOTES

1. Thus most modern translations. See, for instance, *The New Testament in Today's English Version,* published by the American Bible Society, New York (2d ed., 1966), pp. 73, 126. And cf. Brandon, *Jesus and the Zealots,* p. 238, n. 3, and p. 351, n. 1.
2. *Ibid.*
3. Brandon, *op. cit.,* p. 351. And see Winter, *op. cit.,* p. 148.
4. Stauffer, *Jerusalem und Rom im Zeitalter Jesu Christi,* pp. 123, 125 ff.
5. By Winter, *op. cit.,* pp. 62 ff.
6. E.g., Targumim *ad* Genesis 40:19, 22; *ad* Deuteronomy 21:23; *ad* Joshua 8:29; 10:26; *ad* II Samuel 4:12; 21:12; *ad* Esther 2:23; 5:14; 7:10; 9:13.
7. The root *shelov* occurs in Exod. 26:17 ("boards set one against another") ; I Kings 7:28; J Ta'anit IV 7.

   That *shelov* is the true source of the Hebrew *tselov,* as distinguished from the Aramaic *tselov,* is submitted on the authority of Ben Yehuda, *Thesaurus Totius Hebraitatis,* Vol. XI, p. 5482.
8. Bezold, *Babylonisch-Assyrisches Glossar,* p. 106b.
9. *Zaqapu* and *Suqalulu: ibid.,* pp. 115a and 284b.
10. E.g., *Zaqaf* for "hang," and *Zaqifa* for "stake": B Babba Metzia 59b and 83b; B. Avodah Zarah 18b; B Megillah 16b.
11. Kittel, "Gekreuzigt Werden," p. 284.
12. B Sanhedrin 46b; Sifrei Devarim 221; Midrash Tanna'im, Devarim 21,22 (ed. Hoffmann, p. 132). The midrashic version is: "He is hanged alive in the way practiced by the government," while the talmudic version leaves out the word "alive."
13. E.g., Gaster, *The Dead Sea Scriptures,* p. 243; Dupont-Sommer, *The Essene Writings from Qumran* (English trans. by Vermes) , p. 269.
14. "Affront to God" is the paraphrase used by the translators of the Bible for the Jewish Publication Society of America (Philadelphia, 1962, p. 364) . The King James version is, "for he that is hanged is accursed of God," which is the more literal translation.
15. Josephus, *Antiquities,* 13,4,2; and *Wars,* 1,4,6.
16. I Macc. 7:15.
17. Buechler, "Die Todesstrafen der Bibel und der nachbiblischen Zeit," p. 703; Dupont-Sommer, *op. cit.,* p. 269, n. 2; Daniel-Rops, *op. cit.,* p. 177.
18. M Sanhedrin VII 1.

19. The King James version is inaccurate, rendering the words given in the text as "and he be to be put to death." The correct translation is in the past tense, not in the future.

20. B Sanhedrin 46b: proceedings in court are to be protracted until shortly before sunset, so that execution is to follow sentence immediately. And see note 118, p. 369, *supra*.

21. M Sanhedrin VI 4.

22. Stauffer, *Jerusalem und Rom im Zeitalter Jesu Christi*, p. 123.

23. Yonathan ben Uziel, Deut. 21:23.

24. M Sanhedrin VI 4; Sifrei Devarim 221. And cf. Gal. 3:13.

25. There is, however, a strong dissent to the effect that we have here an express biblical injunction to execute certain criminals (to wit, idolaters) by hanging them alive: Rav Hissda, in B Sanhedrin 34b. If this were the correct view, then Phinehas would, at any rate, have disobeyed the divine command, by taking a javelin and thrusting it through the bodies of the offenders (Num. 25:7-8), instead of hanging them, and he would hardly have deserved the praise that God showered on him for his valiant deed (25:11-13). Be that as it may, the fact that, by a legitimate and grammatical interpretation, there is to be found some biblical authority for hanging alive has led some scholars to assume that such hangings may have been known and practiced in ancient Israel; but so far no evidence whatever has come to light to support any such theory.

26. That the word *hoqa* stands for "hanging" was sought to be proved by the occurrence of the same word in II Sam. 21:9. The talmudic tradition is that the Gibeonites did hang the sons of Saul: B Sanhedrin 34b; but they may well have hanged their victims according to their own laws and customs, and the fact that they did has no bearing on the laws and customs of the Israelites.

27. See notes 3 and 22, *supra*.

28. Hentig, *op. cit.*, Vol. I, p. 254; Herodotus III, 125 and 159.

29. The exact dates of these translations are unknown: they appear to be first mentioned and referred to in the eleventh century. For particulars, see Zuntz, *Die gottesdienstlichen Vortraege der Juden*, Chap. 5.

30. Midrash Ruth Rabba 1.

31. M Sanhedrin VII 3: strangulation is effected by two men (the two witnesses) pulling ties wrapped around the convict's neck, each to opposite sides, until suffocation ensues. See my "The Penology of the Talmud," Chap. II.

32. It is to be observed, though, that there is no resemblance, in operation, between hanging and the mishnaic strangling described in the previous note. The view has recently been proffered that, in substituting hanging for strangling, the translators relied on a pre-mishnaic tradition: see Joseph Heinemann, "Targum Shemot 22,4 Vehahalakha Hakedumah," p. 296—a hypothesis which can be

neither proved nor disproved; but it is strange that a tradition of such long standing should have left no trace or clue other than in this late translation.

33. M Sanhedrin VI 4. And see note 44, p. 363.
34. J Hagigah II 8; Rashi (Shlomo Yitzhaki) *ad* Sanhedrin 44b.
35. Graetz, *op. cit.,* Vol. III, p. 152; Dubnow, *op. cit.,* Vol. II, p. 117; *et al.*
36. M Sanhedrin VI 4; B Sanhedrin 46a.
37. It was the same Simon ben Shetah who acquitted a murderer caught *in flagrante delicto* by one witness, only because there had been no second witness present: B Sanhedrin 37b. In another case, he ruled that circumstantial evidence, however strong and conclusive it may seem, as, e.g., finding a corpse and seeing a bloodstained man fleeing from the scene with a knife in his hand, was never sufficient to support a conviction: *ibid.,* and B Shevu'ot 34a. Where a court had convicted one of two false witnesses of perjury and executed him without having tried and convicted the other, he denounced the execution as judicial murder: T Sanhedrin VI 6. While insisting on careful and probing cross-examinations of witnesses, he warned of pitfalls, lest the witness might, by confusing questioning, be induced to lie: M Avot I 9. And it was Simon ben Shetah who, presiding over the Sanhedrin, upheld the dignity and power of the court even as against the king's majesty, by successfully insisting that the king should appear and defend himself in court against a claim brought against him: B Sanhedrin 19a.
38. Witches and sorcerers are liable to stoning: M Sanhedrin VII 4.
39. Maimonides, Commentary *ad* M Sanhedrin VI 6; Rashi (Shlomo Yitzhaki) *ad* B Sanhedrin 45b.
40. M Sanhedrin VII 11.
41. B Sanhedrin 67b.
42. Baron, *Social and Religious History of the Jews,* Vol. I, p. 211, writes that at that time "Jewish women, generally more illiterate and superstitious than men, were irresistibly attracted to the magic arts. The Talmud repeatedly speaks of 'the majority of women being witches' (J Sanhedrin VII 19 and 25, B Sanhedrin 67a) and says that the most pious of women is engaged in sorcery (Soferim 15). Official Judaism protested vainly. Not even Simon ben Shetah's fanatical execution of eighty women in Ascalon, evidently carried out with great difficulty because of Ascalon's independence, could stop a practice rooted in the conditions of the age."
43. Cf. Hansen, *Zauberwahn, Inquisition una Hexenprozess im Mittelalter,* p. 13.
44. M Sanhedrin IX 6. And see note 34, p. 362.

45. B Sanhedrin 8b and 80b. And see Allon, *Mehkarim Betoledot Yisrael*, Vol. I, p. 103.
46. B Sanhedrin 82a. And see note 25, p. 379.
47. *De Legibus Specialibus*, I 55.
48. Winter, *op. cit.*, pp. 74 ff, has put forward the theory that the particular mode of strangulation prescribed in the Mishna was contrived as a means of execution in secret: with the cessation of criminal jurisdiction in the year 70 (see note 43, p. 346), the Jewish courts in Roman-occupied Judaea exercised criminal jurisdiction clandestinely and had to avoid modes of execution which had to be carried out in public. "The methods formerly in use—burning, stoning, beheading—would have been a flagrant contravention of Imperial rule. Strangling and the similar procedure that went under the name of 'burning' provided convenient ways of escaping detection. Such was the reason why the rabbis, otherwise so meticulous in their compliance with the letter of the Torah, resorted to the expedient of execution by strangling, thereby bringing into their statute book a new form of inflicting capital punishment of which the Old Testament had known nothing" (Winter, *ibid.*). This theory presupposes that the cessation of criminal jurisdiction was the result of a Roman decree, and that the continuation of the exercise of such jurisdiction would have been contrary to Roman law; while under Jewish law nothing prevented the continuation of such jurisdiction. This is a misconception of both Roman and Jewish law: we have no information of any Roman decree to the effect that the criminal jurisdiction of local Jewish courts was to cease in the year 70; but, on the other hand, there is ample material in the Jewish sources to indicate that it was precisely under Jewish law that criminal jurisdiction ceased with, and because of, the destruction of the temple in that year: B Sanhedrin 52b; B Ketubot 30a; *et al.* Apart from the emergency measures already mentioned, the Jewish courts would no longer impose capital punishment—not because any Roman decree forbade it, but because their competence under their own law had ceased; they had nothing to hide from the Romans, because they would not unlawfully assume any jurisdiction from which they had been ousted by the only law they recognized as binding upon them. And see my "The Penology of the Talmud," at p. 61.
49. For a detailed description of the consequences of crucifixion from the medical point of view, and the possible causes of death thereby induced, see Blinzler, *Der Prozess Jesu*, pp. 185 ff.
50. B Sanhedrin 43a. This charitable custom reported of the "dear women of Jerusalem" has grown into law: Maimonides ruled that, when being led to his execution, the convict is to be given a drink of wine with incense, so that he may get intoxicated and insensible—and only then is he to be executed (Mishneh Torah, Hilkhot Sanhedrin 13,2).

51. Justinus, 22,7.
52. Mommsen, *op. cit.*, p. 918.
53. Suetonius, *Claudius*, 34.
54. Mommsen, *op. cit.*, p. 919.
55. *Apologiae*, 1,35; *Dialogus*, 97,3.
56. Hentig, *op. cit.*, Vol. I, pp. 255-256.
57. This theory attracted such novelists as George Moore (*The Brook Kerith*) and D. H. Lawrence (*The Man Who Died*).
58. Schonfield, *op. cit.*, pp. 155 ff.
59. *Autobiography*, 75.
60. Since the blood of a living person is pure, but the blood of the dead is impure and may not be touched by anyone who must, for sacrificial or other ritual purposes, keep himself pure, the question arose as to when the blood of the convict on the cross becomes impure—the exact time of his death on the cross not always being readily ascertainable: M Ohalot III 5. Maimonides, in his Commentary *ad loc.*, maintains that death would normally result from the loss of the blood that is dripping from the man on the cross; but the dripping might continue even after death. The same rule is found in T Ohalot IV 10 without express reference to crucifixion; and the question may, indeed, arise not only in the case of a man dying on the cross, but also in cases of stoning or slaying and other executions or deaths entailing the loss of blood.
61. M Shabbat VI 10.
62. B Shabbat 67a.
63. J Shabbat VI 9.
64. Maimonides, Mishneh Torah, Hilkhot Shabbat 6,10.
65. Maimonides, Commentary *ad* M Shabbat VI 10.
66. Plinius, *Historia Naturalis*, 28,36.
67. Hentig, *op. cit.*, Vol. I, p. 257.
68. B Sanhedrin 46b. And see note 12, p. 379.
69. Josephus, *Antiquities*, 17,10,10; *Wars*, 2,5,2.
70. Josephus, *Antiquities*, 20,5,2.
71. Josephus, *Wars*, 2,12,6.
72. *Ibid.*, 2,13,2.
73. *Ibid.*, 2,14,9.
74. *Ibid.*, 5,11,1.
75. M Yevamot XVI 3.
76. J Yevamot XVI 3.
77. B Yevamot 120b. And see Maimonides, Mishneh Torah, Hilkhot Geirushin 13,18.
78. Hentig, *op. cit.*, Vol. I, p. 257, n. 1.
79. Rashi (Shlomo Yitzhaki) *ad* B Yevamot 120a.
80. Tossaffot *ad* Yevamot 120a (*q.v.* "Ve'ein Me'idin").
81. T Gittin VII 1; B Gittin 70b.
82. B Gittin 70b.

83. Strauss, *op. cit.,* pp. 136–137; Craveri, *op. cit.,* pp. 395 ff.
84. Paulus, 3,5,8 and 5,21,4.
85. Mommsen, *op. cit.,* p. 918.
86. *Ibid.,* pp. 918 ff.
87. *Annales,* 14,48.
88. Hentig, *op. cit.,* Vol. I, p. 254.
89. *In Verrem,* 5,64.
90. Goguel, *op. cit.,* Vol. II, p. 535.
91. *Ibid.,* p. 539.
92. Winter, *op. cit.,* p. 106.
93. Olmstead, *op. cit.,* p. 241, relying on John 19:35.
94. Goguel, *op. cit.,* Vol. II, p. 535.
95. Nicholas de Lyra (fourteenth century), quoted by Goguel, *ibid.,* p. 543: "Talis enim potatio aceti mortem accelerat, ut dicunt aliqui."
96. B Keritot 18b.
97. Renan, *op. cit.,* p. 439.
98. Strauss, *op. cit.,* p. 136; Klausner, *Jesus von Nazareth,* p. 490. In the words of Craveri (*op. cit.,* p. 396): "We may dismiss Matthew's statement that the wine was mixed with gall and vinegar. Once again the insistence on fulfilling a Biblical prophecy produced nonsense."
99. Cf. Jer. 7:33 and 16:4: "Their carcasses shall be meat for the fowls of heaven and for the beasts of the earth." Or Ps. 79:2: "The dead bodies of thy servants have they given to be meat unto the fowls of the heaven, the flesh of thy saints unto the beasts of the earth."
100. For a talmudic tradition that the "pierced" one is indeed the Messiah, see B Sukkah 52a.
101. Strauss, *op. cit.,* pp. 143–144.
102. Goguel, *op. cit.,* Vol. II, p. 462.
103. *Ibid.,* p. 545, n. 1.
104. Suetonius, *Augustus,* 67.
105. Suetonius, *Tiberius,* 44.
106. Firmicus Maternus, 8,6; Victor, *Caesares,* 41. For further sources see Mommsen, *op. cit.,* p. 920, n. 6.
107. Eusebius, *Historia Ecclesiae,* V 21.
108. Keim, *op. cit.,* p. 347.
109. A person condemned to death was stripped of what he had on himself before execution, and his executioner had the right to claim it as his property: see Berger, *op. cit., q.v.* "Spolia," p. 712. Craveri (*op. cit.,* p. 398) writes that "the sharing out of his clothes among the soldiers on guard followed a Roman custom: the *lex de bonis damnatorum* required this division of the *spolia.*" To the same effect, see Strauss, *op. cit.,* p. 136; Goguel, *op. cit.,* Vol. II, p. 536; *et al.*
110. E.g., Blinzler, *Der Prozess Jesu,* p. 52.

342

111. Schonfield, *op. cit.*, pp. 165 ff. and *passim*.
112. Digesta, 48,24,1; Tacitus, *Annales*, 6,29.
113. Cicero, *Pro Rabirio Perduellionis Reo*, 5,16; Hentig; *op. cit.*, Vol. I, p. 254.
114. Mommsen, *op. cit.*, p. 989.
115. Ulpian, Digesta, 48,24,1; Paulus, Digesta, 48,24,3.
116. *Wars*, 4,5,2.
117. M Sanhedrin VI 5.
118. Semahot II 7 and 11.
119. J Kilayim IX 4; J Terumot VIII 10; M Shabbat XXIII 4; M Sanhedrin VI 5.

On Rejecting Treasures

By Abba Hillel Silver

Nor did the Jews reject "the still greater treasure which God was offering them" in the coming of Jesus of Nazareth. What they rejected was the Messianism of Jesus, Paul's onslaught on the Law, his gospel of redemption through the atoning death and resurrection of Jesus, and the doctrine of God incarnate in man.

How could it have been otherwise? As a Messianic movement Christianity failed, as have all such movements in Jewish history and in the history of other peoples. The new order of things, the Kingdom of God, which was expected hourly, did not materialize. It has not materialized in the two thousand years which have elapsed since that time. The appearance of Jesus did not mark the end of history, and the mission and teachings of the Christian Church today are not greatly influenced by considerations of his Second Coming. The postponed Parousia has long since lost its theologic import for considerable sections of Christendom, even as the coming of the Messiah has for considerable sections of Jewry.

The Jews did not reject the God concept of Jesus, for that was Jewish in essence and Jesus derived it from the Torah. "The New Testament adds nothing to the content of the idea of God which is not already present in the literature and faith of Israel. It is often argued that Jesus held a unique conception of God, by which is usually meant the fatherhood of God. We have seen, however, . . . that the divine characteristics which the

85

term 'fatherhood' denotes are fully evident in the Old Testament." [1]

The ethics of Jesus, too, were standard Jewish ethics except as regards nonresistance, nonconcern with the material needs of life, and the love of one's enemies—extreme doctrines not part of normative Jewish thought. These ideas were undoubtedly entertained by some apocalyptic groups in Jewry, but were certainly not of a nature to take one out of Judaism. Jesus' moral code, with the exceptions noted, was the code of Pharisaic Judaism in his day. The morality which the Church taught the heathen world—again with the exceptions noted—and which appealed so strongly to it, was Jewish morality, the healthy-minded, clean, and regenerative morality of Israel.

"In what way did the teaching of Jesus differ from that of his contemporaries?" query the editors of *The Beginnings of Christianity*, and they reply:

Not by teaching anything about God essentially new to Jewish ears The God of Jesus is the God of the Jews, about whom he says nothing that cannot be paralleled in Jewish literature. Nor was it in his doctrine as to the Kingdom of Heaven that Jesus differed markedly from the Jewish teachers. . . . The differences which are important concern three subjects of vital and controversial interest, resistance to the oppressors of Israel, the fate of the People of the Land, and the right observance of the Law. On the first point he conflicted with the tendency to rebellion which ultimately crystallized into the patriotic parties of the Jewish war in c.e. 66; with the second and third he conflicted with the Scribes.[2]

As we shall have occasion to show, the pacifism of Jesus was not directed specifically to the Zealots, the Sicarii, those who sought to rebel against Rome. It was a thoroughgoing doctrine of nonresistance applicable to all of life's situations and directed to all men. On this score Jesus did differ from the prevalent prophetic-Pharisaic teachings of Judaism, although his views were surely not unknown in certain mystically-minded groups in Israel: "And if anyone seeketh to do evil unto you, do well unto him, and pray for him and ye shall be redeemed of the Lord from

all evil." [3] It was not a doctrine which was calculated to arouse
any widespread active hostility in his day. It was not until the
war with Rome began a generation later that the advocacy of
pacifism became contentious and dangerous.

As regards the fate of the "People of the Land"—the *'Ame
Ha-arez*—the authors of *The Beginnings of Christianity* maintain
that Jesus offered the opportunity of entering the Kingdom of
God to publicans and sinners through a repentance which "could
be obtained rather by attention to principles than by . . . an extreme and meticulous attention to the details of the Law, such
as rendered repentance impossible to ordinary badly educated
men."

There appears to be some confusion here between the repentance of publicans and sinners and the relation of the *'Ame Ha-arez*
to matters of ritual purity and the tithes. The publicans and sinners were not necessarily the "People of the Land."

The publican was considered a moral outcast not because he
did not observe meticulously all the details of the Law. He was,
as a rule, an unscrupulous and pitiless taxgatherer, serving a hated
and usurping government, who shamefully mulcted the people
of their last extractable *prutah*. His repentance would be indicated only by a radical change in the conduct of his calling. This
is the advice which John gave to the publicans who came to him
to be baptized: "They said to him, Master, what shall we do?
And he said to them: Extract no more than that which is appointed you" (Luke 3:12–13). This is the advice which any
Rabbi of that day would have given them. It had nothing to do
with scrupulosity in the matter of the observance of the laws of
the Torah. If a man sinned he could readily repent and be forgiven. Restitution, wherever possible, and sincere contrition were
all that was required. A man did not have to be a scholar, a
saint, or a pietist to have his repentance accepted.

Jesus befriended publicans and sinners, and dined with them
in the hope of leading them on to repentance. This is the act of
a loving moral guide and teacher. He taught men, as he did in the
parable of the Pharisee and the Publican (Luke 18:9–14), the

346

superiority of sincere repentance over self-righteousness. This, too, is profoundly spiritual. It could hardly be maintained, however, that such attitudes and instructions were unknown and unshared by others, Rabbis and teachers, in his day. They could not have been subjects of controversy in the days of Hillel, a contemporary of Jesus and a leader of the Pharisees, who taught: "Be a disciple of Aaron, loving peace, and pursuing peace, loving all thy fellow-creatures, and drawing them nearer to the Torah." [4]

There is no mention in the New Testament of the technical term "People of the Land." The term "publicans and sinners" is not a synonym for it. There was no animosity between the "People of the Land" and the Pharisaic teachers in the days of Jesus.

The *'Am Ha-arez* is very often placed in the Mishna and the Tosefta in juxtaposition to the *Ḥaber* ("Associate" or "Fellow"). Both are technical terms. The *Ḥaberim* were the more exacting Jews, who formed themselves into associations or *Ḥaburot* for the sole purpose of being in a position to observe more strictly and with greater security the laws of ritual cleanness and of tithing. All those who did not join the *Ḥaburot*, whether priest or layman, were to that extent known as *'Ame Ha-arez*. In the eyes of the *Ḥaber* every Jew who did not obey the laws of Levitical purity and proper tithing in their highly developed form was an *'Am Ha-arez*. Such a man need not at all be a sinner or an ignorant man, or of a disposition inimical to the Sage or the Scribe. An *'Am Ha-arez* could be a teacher of the Law to the children of a *Ḥaber*.[5] The marriage of the son of a *Ḥaber* to the daughter of an *'Am Ha-arez*, or vice versa, is considered a matter of common occurrence.[6] The Tosefta relates that Rabban Gamaliel the Elder married his daughter to Simon b. Nathaniel—a priest and an *'Am Ha-arez*.[7] A *Ḥaber* and an *'Am Ha-arez* may belong to the same family. An *'Am Ha-arez* may at any time join a *Ḥaburah*, and the doors were always open to welcome him.[9]

The highly particularized laws of ritual cleanliness which entered so considerably into the daily life of the *Ḥaber* interfered perforce with close neighborly contacts with the 'Ame Ha-arez, but we have no reason to think that this led to animosity and bitterness—any more than we have reason to think, or any evidence to show, that the masses of the people resented the Pharisees, whose rigorous religious discipline they admired, even though they could not always follow their example. Josephus frequently emphasizes the fact that the Pharisees had great influence with the multitude,[10] that they were able greatly to persuade the body of the people,[11] and that the multitude sided with them against the Sadducees.[12]

The 'Ame Ha-arez included all the elements of the population who were not in Haburot. Just as the Haburot counted among their membership men from every walk of life, so did the 'Ame Ha-arez include men from all classes of society, the scholar and the priest, the merchant and the farmer, the rich and the poor. If Jesus defended the 'Ame Ha-arez, for which there is no evidence, he was certainly not defending the "common people" against any aristocracy either of wealth or of learning.

The bitter criticisms of the 'Ame Ha-arez which one finds occasionally in Rabbinic sources all date from the second century onward. The authorship of the statement, attributed to Hillel: "An 'Am Ha-arez cannot be a Hasid," is doubtful. In Abot De Rabbi Nathan [13] it is attributed to Akiba (2 c.), and we think with greater likelihood. A demoralization spread in the religious life of the people consequent upon the wars with Rome, the destruction of the Temple and the scattering of the priesthood, the Hadrianic persecutions and the closing of the schools and synagogues. Laxity in the observance of all laws set in. The Christian Church under Pauline inspiration was energetically pressing its attack on the Law generally. Pharisaic "legalism" became a controversial issue. The Rabbis therefore reached out for a stricter discipline and a greater stability in doctrine. Periods of great social decomposition create a desire among the faithful for a more vigorous discipline.

In the second century the center of the people's life was shifting from Judaea to Galilee. The religious laxity of the Galileans and their general ignorance of the Law were proverbial. Their religious standards and their educational facilities were inferior to those set by the Rabbis. The term 'Am Ha-arez now came to include not only those who did not live up to the strict observance of Levitical purity and tithes as the Haber understood it, but all those who disregarded moral and religious standards, who neither studied the Law nor taught it to their children, who would not cooperate in the heroic efforts of the Rabbis to save Judaism from total destruction.

All these conditions were non-existent in the days of Jesus. It is doubtful, therefore, whether the fate of the "People of the Land" could have been a subject of vital and controversial interest to him or to his contemporaries.[14]

On the matter of the right observance of the Law—the Sabbath law, for example, or the law of divorce—the attempts to draw a critical distinction between the teaching of Jesus on these subjects and that of the Rabbis have not proved convincing. On the subject of divorce, the Rabbis themselves differed as to the correct meaning of the Biblical law which grants a man the right to divorce his wife if "he found some unseemly thing in her" (Dt. 24:1). Jesus took the position also taken by Bet Shammai, that no man may divorce his wife, save on account of adultery. If Mark (10:1–12) represents the true position of Jesus, he seems to have been opposed to divorce altogether. This is doubtful. Matthew 19:9 appears to reflect his true position. Certainly the clear meaning of the law in the Torah was to make possible the annulment of an unsatisfactory marriage, not to prohibit divorce altogether.

As regards Sabbath observance—"that the Sabbath was made for man and not man for the Sabbath" (Mark 2:27)—this did not represent any break with the basic attitude of Pharisaic Judaism. In the second century of the Common Era, when Sabbath laws had been elaborated much further by the Rabbis and culminated in the thirty-nine chief categories of prohibited work, R. Jonathan b. Joseph (2 c.) employed the almost identical words of the Gospel: "The Sabbath is committed to your hands, not you to its hands." [15] Both the Gospel and the Rabbis were probably quoting a popular folk saying long in vogue among the people.

It was an established principle that in the case of danger to human life, in war, in sickness or accident, all the laws of the Sabbath may be suspended. Even when the danger was not clear, the Sabbath law was to be suspended. Quick action in its suspension is praised, delay condemned.[16] Jesus' controversy with the Pharisees over the charge that his disciples plucked ears of corn unlawfully on the Sabbath day and ate them because they were hungry (Mark 2:23-28) could have involved no real difference of opinion as regards the law. Such action could quite properly be justified under the law on the ground that it was necessary to preserve life. This is true also of the other Gospel references to the Sabbath. They are rather the reflections of the antinomist controversy, developed in later times by other men, which sought to establish that "the Son of man is Lord even of the Sabbath day" (Matt. 12:8), that he could abolish the Biblical law of the Sabbath altogether, as well as all other laws, and that "Christ has redeemed us from the curse of the law" (Gal. 3:13).

Some Jewish rigorists sought to make the Sabbath a day of total inactivity, even to the point of refusing to engage in self-defense on it. But long before the days of Jesus, during the Maccabean revolt, this strict view of Sabbath observance, which was probably held by the Ḥasidim, had been relaxed.[17] It was relaxed in other regards by the Sages and Rabbis of later generations in order to make it a joyous day as well as a holy day. Numerous legal fictions and simple expediencies like the 'Erub (enlarging the private domain within which certain activities on the Sabbath, otherwise prohibited, could be carried on) were evolved to liberalize the inflexible Biblical injunctions not to go out of one's place on the Sabbath (Ex. 16:29), not to kindle any fire in one's dwelling place (Ex. 35:3), and not to do any manner of work (Ex. 20:10). Here as in the case of Prosbul, which Hillel instituted as an economic necessity to circumvent the scriptural ordinance concerning the annulment of debts in the year of release (*Shmiṭah*)—"for he saw that people were unwilling to lend money to one another" [18]—the motive was not "to bind heavy burdens, hard to bear, and lay them on men's shoulders" (Matt. 23:4), but to lift what in the course of time had turned out to be heavy burdens.

This, too, was the case with the dissolution of vows. Scripture makes no provision for it. Vows, often made thoughtlessly or under great stress, turned out at times to be chains too heavy for men to bear. The Rabbis accordingly declared that under certain conditions a Sage or three private persons could declare a vow invalid and absolve the taker of the vow from its consequences. The teachers of the Mishna knew that "the rules about release from vows hover in the air and have naught [in Scripture] to support them"; [19] nevertheless they prescribed these rules to make it easier for men. Similarly the Rabbis declared: "There never has been a 'stubborn and rebellious son,' and there never will be" and "there never was a condemned city and never will be." [20] They surrounded these inoperative Biblical laws which prescribed the death penalty for the rebellious son (Dt. 21:18–21) and for the city beguiled into idolatry (Dt. 13:13–18) with so many restrictions that to all intents and purposes they abrogated them. Other Biblical laws such as the ordeal by means of the Bitter Waters for the woman suspected of adultery (Num. 5:11) and the rite of the breaking of the heifer's neck in the case of the slain found in the field (Dt. 21:1f.) were likewise abrogated.[21]

To return to the Sabbath. The Jewish people throughout the ages loved the Sabbath and welcomed it as a queen and bride. It was not a day of gloom and austerity. "The Holy One, blessed be He, said to Moses: I have a precious gift in my treasure-house, called the Sabbath, and I desire to give it to Israel." [22] "They who keep the Sabbath and hail it with delight will rejoice in Thy Kingdom. The people who sanctify the seventh day will be filled and delighted with Thy goodness. For Thou didst find pleasure in the seventh day and didst sanctify it. Thou didst call it the most delectable of days, a remembrance of creation itself." [23]

351

It is of interest to note that the Sabbath had a strong attraction for many non-Jews in the pagan world, and it retained its hold for centuries upon Judeo-Christians. "The Church had to fight against the translation of the Jewish Sabbath into the Christian Sunday for nearly the whole of the first millenium of its existence." [24]

The above considerations lead one to the conclusion that there were no such decisive differences on the subject of law between Jesus and his contemporaries as to make inevitable a complete break. The break was due to other causes and was made inevitable by other hands.

Certainly the Jews did not reject Jesus because of his alleged total abandonment of the Torah, for Jesus never abandoned the Law in whole or in part. On the contrary, he made it abundantly clear that he came not to abolish the Law and the prophets but to fulfill them. "Whoever then relaxes one of the least of these commandments and teaches men so, shall be called least in the Kingdom of Heaven; but he who does them and teaches them shall be called great in the Kingdom of Heaven" (Matt. 5:17–19). Jesus did not oppose even those laws which the Scribes and Pharisees developed out of the Torah and which the Sadducees, for example, opposed. He denounced these teachers because he believed that they were not practicing what they preached—and what true prophet and teacher in Israel ever failed to denounce pretense and hypocrisy? "The Scribes and the Pharisees sit in Moses' seat; so practice and observe whatever they tell you, but not what they do; for they preach, but do not practice" (Matt. 23:2–3). He denounced them for giving tithes of mint and dill and cinnamon but ignoring "the weightier matters of the law, justice and mercy and faith; these you ought to have done, without neglecting the others" (Matt. 23:23). Centuries before, Amos and Isaiah had uttered the selfsame diatribe. Jesus' attack was certainly no new note to Jews who in their synagogues on Sabbaths and holidays listened to the readings from the prophets. They knew that Isaiah had said: "Bring no more vain offerings . . . I cannot endure iniquity along with the solemn assembly"

(Is. 1:13), and that Hosea had proclaimed, "I desire mercy and not sacrifice, the knowledge of God, rather than burnt offerings" (Hosea 6:6).

Jesus taught the Law "as one who had authority" (Mark 1:22), that is, not as the Rabbis taught it; not, for example, as Hillel taught it, in accordance with a generally accepted technique of Halachah employed in the Schools, but as a prophet would have taught it, *mi-pi Ha-Geburah*, on direct authority received from God. All the apocalyptists spoke in the name of revelation. Jesus saw his rôle as that of a prophet announcing the approach of the Millennium. He accordingly did not feel himself restricted to the Pharisaic technique of interpreting the Torah. It was generally accepted that with the coming of Messianic times prophecy would return to Israel. In fact, the return of prophecy would be one of the signs heralding the coming of the Messiah. A prophet was assured privileges under the Law which were not possessed by any other religious teacher. No prophet, of course, could advocate the abrogation of any fundamental Biblical law, such as the prohibition of idolatry, without branding himself a false prophet, deserving of death. But a prophet had considerable leeway in other matters. A prophet whose credibility was well established could, for example, order the temporary suspension of any law of the Torah (short of idolatry) in order to meet an emergency, and the people were obligated to obey him.[25]

Jesus evidently sought to exercise this prophetic privilege, but only in his exposition of the Law, for he announced no new laws nor did he attempt to abrogate any existing law, and he never questioned the authority of the Torah as such. When he told his disciples, "Do you not see that whatever goes into a man from outside cannot defile him?" (Mark 7:18), he was directing himself specifically to the criticism made by the Pharisees against some of his disciples who ate with hands unwashed, thus violating "a tradition of the elders" (Mark 7:2-3). The law of the washing of the hands was not a Biblical law and was not in common practice among the people. The inference drawn in Mark that "thus he declared all foods clean" (7:19) is clearly unwarranted and is not mentioned in Matthew 15 where the episode is also recorded. It is out of keeping with Jesus' consistent and positive attitude toward the Law. Mark here reflects the later Pauline influence. This seems to be the case also with the claim, attributed to Jesus, to forgive sins (Mark 2:5–12; Matt. 9:2–8). This has no basis in Jewish law. The core of Pauline Christianity was Jesus' rôle in the forgiveness of sin—by his death and during his life. This authority came with the possession of the Holy Spirit. According to John, Jesus bestowed the authority to forgive sins also upon the apostles, after he had breathed the Holy Spirit on them (John 20:23). Jesus' assumption of the rôle of prophet certainly did not please the Rabbis, but it was not on that score that the Jewish people rejected him.

The Jews would certainly not reject Jesus on the strength of his conception of the rôle of Israel in history. "Salvation is from the Jews" (John 4:22), he told the woman of Samaria. The charge which he gave to his disciples was specifically limited to Jews: "Go nowhere among the Gentiles, and enter no town of the Samaritans, but go rather to the lost sheep of the house of Israel. And preach as you go, saying: 'The Kingdom of Heaven is at hand' " (Matt. 10:5–7). His mission was exclusively to the Jews. This was a deviation from the prophetic tradition. The prophets of Israel never restricted their prophecies to the Jewish people. "I appoint you a prophet to the nations," was the word of the Lord to Jeremiah. "See, I have set you this day over nations and kingdoms" (Jer. 1:10). (The text of Matt. 28:19, "Go therefore and make disciples of all nations, baptizing them in the name of the Father and the Son and the Holy Spirit," is clearly of a later time.)

Jesus would not heal the daughter of the Canaanite woman who pleaded with him. He would not answer her. He was sent only to the lost sheep of the house of Israel. "It is not fair to take the children's bread and throw it to the dogs"—a sentiment which cannot be paralleled for severity in the whole literature of Judaism. It was only after the distraught mother pleaded,

"Yes, Lord, yet even the dogs eat the crumbs that fall from their master's table," that Jesus recanted: "O woman, great is your faith! Be it done for you as you desire" (Matt. 15:21–28).

It has been correctly observed "that Christianity in the first century achieved a synthesis between the Greco-Oriental and the Jewish religions in the Roman Empire." [26] Whether this synthesis was actually achieved in the first century or somewhat later is not of great moment. Three stages may be noted in its consummation—in the transition from Judaism to Christianity. The first stage is Jesus and the gospel of the Kingdom, the second is Paul and the piacular sacrifice on the cross, the third is the Gospel of John and the Word become flesh. Each was distinctive and all three were ultimately merged, though not without great controversy and confusion, in the final orthodox version.

Paul is the bridge between the Judaic gospel of Jesus concerning the coming of the Kingdom of God and the urgent need for repentance, and the thoroughly Hellenistic Logos gospel of John, wherein the Word which was God became flesh in Jesus, the Son of God, one with the Father, who was sent by God to overcome the dominion of Satan in the world and, having accomplished his mission, returned to God.

"When Jesus came into Galilee, spreading the gospel of the Kingdom of God and saying the time is fulfilled and the Kingdom of God is at hand" (Mark 1:14), he was voicing the opinion widely held that the year 5000 in the Creation calendar which was to usher in the sixth millennium—the age of the Kingdom of God—was "at hand." [27] Induced by the popular chronology of the day, the mass of the people came to believe that they were on the threshold of the Millennium. The advent of the Millennium carried along with it the appearance of the Messiah and his appointed activities. Jesus' essential mission was messianic, and he sought to save men from the "birth throes" of the messianic times by calling them to swift and thoroughgoing repentance so that they may be found worthy to enter the Kingdom.

There wás nothing in Jesus' doctrine of repentance and the approaching Kingdom of God which the Jews of his day needed to reject in defense of their faith. There was nothing in it which endangered their faith. There were apocalyptically-minded Pharisaic Jews who believed that the order of the world was about to change and that they were on the threshold of the Millennium. There were those who did not believe it. It was not an issue involving a fundamental creed. To those who did believe in the approaching cosmic catastrophe, thoroughgoing repentance and austerities would logically recommend themselves.

Because there were many at that time who were expecting the coming of the Messiah, or his forerunner, to announce the beginning of a new age, the generation abounded in Messianic movements, each one fraught with grave political consequences for the peace of the nation. The Roman imperium was ruthless in the suppression of all such messianic claimants because they were suspected of seeking the overthrow of Roman authority and the reestablishment of Jewish independence. The Jewish Messiah, when he appeared, would be proclaimed King of the Jews.

When Jesus was put to death, his faithful followers were confronted with a dreadful dilemma and embarrassment. It was to them a crushing catastrophe. Their master had been arrested, tried, condemned, and crucified. Did that not prove that he was not the true Messiah, that he was no different from the many others who had recently appeared as pretenders to that rôle and who had been liquidated by the Romans? If Jesus were the true Messiah, why did he die? Was not his mission a failure?

Two answers were soon supplied by the faithful. He died, it was true, but he was soon resurrected. He was seen alive after his entombment. Where is he now? He ascended to heaven and will soon reappear on earth to complete his mission and usher in the Millennium.

But why did he die? In order to atone by his death for the Original Sin with which mankind was fatefully burdened since Adam. Jesus had called upon men to repent of their own personal sins in preparation for the Kingdom, but there was also a collective sin, it was argued, the primordial sin of Adam, in which all men shared and for which no individual could atone. It was necessary for the Messiah, who had been sent by God, to take upon himself the universal sin of mankind, and by his death to atone for it so that the tragic debt would be paid for all time.

This was Paul's contribution to the theologic complex of Christianity—vicarious expiation, for which Biblical proof was soon sought and discovered in Isaiah 53. It was the second step in the development of Christian theology. With Judaism, Torah was central; with Jesus the Kingdom; with Paul it was the redemptive rôle of Jesus.

The third step was taken in the Diaspora in the course of the missionary preaching about the resurrected redeemer to the Roman world. Here the Hellenistic idea of the Logos was widely current both among Jews and among pagans—the Logos, the Word of God, the instrument by which God, the Transcendant, worked His will in the world. Logos took on many degrees of personification, from what might be called a pure abstraction among the Jews to a God subaltern and co-worker with the Supreme Deity. It was necessary to come to terms with this Logos idea, whether as attribute, instrument, or divine personality, if the Christian gospel was to be widely accepted. This fusing or reconciliation was achieved and is reflected in the Gospel of John. "In the beginning was the Word . . ."

This was the third stage. Jesus became the Logos, the incarnate Word of God, the God made flesh. Orthodox Christianity, after many bitter disputes, finally accepted and fused all three doctrines into one—the historic messianic rôle of Jesus, the resurrection and the atonement death of Jesus preached by Paul, and the Incarnation as reflected in the Fourth Gospel.

Paul marks the dividing line between Judaism and Christianity. He was a Jew of the Diaspora, a rigorous monotheist, and a bitter foe of all forms of idolatry. He had observed the ceremonial law of Judaism, but reluctantly, and at a later stage abandoned it and "died to the Law" (Gal. 2:19). His final disillusionment came when he saw that some of the very champions of the Law among Judeo-Christians, like Peter and Barnabas, were acting insincerely and inconsistently in the matter (Gal. 2:11–14).

Paul claims to have been extremely zealous, before his conversion, for the traditions of his fathers. But he must have been impatient with the Law even before he was converted or he could not have spoken of the Law as "a curse" from which men were finally redeemed by the atonement of Jesus. How could the vision of the resurrected Jesus on the road to Damascus have made him such a bitter and violent enemy of the Law? Certainly Jesus was not one. There must have been other Jews, even before the days of Paul, especially in the Hellenistic Diaspora, who fretted under the restraints of the Mosaic ceremonial code, who found the Law a serious hindrance to their free social and economic contacts with the non-Jewish world, and who in their hearts preferred a purely spiritual Judaism which was based solely on faith in the One God of Abraham, and not cumbered with the legislation which Moses ordained. But they had no authority upon which to base their views such as Paul found in Jesus the Messiah who by his appearance ushered in a new age and a new dispensation. In any event, it is clear that Paul wished to bypass Moses and the covenant of Sinai altogether and return to the original covenant of Abraham, to the universal monotheistic faith, which all the nations of the earth could share. Paul wanted to reject the Torah, but he could not reject it outright. The Torah was needed to substantiate and bear witness to Jesus and to his rôle in history. Paul therefore appealed from Moses to Abraham—from the Sinai covenant, which in his view was a restrictive, negative, and temporal covenant, to the covenant of Abraham which was universal and eternal.

Five hundred years later Mohammed adopted the same line of Paul in rejecting both Judaism and Christianity. He, too, went back to the universal monotheism of Abraham. To quote from a recent study:

He [Mohammed] stated that he did not come to abrogate the Old and New Testaments, but rather to fulfill the spirit and letter of the Book. He maintained that Abraham was neither a Jew nor a Christian, but the true expounder of ethical monotheism, and that the Koran, as revealed to him by Allah, through the angel Gabriel, embodied the true revelation which the Jews and the Christians had failed to follow. Tracing his genealogy to Abraham through his son Ismael, Mohammed claimed to be the rightful heir to Abraham's high rank.[28]

The Law which was given to Moses at Sinai was, according to Paul, a punishment for the sins of the people of Israel. The Ten Commandments were "a dispensation of condemnation." Any written code of laws kills; only the spirit gives life (II Cor. 3:6). The Torah is such a written code. It is not merely the law of the Rabbis which Paul condemns. Actually, the law of the Rabbis was not yet as extensively developed in his day as in the subsequent centuries. It is the laws of the Torah which he principally had in mind. "Where there is no law, there is no transgression" (Rom. 4:15).

At times Paul argues that while the Law itself is not sin, it suggests and arouses sin. "If it had not been for the Law, I should not have known sin" (Rom. 7:7). Paul here has in mind not merely the ceremonial law, but the ethical law as well. "I should not have known what it is to covet if the law had not said, 'You shall not covet' " (ibid.). At other times Paul argues that the Law is too weak to safeguard against the promptings of the flesh, the evil inclinations, within him (Rom. 8:3). At best the Law was a regrettable interlude, a custodian until the true faith was revealed. "Now that faith has come, we are no longer under a custodian" (Gal. 3:25).

Paul was not interested in the healing miracles and exorcisms which others reported about Jesus and which are found so plentifully in the Gospels. He shows little interest in the human career of Jesus altogether. The sole miracle which profoundly stirred and affected his life was the miracle of the resurrection. He knows nothing of Jesus as God incarnate, and nothing of the

Virgin Birth. He was especially eager to preach his gospel to the Gentiles and to convert them to the faith of "Christian" monotheism, thereby erasing all distinctions between Jew and non-Jew according to the promise made to Abraham: "in you all the families of the earth will be blessed" (Gen. 12:3).

The Law, as Paul saw it, was *the* stumbling block to the conversion of the Gentile world to the true faith. The demands of the Law—Sabbath observance, circumcision, the dietary regulations, the laws of purity—were sufficiently exacting to discourage many from accepting the faith. His passionate devotion to the resurrected Christ and the salvation which he was convinced flowed from him for all mankind, and his proselytizing zeal, made him bitterly intolerant of the Law. "Christ is the end of the Law" (Rom. 10:4). The covenant of Sinai is Hagar, bearing children for slavery. The covenant of Abraham is Sarah. "Cast out the slave and her son!" (Gal. 4:30)

Nevertheless, Paul was prepared to practice the Law himself, if by so doing he might win over those under the Law to the true faith (I. Cor. 9:2). For this reason he advised the faithful to avoid eating of food which might have been sacrificed to idols, a very grave matter in the eyes of law-abiding Jews, not because he regarded the act itself as unlawful, for "all things are lawful," but so as not to give offense and make the work of conversion more difficult (I Cor. 10:23–33). The faithful should not make an issue of food or Sabbath observance, of clean or unclean, or of circumcision, but "pursue what makes for peace" (Rom. 14:13f.).

Paul was thus ambivalent on the subject of the Law, even as he was on the election of Israel, his other troublesome theologic inconsistency. Paul assigned to the Jewish people a special rôle in the new dispensation. Like Jesus, he too evidently believed that "salvation is from the Jews." "God has not rejected this people whom he foreknew" (Rom. 11:2). "As regards the gospel they are enemies of God for your sake: but as regards election they are beloved for the sake of their forefathers. For the gifts and the call of God are irrevocable" (Rom. 11:28–29). It is an advantage to be born a Jew. "Then what advantage has the Jew? . . .

Much in every way. To begin with, the Jews are entrusted with the oracles of God. What if some were unfaithful? Does their faithlessness nullify the faithfulness of God?" (Rom. 3:1–3). "They are Israelites, and to them belong the sonship, the glory, the covenants, the giving of the Law, the worship and the promises; to them belong the patriarchs, and of their race, according to the flesh, is the Messiah" (Rom. 9:4–5).

The universalism of Paul was not free of local patriotism. Israel "after the flesh" was still the chosen people. At times there appears to be no contradiction in his mind between a national faith and its universal mission. At other times there decidedly is.

The total effect of Paul's disquisitions on the Law and his ambivalence was to denigrate its sanctity in the eyes of assimilation-minded Jews and to nullify it completely as far as Gentiles seeking conversion were concerned.

There was violent resistance among the early Judeo-Christian brotherhoods of Palestine and elsewhere to Paul's attitude toward the Law. They looked upon the Law—the Torah—as sacred and eternally binding upon themselves and their descendants, and not as a punishment but a privilege. The Jewish-Christian Ebionites, according to Irenaeus (2 c.), rejected Paul because he was an apostate from the Law.[29] The early Christians among the Jews saw no contradiction between their loyalty to traditional Judaism and their belief in the Messiahship of Jesus. They were aware of no new covenant or dispensation. Jewish Christians who observed the Sabbath and the festivals, circumcision, the dietary laws, and the laws of purity persisted well into the third century. Orthodox Christianity attacked them bitterly. "It is monstrous," wrote Ignatius (2 c.), "to talk of Jesus Christ and to practice Judaism."[30] Some Rabbis, on the other hand, like Simon the Pious (3 c.) and Simon ben Lakish (3 c.), defended these Judeo-Christians, and did not wish to exclude them from the Jewish community.[31]

The "burden of the Law" was regarded by loyal Jews not as a burden at all, but as a wholesome discipline. The purpose of the Law was to increase personal holiness [32] and to refine the spirit of man,[33]—not to make him aware of his inability to fulfil it and thus force him to rely exclusively upon grace and redemption. God wished to increase the merits of Israel, wherefore he multiplied for them laws and commandments.[34] The Jews found the Torah and its statutes and ordinances "perfect, reviving the soul; rejoicing the heart . . . enlightening the eyes . . . more to be desired than gold, even much fine gold; sweeter also than honey and the honeycomb" (Ps. 19:8–10).

With everlasting love hast Thou loved the House of Israel, Thy people. Torah and commandment, statute and judgment hast Thou taught us. Therefore, O Lord our God, when we lie down and when we rise up we will meditate on Thy statutes. We will rejoice in the words of Thy Torah and in Thy commandment forever; for they are our life and the length of our days. Blessed art Thou, who lovest Thy people, Israel.[35]

The Jewish people—Pharisees, Sadducees, and Essenes alike—could not have accepted Paul's conception of the Law under any circumstances. It was utterly alien to them, as it was to the Jewish-Christians of Palestine, as it would have been to Jesus himself, who did not oppose the Law at all and who did not seek to abrogate it for the sake of making proselytes among the Gentiles. Paul's position cut at the very roots of their faith. There has always been a debate among Jews as to the extent to which one is free to interpret the Written Law and by what technique, and whether the Oral Law is binding and to what extent. Orthodox, Conservative, and Reform Jews have continued the debate to this day. But no organized Jewish religious group ever maintained that the Law could be dispensed with altogether, that the Law was a curse or that faith alone was sufficient.

In fact, it was the Law around which the faithful in Israel rallied in the disastrous days which followed the destruction of the Temple and the collapse of the state, and again during the savage Hadrianic persecutions. The spiritual chaos of those times, the crushed and beaten morale of the people, the danger of complete prostration, are nowhere so movingly portrayed as in the Apocalypse of Baruch (2 c. c.e.), written contemporaneously with some parts of the New Testament; and its exalted faith, rising from amidst the ruins, reflects the indestructible strength and nobility of a Judaism based on Torah:

> "For the shepherds of Israel have perished,
> And the lamps which gave light are extinguished,
> And the fountains have withheld their stream whence
>   we used to drink,
> And we are left in darkness,
> And amid the trees of the forest,
> And the thirst of the wilderness."
> And I answered and said unto them:
> "Shepherds and lamps and fountains come from the Law:
> And though we depart, yet the Law abides.
> If therefore you have respect to the Law,
> And are intent upon wisdom,
> A lamp will not be wanting
> And a shepherd will not fail,
> And a fountain will not dry up." [36]

One is forced to the conclusion that not all the Jews who lived in the century in which Paul and other Christian antinomists preached regarded the Law as a curse! Many looked upon it lovingly, as a blessing and a refuge, even as centuries before it had been for the sorely afflicted "a lamp to my feet and a light to my path" (Ps. 119:105). One hundred and seventy-six verses are devoted in this psalm to an exuberant laudation of the Torah.

The Christian Church itself soon came to have laws—ceremonial laws—of its own, and in time they were codified into canons of religious and ecclesiastical practices—baptism, the eucharist, the sacraments, communion feasts, fasts and Sunday laws, penance and unction, priesthood and confession, ecclesiastical regulations and privileges, tithes, pilgrimages and shrines, rituals, incense and vestments—an Halachah quite as meticulous and burdensome as that of the Scribes and the Pharisees. The Church, too, came to acknowledge the importance of canons in the regulation of faith and discipline. The great experiment in building a Church on pure faith did not succeed!

Certainly, no one who is acquainted with the determined and persistent struggle for the pure monotheistic faith among the people of Israel since the days of Moses and the Prophets could have assumed for a moment then or since that Judaism would find lodgement for the concept of a God such as one finds in the Fourth Gospel, a God who came down to earth, assumed human form, and suffered death for the salvation of men—a doctrine which Jesus himself never taught. These ideas were known to the Jews long before the time of Jesus, and had been rejected by them. They were popular and current in the ancient world. As Professor Murray correctly states:

The idea of an "only begotten son" of God was regular in the Orphic systems, and that of a son of God by a mortal woman, conceived in some spiritual way, and born for the saving of mankind, was at least as old as the fifth century B.C. . . . That this Saviour "suffered and was buried" is common to the Vegetation or Year religions, with their dying and suffering gods; . . . That after the descent to Hades He should arise to judge both the quick and the dead is a slight modification of the ordinary Greek notion, according to which the Judges were already seated at their work, but it may have come from the Saviour religions. The belief in God as a Trinity, or as One substance with three "personae," . . . is directly inherited from Greek speculation. . . .[37]

Judaism had resisted these notions for centuries.

It is understandable that Fourth Gospel ideas should have found acceptance among those in the pagan world who had long been habituated to them through mystery religions, or among pagan proselytes to Judaism to whom such ideas would appear neither strange nor startling and among whom the Christian propaganda actually made its first converts. These concepts might not be strongly resisted by those who, in the Hellenistic world, entertained the current ideas of a Logos, the Word made flesh, the Incarnation of divine wisdom and the mediator between God and man. They certainly could not be accepted by Torah-trained Jews to whom the concept of the unity of God, simple and undifferentiated, was the very bedrock of their faith.

364

The Jewish people could not but reject such a doctrine unless it were prepared to abandon the most treasured and essential conviction for which it had struggled through the centuries and of which it believed itself to be the covenanted guardian and spokesman to the world. It could not accept a renewed mythologizing of God, which it had resisted for a thousand years, even though the concept of a born, dying, and resurrected God might now be presented as a metaphysical idea and not as a concrete event which took place on a specific date in history or as a trinitarian conception of monotheism. Judaism could find no room in its monotheism for the concept of Jesus as "Son of God, born of the Virgin Mary" (The Apostles' Creed), or as "Very God of Very God" (Nicene Creed), or as "Perfect God and Perfect Man" (Athanasian Creed).

It was not the rejection of the Rabbinic law which made of Christianity a Gentile faith; the Sadducees had also rejected it, and centuries later, the Karaites, who remained, however violently opposed, a minority within the borders of Judaism. Though some Rabbinic authorities would have nothing to do with the Karaites, others like Maimonides urged that they be treated as erring brothers and ministered to as members of the household of Israel. It was the rejection of *all* authority to the Law and the idea of a God incarnate which placed Christianity outside the bounds of Judaism. Here was the fork of the road!

Judaism rejected no treasure. Judaism rejected nothing in the teachings of Jesus which, if accepted, would have added one cubit to its stature or in any way reenforced its monotheism or its moral code. It was to the Gentile world that Christianity made its monumental contribution. It was upon the Gentile world that Christianity, profiting from the momentum of the frontal attack upon polytheism and idolatry which Judaism in its proselytizing activity had been carrying on, and equipped with much of Judaism's lofty and cleansing moral code, made its powerful impact. Where Judaism in its proselytizing efforts could attain only a limited success because it would not yield in its requirements for full acceptance of the Law on the part of those who sought conversion, Christianity, making no such requirements, scored heavily. Christianity was able to bring large sections of the Gentile world—then in the throes of a prolonged spiritual crisis resulting from the breakdown of its ancient beliefs and the failure of its ethical philosophies to satisfy the spiritual needs of men —to a vision of a noble faith and a clean way of life which it derived from Judaism. In so doing, Christianity contributed mightily to the spiritual progress of mankind. One cannot but salute in reverence and admiration its many teachers and leaders who through their devotion, courage, and often through their martyrdom, carried the message of their faith through the centuries to the far-flung corners of the earth.

Maimonides and other Jewish spokesmen regarded Jesus as well as Mohammed as divine instruments in preparing the way for mankind's universal conversion to faith in the one true God. Maimonides wrote: "All these teachings of Jesus the Nazarene and the Ishmaelite [Mohammed] who arose after him were intended to pave the way for the coming of the King Messiah and to prepare the whole world to worship God together as one." [38]

But it was not the pristine monotheism of Judaism which Christianity in its missionary zeal conveyed to the Gentile world, nor exclusively its sturdy, practical, this-worldly ethics. It was a syncretistic faith—strongly salvationist in character, with a major accent on the promise of immortality—far in advance of anything in the Greco-Roman world, but not the uncompromising monotheism of Judaism. Its moral idealism excelled anything the ancient world had to offer, but it was unlike Judaism in that it was oriented toward a Kingdom not of this world.

Thus a mighty stream of influence flowed out of Judaism at the beginning of the common era and, dividing from it, watered benignly many lands and cultures. Other streams were in time to flow out of it and, again dividing, were to pursue their independent courses through history. But the river which is Judaism, replenished by the ageless springs of its own inspiration, continued to follow its own course to its appointed destiny known only to God.

[1] Otto J. Baab, *The Theology of the Old Testament* (1949), p. 270.

[2] F. J. Foakes Jackson and Kirsopp Lake, *The Beginnings of Christianity*, I, 288–289.

[3] *Test. of Joseph* 18:2 (2 c. B.C.).

[4] Abot 1:12.

[5] Tosef. Demai II, 18.

[6] *Ibid.*, II, 5, 16, 17.

[7] Tosef. 'Ab. Zar. III, 10.

[8] Demai 1:9.

[9] Tosef. Demai 2:3, 5; Bakorot 30b.

[10] Josephus, *Antiquities*, XIII, 11:5.

[11] *Ibid.*, XVIII, 1:3.

[12] *Ibid.*, XVIII, 4.

[13] Ed. Schechter, p. 82.

[14] See the author's essay "The 'Am Ha-arez in Soferic and Tannaitic Times," *Hebrew Union College Monthly*, Dec. 1914, Jan. 1915, Feb. 1915.

[15] Yoma 85b.

[16] J. Yoma 8:5.

[17] Josephus, *op. cit.*, XII, 8:3.

[18] Giṭ. 36a.

[19] Ḥag. 1:8.

[20] San. 71a.

[21] Sotah 9:9.

[22] Shab. 10b.

[23] From the Sabbath Day Ritual in the Prayer Book.

[24] A. Marmorstein, *Studies in Jewish Theology* (1950), p. 224.

[25] Maimonides, *Hilch. Yesode Ha-Torah*, 9:3; San. 90a.

[26] Jackson and Lake, *op. cit.*, I, Prologomena I (1939), Preface, p. vii.

[27] See the author's *Messianic Speculation in Israel* (1927), pp. 6, 16f.

[28] Abraham I. Katsh, *Judaism in Islam* (1954), p. xvi.

[29] *Against Heresies*, I, 26.

[30] *To the Magnesians*, X, 3.

[31] See Marmorstein, *op. cit.*, pp. 197f.

[32] *Mechilta*, III, 15.

[33] Gen. R. 44:1.

[34] Mak. 3:16.

[35] From the Prayer Book—a prayer composed probably before the common era.

[36] *Baruch*, 77, 13–16, ed. R. H. Charles.

[37] Gilbert Murray, in *The History of Christianity in the Light of Modern Knowledge* (1929), pp. 77–78.

[38] *Mishneh Torah, Hilch. Melachim*, Chap. 11 (ed. Rome, c. 1480).

Jesus vis-à-vis Paul, Luther, and Schweitzer

By Walter Kaufmann

The problem of happiness is scarcely considered in the Old Testament. Man is destined to be free. Whether liberty will make him happy is somehow beside the point. What matters is God's will, God's challenge.

In the New Testament, each man's overruling concern with his eternal happiness — his salvation — is central and defines the whole milieu. A similar concern had earlier found expression in Buddhism, also in the Orphic religion that probably influenced Plato's later thought. The change in the climate of opinion in the Near East between the age of the prophets and the time of Jesus has been noted above (§§ 39-40). Nation upon nation had lost its independence and its cultural initiative. Otherworldliness had spread, and millions had come to accept this world with resignation, hoping for the next. The era that, reeling from climax to climax, had witnessed Genesis and Deuteronomy, Hebrew prophecy and Attic tragedy, Greek temples and Thucydides, was long since drowned in Alexander's conquests and unprecedented syncretism. All kinds of mystery religions merged their dreams

219

of supernatural salvation. Large masses of people felt that in this world nothing was left to live for.

Jesus did not have to persuade his listeners that they ought to be concerned about salvation, any more than the Buddha did. They came to hear him because he was offering a way. Conversely, when most men do not worry about salvation, Jesus' message is not easily made relevant to them.

According to the Gospels, Jesus' conception of salvation was radically otherwordly, and opposed to any this-worldly messianic hopes — not only to chauvinistic dream of glory but also to swords beaten into plowshares and liberty and justice for all. The "kingdom is not of this world" (John 18:36). The perspective of the prophets is reversed. They, too, had taught humility and love, but not this preoccupation with oneself. The accent had been on the neighbor and the stranger, the orphan, the widow, and the poor. Social injustice cried out to be rectified and was no less real because it meant a lack of love and a corruption of the heart. Man was told to love others and to treat them justly — for their sake, not for his own, to escape damnation. To the Jesus of the Gospels, social injustice as such is of no concern. Heaven and hell-fire have been moved into the center.

But does not Jesus give a central place to the commandment "Love your neighbor as yourself"? It has often been said that this is the essential difference between the New Testament and the Old. Yet this commandment is taken from the Law of Moses, and the New Testament itself designates this as the ground that Jesus and the Pharisees had in common. Consider what may well be the most famous parable in the Gospels — the Good Samaritan (Luke 10). "Behold a lawyer stood up to put him to the test, saying: Teacher, what shall I do to inherit eternal life? He said to him: What is written in the Law? How do you read? And he answered: You shall love the Lord your God with all your heart, and with all your soul, and with all your strength, and with all your mind; and your neighbor as yourself. And he said to him: You have answered right; do this, and you will live." Nor is there any disagreement about the point of the parable. Having related the different conduct of priest, Levite, and Samaritan, Jesus asks his interrogator: "Which of these three, do you think, proved neighbor to the man who fell among the robbers? He said: The one who showed mercy on him."

One may doubt the authenticity of this parable. If Jesus had really told it, why should three of the evangelists have omitted it entirely? But if Jesus never told it, it would be easy to understand why, in time, it should have been attributed to him. This consideration is certainly not conclusive; and what matters here is that, in telling the story, the third Gospel underlines the fact that, in questions of this sort, Jesus did not differ with the Pharisees; certainly they did not uphold the conduct of the priest and the Levite in the parable.

"Teacher, what shall I do to inherit eternal life?" The concern with the life to come was by then characteristic of much Jewish thinking. But the Jesus of the Gospels went much further in his otherwordliness than the Pharisees did, not to speak of the Sadducees. Salvation became with him the central motive for loving one's neighbor.

Consider the rich man who, according to Luke (18:18 ff.), asked Jesus the identical question. To him, Jesus cites five of the Ten Commandments before adding: "One thing you still lack. Sell all you have and distribute it to the poor, and you will have treasure in heaven; and come, follow me." It is no longer the poor that require love and justice; it is the giver who is to accumulate treasure in heaven. The social order, with which Moses and the prophets were centrally concerned, counts for nothing; the life to come is everything. If what truly matters is treasure in heaven, what do the poor gain from what they are given?

If, to gain salvation, we must give up all property and follow Jesus, then either salvation requires the complete disintegration of the social order, or salvation is denied to the vast majority of men and restricted to a few. The Jesus of the Gospels was clearly prepared to accept both consequences: he was willing to countenance the disappearance of any social framework and resigned to see only a few saved.

To begin with the last point, Jesus, according to all three Synoptic Gospels, actually reassured his disciples: "If any one will not receive you or listen to your words, shake off the dust from your feet as you leave that house or town. Truly, I say to you, it shall be more tolerable on the day of judgment for the land of Sodom and Gomorrah than for that town" (Matthew 10:14 f.; cf. 11:24; Mark 6:11; Luke 10:10 ff.). Far from being an isolated dictum, the prospect of damnation is one of the central motifs of the Gospels.

Returning once more to the story of the rich man: at the end, those who heard Jesus' words ask him, understandably: "Then who can be saved? But he said: What is impossible with men is possible with God." Here it is suggested that salvation is a gift of divine grace. Inequality is instituted by God: some are chosen, others rejected.

Indifference to the social order is expressed in Jesus' next words: "Truly, I say to you, there is no man who has left house or wife or brothers or parents or children, for the sake of the kingdom of God, who will not receive manifold more in this time, and in the world to come eternal life." If one wants a briefer formulation for this rigorous indifference to the social and political realm, there is the famous "Render to Caesar what is Caesar's" (Matthew 22:21; Mark 12:17; Luke 20:25).

This phrase should be understood in its historic context. The question is one of subordination or resistance to a foreign oppressor — a perennial issue. And the answer is: oppression is unimportant; "render to God what is God's"; the social sphere is not God's and merits no concern.

Jesus' association with the publicans illustrates this point, too. The publicans, who collected taxes for the Roman conquerors, were the quislings of their day. To Jesus, this was utterly irrelevant. The one thing needful was salvation.

Only an age in which salvation had all but lost meaning could misconstrue Jesus' moral teachings the way liberal Protestantism did. The morality of the Sermon on the Mount, too, is centered not in the neighbor but in salvation. Each of the nine Beatitudes in the beginning announces a reward, and they conclude with the promise: "Rejoice and be glad, for your reward is great in heaven." In the Sermon itself, promises and threats alternate continually: "shall be called great in the kingdom of heaven"; "will never enter the kingdom of heaven"; "judgment"; "hell fire"; "your whole body should be cast into hell"; "if you love those who love you, what reward have you?"; "will reward you"; "have their reward"; "will reward you"; "your heavenly Father also will forgive you"; "neither will your Father forgive your trespasses"; "they have their reward"; "will reward you"; and more in the same vein.

The point is clearly stated both in the middle and at the end. "Do not lay up for yourselves treasures on earth, where moth and rust consume, and where thieves break in and steal, but lay up for yourselves treasures in heaven, where neither moth nor rust consumes and where thieves do not break in and steal." At the conclusion, those who do as told are called "wise," and those who do not are called "foolish." Actually, *phronimos* might be translated as "prudent" and *moros* as "moronic."

Moses and the prophets had also often referred to the future, though categorical demands were more characteristic of their style and pathos. But the future they envisaged was a social future; for Micah and Isaiah it even involved the whole of humanity. The Jesus of the Gospels appeals to each man's self-interest.

This may strike some modern readers as paradoxical because liberal Protestantism has persuaded millions that the essence of Christianity is altruism and self-sacrifice. But our analysis may help to explain why so many people take it for granted that morality depends on the belief in God and immortality. It is not uncommon to hear people admit that if they lost their belief in a life after death, no reason would remain for them to be moral. In fact, they cannot see why anyone lacking this belief should be moral; and this accounts in large measure for the widespread horror of atheism.

In the Gospels, one is to lose oneself only to find *oneself*. Sacrifices are demanded, but only of what moth and rust consume. We are taught to give up what is of no account. In what truly matters, we are expected to see to our own interest. The "reward" is always *my* reward. Really sacrificing oneself for the sake of others, for the chance, uncertain as such matters are in this world, that our neighbor or society might benefit — or foregoing one's own salvation for the salvation of others, as Mahayana Buddhism says its saints do — the Gospels do not ask of man.

There are, therefore, no grounds for differing with the formulations of by far the best, most comprehensive, and most careful study of "The Social Teachings of the Christian Churches" — that of Ernst Troeltsch. He does not overstate the case when he calls Jesus' moral teachings, as recorded in the Gospels, "unlimited and unconditional individualism"; when he remarks that "of an ideal for humanity there is no thought"; or when he claims that "any program of social renovation is lacking" (39, 41, 48).

The relation of the Gospels to the prophets has often been presented in a false light by those lacking either Troeltsch's scrupulous scholarship or his forthright honesty. The claim that the great innovation of the Gospels lies in a reputed distillation of the older moral teachings is practically a cliché. It is nonetheless false, bars any real understanding of the history of social thought in the past 2000 years, and leads to countless further errors in historical interpretation. As we have seen, there is a crass discontinuity, best summarized in the word otherwordliness.

Much has been made of the Golden Rule; and when it was found that Hillel, the Pharisee, an older contemporary of Jesus, had condensed the morality of Moses and the prophets into the so-called negative formulation of the Golden Rule, which is also encountered, 500 years earlier, in Confucius, Protestant theologians were quick to call this the Silver Rule and to claim that

Jesus' formula was far superior.* In reply to that, three things need to be said.

First, the negative version can be put into practice while the positive version cannot; and anyone who tried to live up to Jesus' rule would become an insufferable nuisance.

Second: no such formula should be overestimated in any case; try, for example, to derive a sexual ethic from Jesus' rule. This example also illustrates the first point.

Finally, there are the wonderful words with which Thomas Hobbes concluded Part III of his *Leviathan:* "It is not the bare Words, but the Scope of the writer that giveth the true light, by which any writing is to bee interpreted; and they that insist upon single Texts, without considering the main Designe, can derive no thing from them cleerly; but rather by casting atomes of Scripture, as dust before mens eyes, make every thing more obscure than it is; an ordinary artifice of those that seek not the truth, but their own advantage."

When we consider the main design, it appears that the Gospels reject all concern with social justice and reduce morality to a prudent concern for one's own salvation; indeed, that morality itself becomes equivocal. No agreement can be had on where Jesus stood on moral questions — not only on pacifism, the courts, and other concrete issues: most of his formulations do not seem to have been meant literally. Parable and hyperbole define his style. Specific contents are disparaged.

Superficially, of course, a very different view suggests itself. The Pharisees had tried to build what they themselves called "a

* "Once a pagan went to Shammai and said: Accept me as a proselyte, on condition that you teach me the whole Law [Torah] while I stand on one leg. Shammai pushed him away with a measure that he had in his hand. He went to Hillel who accepted him as a proselyte. Hillel said to him: What you don't like, don't do to others; that is the whole Law; the rest is commentary; go and learn!" (Talmud Babli, Sabbath 31a). Hillel died about A.D. 10. Other similar formulations, some of them earlier, are listed in Strack's and Billerbeck's *Kommentar*, I, 460. That in the Letter of Aristeas, which is much earlier, combines the positive and negative forms, but I find Hillel's pithy four-part formulation superlative.

fence around the Law" — for example, by demanding that the observation of the Sabbath should begin a little *before* sunset, to guard against trespasses. It might seem that Jesus, in the Sermon on the Mount, was similarly erecting a fence around *morality*. For he introduces his most extreme demands: "Till heaven and earth pass away, not an iota, not a dot, will pass from the law until all is accomplished. Whoever then relaxes one of the least of these commandments and teaches men so, shall be called least in the kingdom of heaven. . . . Unless your righteousness exceeds that of the scribes and Pharisees, you will never enter the kingdom of heaven." Then Jesus goes on to say that it is not enough not to kill: "Whoever says, 'You fool!' shall be liable to hell fire." It is not sufficient not to commit adultery, nor — the omission of any reference to the Tenth Commandment is surprising — not to covet one's neighbor's wife, but "every one who looks at a woman lustfully has already committed adultery with her in his heart. If your right eye causes you to sin, pluck it out and throw it away." (We shall return to this saying later in this chapter).

On reflection, the old morality is not protected but undermined, not extended but dissolved; and no new morality is put in its place. Where murder is not considered importantly different from calling a man a fool, nor adultery from a lustful look, the very basis of morality is denied: the crucial distinction between impulse and action. If one is unfortunate enough to have the impulse, no reason is left for not acting on it.

Again, it might well be asked: "Then who can be saved? But he said: What is impossible with men is possible with God." At this point one can understand Luther's suggestion that the moral commandments in the Bible were "ordained solely that man might thus realize his incapacity for good and learn to despair of himself" (see § 31 above).

Jesus' few remarks about the Jewish ceremonial laws have to be placed in this context. He speaks not as a reform Jew or a liberal Protestant; he does not, like the prophets, unequivocally reject specific rituals to insist instead on social justice; rather, he depreciates rules and commandments as such, moral as well as ceremonial. What ultimately matters is the other world.

As was shown in Chapter VI, it is not only in time that the Gospels are closer to Ezekiel and Daniel than to the pre-exilic prophets. Jesus and the evangelists lived in an age in which apocalypses flourished, and the atmosphere was apocalyptic. In the oldest Gospel, Mark's, "he said to them: Truly, I say to you, there are some standing here who will not taste death before they see the kingdom of God come with power" (9:1; cf. 13:30; Matthew 10:23). The end is at hand, and Jesus himself is understood in the Gospels as an intrusion of the other world into this world. It was not morality or ceremonial law that became the central issue between Jesus and the Pharisees, but the person of Jesus.

Almost all scholars agree that the Sermon on the Mount is not a sermon Jesus delivered in that form, but Matthew's compilation of some of the most striking dicta. (Luke constructed all kinds of situations to frame some of the same dicta.) It is doubly revealing that Matthew should have said, right after the end of the Sermon: "The people were astonished at his teaching" — why? — "for he taught them as one who had authority, and not as their scribes." Moral questions could be argued; one was used to different opinions. Matters of ceremonial law were debated too much, if anything, with a vast variety of views. It was Jesus' conception of his own person that caused astonishment; and if he said half the things about himself that the Gospels relate, it must have seemed the most shocking blasphemy to the Pharisees. The three Synoptics agree that the scribes condemned Jesus not for being too liberal but for blasphemy — for what he said about himself. They relate that he not only called himself the Messiah, or — to use the familiar Greek translation of that term — the Christ, but that he went on to say, alluding to Daniel: "You will see the Son of Man sitting at the right hand of Power, and coming with the clouds of heaven."* Then, they say, the high

* For the history of this conception, see Baeck, "The Son of Man" in *Judaism and Christianity,* translated with an introduction by Walter Kaufmann.

priest tore his mantle, said, "You have heard his blasphemy," and they condemned him.

Whether this is how it actually happened, we have no way of knowing for sure; but this is the Christian story, as related in the Gospels. It was only in recent times, when salvation had ceased to be meaningful for large numbers of liberal Protestants, that men who did not believe any more in "the Son of Man sitting at the right hand of Power, and coming with the clouds of heaven" began to see Jesus as primarily a moral teacher. The apocalyptic tradition suggested by these words, derived from Daniel and Ezekiel, seemed dated. Neither the Catholic church nor the Greek Orthodox church, nor the overwhelming majority of Protestant denominations have ever accepted this liberal view; but it is still popular with a large public that knows what it likes — without *knowing* what it likes.

Let us return once more to the parable of the Good Samaritan. Asked, "What shall I do to inherit eternal life?" Jesus retorts, "What is written in the law?" and receives the reply: "You shall love the Lord your God with all your heart, and with all your soul, and with all your strength, and with all your mind; and your neighbor as yourself." Although Luke has Jesus agree with this, this is not the teaching of the Gospels. On occasion we are given the impression, noted at the beginning of this chapter, that this constituted an area of agreement between Jesus and the Pharisees. But the fourth Gospel denounces this idea constantly:

"Unless one is born of water and the Spirit, he cannot enter the kingdom of God" (3:5). "He who does not believe is condemned already, because he has not believed in the name of the only Son of God" (3:18). "He who does not honor the Son does not honor the Father who sent him" (5:23). "He who believes has eternal life" (6:47). "I am the living bread which came down from heaven; if any one eats of this bread, he will live for ever" (6:51). "No one comes to the Father, but by me" (14:6).

This list could easily be lengthened. In the other Gospels these themes are not nearly so prominent; but, according to Matthew, Jesus said: "Every one who acknowledges me before men, I also

will acknowledge before my Father who is in heaven; but who
ever denies me before men, I also will deny before my Father
who is in heaven" (10:32 f.). Luke 12:8 f. agrees almost literally,
and there is a parallel passage in Mark (8:38).

It is exceedingly doubtful that Jesus himself said all these
things, especially those ascribed to him in the Gospel according
to John. Enslin remarks, in *The Literature of the Christian Movement,* that the Jesus of the fourth Gospel is really not very attractive, and that if it were not for the other three Gospels and
the fact that most readers create for themselves "a conflate," the
Jesus of St. John would lose most of his charm. Surely, the same
consideration applies to all four Gospels. Most Christians gerry-
mander the Gospels and carve an idealized self-portrait out of
the texts: Pierre van Paassen's Jesus is a socialist, Fosdick's a
liberal, while the ethic of Reinhold Niebuhr's Jesus agrees, not
surprisingly, with Niebuhr's own.*

The problem these men confront is not of their making. The
Jesus of the Gospels confronts the serious Christian less as a challenge than as a stumbling block, to use Paul's word. It should
be fruitful to consider how three of the most eminent and earnest
Christians of all time have sought to solve this problem — three
men of very different background and temperament, one in the
first century, one in the sixteenth, and one in the twentieth: Paul,
Luther, and Schweitzer.

Those who see Jesus as essentially a moral teacher often see
Paul as the real Judas. Clearly, Paul's letters bear the stamp of
his personality; and since they were written earlier than any of
our Gospels, they may well have influenced the Gospels, especially that according to John.

Jesus had spoken Aramaic, to Jews; Paul wrote Greek, to Gentiles. Jesus had grown up in Nazareth and taught in Galilee and

* For Niebuhr, see my *Critique,* § 68.

Jerusalem; Paul grew up in a town where Hellenism flourished, and he traveled widely in the Hellenistic world and became a Roman citizen. Jesus had spoken elusively and, according to the Gospels, did not mind puzzling his listeners; Paul preached a doctrine and tried to back it up with arguments — which, to be sure, have to be understood in their contemporary climate of opinion.

Paul had not known Jesus, had not listened to his stories, had not heard his commandments. Jesus appeared to him as the Lord had appeared to the ancient prophets. Paul knew that such an appearance meant a call to go and bear witness of the Lord's revelation; but the Lord now is "Jesus Christ our Lord." Is this a betrayal of Jesus of Nazareth?

To justify an affirmative reply, one must reject as apocryphal all the manifold indications in the Gospels that Jesus did not consider himself an ordinary human being. Yet we have already tried to show that this seems to have been the crucial issue between Jesus and the Sadducees and Pharisees; and presumably it was this, too, that led to the ironic inscription on the cross: King of the Jews. It is the unequivocal centrality of this idea in Paul that is new, also the doctrinal formulations. With this further development, Christianity as a separate religion was born.

What else was Jesus' legacy? If individual salvation counts for everything and is conceived as otherworldly; if action is deprived of its significance and the distinction between deed and impulse is dissolved, what remains but faith in the person around whom the lines were drawn, faith that he was the Messiah, the Christ? Now one could wait for the kingdom to come with power, and meanwhile recall his life and his stories and sayings; or one could accept in all seriousness, with all its implications, as Paul did, the idea that the Messiah had come, and that this must be the clue to salvation.

At this point Paul transformed Jesus' preaching and assimilated the crucified and resurrected Savior to the mystery religions that were prevalent throughout the Roman world. The pagan sacraments found their way into the new religion. Around A. D. 200, when it was still obvious to many educated people where

379

the sacraments had come from, Tertullian said boldly that Satan had counterfeited the Christian sacraments in advance. In our time, Toynbee, once again aware of scores of borrowings from Hellenistic folklore in our Gospels, concludes that God chose to reveal himself in folklore (*A Study of History*, Vol. VI, Annex).

Understandably, many Protestants feel that these Hellenistic elements were merely features of the age that are dispensable today, and that we must go back to original pre-Hellenic, pre-Pauline Christianity. Toynbee, in *An Historian's Approach to Religion*, asks in this vein: "In what sense did Christians, in those very early days before the statement of Christian beliefs began to be Hellenized, mean that Jesus was the Son of God, that He rose from the dead, that He ascended into heaven?" It is widely felt that this is the right question. In fact, however, these "very early days" are a figment of the imagination, and the question is unfair to Paul.

Even some of the later books of the Old Testament are by no means pre-Hellenistic; Jewish literature of the period between the Testaments (the *Apocrypha*, for example) shows strong Hellenistic influence; and the hopes, beliefs, and expectations of the Jews of Jesus' time owed a great deal to Hellenistic thought. Some recent studies have tried to show how deeply Jewish Paul was, notably, W. D. Davies' *Paul and Rabbinic Judaism: Some Rabbinic Elements in Pauline Theology*. And the literature about the Dead Sea scrolls has made it a commonplace that Hellenistic elements — which, it was previously supposed, Paul might have introduced into Christianity — were well established in at least some Jewish circles in the time of Jesus. Some people put this last point rather oddly, saying: These things, which we considered Hellenistic, were really Jewish. It would be more accurate to say that the Judaism of Jesus' time was no longer pre-Hellenistic.

Still, some circles had resisted syncretism more than others, and one need only read the Book of Acts in the New Testament to see that the Jerusalem group, dominated by Peter and James, was inclined to resist more than Paul was. But how could one possibly go back to the religion of this group? They lived in the expectation that they would soon see Jesus return "sitting at the right hand of Power, and coming with the clouds of heaven." They believed that Jesus had assured them that some of them would "not taste death before they [would] see the kingdom of God come with power." Meanwhile, they were willing to preach and make converts, but few Jews were converted, and practically no Gentiles. Was Jesus' legacy, then, a hope that proved vain?

A Jew might say so; a heretic might; but Paul, far from wishing to betray his Lord, refused to see it that way. Never having heard the preaching *of* Jesus, he felt free to develop a new teaching *about* Jesus; and he transformed a message of parables and hyperboles into a theological religion. What he said was clearly different from what Jesus had said; but Jesus' teaching had been so utterly elusive that neither Peter nor James, the brother of Jesus,* nor the other disciples who had listened to him day after day were able to point to anything clear or definite to combat Paul. That they *wanted* to fight Paul's new doctrines, the Book of Acts makes very clear; but the truly extraordinary fact is that these men, whose authority seemed clearly established because they had known Jesus and heard his teaching, had to capitulate to the strong convictions of Paul — himself a recent convert, discredited by his anti-Christian past — because they could not pit any notion of Jesus' legacy against his.

I can see no good reasons for supposing that this was their fault. Indeed, it is not at all uncommon for a teacher to exert a strange and strong fascination on his students — by the force of his personality, his way of speaking, gestures, metaphors, intensity — although they cannot say just what he taught them. It is hardly reasonable in such cases to insist: But he must have taught them something — indeed, something of crucial significance — that we, by painstaking reflection, should be able to recover. It is even less reasonable to assume this when the whole

---

* See, e.g., Galatians 1:19, 2:11 ff.; *Harper's Bible Dictionary* (1959 ed.), 301, "James the brother of Jesus"; and *Encyclopaedia of Religion and Ethics*, VIII, 661, "The Position of James the Lord's Brother at Jerusalem."

climate was thoroughly authoritarian, when the master was surrounded by an air of mystery and constant reports of miracles that could not possibly be questioned, and when there were ocsional suggestions that everything would become clear soon when the world would end. The four evangelists agree in ascribing to Jesus evasive and equivocal answers to plain questions; some of the parables are so ambiguous that different evangelists interpret them differently; and it was evidently unthinkable for a disciple to ask searching questions and persist.

Paul did not villainously overturn the purest teaching that the world had ever heard: he filled a vacuum. Had it not been for him, there would not have been far-flung churches that required Gospels, cherished, and preserved them; there would have been no large-scale conversion of Gentiles; there would have been no Christianity, only a short-lived Jewish sect.

What is ironical, though there are parallels, is that Jesus' dissatisfaction with all formulas and rules should have given way within one generation to an attempt, not yet concluded, to define the most precise dogmas. It is doubly ironical because, according to the Gospels, Jesus constantly inveighed against hypocrisy: indeed, the Gospels have made Pharisee and hypocrite synonymous. Yet the hypocrisy possible within a legalism that prominently emphasizes love and justice is as a mote compared to the beam of the hypocrisy made possible where dogma and sacraments have become central. If "he who eats me will live because of me" (John 6:57), why worry about loving one's enemies?

According to Micah, God demands "only to do justice, to love mercy, and to walk humbly with your God"; according to John, "This is the work of God, that you believe in him whom he has sent" (6:29). Since the Reformation, in spite of the Reformers who pitted their doctrine of justification by faith *alone* against the Catholic doctrine of justification by faith and works, the prophetic ethic has been so widely accepted, however far one falls short of it, that the contrast of these two quotations may strike some readers as almost black and white. But those who study the *Documents of the Christian Church*, selected and edited by

Henry Bettenson for the Oxford University Press, will find that neither the church councils nor the Reformers would have been likely to question this juxtaposition. The body of Bettenson's book happily belies the misleading singular in the title; but one finds that the documents of the various Christian churches agree in rejecting the supremacy of Micah's imperatives, that there is scarcely a reference to love, justice, mercy, or humility, and that what mattered most throughout was right belief about Christ and the sacraments. To this day, it is dogma that keeps the churches apart — different beliefs, creeds, and sacraments — not morality, not the Sermon on the Mount. Only one motif from the Sermon on the Mount was echoed constantly: the threat of hell. As dogma upon dogma was carefully defined, in an effort to determine what precisely one had to believe in order to be saved, the refrain was always: if anyone believes otherwise, "let him be anathema" — let him be damned, let him go to hell!

The Rule of Saint Francis represents a notable exception. Without taking issue with the doctrines and dogmas of the Catholic church, and while fully subordinating his judgment to the church's, he tried to create an island of love in an unloving world. He lived to see corruption and hatred in his order, and soon after his death the Franciscans came to vie with the Dominicans in implementing the Inquisition.

For Paul, as for Jesus, social justice and political arrangements seemed irrelevant. He accepted the prevailing order, sometimes with contempt because it was merely secular, sometimes with respect because it was ordained by God.

Jesus' "render to Caesar what is Caesar's" is elaborated in Paul's fateful Letter to the Romans: "The powers that be are ordained by God. Whoever therefore resists these powers, resists the ordinance of God; and whoever resists shall incur damnation" (13:1 f.). That had not been the view of Elijah and the pre-exilic prophets. But now moral courage before royal thrones and despots gives way to resignation and submission — not from lack of courage (neither Paul nor Luther, who echoed Paul's injunctions, was timid), but because this world has ceased to matter.

The ancient notion of the equality and brotherhood of men is reinterpreted in a purely otherworldly sense; even coupled with a Platonizing, anti-egalitarian, organic metaphor: "As the body is one and has many members, and all the members of the body, though many, are one body, so it is with Christ. For by one Spirit we were all baptized into one body — Jews or Greeks, slaves or free — and all were made to drink of one Spirit. . . . Now you are the body of Christ and individually members of it. And God has appointed in the church first apostles, second prophets, third teachers, then workers of miracles. . . . Are all apostles? Are all prophets? Are all teachers? Do all work miracles?" (I Corinthians 12). The foundation is laid for an elaborate hierarchy and for radical inequalities even within the church, while in the social order outside it inequality and injustice are accepted as fated. "Every one should remain in the state in which he was called. Were you a slave when called? Never mind" (I Corinthians 7). If you can become a free man, fine; if not, it does not really matter.*

In the same spirit, Paul says in the same chapter: "But because of fornication, each man should have his own wife, and each woman her own husband. . . . To the unmarried and the widows I say that it is well for them to remain single as I do. But if they cannot exercise self-control, they should marry. For it is better to marry than to burn." Later, in the same chapter, Paul explains: "I want you to be free from care. The unmarried man cares for the things of the Lord, how to please the Lord; but the married man cares about the things of this world, how to please his wife." It is the importance of the social order, it is this whole world that is rejected here. Paul, like Plato, believes that marriage would distract the elite from that other world on which they should concentrate. At least by implication, Paul, too, introduces the conception of an elite. Henceforth, there are, as it were, first- and second-class Christians. "He who marries his betrothed does well; and he who refrains from marriage will do better."

* The New English Bible offers a footnote to verse 21: "*Or* but even if a chance of liberty should come, choose rather to make good use of your servitude." Contrast Exodus 21, discussed in § 49 above.

For Paul, the otherworldly equality in Christ has a vivid meaning that was soon to be lost. His advice seems to hinge on his conviction that the end is at hand: "I think that in view of the present distress it is well for a person to remain as he is. . . . I mean, brethren, the appointed time has grown very short; those who have wives shall be as though they had none, and those who mourn as though they were not mourning, and those who rejoice as though they were not rejoicing, and those who buy as though they had nothing, and those who deal with the world as though they had no dealings with it. For the form of this world is passing away."

Equality has its place only as this world passes away and all distinctions are lost. Equality is not the final triumph of love and justice, presented to man as a challenge and a task; it is what remains after the diversity of the phenomenal world drops away. But this event is for Paul not so distant that it is almost void of meaning; on the contrary, "the appointed time has grown very short."

In this context, the preceding chapter is readily understood, too: "To have lawsuits at all with one another is defeat for you. Why not rather suffer wrong? Why not rather be defrauded?" This is a significant variation on the theme, "I want you to free from care." One should not become involved in this world and take it seriously. The end of this world is at hand, and the other world alone matters.

Even in the other world, however, inequality appears, as it does in the Gospels. Men are not equal even in the eyes of God. Not only are there first- and second-class Christians; not only are some called to be free and some to be slaves; there are the elect and the damned. Once convinced of a truth, Paul, like the rabbis, looks to Scripture, to the Old Testament, to find it there. "When Rebecca had conceived children by one man, our forefather Isaac, though they were not yet born and had done nothing either good or bad, in order that God's purpose of election might continue, not because of works but because of his call, she was told, 'The elder will serve the younger'" (Romans 9). The story is found in Genesis, as is the story of the Garden of Eden; but the doctrines Paul derives from them are alien to the mainstream of Old Testament religion and opposed to the very core of Hebrew prophecy.

The prophets do not *predict* disaster; they threaten disasters that are bound to happen if the people persist in their ways, but the hope is always that they will not persist in their ways and thus avoid the disaster. Jonah, annoyed that his prophecy will remain unfulfilled, tells God that this was why he fled in the first place to avoid making the prophecy: "Is not this what I said when I was yet in my country? That is why I made haste to flee to Tarshish; for I knew that thou art a gracious God and merciful, slow to anger, and abounding in steadfast love, and repentest of evil." But part of the point of the Book of Jonah is clearly that the prophet who has led men to repentance, who has made them change their ways to avoid imminent disaster, has done his job and should be glad when his prophecies are not fulfilled.

Paul from Tarshish is the great anti-Jonah. Like the Pharisees and millions of rabbis, ministers, and theologians ever since, he finds verses to corroborate his doctrines. Since the Old Testament is a collection of history and poetry, laws and wisdom, folklore and traditions, verses can always be found for every situation. But there is no want of central ideas, of great currents that flow through this great garden and water it — no want of backbone. And it is one of these central conceptions and the very backbone of Hebrew prophecy that Paul ignores: the idea of *t'shuvah*, return, repentance.

Paul's whole argument for the impossibility of finding salvation under "the Law" and for the necessity of Christ's redemptive death depends on this. If, as the rabbis were still teaching in Paul's day, God could at any time freely forgive repentant sinners, Paul's theology collapsed and, in his own words, "then Christ died in vain" (Galatians 2:21). If God could forgive the men of Nineveh simply because they repented of their wicked ways, though they had not been converted, circumcised, or baptized — and this is the teaching of the Book of Jonah, which is also implicit in many other books of the Old Testament — then

Paul's doctrines, which have become the very core of Christianity, lose their point and plausibility and come to look bizarre.

Consider the Christian story the way it looks to an outsider. God causes a virgin, betrothed to Joseph, to conceive his own son, and this son had to be betrayed, crucified, and resurrected in order that those, and only those, might be saved who should both believe this story and be baptized and eat and drink on regular occasions what they themselves believe to be the flesh and blood of this son (or, in some denominations, merely the symbols of his flesh and blood); meanwhile, all, or most, of the rest of mankind suffer some kind of eternal torment, and according to many Christian creeds and teachers they were actually predestined for damnation by God from the very beginning.

Paul did not contribute all the elements of this story — not, for example, the virgin birth, of which most scholars find no trace in his letters. But he did contribute the central ideas of Christ's redemptive death and justification by faith. Protestants and Catholics may argue whether Paul taught justification by faith *alone* or justification by faith and works; it is plain and undisputed that he did not allow for justification by works alone. It is no longer enough "only to do justice, to love mercy, and to walk humbly with your God."

In a long note on Paul, in the third volume of his classical work on *Judaism*, George Foot Moore declared himself utterly unable to understand how a Jew of Paul's background could ignore such a central idea as that of repentance and forgiveness. But the history of religions abounds in parallels. The great religious leaders of humanity have generally been richer in passion than in justice or fairness; their standards of honesty have been far from exemplary; and with an occasionally magnificent one-sidedness, they have been so obsessed by some features of the positions they opposed that they thoroughly misunderstood and misrepresented the religion they denounced. If they deserve blame for this, how much more blameworthy are those who use them as historical authorities, turning to Luther for a portrait of Catholicism, or to the New Testament to be informed about Judaism!

When Paul turned his back on the old notion of forgiveness for the repentant sinner and embraced the doctrine of predestination, he gave up the idea of the equality and fraternity of all men. To cite Troeltsch once more: "The idea of predestination breaks the nerve of the idea of absolute and abstract equality"; and henceforth "inequalities are accepted into the basic sociological scheme of the value of personality" (64, 66).

I am rejecting two clichés: that of the Judaeo-Christian tradition as well as the claim that Western civilization is a synthesis of Greek and Christian elements. Against the former, I stress the discontinuity between Jesus and the pre-exilic prophets: one might as well speak of the Judaeo-Islamic tradition or of the Greco-Christian tradition. Against the latter, I point to the fact that Christianity itself was a child of Greek and Hebrew parents; that the Gospels are a product of Jewish Hellenism; and that Paul, though he claimed to have sat at the feet of Gamaliel, was in important respects closer to Plato and to Gnosticism than to Micah or Jonah.

Paul's decisions have occasionally been explained as highly expedient. When the Jews did not accept the Gospel, the new teaching could survive only by turning to the Gentiles, by abrogating circumcision and the dietary laws, which stood in the way of mass conversions, and by emphasizing faith and preaching obedience to the powers that be. But expediency in this case did not involve any compromise of principle or any sacrifice of Paul's convictions. His innovations make sense in the context of his profound otherworldliness: this was the meeting ground of the Gospel and the mysteries, of Jesus and Gnosticism. Jesus, who had stood in the apocalyptic tradition, was readily assimilated to Hellenistic ideas about salvation. Twelve centuries before St. Thomas wrought the so-called medieval synthesis, Paul fashioned an impressive synthesis of two great heritages. He even found a place for that curious equation of virtue, happiness, and knowledge which we find in Plato: but by knowledge Paul meant the knowledge of faith; by happiness, salvation; and his virtues were not the virtues of Plato.

Paul was not the first to attempt such a synthesis: Philo of Alexandria had fused Plato and the Hebrew Scriptures in an intricate philosophy at least a generation earlier. Nor was Paul's synthesis entirely deliberate: it grew out of the Hellenistic Judaism of that age. But its historic effect has been staggering. No doubt, it would have astonished and distressed Paul himself.

From his letters one gathers that he placed the primary emphasis on faith when he made converts, and that he was shocked when the new congregations took him by his word and did not live up to the moral standards that he had simply taken for granted. In his letters he frequently gives expression to his exasperation. It was therefore in a sense in keeping with Paul's spirit that the new church should have made the Old Testament part of its canon, along with the New. Paul, like the other early Christians who had been raised as Jews, lived in the Hebrew Scriptures, constantly citing them, understanding contemporary events in terms of them, and looking to them for guidance and truth. One cannot read the Gospels or Epistles without being aware of this. The Old Testament was the authors' canon, and much of what they said was meant to be understood against the background of the Hebrew Scriptures — or their Greek translation, the Septuagint. This was so plain that those who later canonized their works retained what they then called the Old Testament to distinguish it from the New Testament.

Eventually, the message of the prophets came to life again. For over a thousand years it slept quietly in the midst of Christendom. Then, early in the sixteenth century, their voice was suddenly heard again, and a new era began. It is customary to date the Modern Age from 1453, when the Turks took Constantinople; or from 1492, when Columbus discovered America; or from the day in 1517 when young Martin Luther nailed his 95 Theses on the cathedral door in Wittenberg. But if a striking symbol is wanted, one could also reckon the end of the Middle Ages from the day when Michelangelo placed above the pope's most holy altar in Rome, the capital of Nero and the Inquisition, not the Mother of God, nor the Christ, nor the expulsion from Paradise, but Jonah.

Human history cannot boast of a more vivid, valiant, and vindictive character than Luther. He performed three apparently unrelated feats, each of which would have sufficed to make him one of the outstanding figures of all time: he smashed the unity of Western Christendom; he translated the Bible and put it into every household that his influence could reach; and he developed a new *Weltanschauung*.

With nothing to begin with but passion and the power of his language, this simple monk dealt the papacy a blow compared to which the drawn-out efforts of generations of German emperors with huge armies and vast resources seem as nothing: he surpassed the very imagination of the supple scheming of Henry IV and the refined hatred of Frederick II.

Then he put his genius at the disposal of the Bible and, translating it, created a new language: modern German. Though he found God's revelation above all in Paul, particularly in the Letters to the Romans and Galatians, his heart caught fire as he read the Hebrew Scriptures; and, far more than the King James Version almost a century later, he communicated much of their austere simplicity, laconic majesty, and the immediacy of the experience with which so much of the original is still alive. Though it was the New Testament — and really only a very small part of this — that became the center of his new religion, he not only left the Old Testament in the Protestant Bible, he helped it to a popularity it had never before had in the Western world.

Finally, the reformer and translator fashioned a new religious and political world view, based on the Bible and his break with Rome. It, too, bears the distinctive stamp of his unique personality. Luther thought he was offering a return to Paul. He felt that he was fighting corruption and re-establishing the ancient and pure doctrine. Yet his message was a reflection and projection of his own genius, not the Gospel according to Paul but a characteristically Lutheran piety.

A sincere Christian could scarcely differ more from the mild and milk-faced Jesus of Hofman's popular paintings than Luther did. Not even Calvin outdoes him in this respect. Fanatical from beginning to end, as monk, Reformer, and politician, Luther did whatever he did with all his heart, all his soul, and all his power: fiery, fierce, with the force of a bull rhinoceros — but thoroughly devoted to Christianity, which was the one constant in his life. Monk or married, preaching rebellion or obedience, it was Christianity that he had at heart. And moderation was not for him. Even apart from his doctrinal differences with the followers of Aquinas, Aristotelianism with its subtleties, its praise of wisdom and philosophy, was antithetical to Luther's vision of Christianity: radical through and through, and opposed alike to wisdom, reason, and subtlety.

He was thirty-three when he nailed his 95 Theses to the cathedral door in Wittenberg. Before this, he had tried to gain salvation through works. For salvation was still central for him as it had been for Jesus' and Paul's original audience. "Works" had not meant to Luther middle-class decency or a respectable regard for convention. Being a Christian meant something extraordinary, extreme, exalted. Works led to no conclusion; there is no end to works, no final salvation. Striving for salvation through works is like struggling against quicksand.

Luther believed in the devil and in hell, as Jesus and Paul had done. A life devoted to the quest for salvation through works became intolerable for him: one could never cease without perishing. And cease one must, if only sometimes. There are moments of weariness, discouragement, temptation, disgust. Not only moments. Hamlet's famous advice to his mother, how continence breeds more continence and virtue makes virtue ever easier, is surely one of those half-truths which owe their popularity to wishful thinking, as does much glib talk about sublimation. Luther knew through the torture of his own experience how continence bred the half-crazed desire for incontinence, and virtue like a cancer could corrode the soul with the obsession to do evil. There is a peace of mind born of transgression which is sweeter than that of good conscience: the peace that attends virtue is a guarded joy, dependent on past triumphs and continued perseverance; *relative* to these, not absolute — not extraordinary, extreme, exalted. But still finding oneself in and after evil, knowing all the joy of sin and feeling that sin is not the great power virtue thinks it, not the menace against which we must at all times be on our guard, but a foe to whom one can concede a battle and survive — this sense of peace which comes of saturation and the new experience of a deadness to desire is indeed a peace surpassing unreflective understanding. Hence, not only must salvation through works be abandoned but a place must be found for sin. It is hardly an exaggeration to say that for Luther the Gospel, the glad tidings, was that one could sin and yet be saved, and that sin need not even be rationed.

Paul and Luther notwithstanding, salvation through works never was the doctrine of the Jews or the Catholics. The Old Testament was, for the most part, not at all concerned with individual salvation in another world or life; and the Pharisees who did believe in immortality never failed to supplement their teaching of the Law with the prophetic doctrine of repentance and forgiveness. They did *not* believe that salvation required unexceptional fulfillment of all laws, moral and ceremonial, or that they, and only they, could point to perfect records and hence were entitled to salvation while the rest of mankind was less fortunate. Nor did the Catholic church, prior to Luther, teach that only the perfect ascetic could win redemption while the rest of mankind would be damned. Paul and Luther passionately, but erroneously, projected their own frantic efforts on two great religions within which they had failed to realize their self-imposed conception of salvation.

At no time had the church accepted Jesus' hyperbolic counsels. How could it? How could an institution which expects to outlast centuries take as its motto, "Take no thought for the morrow"? How could it reach men with the teaching, "Whoever then relaxes one of the least of these commandments and teaches men so, shall be

called least in the kingdom of heaven"? How could it discipline
men if it accepted the command, "Resist not evil"? How could it
possibly accept the Sermon on the Mount and its eloquent conclusion: "Every one who hears these words of mine and does not do
them will be like a foolish man who built his house upon the sand;
and the rain fell, and the floods came, and the winds blew and beat
against that house, and it fell; and great was the fall of it"? Organized Christianity could be defined as the ever renewed effort to get
around these sayings without repudiating Jesus. This is what the
Roman Catholic and the Greek Orthodox church, Luther and
Calvin, Barth and Schweitzer have in common.

Luther and the church against which he rebelled agreed that
there must be some dispensation from the stern demands of Jesus,
and that sin must not be considered a bar to salvation.

Their difference? A joke may crystallize it. A hostess offers a
guest some canapés. Says the guest: "Thank you. I have already
had three." Says the hostess: "Had three? You've had five; but who
counts?" What enraged Luther was that the church counted.

Lutheran children are often brought up on Luther's protests
against the sale of indulgences and are appalled to learn how freely
people sinned with the assurance that a small formality would soon
restore them to their former state of grace — or even how a man
planning a robbery might obtain indulgence in advance. They are
less likely to be told how Luther, on the Wartburg, wrote his friend
Melanchthon on August 1, 1521: "If you are a preacher of grace, do
not preach a fictitious, but a true, grace; and if the grace is true,
carry a true, and not a fictitious sin. God does not work salvation for
fictitious sinners. Be a sinner and sin vigorously [*esto peccator et
pecca fortiter*]; but even more vigorously believe and delight in
Christ who is victor over sin, death, and the world." And later on
in the same letter he writes: "It is sufficient that we recognize
through the wealth of God's glory, the lamb who bears the sin of
the world; from this, sin does not sever us, even if thousands, thousands of times in one day we should fornicate or murder."

Luther and the church agreed on the compatibility of sin and
salvation; but Luther insisted on justification by faith alone, *sola*

fide. Not by works and not through any mediator other than Christ. Works are by their nature inconclusive: even if one should persist in works, all one's accomplishments are dwarfed by what one *might* have done. If salvation involves, as both Jesus and Paul taught, an assurance even now, a conviction, a triumphant sense of ultimate redemption, it cannot be found in works. But faith is ultimate; faith is conclusive; faith is final. A verse in the Book of Habakkuk (2:4.), cited in the first chapter of Paul's Letter to the Romans, becomes the cornerstone of Luther's religion: "The just shall live by faith."

Faith for Luther is not merely assent to certain propositions, though this is a necessary element of faith: it is a liberating experience which suffuses a whole life with bliss. Care is dead, also worry about sin. One is saved in spite of being a wretched and incorrigible sinner. It is like knowing that one is loved — loved unconditionally with all one's faults. And the Catholic church would still keep count of faults and impose penances or sell indulgences! As if the glad tidings were not that our sins no longer matter.

What is wrong with the indulgences is not that they make sin compatible with ultimate salvation, but that they are incompatible with the glad tidings of salvation by faith alone. What is wrong with all the preaching of pleasing God by works is that the Gospel can be understood only when we have experienced the impossibility of pleasing God by works. What is wrong with the church's assumption of the role of mediator between God and man, wrong with the hierarchy and faith in intervention by the saints, is once again that all this stands opposed to the glad tidings. Christ loves us! That means that his love need not be earned by works. In fact, we brazenly exclude ourselves from the redeeming power of his love if we insist that we deserve it or must, by some future works, still earn it.

The glad tidings that Christ loves us permeate Luther's prose; and more than 400 years later we can still experience their intoxicating power. But if, instead of trying to re-experience Luther's faith, we step back to look at it with some detachment, we find that Luther's version of Christianity falls within our previous definition:

it gets arounds the Sermon on the Mount without repudiating Jesus.

With the radical power of his language, Luther himself expressed this again and again. "The law is fulfilled not insofar as we satisfy it, but insofar as we are forgiven for not being able to do anything" (XII, 377°). "The hearts that are filled with God's bliss do not fulfill the Ten Commandments; but Christ has brought about such a violent salvation that he deprives the Ten Commandments, too, of all their claims" (VII, 1516°). And in a letter to his young friend Jerome Weller: "You must believe that this temptation of yours is of the devil, who vexes you so because you believe in Christ. You see how contented and happy he permits the worst enemies of the gospel to be. Just think of Eck, Zwingli, and others. It is necessary for all of us who are Christians to have the devil as an adversary and enemy; as Saint Peter says, 'Your adversary, the devil, walks about' [I Peter 5:8]. . . . Whenever the devil pesters you with these thoughts, at once seek out the company of men, drink more, joke and jest, or engage in some other form of merriment. Sometimes it is necessary to drink a little more, play, jest, or even commit some sin in defiance and contempt of the devil in order not to give him an opportunity to make us scrupulous about trifles. We shall be overcome if we worry too much about falling into some sin. So, if the devil should say, 'Do not drink,' you should reply to him, 'On this very account, because you forbid it, I shall drink, and what is more, I shall drink a generous amount.' Thus one must always do the opposite of that which Satan prohibits. What do you think is my reason for drinking wine undiluted, talking freely, and eating more often, if it is not to torment and vex the devil who made up his mind to torment and vex me? . . . When the devil attacks and torments us, we must completely set aside the Ten Commandments. When the devil throws our sins up to us and declares that we deserve death and hell, we ought to speak thus: 'I admit that I deserve death and hell. What of it? Does this mean that I shall be sentenced to eternal damnation? By no means. For I know One who suffered and made satisfaction in my behalf. His name is Jesus Christ, the Son of God. Where he is, there I shall be also'" (July [?], 1530).

Many will say, no doubt: Luther was terrible, but the Sermon on the Mount shows Jesus to have been the greatest moral teacher of all time. This facile view lacks that impassioned seriousness which commands respect for Luther. It is fashionable to pay lip service to the Sermon on the Mount even if one works for, or constantly patronizes, million-dollar industries that involve systematic efforts to increase the frequency of lustful looks. Luther had tried with all his might to eradicate all lustful thoughts from his tormented mind: as a monk he had denied himself food and sleep, scourged himself, prayed, done penance — all to no avail.

He was not the kind of man that practices law while avowing belief in Jesus' ethic; not one to extol the Sermon on the Mount as the best rule of conduct, while making elaborate plans for the future; not one to hail Jesus as a moral genius while thinking nothing of calling another man a fool. When he arrived at the conclusion that one could not live by Jesus' moral teachings, he said so outright.

A number of conclusions are open to us at this point. We can say that Hillel, the Pharisee, was a greater moral genius when he said a generation earlier: "Do not judge your neighbor till you have seen yourself in his position" (Mishnah Avoth, 2:5). For this is an attainable ideal, not moral utopianism; and as one approximates it, one becomes a better man. Or one could become a Buddhist. Or, convinced of the futility of good works and the liberating force of sin, one might adopt a pagan ethic depriving "even the Ten Commandments of all their justice." But Luther had the unshakable conviction that the Bible was the word of God, that all religious and all moral truth was to be found in it, and that Christ was the Truth — if not in one sense, then in another.

The problem here, unlike the solution, was not a function of Luther's personality or outlook. As long as we do not realize this, we cannot hope to understand either Luther or Christianity. The same problem confronts everybody who takes Christianity seriously. This is perhaps best shown by considering a man whose Christianity is in some ways antithetical to Luther's: Albert Schweitzer.

Schweitzer, organist, Bach scholar, and New Testament scholar, who at thirty turned his back on his manifold achievements to practice medicine among the natives in Central Africa, is to many minds the one true Christian of our time — the one outstanding personality whose scholarly and thorough study of the Gospels led him to realize their ethic in his life. This view depends on ignorance of Schweitzer's writings. For Schweitzer, like Luther, takes the Sermon on the Mount too seriously to claim that he accepts it. Like Luther, he repudiates it without repudiating Jesus.

His study of the texts and his definitive work on outstanding previous interpretations led him to the conclusion that Jesus' moral teachings must be understood as a mere "interim ethic" — designed and appropriate only for the interim, which Jesus firmly believed to be quite brief, before the kingdom of God would come with power. Schweitzer's result implies not only that Jesus' ethic is inapplicable today but that it has *never* been applicable and that Jesus' most central conviction was wrong.

With this, one might expect Schweitzer to give up Christianity — unless he accepts traditional Christian solutions of this problem. He does neither. He disagrees with the early Christians and the medieval church, and repudiates Luther's belief that he was returning to the ancient teaching — and yet Schweitzer considers himself a Christian and a Protestant.

Let us concentrate on two major issues: otherworldliness and remission of sins. Far from denying the essential otherworldliness of Jesus' outlook, Schweitzer has used his vast scholarship to establish its importance against the entrenched preconceptions of liberal Protestants. Jesus' otherworldliness is, to Schweitzer's mind inseparable from Jesus' firm conviction that *this* world was about to come to an end. When this expectation was not realized, belief in the beginning of the kingdom did not all at once evaporate, but the event was moved into the future; and as generation after generation

397

passed, it was gradually projected into an infinite distance. As this happened, otherworldliness changed its character.

Paul, according to Schweitzer, had retained the belief in the impending end of this world, even after most other Christians had become resigned to the vague prospect of an indefinite future. Paul believed that the kingdom *had* come with Christ's death and resurrection, and that this would soon become manifest through a transformation of the natural world. But Paul was wrong, and the indefinite postponement of the expectation of the kingdom became universal.

In the perspective of this infinitely distant hope, the Christian negation of this world acquired a new and, Schweitzer feels, unfortunate importance. Originally, the negation had been almost void of content: this world was depreciated as something that was about to pass away, and one concentrated on the other world because it was about to be the only one. But now *this* world is negated even though it is assumed to have duration; and — though Schweitzer himself does not sharpen the contrast in this manner — it is the affirmation that is almost void of content now: an essentially positive outlook is converted into a primarily negative one.

The triumphant conviction that the kingdom was about to come — or had come, as Paul believed — is gone beyond recall; and the conviction that the affairs of this world do not matter any more is no longer a mere corollary, but broadens out into pervasive resignation. In Schweitzer's words: "By their negation of this world as well as by the conception that the kingdom will eventually come all by itself, the believers are sentenced not to undertake anything to improve the present. Because Christianity must pursue this course, it cannot be to the Greco-Roman world in which it appears what it ought to have been to it. The ethical energies contained in Christianity cannot regenerate the world empire and its peoples. Christianity triumphs over paganism: it becomes the state religion. But in accordance with its nature, it must leave the world empire to its fate."

Thus Schweitzer stands opposed to Christian otherworldliness, both in its hopeful, eschatological form, which he associates with

Jesus and Paul and considers inseparable from clearly erroneous beliefs, and in its subsequent negativistic form which he considers a
moral disaster. Judged by his moral standards, which are shared by
millions who do not care to press the point, Christianity did not do
what it ought to have done; and Schweitzer has the rare honesty to
insist that *Christianity failed morally not because Christians have
not been Christian enough, but because of the very nature of
Christianity.*

Discussions of Christianity and liberty are full of such phrases
as the following, from a recent book by R. M. Thompson: "The
Christian Ethic, which reverences personality and recognizes the
individual's right to a full and free life in cooperation with his fel-
lows, is the only hope for a world that subordinates man to collective materialism." In line with these glib generalities, it is often supposed that Christianity spread the idea of liberty in the West: the
suffering of the Christian slave is stressed, the problem of the Christian slaveholders ignored; the Christian martyrs of the early pagan
persecutions are emphasized; the martyrs, Christian and non-Christian, of subsequent Christian persecutions overlooked; and it is
scarcely ever doubted that, in principle, Christianity was always
on the "right" side, regrettable lapses notwithstanding.

In fact, neither Jesus and Paul nor the early church, nor medieval
Christianity, nor Luther recognized "the individual's right to a full
and free life." Nor need one think only of Jesus' saying that it is
better to live "maimed" and go to heaven "than with two hands to
go to hell, to the unquenchable fire" (Mark 9:43); or of Paul's view
of marriage. Take the article on slavery in the Encyclopaedia of
Religion and Ethics, which is written from a distinctly Christian
point of view.

"The abolitionist could point to no one text in the Gospels in
defence of his position." The church "tended to make slavery
milder, though not to abolish it, and, owing to its excessive care for
the rights of the masters, even to perpetuate what would otherwise
have passed away." "Legislation forbade Christian slaves to be sold
to pagans or Jews, but otherwise tended to recognize slavery as a
normal institution." "The general tone of this legislation can hardly

be said to favor the slave." "In Spain slavery was a prominent feature of medieval society. . . . Here, as elsewhere, the Church was a
slave-owner."*

If Schweitzer is scrupulously correct up to this point, his transition to his own this-worldly ethic gives us pause: both for his history
and for his logic. In the Renaissance he finds a turning point: the
Christian negation of this world is finally opposed by a new attitute
of affirmation; and this new positive outlook is blended with the
ethic of late Stoicism, as we find it in the writings of Cicero, Seneca,
Epictetus, and Marcus Aurelius. "From this originates, as something
absolutely new in the cultural history of Europe a *Weltanschauung*
characterized by an ethical affirmation of world and life. This constitutes the fundamental difference between the Europeans of
classical antiquity and those of modern times. The modern European has a different spirit because he has achieved faith in progress,
a will to progress, the conception of a further and higher development, and the idea of universal love of man." The similarity between
the ethic of Jesus and that of late Stoicism made it possible for modern Protestantism to adopt these new attitudes. "Thus the transition
of Christianity from an ethical negation of life and world to an ethical affirmation of life and world takes place in modern times, quietly
and without a struggle."

Once again the faith in the kingdom of God becomes central —
although the kingdom is now no longer conceived as "eschatological, cosmic, and eventually coming all by itself" but as something
"uneschatological, spiritual-ethical, for whose realization men, too,
must work." Only after this complete transformation, "the kingdom
of God can regain in our faith the importance which it had for Jesus
and original Christianity. But it must have this importance if Christianity is to remain, in its inmost nature, what it was in its beginnings: a religion dominated by the idea of the kingdom of God. The
role which the kingdom of God plays in the faith constitutes the
essence of the faith. *The conception of the kingdom and its realization is only of secondary significance.* Although modern Protestant
Christianity is modern, it is nevertheless also truly in accordance

* Cf. Troeltsch, 19; Westermarck, I, 693 ff.

with the Gospel because it is again a religion with a living faith in the kingdom of God" (my italics).

The logical enormity of Schweitzer's argument is obvious. Few men have done more than he to demonstrate the complete incompatibility of Jesus' conception of the kingdom with any social or thiswordly aspirations. He has fought the errors of Harnack, who maintained in his famous Berlin lectures on "The Essence of Christianity" that Jesus brought a revolutionary and prophetically modern notion of the kingdom. Schweitzer denies Jesus all originality at this point: "All evidence is lacking that Jesus had a conception of the kingdom and of the Messiah differing in any way from the late Jewish eschatological one." And he adds: "It is hard for us to resign ourselves to the fact that Jesus, who possesses the spirit of God in a unique manner and who is for us the highest revelation of religious and spiritual truth, does not stand above his time in a manner appropriate to the significance which he has for all time."

This is not a passing concession but a central motif of Schweitzer's thought. Among Jesus' ideas are some "which we can no longer experience as truth or accept. Why is Christianity sentenced to this? Is this not a wound for which there is no balm? Should it be impossible to maintain Jesus' freedom from error in religious matters? Does he not cease, then, to be an authority for us? . . . I have suffered deeply from having to maintain something out of truthfulness which must give offense to the Christian faith." And again: "All attempts to escape the admission that Jesus had a conception of the kingdom of God and its impending arrival which remained unfulfilled and cannot be taken over by us, mean trespasses against truthfulness."

Nevertheless, Schweitzer maintains that his social and ethical conception of the kingdom is "truly in accordance with the Gospel because it is again a religion with a living faith in the kingdom of God"; and "the conception of the kingdom and its realization is only of secondary significance." Here we are close to the ancient *credo quia absurdum*. Jesus' otherworldly kingdom is rejected in favor of an affirmation of *this* world; his disparagement of social problems is considered most unfortunate and countered with an ethic of social regeneration — and then we are assured that this apparently diamet-

rical opposition "is only of secondary significance" because the new
ideal can borrow the ancient name: "kingdom of God." This phrase,
of course, reflects not an artful attempt to deceive, but the believer's
sincere, if entirely subjective, sense of continuity.

Schweitzer's subjective logic must be seen in the light of his subjective history. The quotes given here have been taken from his important essay on "The Idea of the Kingdom of God in the Course of
the Transformation of the Eschatological Faith into an Uneschatological One." In the whole careful historical account, which is full of
names and dates, we find no reference whatever to either the Old
Testament or John Calvin. Yet it was in Calvinism rather than in
Lutheranism — to which Schweitzer devotes a large part of his essay
— that the modern affirmation of this world found its expression. It
was here that the idea of refashioning society took hold. And Calvinism was inspired much less by late Stoicism than by the Old Testament. Indeed, Schweitzer's own conception of the kingdom is far
closer to that of the pre-exilic prophets than to that of Jesus.

Schweitzer himself knows how far he stands from traditional
Christianity. Almost half of his essay is devoted to developing the
proposition: "Christianity ceased to be the religion of faith in the
kingdom of God and became the religion of faith in the resurrection
and the remission of sins." Jesus, according to Schweitzer, still believed, like the Jews of his time, that God could freely forgive a
repentant sinner without Jesus' sacrifice or any other intervening
mechanism. Schweitzer himself belongs to those "who cannot reconcile it with their conception of God that he should have required a
sacrifice to be able to forgive sins."

Jesus did believe, Schweitzer maintains, that his atonement would
cause God not to exact the penance of a pre-messianic time of trou-
bles, "but to let the kingdom of God commence soon without this
frightful prelude." Schweitzer leaves no doubt that he considers
Jesus' view to have been factually mistaken, but he does not say
whether he can reconcile Jesus' conception of God with his own.

That Schweitzer finds Paul's view of God unacceptable is clear.
"Paul creates the conception of justification solely by faith in Jesus
Christ." This faith wins complete remission of sins. "The possibility

of further sinning after the attainment of faith is not considered by
him." Only when the kingdom failed to come, and generation after
generation was born into a sinful world, did the church become
aware of a great problem — and solved it: baptism won forgiveness
for all previous sins, including original sin, and subsequent sins had
to be forgiven subsequently, by the church. "Augustine (354-430)
introduces the principle that forgiveness for all sins committed after
baptism is to be found in the church, if only an appropriate penance
is performed. Outside the church there is no pardon. And whoever
does not believe in the continual remission of sins within the church,
commits the sin against the Holy Spirit. Among the new conceptions
which had in the course of time developed in connection with the
attainment of the continual remission of sins, we encounter in
Augustine the notion of purgatory and the idea that prayers, alms,
and sacrificial masses of the survivors can help the departed souls to
attain remission of sins." But Augustine still understood the sacrifice
of Christ in the mass "only in a spiritual sense. It was under Pope
Gregory I (590-604) that the realistic conception prevailed that in
the mass Jesus is again and again sacrificed sacramentally in order
that the atonement thus provided may profit the living and the
dead."

Luther, finally, breaks with these traditions and understands baptism as effecting not only the remission of sins previously incurred —
it assures man of the full benefits of Christ's atoning death and of
continual forgiveness. "He thinks that he is restoring the original
simple doctrine from which the Catholic church has deviated. Yet
it is not he but the Catholic church that maintains the original conception of baptism. His conception, however, is religiously justified."

Later, Schweitzer sums up once more: "Historically, both Luther
and modern Protestant Christianity are in the wrong; but religiously
they are right." In other words, Luther and modern Protestantism
have not only broken with Catholic traditions; they have broken
with Jesus' teaching and early Christianity, too. But they are right
because all previous Christianity, including even Jesus' teaching, has
been wrong. And — here comes the leap of faith beyond the bounds

of rationality — if modern Protestantism and Albert Schweitzer are right, then their views must after all be "truly in accordance with the Gospel" because Christ was the Truth — if not in one sense, then in another.

Here Luther and Schweitzer face the same problem and resort to the same *salto mortale*: they not only repudiate the Sermon on the Mount and Jesus' teaching without repudiating Jesus; they claim that their own convictions are, even if not historically or empirically, in some higher sense the essence of the Gospel. Superficially it often seems that certain doctrines are held to be true because they are encountered in the Gospels; in fact, we are confronted with the postulate that certain views must represent the real meaning of the Gospel because they are so firmly held to be religious truth.

It would add little if we went on to consider some Catholic thinkers. On the whole, Catholics have concerned themselves less with the figure of Jesus than have Protestant writers: it was only after the Reformers' protest against the church's assumption of the role of mediator, after their insistence that Christ was the only mediator man required, and after their call for a return to the authority of Scripture, that Jesus was once again moved into the center from which he had disappeared after the first century. And the point of this chapter is not to cover twenty centuries of Christian thought but rather to follow up the chapter on the Old Testament by showing how I see Jesus.

Because most accounts of Jesus are highly subjective, it seemed best to relate my own reading of the Gospels to the views of some of the most eminent Christian interpreters. Whether the choice of Paul, Luther, and Schweitzer was justified depends on how fruitful it has proved to be. As for Calvin, he will be cited in the next chapter in a manner that should indicate how he fits into our picture.

Only one further view will be quoted here. Early in the nineteenth century — about 1818 — William Blake said: "There is not one Moral Virtue that Jesus Inculcated but Plato & Cicero did Inculcate before him; what then did Christ Inculcate? Forgiveness of Sins. This alone is the Gospel. . . ." And again:

If Moral Virtue was Christianity,
Christ's Pretensions were all Vanity. . . .

My account of the New Testament is less positive than my analysis of the Old Testament. Even those who might concede that this
makes for a wholesome antidote may feel that it is odd in a book
that attacks the double standard and pleads for honesty.

Heresy and polemics inveigh against traditional views, stressing
their shortcomings and points that have been widely overlooked. As
a result, they rarely give a balanced picture. That is true of Jesus'
and Paul's polemics as well as of Luther's.

Still, I shall not plead guilty to a charge of gerrymandering the
Bible. It is essential to recognize the discontinuity between the
prophets and Jesus, also the modern falsification of the New Testament idea of love. If Jesus and Paul believed that the world was
about to end, and that "few are chosen" to escape eternal torment,
that is not a marginal belief that can be safely ignored. And their
praise of love was intimately related to this central conviction. I
have tried to show this in the case of Jesus; it is no less obvious in
Paul's.

Consider Paul's great hymn on love, I Corinthians 13: "If I give
away all I have, and if I deliver my body to be burned, but have not
love, *I gain nothing.*" Or, as the King James Bible puts it: "It profit-
eth me nothing." Long familiarity has dulled the bite of these words.
Jesus and Paul teach us to love others — for our own profit.

This analysis does not depend on partiality but on a contexual
reading. It is the traditional reading that depends on ignoring what
is not considered timely and attractive.

From a scholarly point of view, the fashionable picture of Jesus is
fantastic. It disregards Jesus' concern with the end of the world and
his appeal to every man's interest in his own salvation, and it is derived in very large measure from two sayings that are missing in

most ancient manuscripts (a fact duly acknowledged not only in scholarly works but also in the Revised Standard Version of the Bible): "Let him who is without sin among you be the first to throw a stone" (John 8:7) and "Father, forgive them; for they know not what they do" (Luke 23:34).

Even so, something besides gerrymandering has been at work here. These two sayings, as well as a few others, do somehow leap out of their context and haunt the mind. Actually, they have not haunted as many minds as one might wish: historically, they have been staggeringly ineffective. But there are two levels worth distinguishing. Take Shakespeare's line, "Ripeness is all." It surely cannot mean much to most readers. But those who after the experience of a lifetime suddenly are ripe for this insight will feel hit by it and note that it says in three words what, but for that, might well have seemed ineffable. It may have taken the experience of well over eighteen centuries of history for men in some parts of the world to be struck in somewhat the same way by some verses in the Gospels and Epistles. The claim that these sayings changed the course of history is false; but a book containing words like these is obviously .not merely of historic interest.

One may wonder whether the Gospels did not at least spread sympathy for suffering, if only by moving into the center of a great religion the symbol of Christ crucified. Did this not produce in literature, art, and morality a new preoccupation with man's misery, a new note of compassion? Such pleasant suggestions conflict with the historic evidence. These concerns were common in the Hellenistic world — the motif of the tormented body and anguished face of a man, for example, is encountered in the sculptured giants of the Pergamon altar and in the Laocoon group — but they vanished with Hellenism and were largely absent during the first twelve centuries of Christianity. When the Gothic developed a taste for such motifs, the crucifixion was available; but in Byzantine and Romanesque art it had not been treated in any such manner. Nor was the age of the Gothic remarkable for compassion. Neither do the Christian fathers, Augustine and Aquinas, Luther or Calvin, impress us with the importance of compassion. These things were undeniably present in the Gospels, and we may find inspiration in them. But they do not issue the unequivocal challenge that the prophets fling at us.

The place of the child in the Gospels affords a parallel example. Many verses reflect the unusual feeling of the Jewish father for his son, which is familiar to us from the Old Testament. We need only to recall David's attitude toward Absalom, Jacob's toward Joseph and Benjamin, and Abraham's toward Isaac, especially the suggestion in Genesis that Abraham made the supreme sacrifice by being willing to sacrifice his son, "the only one, whom you love." And if some other Near Eastern religion had become the state religion of the Roman empire, we might well have had just as many Madonnas in Western art. The motif of a woman nursing a baby is found in ancient Egyptian art — the Brooklyn Museum owns two examples from around 1800 B.C., one in limestone, the other in copper — and statues of Isis with her mysteriously conceived son, the god Horus, on her lap were common indeed. Some Hellenistic examples might well be taken for Gothic Madonnas by those not familiar with Egyptian art. For all that, these motifs are present in the New Testament and move us.

Regarding social ideas, the matter has been well stated by Troeltsch: "In sum: the egalitarian-socialist-democratic conceptions of natural and divine law, and of Christian liberty founded on such law, never issue from the dialectic of the pure Christian idea, but are brought about in all instances only by political and social revolutions; and even then they are related only to those elements in Patristic ethics which are not derived from the development of Christian ideas. Wherever these ideas are to be realized by force, and a revolution is to be given a Christian basis, it is always, here also, the Old Testament that must help out" (411). For "with the New Testament alone, no social teachings at all can be generated" (254).

Similar considerations apply to Jesus' denial of the crucial distinction between impulse and action, which we have discussed. It, too, has been misrepresented. Liberals have spread the myth that Jesus protested against Jewish legalism and extolled pure morality. The Gospels do not support either claim. The Jesus of the Gospels was no liberal Protestant. But sayings like, "Every one who looks at a woman lustfully has already committed adultery with her in his heart," also leap out of the context; and the modern reader happily forgets the following words, which are not so readily assimilated to Freud's heritage: "If your right eye causes you to sin, pluck it out and throw it away; it is better that you lose one of your members than that your whole body be thrown into hell. And if your right hand causes you to sin, cut it off and throw it away; it is better that you lose one of your members than that your whole body go into hell." Indeed, if one interprets this dictum as an exhortation to purge lust from one's heart, it becomes a counsel of repression and, in practice, self-deception.

"The spirit bloweth where it listeth" (John 3:8), and one man feels addressed by one saying while another man's heart opens up for another. At different times in his life, the same person may respond to different verses, and interpret the same verses differently. It is one of the marks of the greatest books that they have this power to speak to us in moments of crisis. Unquestionably, the New Testament possesses this power to a rare degree.

Some will say, no doubt, that I am "against" it. But to adopt a simplistic stand "for" or "against" Jesus and Paul, Luther or Schweitzer, would not be in keeping with the aims of this book. According to Matthew and Luke, Jesus said: "He that is not for me is against me." By that token, I should indeed be against Jesus. But according to the oldest Gospel, that of Mark, Jesus said: "He that is not against us is for us."

I have tried to determine honestly what the Jesus of the Gospels, Paul, Luther, and Schweitzer say to us. Some of my results are controversial, but they are not prompted by malice. My Luther is neither the democratic milksop of the celebrated motion picture sponsored by the Lutheran churches of America, nor the hateful devil of much anti-German propaganda, but one of the most impressive figures of world history. My Paul is neither the infallible saint of many believers nor the traitor to Jesus that many liberals have found in him. And my Jesus is closely related and indebted to Albert Schweitzer's.

My heresy is hardly that I go along with such highly regarded scholars as Schweitzer and Troeltsch, but that I refuse to make amends for honesty. It is pretty well known by now that scholarship may lead one to attribute to Jesus views that are not in favor today; and such honesty is forgiven, no less, if only it is coupled immediately with the protestation that facts, if inconvenient, are irrelevant, and that in a higher sense, whatever that may mean, all that was good and true and beautiful was really taught by Jesus. In such contexts, "really" means "not *really*, but — *you* know."

Perhaps it is the essence of organized religion to read current insights into ancient books and rites. But if one does this, disregarding Jesus' counsel not to do it, one should realize that one could do it with almost any religion. I'am not against Jesus but against those who do this with Jesus' life and teachings, or with anyone else's. It is well to forgive them; for they know not what they do. But it is also well for us to realize what they do, lest we should do it, too. Perhaps I myself have done this in the case of the Old Testament? I do not think so, but shall return to this question once more in Section 70 in the next chapter.

Judaism Despite Christianity

The "Letters on Christianity and Judaism"
between Eugen Rosenstock-Huessy and Franz Rosenzweig

By Franz Rosenzweig

Franz to Eugen

Dear R.,

I want to begin to answer you at once. (I got your letter yes-

101 This work, which went through several editions in Germany, was *Beiträge zu einer Kritik der Sprache*, first published in 1901–1902, by Fritz Mauthner (1849–1923), a radical skeptic of the day. "Fritz Mauthner wrote 6000 pages and proved in one and a half million words that all words lie. And he got his books printed and they are in all the libraries of the world because in their heart of hearts, all academic people treat languages as rudiments of a barbaric age. How they would prefer to think without words!" (from Eugen's essay "A Horse Block" [1945], now printed in *Die Sprache des Menschengeschlechts* [Heidelberg: Verlag Lambert Schneider, 1963–1964], vol. 1, p. 23–31).

102 Comte Josephe de Gobineau (1816–1882), among other things a notorious anti-Semitic race theorist.

103 The Army group von Strantz organized lecture courses for the troops.

terday. I was thinking that the 103rd Division would perhaps have come to Mackensen, and my letter would have had to make the journey twice over.) I am suffering from a paper shortage as you see.

Our present correspondence is suffering from the fact that on the one hand we could not put it off, while on the other hand it is still too soon for it. I can see that very clearly, because I am the one who was responsible for the long gap (of the winter of 1913–1914). I could not write to you then, though you were continually sounding me and were offended because of my silence. I could not, because I thought I had done with you as you were up to then, and as I had dug you out at the end of our time in Leipzig, up to certain undiscoverable fragments (I won't say which parts of your body), put you together, and exhibited you in my museum in a gallery on a revolving pedestal, with a piece of dark blue stuff, which made a good background to you. That you were walking about alive despite this statue was almost an insult to me. I had to ignore it, and to appease my pangs of conscience with the idea that I had "put the matter off." That you were in fact walking about very much alive I realized, of course, when you were in Berlin in the spring, but I didn't feel myself strong enough, not indeed physically, but spiritually, to challenge you all over again (since it would only have been done as a challenge, and will so be done again); to my mind I was not actual enough, not tested enough, not enough on the spot, and to me there would have been no point in a merely theoretical controversy. Formerly, I had confronted you as a point of view, as an objective fact, and you were the first to summon me to an analysis of myself, and thereby cast me down. I would have liked to wait until I could again confront you as a *fait accompli*. 'Till then we could have kept our guest rooms ready for each other, and put some little cheap flowers in them as a token of our feeling for one another. That does, and would have done.

"Then the War came." And with it came a time of waiting against one's will, a chasm that one does not make artificially for oneself, but that was opened blindly in every life; and now it is no longer any good to wait deliberately; fate is now so calmly patient with individuals (from indifference towards them, be-

108

cause it has its hands full with nations) that we individuals ought just now to be impatient, unless we want simply to go to sleep (for fate certainly won't wake us up now). So now we are talking to each other theoretically, *faute de mieux*. But for that reason everything that we say to each other is incomplete, not incomplete like the flow of life that completes itself anew in every moment, but full of static incompletenesses, full of distortions.

You "leave me alone." You "don't know why." You "stop at me." Nevertheless, I reply and give you an answer that is theoretically correct, interesting, and I'm sure you will agree with it. You want to know what business I have on that galley[104]—but it were better you did not agree, did not know, but *just saw me set sail on that galley* without knowing what business I had on it, rather than that *my galley should now be lying idle in a neutral port since the beginning of the war*, and that I should incur your intellectual sympathy, since the *vis major* of the war prevents me from acquiring your active hatred; for there is in the delay the danger of indifference, which lies beyond love and hate, and that would be the worst of all.

Now to the point. You could have formulated your objection still more strongly; I should like perhaps later to do it for you. But first let's stick to your formulation. Yes, the stubbornness of the Jews is a Christian dogma. So much so that the Church, after she had built up the substantial part of her particular dogma— the part having to do with God and Man—in the first century, during the whole of the second century turned aside to lay down the "second dogma" (the formal part of her dogma, i.e. her historical consciousness of herself). And in its aftereffects this process continued through the third and fourth centuries and beyond; and Augustine applied himself to it personally, though the Church had already for some time been moving away from it. That is, it had been becoming a Church of writings or rather of tradition, instead of spirit; in other words, it was becoming exactly the Church that history knows. Paul's theory concerning the relation of the Gospels to the Law could have remained a

104 See note 93.

"personal opinion"; the Hellenizing "spiritual" Church (of John's Gospel) of the first century, in the marvelous naïveté of her "spiritual believers," had scarcely worried about it. Then came gnosticism, which laid its finger on Paul and sought to weed out the personal element from his theory and to develop its objective aspects in distinction from the personal in it. (Paul said: "The Jews are spurned, but Christ came from them." Marcion said: "Therefore the Jews belong to the devil, Christ to God.") Then the Church, which hitherto had been quite naïve in its own gnosticism (in St. John we read that salvation comes from the Jews), suddenly seeing this, pushed the spirit [pneuma] to one side in favor of tradition, and through a great *ritornar al segno* fixed this tradition by returning to its cardinal point, to its founder Paul; that is, she deliberately established as dogma what previously had been considered Paul's personal opinion. The Church established the identity of the Creator (and the God revealed at Sinai) with the Father of Jesus Christ on the one hand, and the perfect manhood of Christ on the other hand, as a definite, correlated Shibboleth against all heresy—and thereby the Church established herself as a power in human history. You know the rest better than I do. (N.B. I have just read all this in Tertullian, of whom I bought a complete edition dating from the thirties of the last century for two marks. I warn you against it emphatically! For the first and last time, as a result of pure folly and stinginess, I am reading an as-good-as-uncollated text. I know now at last why the textual critic is necessary. Scarcely any sentence is understandable; one has to guess at the meaning paragraph by paragraph, though I have a feeling for Tertullian's style. I prefer his rhetoric, as that of a real lawyer, to the professorial rhetoric of Augustine, just because it is more genuine—at least according to our modern ideas.)

Thus, in the firm establishment of the Old Testament in the Canon, and in the building of the Church on this double scripture (Old Testament and New Testament) the stubbornness of the Jews is in fact brought out as the other half of the Christian dogma (its formal consciousness of itself—the dogma of the Church—if we may point to the creed as the dogma of Christianity).

110

But could this same idea (that of the stubbornness of the Jews) also be a Jewish dogma? Yes, it could be, and in fact it is. But this Jewish consciousness of being rejected has quite a different place in our dogmatic system, and would correspond to a Christian consciousness of being chosen to rule, a consciousness that is in fact present beyond any doubt. The whole religious interpretation of the significance of the year 70[105] is tuned to this note. But the parallel that you are looking for is something entirely different. A dogma of Judaism about its relation to the Church must correspond to the dogma of the Church about its relation to Judaism. And this you know only in the form of the modern liberal-Jewish theory of the "daughter religion" that gradually educates the world for Judaism. But this theory actually springs from the classical period in the formation of Jewish dogma—from the Jewish high scholasticism which, in point of time and in content, forms a mean between Christian and Arabian scholasticism (al-Ghazali–Maimonides–Thomas Aquinas). For it was only then that we had a fixing of dogma, and that corresponds with the different position that intellectual conceptions of faith hold with us and with you. In the period when you were developing dogma, we were creating our canon law, and vice versa. There is a subtle connection running all through. For instance, when you were systematizing dogma, we were systematizing law; with you the mystical view of dogma followed its definition, while with us the mystical view preceded definition, etc., etc. This relation is rooted throughout in the final distinction between the two faiths. Indeed with us, too, this theory is not part of the substance of our dogma; with us, too, it was not formed from the content of the religious consciousness but belongs only to a second stratum, a stratum of learning concerning dogma. The theory of the daughter religion is found in the clearest form in both of the great scholastics. Beyond this, it is found, not as dogma but as a mystical idea (see above), in the literature of the old Synagogue, and likewise in the Talmudic period. To find it is no easy task, however. For whereas the substantial dogma in our scholasticism was based on trials, the connection between the old

---

[105] That is, the traditional date of the destruction of the Temple.

111

mysticism and medieval philosophy is brought about by the free religious spirit of the people, not by a fettered relationship to the past. But I should like to quote you one such legend. The Messiah was born exactly at the moment when the Temple was destroyed, but when he was born, the winds blew him forth from the bosom of his mother. And now he wanders unknown among the peoples, and when he has wandered through them all, then the time of our redemption will have come.

So that Christianity is like a power that fills the world (according to the saying of one of the two scholastics, Yehuda ha-Levi: it is the tree that grows from the seed of Judaism and casts its shadows over the earth; but its fruit must contain the seed again, the seed that nobody who saw the tree noticed. This is a Jewish dogma, just as Judaism as both the stubborn origin and last convert is a Christian dogma.

But what does all that mean for me, apart from the fact that I know it? What does this Jewish dogma mean for the Jew? Granted that it may not belong to the dogmas of the substantial group, which like the corresponding Christian dogmas can be won from an analysis of the religious consciousness. It is rather like the corresponding Christian one, a theological idea. But theological ideas must also mean something for religion. What, then, does it mean?

What does the Christian theological idea of Judaism mean for the Christian? If I am to believe E. R.'s letter before last (or before the one before the last?): Nothing! For there he wrote that nowadays König and he are the only people who still take Judaism seriously. The answer is already on the point of my pen— that it was not here a question of theoretical awareness, but whether there was a continual realization of this theological idea by its being taken seriously in actual practice. This practical way, in which the theological idea of the stubbornness of the Jews works itself out, is *hatred of the Jews.* You know as well as I do that all its realistic arguments are only fashionable cloaks to hide the single true metaphysical ground: that we will not make common cause with the world-conquering fiction of Christian dogma, because (however much a fact) it *is* a fiction (and "*fiat*

112

veritas, pereat realitas,"[106] since "Thou God art truth") and, putting it in a learned way (from Goethe in *Wilhelm Meister*): that we deny the foundation of contemporary culture (and "*fiat regnum Dei, pereat mundus,*"[107] for "ye shall be to me a kingdom of priests and a holy people"); and putting it in a popular way: that we have crucified Christ and, believe me, would do it again every time, we alone in the whole world (and "*fiat nomen Dei Unius, pereat homo,*"[108] for "to whom will you liken me, that I am like?").

And so the corresponding Jewish outcome of the theological idea of Christianity as a preparer-of-the-way is the *pride of the Jews.* This is hard to describe to a stranger. What you see of it appears to you silly and petty, just as it is almost impossible for the Jew to see and judge anti-Semitism by anything but its vulgar and stupid expressions. But (I must say again, *believe me*) its metaphysical basis is, as I have said, the three articles: (1) that we have the truth, (2) that we are at the goal, and (3) that any and every Jew feels in the depths of his soul that the Christian relation to God, and so in a sense their religion, is particularly and extremely pitiful, poverty-stricken, and ceremonious; namely, that as a Christian one has to learn from someone else, whoever he may be, to call God "our Father." To the Jew, that God is our Father is the first and most self-evident fact—and what need is there for a third person between me and my father in Heaven? That is no discovery of modern apologetics but the simplest Jewish instinct, a mixture of failure to understand and pitying contempt.

These are the two points of view, both narrow and limited just as points of view, and so in theory both can be surpassed; one can understand why the Jew can afford his unmediated closeness to God and why the Christian may not; and one can also understand how the Jew must pay for this blessing. I can elaborate this argument in extreme detail. It can be intellectualized through and through, for it springs in the last resort from

---

[106] Let there be truth, and let reality perish.
[107] Let there be the kingdom of God, and let the world pass away.
[108] Let the name of One God exist, and let man pass away.

113

that great victorious breaking in of the spirit into what is not spirit that one calls "Revelation."

But now I want to formulate your question in a way that seems profitable to me—but is not such intellectualizing, as an activity of knowing, preparing, acting on the future, like every cultural activity, a Christian affair, not a Jewish affair? Are you still a Jew in that you do it? Is not part of the price that the Synagogue must pay for the blessing in the enjoyment of which she anticipates the whole world, namely, of being already in the Father's presence, that she must wear the bandages of unconsciousness over her eyes? Is it sufficient if you carry the broken staff in your hand, as you do—I am willing to believe it—and yet take the bandages away from your eyes?

Here the polished clarity of antitheses ends; here begins the world of more and less, of compromise, of reality, or, as the Jewish mysticism of the late Middle Ages very finely said for "World of Reality, of Thinghood," "World of Activity, of Matter of Fact"; and as I should prefer to say, the "World of Action." Action alone can here decide for me, but even if it has decided for me, I still always need indulgence? Not as if thought is here entirely left behind; but it no longer goes as before along a proud, sure king's highway, with vanguard, flanks, and countless trains of attendants; it goes lonely along the footpath in pilgrim dress. Something like this:

You recollect the passage in the Gospel of John where Christ explains to his disciples that they should not leave the world, but should remain within it. Even so, the people of Israel—who indeed could use all the sayings of this Gospel—could speak to its members in such a way, and as a matter of fact it does so: "to hallow the name of God in the world," is a phrase that is often used. From this follows all the ambiguity of Jewish life (just as all the dynamic character of the Christian life follows from it). The Jew, insofar as he is "in the world," stands under these laws and no one can tell him that he is permitted to go just so far and no farther, or that there is a line that he may not cross. Such a simple "as little as possible" would be a bad standard, because if I wished to govern all of my actions by the standard "as little as possible from outside Judaism" it would mean, in the circum stances, a diminution of my inner Jewish achievement. So I say to myself as a rule: "as much as possible of the inner Jewish life"—though I well know that in the particular case I cannot anxiously avoid a degree of life outside Judaism. I also know that thereby, in your eyes, I open the way to a charge of soullessness. I can only answer fully at the center and source of my activity; at the periphery it escapes me. But should I then let the citadel fall in order to strengthen these precarious outworks? Should I "be converted," when I have been "chosen" from birth? Is that a real alternative for me? Have I only been thrown into the galley? Is it not *my* ship? You became acquainted with me on land, but you have scarcely noticed that my ship lies in harbor and that I spend more time than is necessary in sailors' taverns, and therefore you could well ask what business I have on the ship. And for you really to believe that it is my ship, and that I therefore belong to it (*pour faire quoi? y vivre et y mourir*)— for you really to believe me will only be possible if the voyage is once more free and I launch out.

Or only when we meet out on the open sea? You might!

Now from the *multum* to the *multa*[109] in your letter. I know Gobineau's book on the Renaissance, and possess without having read them the rest of his books in Reclam. Indeed "everyone" knows his Renaissance, just as "everyone" knows whatever is read by both sexes. Don't you think it is really a remarkable connection? Only what belongs in common to both man and woman belongs to *all* men, and everything else has only sectional interest. For instance, Hans Ehrenberg is now reading Lagarde[110] for the first time in his life. Incidentally, will you be seeing him some time? I don't know the geographical possibilities. He is in a sanatorium in Sedan. He is the strangest phenomenon of the war that I have come across, as far as people go. Everyone has in himself some extreme possibility that is in the highest degree typical of him, and in his case, through the war, and before that already of course through his very strange marriage, and before both of these, that is, before everything else, through his own

109 The important matter . . . the many lesser matters.
110 Paul Anton de Lagarde, née Bötticher (1827–1891), a noted Orientalist and anti-Semitic writer.

115

will to lead an extreme life, this possibility has become an actuality; he is now what might have been "lost" in him when he became a professor.[111]

Yes, I wouldn't have gone to Rickert with the Schelling essay—for personal reasons; but a thousand kilometres as the crow flies makes one enormously indifferent, so it is all right. But after the various rejections I certainly no longer trust your judgment and mine with respect to the value of the work.

Isn't Rüdorffer a pseudonym for Riezler? Anyhow, it is the pseudonym of "a man who stands very near the Chancellor." I have not read him yet. You mean, I take it, the *Weltpolitik der Gegenwart*[112] or is *Nationalität*[113] another, smaller book? Riezler is in the Foreign Office, and son-in-law of Max Liebermann.[114] It is so long since I had any cause to bother myself over the Kantians. Even when I was reading Kant himself (lately it was the *ewigen Frieden*,[115] and in February the *Religion innerhalb der Grenzen*[116]), I did not find any reason to turn to them. I mean the present "schools" have simply the significance of being schools. One must have passed through one of them—it doesn't matter which (I did the Southwest German one)—but afterwards one need only to bother himself further with the Master, the "good Master, long since dead." You indicate the fundamental attitude of the whole Kantian movement, just as Hans also does in his last writing ("last"—in 1911! And we used to take him for a man who was always rushing wildly into print). I was introduced

---

[111] Hans Ehrenberg (1883–1958), a cousin of Franz, commanded an infantry battalion in the war and at the time of this letter was probably enjoying a respite from the horrors of the battlefield. He had been a university professor before the war—hence Franz' reference to "what might have been 'lost' in him." His marriage in 1913 to Else Zimmermann and then the war turned him away from the narrowly academic way of life.

[112] Franz was of course correct in identifying "J. J. Rüdorffer" as a pseudonym of Kurt Riezler, the true author of *Grundzüge der Weltpolitik in der Gegenwart* (Foundations of World Politics in the Present Day), 1914.

[113] Nationality.

[114] The famous painter.

[115] Perpetual Peace.

[116] Religion within the Limits of Reason.

116

to Fechner in Bölsche's volume of essays, *Hinter der Welt-stadt*,[117] and by accident, I read the Zend-Avesta in my first term as a student. Up to then my knowledge of philosophy had been limited to: some of the first volume of Büttner's edition of Eckhart, Plato's Symposium, Schopenhauer's *Uber die Weiber*,[118] Nietzsche's *Der Fall Wagner*;[119] and I was quite captivated by Fechner (he describes, yes, really describes, the world as a great living being, and what is dead in it not as the source of life, but as an unburied corpse of what was formerly alive, since life is itself a source, and doesn't arise from anything else); subsequently, I have read only the little book *Vom Leben nach dem Tode*.[120] Wundt's relation to Fechner as a pupil is, I suppose, only in respect of his being the founder, as Fechner was, apart from everything else, the man who attempted to introduce mathematical methods into psychology (pure, not physiological psychology). Wundt, too, is one of the many people on whom I am not keen; I will look into all these matters as opportunity arises and when the *subject* inspires me (since the author will certainly leave me cold. Heim I am reading to the end just now; he is very good (but ought one not sometime to read M. Kähler himself?) I spent almost an entire week without reading anything, because I was writing something myself, namely, a syllabus for the school of the future!

Two missives were registered to me from your hand from Kassel, but they are not yet here. I discovered the little volume of poetry through a note from Klabund in the *Berliner Tageblatt*. Read it all the same.

And now a request. I have compressed my thoughts into tablet form for you, having regard for the weight restrictions of the field postal service and my paper shortage. If you pour on boiling water everyone can get a pint of strong coffee. So, requite me equal measure, and please explain to me your present idea of the relation between Nature and Revelation. That you have altered

[117] Behind the City of the World, by Wilhelm Bölsche (1861–1939), a novelist, translator, etc., who zealously propagated the theories of Charles Darwin and Ernst Haeckel.
[118] Concerning Women.
[119] The Case of Wagner.
[120] Of the Life after Death.

your opinion on this hasn't just happened during the war, but as long ago as the spring of 1914 you were using the concept "paganism" in your talk in a way that I could not understand. Where do you stand between the E. R. of the night of July 7, 1913 and Kierkegaard? I am asking so roundly and tactlessly because by those same round tablets of mine I have acquired a right at least to ask the question, if not also, I recognize, to obtain an answer. Heim's weakness, so far as I can see at present—I am on the border between the general and the Christian part of the book—as that of his whole circle, is that the history of philosophy ceases for him with Kant and as an alternative to the Idealists he knows only the specialist dogmatic theologians of the nineteenth century. Hence, he does not ask himself: How would it be if philosophy itself adopted the paradox[121] as its basis? But then he would have to concern himself with an immense task in the history of philosophy, and the beautiful short guides would no longer suffice (for, dear friend, only theory is short). Thus he has allowed the question of Christianity and philosophy (and with it, Christianity and the world) to be stultified in the simpler question of "Christianity and Paganism," and he still evades the particularly burning group of questions about the Christian world (Philosophy, Art, the State, Marriage, and so forth). But I want to read on further.

One further question. Has Speech no longer the meaning for you that it used to have? Could you express better what you mean by speaking about it? With cordial greetings, from "The sender" [N.B.: printed on the official letter form].

118